ENERGY DESIGN
FOR ARCHITECTS

ENERGY DESIGN FOR ARCHITECTS

The American Architectural Foundation
Alexander Shaw, Editor

Published by

THE FAIRMONT PRESS, INC.
700 Indian Trail
Lilburn, GA 30247

Library of Congress Cataloging-in-Publication Data

Energy design for architects.

Includes Index.
1. Architecture and energy conservation--United States.
I. Shaw, Alexander, 1944-   . II. American Architectural Foundation.

NA2542.3.E47   1989   721   88-24542
ISBN 0-88173-074-2

Energy Design For Architects
©1989 by The Fairmont Press, Inc. All rights reserved. No part of this publication may be reproduced or transmitted in any form or by any means, electronic or mechanical, including photocopy, recording, or any information storage and retrieval system, without permission in writing from the publisher.

Published by The Fairmont Press, Inc.
700 Indian Trail
Lilburn, GA 30247

Printed in the United States of America

10 9 8 7 6 5 4 3 2 1

ISBN 0-88173-074-2   FP
ISBN 0-13-277766-5   PH

This report was prepared by the American Architectural Foundation on account of work sponsored by the U.S. Department of Energy (DOE), through the Pacific Northwest Laboratory, operated by Battelle Memorial Institute (BMI) under Contract No. DE-AC06-76RL0 1830. The views expressed herein are those of the authors, and do not necessarily reflect the opinion of the DOE or BMI.

While every effort is made to provide dependable information, the publisher, authors, and editors cannot be held responsible for any errors or omissions.

Distributed by Prentice Hall
A division of Simon & Schuster
Englewood Cliffs, NJ 07632

Prentice-Hall International (UK) Limited, London
Prentice-Hall of Australia Pty. Limited, Sydney
Prentice-Hall Canada Inc., Toronto
Prentice-Hall Hispanoamericana, S.A., Mexico
Prentice-Hall of India Private Limited, New Delhi
Prentice-Hall of Japan, Inc., Tokyo
Simon & Schuster Asia Pte. Ltd., Singapore
Editora Prentice-Hall do Brasil, Ltda., Rio de Janeiro

ACKNOWLEDGEMENTS

Project Team

The AIA Foundation of the American Institute of Architects provided the organization and leadership for this book, which is a major update of materials produced for the AIA Energy Professional Development Program. The following were the members of the AIA Foundation team:

>Alexander Shaw, Project Manager/Editor
>
>Earle Kennett, Technical Consultant/Editor
>Paul McClure, Technical Editor
>Karen N. Smith, Graphic/Editorial Assistant
>Allan Assarsson, Graphics

Authors-Advisory Committee

The following wrote sections of the book and advised on its development:

Joe Deringer, AIA	John Holton, AIA
The Deringer Group	Burt Hill Kosar Rittelmann
Benjamin Evans, FAIA, FIES	Eino Kainlauri, Ph.D., AIA
Virginia Polytechnic Institute	Iowa State University
Gregory Franta, AIA	Donald Mirkovich, AIA
The ENSAR Group	Mirkovich and Associates

Support and Guidance

This effort was made possible through the Research Utilization Program under the guidance of Marvin Gorelick of the U.S. Department of Energy, Office of Buildings and Community Systems. This publication is one of many ongoing efforts to transfer lessons from the U.S. DOE buildings research programs to building practitioners. Bryan Mohler of the Pacific Northwest Laboratory, operated for the DOE by Battelle Memorial Institute, provided project management support.

Sponsors

This work was supported by the U.S. Department of Energy, Assistant Secretary for Conservation and Renewable Energy, Office of Building and Community Systems, under prime contract DE-AC06-76RLO with Battelle Memorial Institute, Pacific Northwest Laboratory, Richland, Washington.

Disclaimer

The statements contained in this document are those of the AIA Foundation and do not necessarily reflect the views of the foregoing sponsors. The sponsors and the AIA Foundation make no warranty, express or implied, and assume no responsibility for the accuracy or completeness of the information herein.

CONTENTS: TOPICAL

1 ENERGY DESIGN

    INTRODUCTION 1
    ENERGY DESIGN PROCESS 6

2 ENERGY FUNDAMENTALS

    ENERGY USE IN BUILDINGS 21
    COMFORT & HEALTH 44
    COST OF ENERGY 58
    CLIMATE 64
    THE BUILDING DESIGN PROCESS 73
    CODES AND STANDARDS 85

3 DESIGN ELEMENTS

    SITING 93
    SPACE PLANNING 106
    BUILDING ENVELOPE 117
    FENESTRATION AND OTHER APERTURES 131
    STRUCTURE AND MASS 165
    ELECTRIC LIGHTING 185
    THERMAL SYSTEMS 202
    PROCESS LOADS AND DOMESTIC HOT WATER 236
    ENERGY MANAGEMENT AND CONTROL SYSTEMS 240
    CONSTRUCTION AND COMMISSIONING PROCESS 254

4 DESIGN ANALYSIS

    BUILDING TYPES 267
    ANALYTICAL TECHNIQUES 283
    ECONOMIC ANALYSIS 298

GLOSSARY 317

INDEX 327

CONTENTS: DETAILED

1 ENERGY DESIGN

1.1 INTRODUCTION 1
1.2 ENERGY DESIGN PROCESS 6

2 ENERGY FUNDAMENTALS

2.1 ENERGY USE IN BUILDINGS
    2.1.1 Thermodynamics 21
        First Law of Thermodynamics (21);
        Second Law of Thermodynamics (21)
    2.1.2 Heat Transfer 22
        Conduction (23); Convection (23); Radiation (23)
    2.1.3 Phase Changes 24
    2.1.4 Building Energy Flow 25
        Energy-Flow Diagram (26); Definitions for Building
        Energy Flow Diagram (27)
    2.1.5 Heat Gain and Loss 29
    2.1.6 Design Strategies 32
        Introduction (32); Increase/Decrease Internal Heat
        Gain (33); Increase/Decrease Solar Heat Gain (35); Increase/Decrease
        Envelope Heat Gain/Loss (36); Increase/Decrease Ventilation
        Heat Gain/Loss (39); Increase/Decrease Stored Energy (41);
        Design Concept Analysis (43)

2.2 COMFORT & HEALTH
    2.2.1 Introduction 44
    2.2.2 Thermal Comfort 44
        Conductive Heat Transfer (45); Radiant and Ambient
        Temperatures (45); Humidity (46); Air Velocity (46)
    2.2.3 Psychrometric Chart 48
    2.2.4 Indoor Air Quality 50
        Problem Areas (50); Design Strategies (52); Source
        Control (53); Concentration Reduction (55); Natural
        Ventilation (55); Local Ventilation (55); Mechanical
        Ventilation With Air-to-Air Heat Exchangers (56); Air
        Cleaning (56); Air Filtration (56); Electrostatic
        Precipitators (56); Air Ionizers (57);
        Absorption (57); Adsorption (57)

2.3 COST OF ENERGY
    2.3.1 Introduction 58
    2.3.2 Electricity 58
    2.3.3 Natural Gas 62
    2.3.4 Delivered Fuel 62
    2.3.5 Cogeneration, District Heating and Cooling 63

2.4 CLIMATE
- 2.4.1 Introduction ... 64
- 2.4.2 Climatic Analysis ... 64
  Climatic Zones and Regions (64); Temperature (66); Sun (68); Wind (69); Recurrent Weather Events and Anomalies (70); Limitations of Climatic Data (70)
- 2.4.3 General Design Considerations in Relation to Climatic Data ... 70
- 2.4.4 Sources of Climatic Data ... 71

2.5 THE BUILDING DESIGN PROCESS
- 2.5.1 Introduction ... 73
- 2.5.2 Predesign ... 73
  Problem Definition (74); Design Strategies (77); Programming (79)
- 2.5.3 Design ... 82
  Schematic Design (82); Design Development (83); Construction Documents (83)
- 2.5.4 Construction Management and Commissioning ... 84
- 2.5.5 Redesign ... 84

2.6 CODES, STANDARDS, AND REGULATORY ISSUES
- 2.6.1 Introduction ... 85
- 2.6.2 Model Building Codes ... 85
- 2.6.3 Model Energy Code ... 87
- 2.6.4 Standards-Developing Organizations ... 89

3 DESIGN ELEMENTS

3.1 SITING
- 3.1.1 Introduction ... 93
- 3.1.2 Orientation and Configuration ... 93
- 3.1.3 Underground Design ... 95
  Underground Characteristics (95); Underground Construction (96); Berming (97)
- 3.1.4 Microclimate ... 97
  Topography (99)
- 3.1.5 Sun Control ... 101
  Shading Patterns (101); Reflection (101); Skyvault (102)
- 3.1.6 Wind Control ... 103
  Wind Patterns (103); Windbreaks (103)

3.2 SPACE PLANNING
- 3.2.1 Introduction ... 106
- 3.2.2 Internal Heat Gain ... 106
  Occupants (106); Electric Lighting (107); Equipment and Process Loads (111)
- 3.2.3 Solar Heat Gain ... 111
- 3.2.4 Zoning ... 114

3.3 BUILDING ENVELOPE
- 3.3.1 Introduction ... 117
- 3.3.2 Surface Area-to-Volume Ratio ... 117

3.3.3	U Values	117
3.3.4	Exterior Walls	119
3.3.5	Roof-Ceilings	124
3.3.6	Floors and Slabs	127
	Floors (127); Slabs (128)	
3.3.7	Infiltration	129
3.3.8	Double Envelope	130
3.3.9	Total Envelope Performance	130

3.4 FENESTRATION AND OTHER APERTURES

3.4.1	Introduction	131
	Solar Heat Gain (131); Condensation (132)	
3.4.2	Ventilation and Natural Air Flow	132
	Inlet and Outlet Location (134); Aperture Size (134); Partitions (134)	
3.4.3	Infiltration	135
	Window Frames and Seals (136)	
3.4.4	Multiple Glazing	137
	Air-Flow Windows (139)	
3.4.5	Glazing Materials	140
	Glass Block (141); Heat-Absorbing Glass (142); Reflective Glass (142); Anti-Reflective Coatings (143); Low-e Coatings (144); Plastic Sheets (145)	
3.4.6	Shading Devices	146
	Exterior Shading Devices (146); Interior Shading Devices (147)	
3.4.7	Light Shelves	149
3.4.8	Daylighting	149
	Functional Objectives (150); Daylight Availability (150); Site Criteria (151); Building Configuration (151); Building Orientation (151); Daylight Apertures (152); Glare Control (156)	
3.4.9	Physical Models	156
	Model Geometry (157); Materials (158); Scale (158); Instrumentation (158); Model Testing (158); Measurement of Ev and Eh (159)	
3.4.10	Daylighting Analysis by the Lumen Method	159

3.5 STRUCTURE AND MASS

3.5.1	Introduction	165
3.5.2	Storage Strategies	165
3.5.3	Location of Thermal Mass	166
	Envelope (167); Internal Mass (167); Isolated Mass (167); Exterior Mass (167)	

3.5.4 Materials for Energy Storage 168
Solid Thermal Mass (168); Water Storage (169);
Rock-Bed Storage (169)
3.5.5 Mass Storage for Heating and Cooling 170
Heating (170); Cooling (171)
3.5.6 Passive Heating Systems 172
Direct Gain (172); Indirect Gain (175);
Isolated Gain (179)
3.5.7 Passive Cooling Systems 180
Direct Cooling (181); Indirect Cooling (182);
Isolated Cooling (184)

3.6 ELECTRIC LIGHTING
3.6.1 Introduction 185
Luminance (186); Glare (186)
3.6.2 Light-Distribution Systems 187
Direct Lighting (187); Indirect Lighting (188);
Indirect-Direct (188)
3.6.3 Light-Producing Systems 190
Lamps (190); Luminaires (191); Ballasts (191)
3.6.4 Lighting Controls 192
Selective Switching (192); Dimming (192)
3.6.5 Illuminance Calculation Methods 192
Point Illuminance Calculations (192); Average
Illuminance Calculations (193); Number of Luminaires
for a Space (193); Area Covered by a
Luminaire (194); Zonal Cavity Calculation (194)
3.6.6 Energy Use 196
Thermal Effects (197)
3.6.7 IES Energy Guidelines for Lighting Systems 197
Lighting Needs (197); Lighting Equipment (198);
Daylighting (200); Controls and Distribution
System (199); Lighting Maintenance (199)

3.7 THERMAL SYSTEMS
3.7.1 Introduction 201
3.7.2 Distribution Systems 203
All-Air Systems (204); Air-Water Systems (208);
Air-Water Induction Systems (209); All-Water
Systems (210); Unitary Systems (211); Direct-Expansion,
Water-Loop Heat Pumps (212); Typical Systems (213)
3.7.3 Components 219
Cooling Sources (219); Heating Sources (220); Pumps,
Motors, and Fans (221); Heat Rejection (222);
Heat Exchangers (222)

　　　　3.7.4　Controls 225
　　　　　　　Localized Controls (226); Remote-Limited and
　　　　　　　Multifunction Controls (229); Waste Heat Recovery (232);
　　　　　　　Heat Recovery From Lighting Systems (232)
　　　　3.7.5　Active Solar Systems 233
　　　　　　　Heating (233); Cooling (234); Photovoltaics (234)

3.8 PROCESS LOADS AND DOMESTIC HOT WATER
　　　　3.8.1　Process Loads 236
　　　　　　　Vertical Transportation (236); Miscellaneous Equipment (236)
　　　　3.8.2　Domestic Hot Water 237

3.9 ENERGY MANAGEMENT AND CONTROL SYSTEMS
　　　　3.9.1　Introduction 240
　　　　3.9.2　Centralized Computer-Based EMCSs 240
　　　　3.9.3　Basic Functions 241
　　　　　　　Optimizing Functions (241)
　　　　3.9.4　Operational Functions 243
　　　　3.9.5　Other Functions 243
　　　　3.9.6　EMCS Components 244
　　　　3.9.7　Field Equipment 248
　　　　　　　Field Interface Devices (248); Multiplexer Panels (248);
　　　　　　　Intelligent Multiplexer Panels (248); Sensors (248);
　　　　　　　Actuators (249); Software (249)
　　　　3.9.8　EMCS Evaluation and Selection 249
　　　　　　　Cost Effectiveness (249); Adaptability (250);
　　　　　　　Maintainability (250); Reliability (250);
　　　　　　　Expandability (251); Programmability (251);
　　　　　　　Building Size and Type (252)

3.10 CONSTRUCTION AND COMMISSIONING PROCESS
　　　　3.10.1　Introduction 254
　　　　3.10.2　Project Documentation 257
　　　　　　　Economic Program (257); Energy Economic Goals (257);
　　　　　　　Energy Usage by Subsystem (257) Systems and Control
　　　　　　　Assumptions and Strategies (258) Contractor-Supplied
　　　　　　　Operating and Maintenance Manuals (259)
　　　　3.10.3　Operational Checks 259
　　　　　　　Contractor Requirements Prior to Occupancy (260);
　　　　　　　On-Site Instruction and Training (261); Access Doors,
　　　　　　　Maintenance Valves, and Test Ports (261); Equipment
　　　　　　　and Piping System Identification (262)
　　　　3.10.4　Construction 262
　　　　　　　Record Drawings (263); Special Service and
　　　　　　　Maintenance Tools (264); Inspection (264);
　　　　　　　Warranty Agreements (264);
　　　　3.10.5　Operation 264
　　　　　　　Testing Equipment Efficiency (264); Testing Water
　　　　　　　Systems (265); Inspecting and Calibrating System
　　　　　　　Controls (265); Monitoring Occupant Complaints (265)

4 DESIGN ANALYSIS

4.1 BUILDING TYPES
- 4.1.1 Introduction.. 267
- 4.1.2 Offices... 269
  Design Strategies (269)
- 4.1.3 Educational Facilities.. 271
  Design Strategies (272)
- 4.1.4 Retail Stores... 274
  Design Strategies (275)
- 4.1.5 Apartments (Housekeeping)..................................... 276
  Design Strategies (277)
- 4.1.6 Hotels/Motels (Non-Housekeeping).............................. 278
  Design Strategies (279)
- 4.1.7 Health Facilities... 280
  Design Strategies (280)

4.2 ANALYTICAL TECHNIQUES
- 4.2.1 Introduction.. 283
- 4.2.2 Uses of Energy Analysis Methods............................... 283
  Code Compliance (283); Economic Assessments (284);
  Energy Design Tools (284)
- 4.2.3 Energy Strategy Tools... 284
  Logical Solution Tools (286);
  Predetermined Solution Tools (286)
- 4.2.4 Energy Analysis Tools... 286
  Physical Models (287); Numerical Models (287);
  Special Purpose Tools (287); Load Calculation Tools (287);
  Equipment Sizing Tools (288); Energy Analysis Tools (288);
  Applications (288)
- 4.2.5 User Requirements... 289
  Types of Users (289); Availability (289); Cost of
  Use (289); Documentation (290); Run Time (290); User
  Support (290); Input/Output (291); Tool Structure (291)
- 4.2.6 Technical Capabilities of Different Tools..................... 291
- 4.2.7 Energy Analysis Models.. 293
  Steady State vs. Dynamic Models (293); Single- vs.
  Multiple-Measurement Models (293); Building Mass (296);
  Weather Data Requirements and Availability (296)
- 4.2.8 Selecting Analysis Tools...................................... 297

4.3 ECONOMIC ANALYSIS
    4.3.1 Introduction 298
    4.3.2 Constant Dollar Calculations 301
          Equivalence (301); Present-Worth Method (301);
          Equivalent-Annual-Cost Method (302);
          Interest Formulas (302)
    4.3.3 Life-Cycle Cost/Benefit Analysis 307
    4.3.4 Payback and Break-Even Analysis 311
          Payback (311); Break-Even Analysis (311)
    4.3.5 Rate of Return on Investment 311
          Rate of Return on Extra Investment (312)

GLOSSARY 317

INDEX 327

LIST OF FIGURES

Section 1 ENERGY DESIGN

Figure 1.1.1 - Energy End Use in the United States 1
Figure 1.1.2 - Total U.S. Energy Use 2
Figure 1.1.3 - Building Sizes 2
Figure 1.1.4 - Energy Use 2
Figure 1.1.5 - Number and Area Distribution of Commercial Buildings 3
Figure 1.1.6 - Commercial Building Energy Use 3
Figure 1.1.7 - End Use Energy 4
Figure 1.1.8 - Electricity Use 4
Figure 1.1.9 - End Use by Fuel Type 5
Figure 1.2.1.1 - Overview of Energy Design Process 7
Figure 1.2.1.2 - STEP ONE: Determine Energy Opportunities and Problems 8
Figure 1.2.1.3 - STEP TWO: Establish Energy Goals 10
Figure 1.2.1.4 - STEP THREE: Optimize Impacts of Building Functions 11
Figure 1.2.1.5 - STEP FOUR: Optimize Impacts of Loads 13
Figure 1.2.1.6 - STEP FIVE: Improve Systems 17
Figure 1.2.1.7 - STEP SIX: Integrate Building Systems 19
Figure 1.2.1.8 - STEP SEVEN: Compare Results with Goals 20

Section 2 ENERGY FUNDAMENTALS

Figure 2.1.1.1 - First Law of Thermodynamics:
                "Energy can be neither created nor destroyed." 21
Figure 2.1.1.2 - Heat Flow 22
Figure 2.1.2.1 - Conduction 23
Figure 2.1.2.2 - Convection 23
Figure 2.1.2.3 - Radiation 24
Figure 2.1.3.1 - Phase Change 24
Figure 2.1.4.1 - Energy Flow Diagram 26
Figure 2.1.4.2 - Energy, Power and Usage 29
Figure 2.1.5.1 - Heat Gains and Losses 30
Figure 2.1.5.2 - Thermal Balance Analysis 31
Figure 2.1.5.3 - Thermal Balance Analysis 32
Figure 2.1.6.1 - Internal Heat Gain 33
Figure 2.1.6.2 - Solar Heat Gain 35
Figure 2.1.6.3 - Envelope Heat Gain 37
Figure 2.1.6.4 - Ventilation Heat Gain 39
Figure 2.1.6.5 - Storage Heat Gain 41
Figure 2.2.2.1 - Comfort Zone 44
Figure 2.2.2.2 - Factors Affecting Human Comfort 45
Figure 2.2.2.3 - Effect of Climate 46
Figure 2.2.3.1 - Psychrometric Chart 47
Figure 2.2.3.2 - Cooling and Heating Design Strategies 49
Figure 2.2.4.1 - Radon Entry Paths 53
Figure 2.3.2.1 - Demand Cost Computation 59
Figure 2.3.2.2 - Total Monthly Cost Factors 59
Figure 2.3.2.3 - 30 and 50 Percent Load Factors 60
Figure 2.3.2.4 - Monthly Energy Charge: Example Rate 61
Figure 2.3.2.5 - Monthly Demand Charge: Example Rate 61

Figure 2.4.2.1 - Climatic Regions in U.S. 64
Figure 2.4.2.2 - Psychrometric Chart 65
Figure 2.4.2.3 - MacroClimatic Regions 65
Figure 2.4.2.4 - Temperature Patterns 66
Figure 2.4.2.5 - Relative Humidity 67
Figure 2.4.2.6 - Solar Radiation 68
Figure 2.4.2.7 - Wind Rose 69
Figure 2.5.2.1 - Energy Budget 74
Figure 2.5.2.2 - Energy Use 74
Figure 2.5.2.3 - Energy Profiles 75
Figure 2.5.2.4 - Energy Profile 77
Figure 2.5.2.5 - Architectural Program Factors 78
Figure 2.5.2.6 - Energy Targets 80
Figure 2.5.3.1 - Energy Savings at Design Stage 82
Figure 2.6.1.1 - Energy Codes and Standards 86
Figure 2.6.3.1 - Model Energy Code Criteria 88
Figure 2.6.3.2 - Model Energy Code U-Values 90

Section 3 - DESIGN ELEMENTS

Figure 3.1.2.1 - Building Shapes in Different Regions 95
Figure 3.1.3.1 - Underground Degree Day Lag 96
Figure 3.1.3.2 - Heat Loss for Subgrade Wall 96
Figure 3.1.4.1 - Solar Geometry 98
Figure 3.1.4.2 - Effects of Water Bodies 100
Figure 3.1.5.1 - Material Temperature and Reflectance 102
Figure 3.1.6.1 - Wind Effects 103
Figure 3.1.6.2 - Wind Speed Reduction 104
Figure 3.1.6.3 - Windbreak Effects 105
Figure 3.2.2.1 - Heat Gain Sources 106
Figure 3.2.2.2 - Space Requirements 106
Figure 3.2.2.3 - Heat Gain per Occupant 107
Figure 3.2.2.4 - Illuminance Values 108
Figure 3.2.2.5 - Reflectance Values 109
Figure 3.2.2.6 - Light Source Comparison 109
Figure 3.2.2.7 - Illuminance Values 110
Figure 3.2.2.8 - Heat Recovery 111
Figure 3.2.3.1 - Solar Radiation 112
Figure 3.2.3.2 - Glazing Characteristics 113
Figure 3.2.4.1 - Zone Planning 114
Figure 3.2.4.2 - Energy Use Groups 116
Figure 3.3.3.1 - Insulation R-Values 118
Figure 3.3.3.2 - Wall Sections 119
Figure 3.3.4.1 - Insulation Detail 120
Figure 3.3.4.2 - R-Values of Materials 121
Figure 3.3.4.2 - R-Values of Materials (continued) 122
Figure 3.3.4.3 - OTTV Terms from Model Energy Code 123
Figure 3.3.5.1 - Roof Sections 124
Figure 3.3.5.2 - Roof System Descriptions 125
Figure 3.3.5.2 - Roof System Descriptions (continued) 126
Figure 3.3.5.3 - TD^{EQR} from Model Energy Code 127

Figure	Title	Page
Figure 3.3.6.1	Perimeter Insulation	128
Figure 3.4.1.1	Condensation Prediction	132
Figure 3.4.2.1	Natural Ventilation	133
Figure 3.4.2.2	Thermosiphon Effect	133
Figure 3.4.3.1	Stack Effect	135
Figure 3.4.3.2	Thermal Break Detail	136
Figure 3.4.4.1	Air Space U-Values	137
Figure 3.4.4.2	Glazing Performance	138
Figure 3.4.4.3	Glazing Performance	138
Figure 3.4.4.4	Solar Transmission	139
Figure 3.4.4.5	Air Flow Window Details	139
Figure 3.4.5.1	Selective Transmittance Spectrum	140
Figure 3.4.5.1	Selective Transmittance Spectrum (continued)	141
Figure 3.4.5.2	Solar Transmission	142
Figure 3.4.5.3	Location of Reflective Film	143
Figure 3.4.5.4	Reflective Properties: Blocking Ultraviolet	144
Figure 3.4.5.5	Glazing Properties	145
Figure 3.4.6.1	Shading Options	146
Figure 3.4.7.1	Light Shelves	148
Figure 3.4.7.1	Light Shelves (continued)	149
Figure 3.4.8.1	Daylighting Configurations	150
Figure 3.4.8.2	Daylighting Clerestories	153
Figure 3.4.8.3	Daylighting Sections	154
Figure 3.4.8.4	Skylight Configurations	154
Figure 3.4.8.4	Skylight Configurations (continued)	155
Figure 3.4.8.5	Skylight Shading Devices	155
Figure 3.4.9.1	Daylighting Measurements	157
Figure 3.4.10.1	Lumen Method Factors	159
Figure 3.4.10.2	Lumen Method	160
Figure 3.4.10.3	Lumen Method	160
Figure 3.4.10.4	Lumen Method	161
Figure 3.4.10.4	Lumen Method (continued)	162
Figure 3.4.10.5	Lumen Method	162
Figure 3.4.10.5	Lumen Method (continued)	163
Figure 3.5.2.1	Average Temperature and Temperature Swing	166
Figure 3.5.3.1	Interior Thermal Mass	167
Figure 3.5.5.1	Thermal Mass for Heating	170
Figure 3.5.5.1	Thermal Mass for Heating (continued)	171
Figure 3.5.5.2	Thermal Mass for Cooling	172
Figure 3.5.6.1	Direct Gain Storage	172
Figure 3.5.6.2	Heat Capacity	173
Figure 3.5.6.3	Sizing Storage	174
Figure 3.5.6.4	Indirect Gain Thermal Storage	175
Figure 3.5.6.5	Recommended Vent Areas	176
Figure 3.5.6.6	Mass Sizing	178
Figure 3.5.6.7	Roof Pond Ratios	179
Figure 3.5.7.1	Cooling Strategies	181
Figure 3.6.1.1	Levels of Illumination	185
Figure 3.6.1.2	IES Luminous Ratios	186
Figure 3.6.3.1	Light Sources	189
Figure 3.6.5.1	Isofootcandle Diagram	193
Figure 3.6.5.2	Three Room Cavities	194

Figure 3.6.5.3 - Cavity Ratio Formulations ... 195
Figure 3.6.5.4 - Room Cavity Ratio Nomograph ... 196
Figure 3.7.1.1 - Cooling Process Sequence ... 201
Figure 3.7.1.2 - Cooling Process Sequence ... 202
Figure 3.7.2.1 - HVAC System Comparisons ... 203
Figure 3.7.2.2 - Comparative Space Needs ... 208
Figure 3.7.2.3 - Single Package Unit ... 212
Figure 3.7.2.4 - Single-Duct Single-Zone ... 214
Figure 3.7.2.5 - Terminal Reheat ... 214
Figure 3.7.2.6 - Dual Duct ... 215
Figure 3.7.2.7 - Multi-Zone ... 216
Figure 3.7.2.8 - Fan-Coil ... 217
Figure 3.7.2.9 - Water-Loop Heat Pump ... 217
Figure 3.7.2.9 - Water-Loop Heat Pump (continued) ... 218
Figure 3.7.2.10 - Common HVAC System Types ... 218
Figure 3.7.3.1 - Typical COPs ... 219
Figure 3.7.3.2 - Compressive Cycle ... 219
Figure 3.7.3.3 - Absorption Cycle ... 220
Figure 3.7.3.4 - Thermal Wheels ... 222
Figure 3.7.3.5 - Heat Pipes ... 223
Figure 3.7.3.6 - Run-Around Coils ... 223
Figure 3.7.3.7 - Air-to-Air Exchangers ... 224
Figure 3.7.3.8 - Flue-Gas Recovery ... 224
Figure 3.7.3.9 - Heat Reclamation Devices ... 225
Figure 3.7.4.1 - Dead Band Control ... 228
Figure 3.7.5.1 - Active Solar Heating ... 233
Figure 3.7.5.2 - System Comparisons ... 233
Figure 3.8.2.1 - DHW Usage ... 237
Figure 3.8.2.2 - DHW System Efficiencies ... 238
Figure 3.9.6.1 - Energy Management Control System BLOCK Diagram ... 245
Figure 3.9.6.2 - Typical closed loop, direct control system. ... 246
Figure 3.9.6.3 - Digital Control Network ... 246
Figure 3.9.6.4 - Transmission Line Characteristics ... 247
Figure 3.10.1.1 - Timely Effort Curve ... 254
Figure 3.10.1.2 - Commissioning Responsibility and Schedule Checklist ... 255
Figure 3.10.2.1 - Programming Assumptions ... 256
Figure 3.10.2.2 - Economic Goals ... 257
Figure 3.10.2.3 - Energy Usage ... 258
Figure 3.10.3.1 - Balancing Plan ... 260
Figure 3.10.3.2 - Access Doors ... 262
Figure 3.10.4.1 - As-Built Drawings ... 263

Section 4 - DESIGN ANALYSIS

Figure 4.1.1.2 - Energy End Use by Building Type ... 267
Figure 4.1.1.2 - Building Types and SubTypes ... 268
Figure 4.2.3.1 - Design Tool Spectrum ... 285
Figure 4.2.7.1 - Energy Tool Descriptors ... 292
Figure 4.2.7.2 - Analysis Tool Descriptors ... 294
Figure 4.2.7.2 - Analysis Tool Descriptors (continued) ... 295
Figure 4.3.2.1 - Life Cycle Cost Format ... 304
Figure 4.3.2.2 - Cost Categories ... 305

Figure 4.3.2.2 - Cost Categories (continued) 306
Figure 4.3.3.1 - Time and Life Cycle Cost 308
Figure 4.3.4.1 - Interest Tables 313
Figure 4.3.4.1 - Interest Tables (continued) 314
Figure 4.3.4.1 - Interest Tables (continued) 315

GLOSSARY

Absorption 315
Dewpoint 318
Direct Gain 319
Indirect Gain 321
Isolated Gain 321
Relative Humidity 323
Solar Azimuth 324
Specific Volume 325

1 ENERGY DESIGN

1.1 INTRODUCTION

With the present energy use patterns and limitations on the availability of fossil fuels (Figure 1.1.1), shortages are inevitable in the future. The rate of energy use in the United States is expected to reach 125×10^{15} Btu by the year 2000 unless conservation is practiced diligently. Technology offers important help in reducing our dependence on fossil fuels, but technology is only part of the answer.

Energy End Use	Total (Quadrillion Btu)	%
Transportation (fuel; excludes lubes, grease)	18.90	27
Space heating (residential, commercial)	11.30	16
Indirect heat (industrial)	7.25	10
Lighting (residential, commercial)	4.07	5.7
Direct heat (industrial)	3.86	5.5
Electrical services (industrial)	3.63	5.1
Air-conditioning (residential, commercial)	3.31	4.6
Feedstock (industrial)	3.20	4.5
Water heating (residential, commercial)	2.44	3.5
Refrigeration (residential, commercial)	2.13	3.0
Cooking (residential, commercial)	0.85	1.2
Other (industrial)	7.51	11
Other (residential, commercial)	1.95	2.7
Total	70.50	99.8

Source: Actual energy use by sector taken from: Energy Information Agency, Monthly Energy Review, U.S. Department of Energy/Energy Information Agency, December 1983.

Figure 1.1.1 - Energy End Use in the United States

Such energy sources as solar, wind, tidal, hydroelectric, biomass, etc., are termed renewable--they are supplied continuously, for free. *Non*renewable energy sources refer to energy that, once used, is not readily available for reuse. The energy resource, e.g., fossil fuels, is permanently converted from a finite source into an exhausted source. Thus, there is a cost involved due to its limited supply. Additional costs are incurred because of inefficiency in energy transformation processes. For example, an electric utility may burn coal to produce the steam to run a generator to produce electricity to power building systems. Because of the several conversions, overall energy efficiency is reduced. That is, although one kiloWatt-hour of electrical energy equals 3413 Btu, three times that many Btu are needed to produce that kiloWatt-hour because of conversion and distribution losses. The energy available at the building (3413 Btu) is called on-site energy. The energy required to produce that energy (10,239 Btu) is called source energy.

Although the United States has only six percent of the world's population, the United States now uses more than 32 percent of the world's fossil fuel resources. The total U.S. energy use, classified into economic sectors, is illustrated in Figure 1.1.2. Note that the energy used directly in residential and commercial buildings is 36 percent of the total U.S. energy use, an increase from 33 percent between 1975 and 1980. This is in addition to approximately 15 percent of energy used for the construction of buildings and an unknown amount used for the transportation of construction materials and equipment.

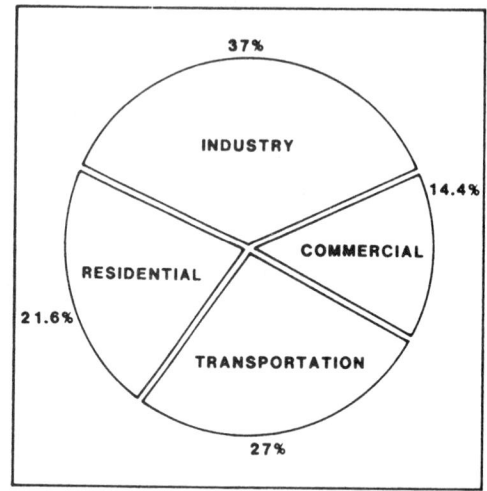

Figure 1.1.2 - Total U.S. Energy Use

The median size of commercial buildings is 3,900 square feet, with 58 percent of the U.S. commercial building stock being less than 5,000 square

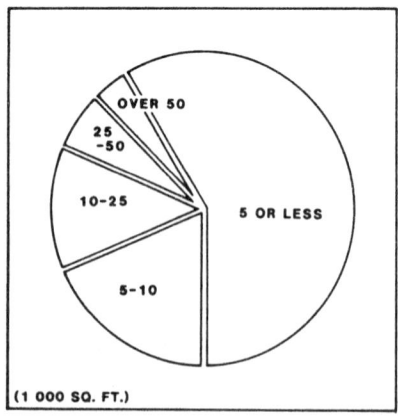

Figure 1.1.3 - Building Sizes

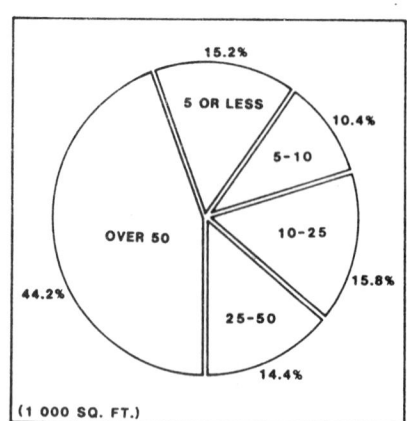

Figure 1.1.4 - Energy Use

feet (Figure 1.1.3 and 1.1.4). Even so, the majority of energy used in commercial buildings goes to buildings larger than 25,000 square feet (Figure 1.1.5).

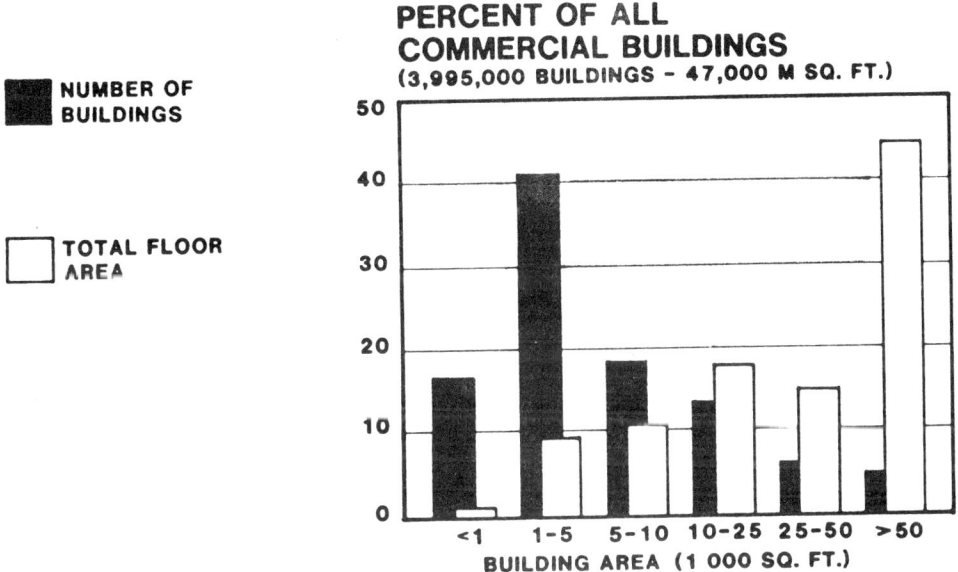

Figure 1.1.5 - Number and Area Distribution of Commercial Buildings

Figure 1.1.6 illustrates the commercial building energy use by floor area and end use.

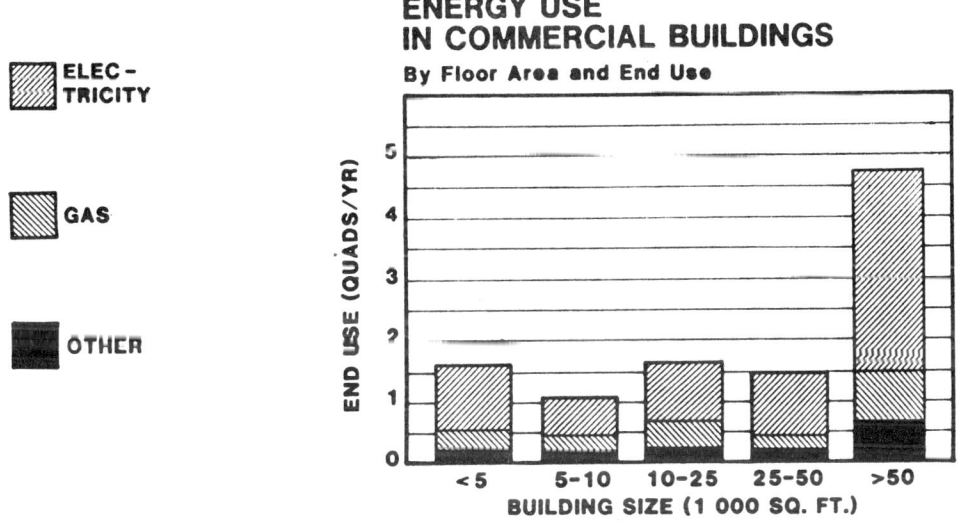

Figure 1.1.6 - Commercial Building Energy Use

Figure 1.1.7 shows the total end use energy breakdown in commercial buildings and can be compared to the largest commercial building end user, office buildings, in Figure 1.1.8.

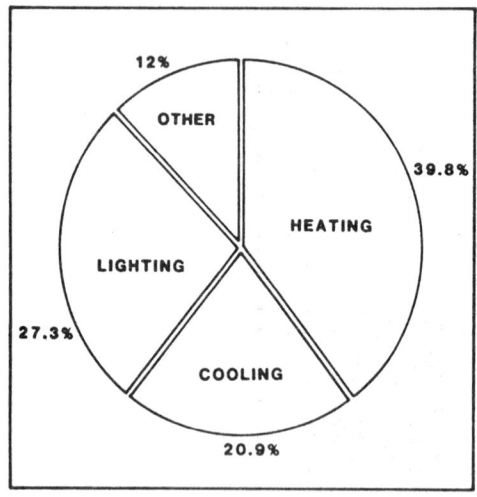
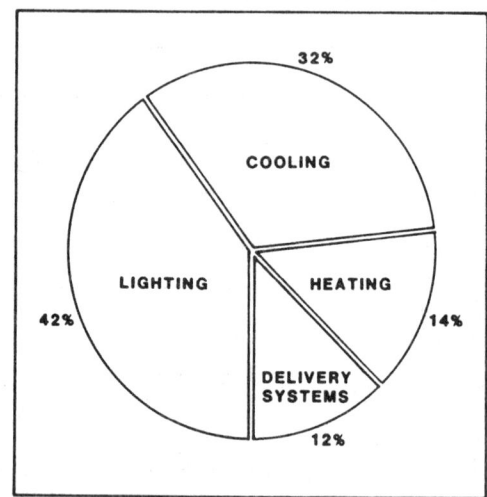

Figure 1.1.7 - End Use Energy   Figure 1.1.8 - Electricity Use

Figure 1.1.9 illustrates the distribution of primary energy use in commercial buildings by fuel types and end use (quads/year). On the average, 67 percent of the energy used in commercial buildings is in the form of electricity and 33 percent fossil fuels. Space heating for residential and commercial buildings represents the second largest U.S. energy end use. Space heating represents a substantial portion of energy end use in many types of commercial buildings, including warehouses, schools, churches and small retail stores. Space heating is a less significant end use of energy in buildings such as offices, laboratories and many large retail stores, where cooling loads and other internally generated loads are predominant.

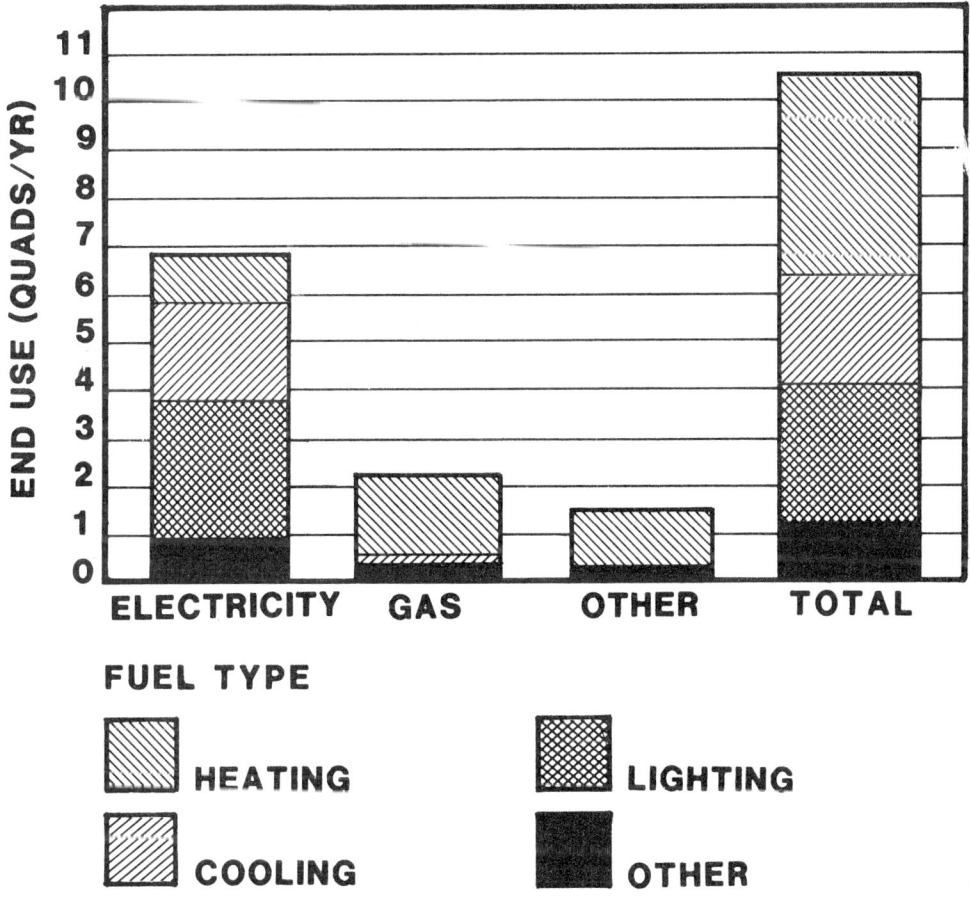

Figure 1.1.9 - End Use by Fuel Type

The amount of energy needed by a building depends on the building's overall energy requirements and the efficiency of the building systems. As mentioned, the three primary space loads are heating loads, cooling loads and lighting loads. How these loads are met will determine the energy efficiency of the whole building.

1.2 ENERGY DESIGN PROCESS

The "energy design process" is a fairly simple sequence of logical steps to be followed in the creation of the building. The process is a reiterative sequence of trial, evaluation, and then retrial to attain greater refinement. The following charts describe this "energy design process". They are intended to offer a comprehensive visual overview of this reiterative effort.

Although energy design is performed in concert with overall building design, there is a distinct approach to determining design alternatives and understanding their implications on the overall energy use of the building being designed.

All aspects of this process are discussed throughout this book. The "Energy Design Procedure" figure summarizes the steps.

STEP 1: The first step in the process is to determine both the inherent energy problems and opportunities.
STEP 2: Establish the energy and cost goals for the particular building under design.
STEP 3: Based on these early decisions the designer should evaluate the energy impacts of building functional requirements such as occupancy schedules, comfort requirements, glazing requirements, form and envelope requirements, etc.
STEP 4: Design decisions should then be made in terms of optimizing the loads caused by the functional requirements of the building. This concept of thermal balance is, in other words, an attempt to reduce or increase heat gains and losses in the building so that the end result will be counteracting gains and losses requiring minimal systems to condition the space.
STEP 5: Once the best energy design based on loads has been identified, the designer must select and design the most appropriate systems to provide for the load requirements (heating, cooling, lighting) that can not be met solely through proper building designs.
STEP 6: These systems should be combined, i.e., integrated, so that the total building energy use can be assessed. System selection should include an understanding of how each will affect the other systems so that when all systems (envelope, lighting, HVAC, etc.) are combined together the most appropriate overall building energy use will be the result.
STEP 7: At this point the result can be compared to the initial energy and cost goals and the design evaluated as to how well the goals have been met. If necessary the building may be redesigned to move closer to the original goals which were set.

The following pages of this section highlight key aspects of each of the seven steps.

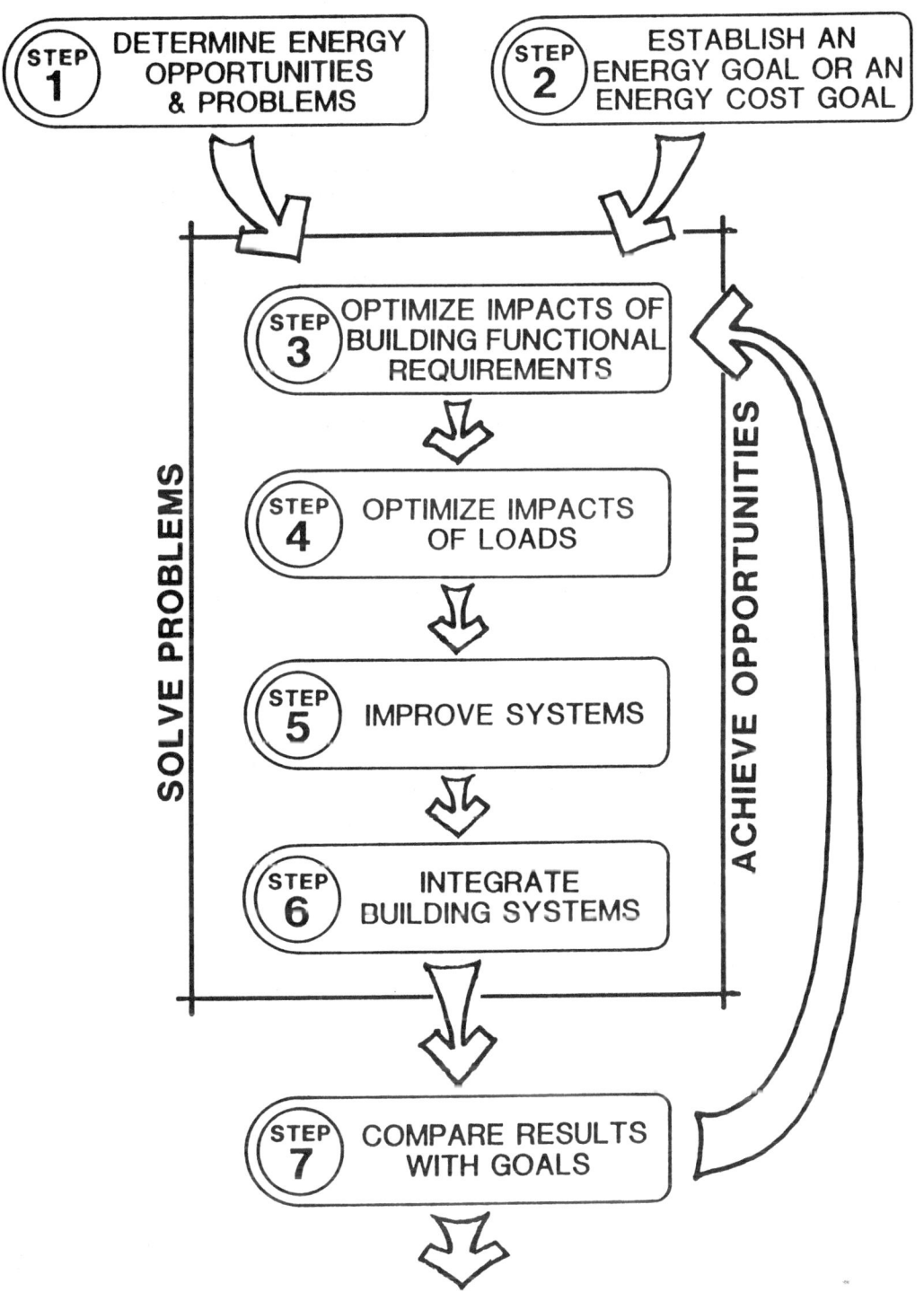

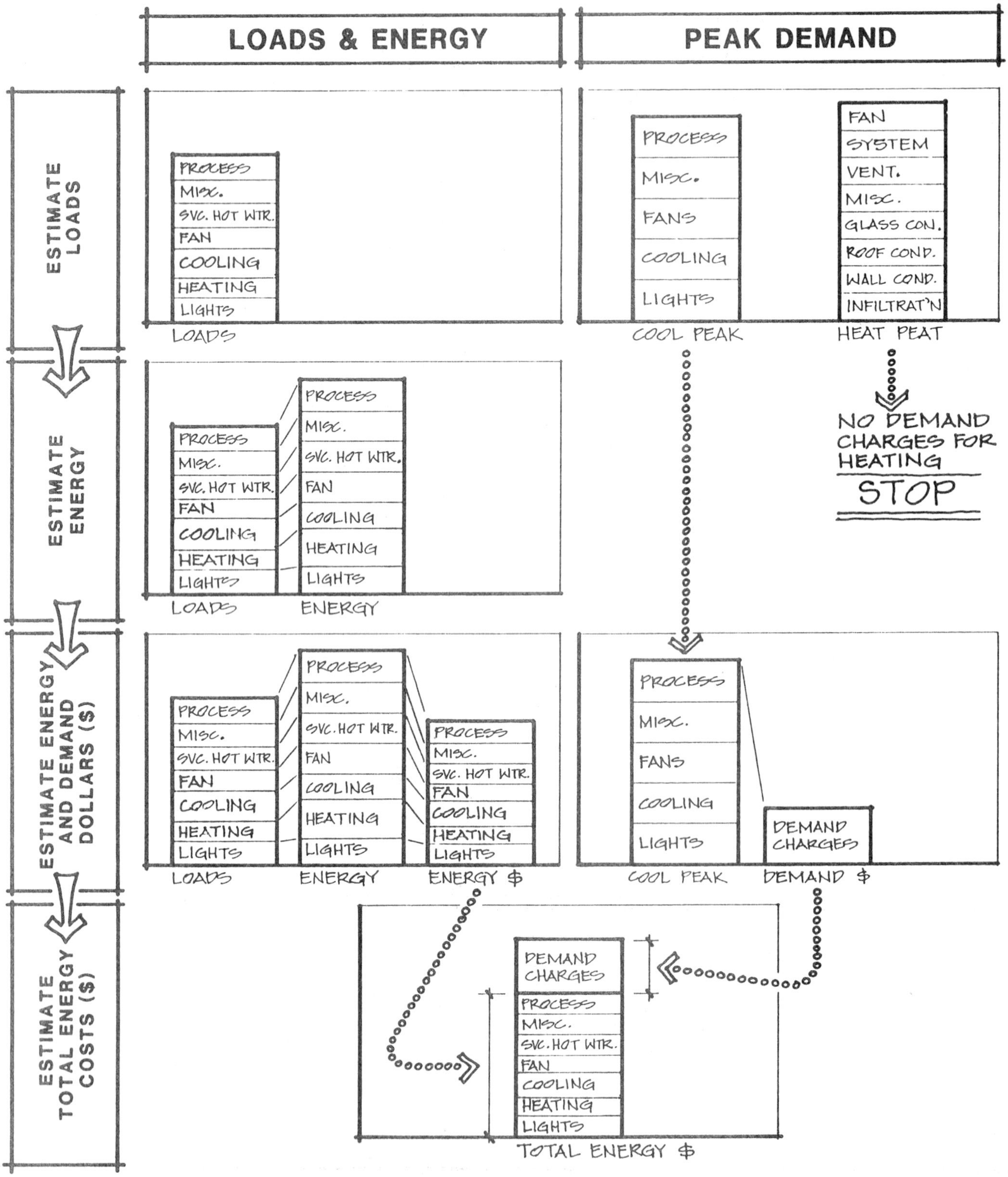

STEP 1: DETERMINE ENERGY OPPORTUNITIES & PROBLEMS

	COMMENTS	SOURCES OF DATA
ESTIMATE LOADS	• Energy loads options (displayed here to show relationships) • Relative magnitudes of energy loads are as important as absolute values • Annual peaks may be sufficient for analysis unless the utility rate structure is complex and requires monthly peak information	• "Typical" building loads information from previous buildings designed. • Data from utility companies based upon their experience • Research studies on typical buildings, (e.g., ASHRAE Special Project 41, TVA Building type studies, etc.)

ESTIMATE ENERGY	• Energy priorities can be very different from load priorities due to efficiencies of heating and cooling systems, (e.g., the example assumes gas heat). For loads, cooling seems a much higher priority than heating, whereas for energy, the apparent priorities reverse.	• BEPS data in "Progressive Architecture" magazine articles (eight articles from April 82 through April 83)
		
		• Utility company data
		
		• The designer's experience with similar buildings
		
		• Research studies on building types
		    Small Office Handbook (PNL, '85)
		    Multi-family Residential Report (PNL, '86)
		    Post Office Energy Target Bands (ANL, '81)

ESTIMATE ENERGY AND DEMAND DOLLARS ($)	• Priorities can shift again markedly when the focus shifts from energy use to energy cost. In the example, the higher cost of electricity compared with gas, makes the priority of cooling appear once again larger than the heating.
	
	• Note that demand costs can vary significantly by location and building situation
		• Bring utility company representatives early in the process to supply information on energy and demand costs for either;
		    - typical building of your type, or
		    - your specific building
		
		• Use research studies for procedures;
		    Small office handbook
		    Multi-family residential report

ESTIMATE TOTAL ENERGY COSTS ($)	• When demand charges are included, priorities can be very different from those apparent in either loads, energy, or energy cost alone. • In the example, the demand charges further increase the priority of <u>all</u> enduses that utilize electricity, for their share of total energy cost increases. Note that heating has relatively low priority now, whereas from the energy perspective it appeared most important.	• Utility company cost data • Energy and demand analysis results from analysis of the specific building OR • Energy and demand mix data from similar or typical buildings

STEP 2: ESTABLISH AN ENERGY GOAL OR AN ENERGY COST GOAL

PRINCIPLES

TYPE OF GOAL

- Meet a set of criteria for the building's components and systems

- Establish an energy target for the building as a whole (e.g., annual Btu/sf/yr)

- Demand target for the building as a whole (e.g., maximum KW)

- Combined energy and demand cost targets

- Environmental quality goals

LEVEL OF GOAL

- Technical limit (e.g., 20-30 kBtu/sf/yr)*

- Excellent (e.g., 30-40 kBtu/sf/yr)

- Good (e.g., 40-60 kBtu/sf/yr)

- Average (e.g., 60-80 kBtu/sf/yr)

- Energy Intensive (e.g., 80+ kBtu/sf/yr)

* Example numbers for an office building

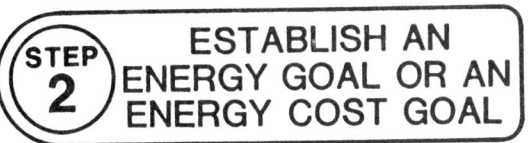

STEP 2: ESTABLISH AN ENERGY GOAL OR AN ENERGY COST GOAL

	EXAMPLES

TYPE OF GOAL	• Meet criteria of ASHRAE 90-75, 90A-1980, 90, 1P, or a state, local, or model energy code
	
	• Use published data from BEPS, or from California, Louisiana, Florida, etc.
	    OR
	  Choose your own energy target, e.g., 45 kBtu/sf/yr for your office building
	
	• e.g., "X" kBtu/sf for your building in the cooling mode
	
	• Use a combination of an energy target and a demand target
	
	• Visual, thermal, acoustical, air quality, etc.

LEVEL OF GOAL	• A building using best available technologies and concepts--maybe a "showcase" building without regard for usual economics • A building using innovative design and technologies, with a strong focus on energy, to units of life cycle cost economics. • Energy is pursued with reasonably high priority up to competitive commercial limits. • Energy efficiency is pursued no more or less rigorously than other design objectives. • Energy efficiency is not considered, or severe programmatic constraints cause high levels of energy use.

PRINCIPLES

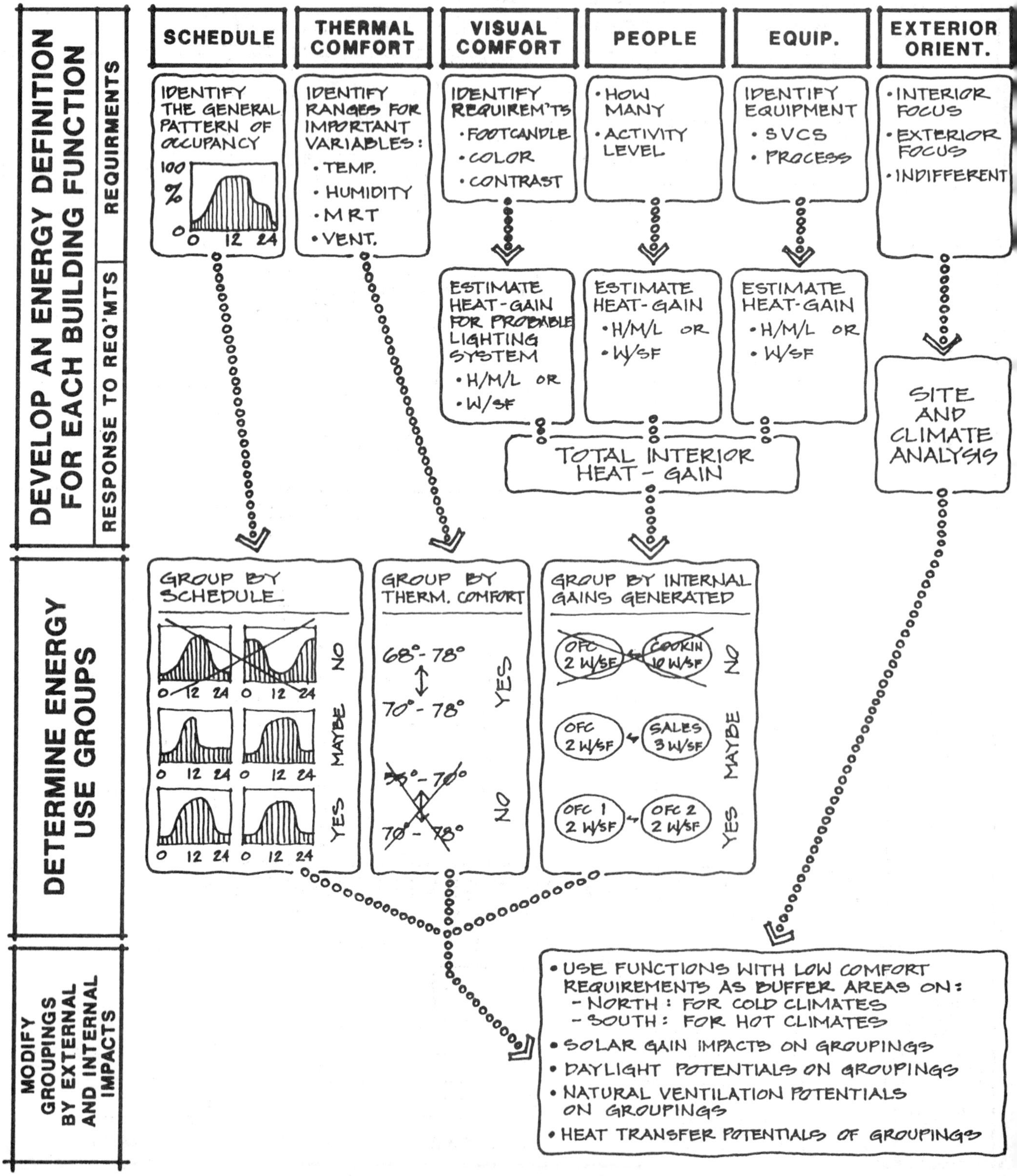

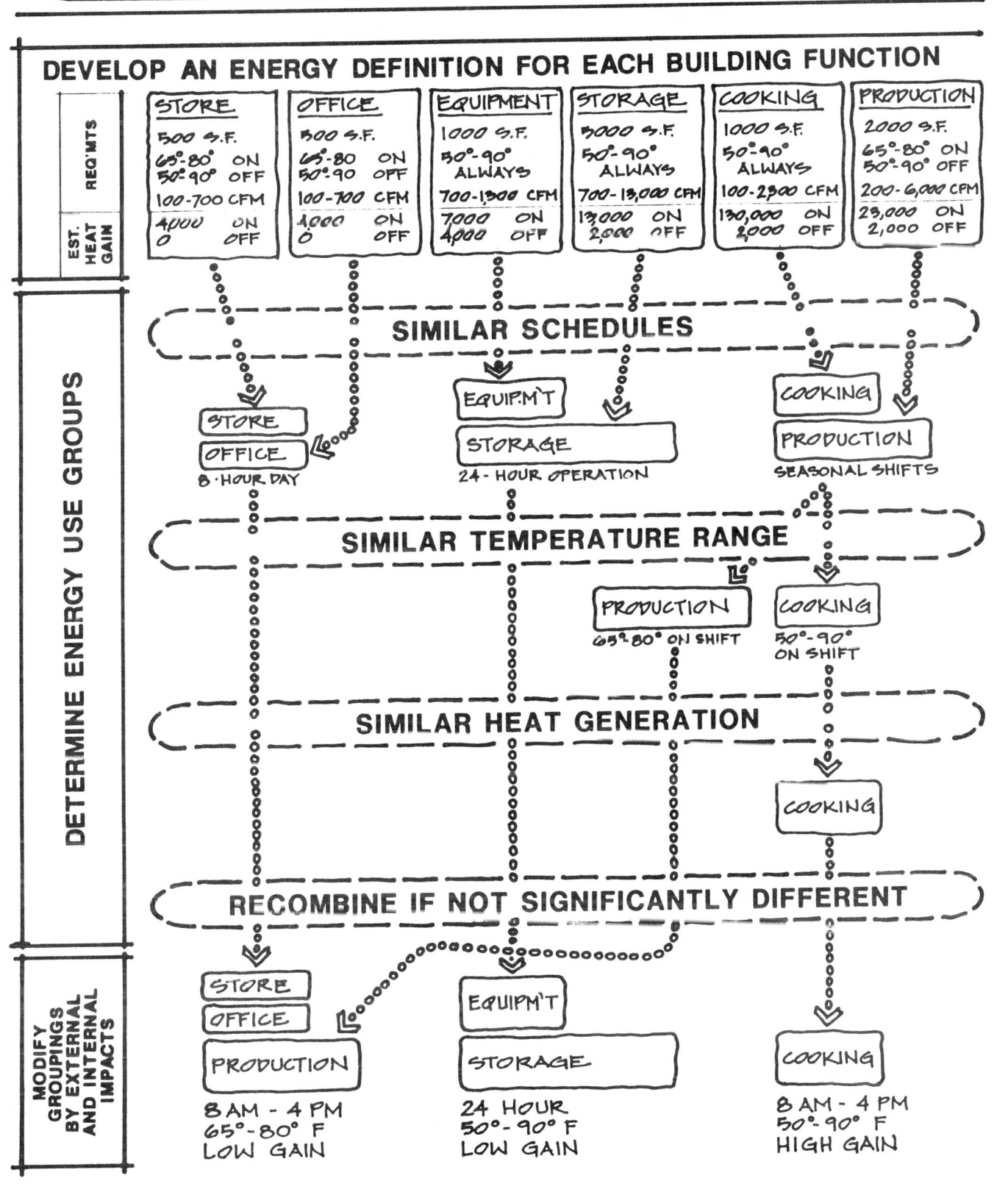

STEP 3: OPTIMIZE IMPACTS OF BUILDING FUNCTIONAL REQUIREMENTS — EXAMPLE

DEVELOP AN ENERGY DEFINITION FOR EACH BUILDING FUNCTION

	STORE	OFFICE	EQUIPMENT	STORAGE	COOKING	PRODUCTION
REQ'MTS	500 S.F. 65°-80° ON 50°-90° OFF 100-700 CFM	500 S.F. 65°-80° ON 50°-90° OFF 100-700 CFM	1000 S.F. 50°-90° ALWAYS 700-1300 CFM	5000 S.F. 50°-90° ALWAYS 700-13,000 CFM	1000 S.F. 50°-90° ALWAYS 100-2300 CFM	2000 S.F. 65°-80° ON 50°-90° OFF 200-6,000 CFM
EST. HEAT GAIN	4000 ON 0 OFF	1000 ON 0 OFF	7000 ON 4000 OFF	13,000 ON 2,000 OFF	130,000 ON 2,000 OFF	23,000 ON 2,000 OFF

DETERMINE ENERGY USE GROUPS

SIMILAR SCHEDULES

- STORE / OFFICE — 8-HOUR DAY
- EQUIP.M'T / STORAGE — 24-HOUR OPERATION
- COOKING / PRODUCTION — SEASONAL SHIFTS

SIMILAR TEMPERATURE RANGE

- PRODUCTION — 65°-80° ON SHIFT
- COOKING — 50°-90° ON SHIFT

SIMILAR HEAT GENERATION

- COOKING

RECOMBINE IF NOT SIGNIFICANTLY DIFFERENT

MODIFY GROUPINGS BY EXTERNAL AND INTERNAL IMPACTS

STORE / OFFICE / PRODUCTION	EQUIPM'T / STORAGE	COOKING
8 AM – 4 PM 65°-80° F LOW GAIN	24 HOUR 50°-90° F LOW GAIN	8 AM – 4 PM 50°-90° F HIGH GAIN

13

STEP 4: OPTIMIZE IMPACTS OF LOADS

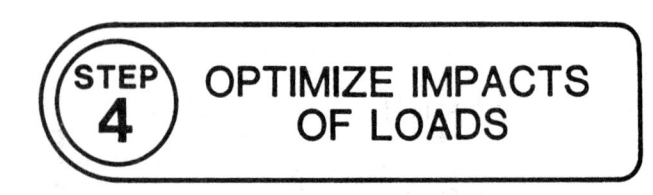

Control Internal Loads

Lighting

a. Select appropriate <u>illumination criteria</u>
   - illumination level
   - glare control (direction/contrast)
   - color quality (full spectrum/limited spectrum)

Note: there is some evidence that full spectrum (including daylight) gives acceptable visible performance at lower levels than partial spectrum illumination.

50-30-10 FC

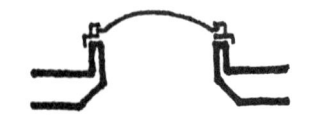

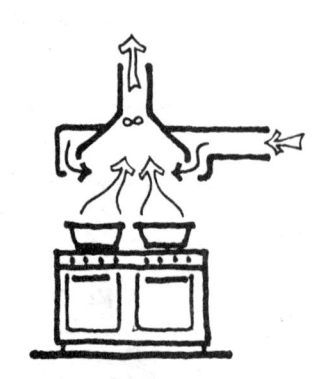

b. Design an <u>efficient system</u>
   - basic system configuration
   - uniform: flexible but efficient
   - task/ambient: efficient but flexibility problems
   - daylight augmented: efficient, perimeter limited, design demanding

c. Provide <u>effective control</u>
   - zoning
   - switching (manual/automatic); investigate lighting condition, occupancy

Equipment Loads

Normally a heat gain (except supermarket freezers); designer needs to know magnitude and duration of gains. Possible actions include:

- Use beneficially:
    Example 1; heat reclaim from refrigeration coil to preheat Domestic Hot Water.

    Example 2; run-around cycle on exhaust to preheat incoming air.

- Control:
    Example; provide shut-off switches on exhaust systems (manual, timed, condition actuated)

Control External Loads

Control Conduction

Use insulation
Eliminate thermal breaks

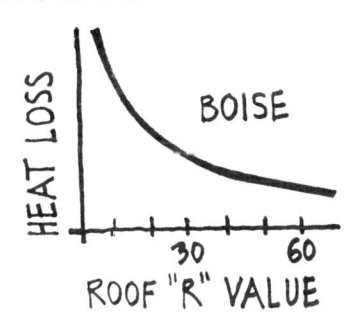

Control Convection

o infiltration/leakage
o ventilation rate

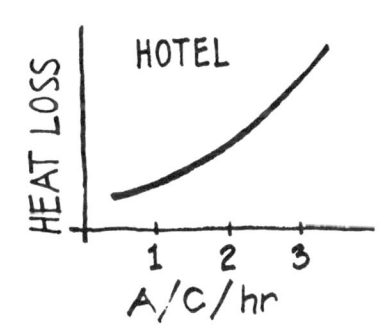

Control Radiation

Shade glass
- fixed
- operable (adjust with season)
- foliage (tracks season with you)

Glass characteristics
- effective aperature (area x shading coefficient); where shading coefficient includes internal shading, external shading, and glass characteristics
- daylighting (area x transmittance)

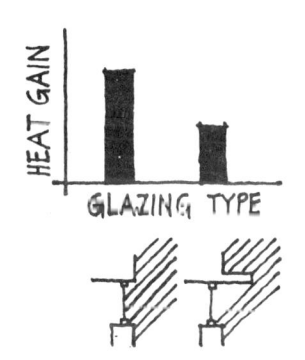

Control Humidity

Site planning:
    Example; control proximity to high evaporative sources

Balance Loads

Move the Load Through the Space

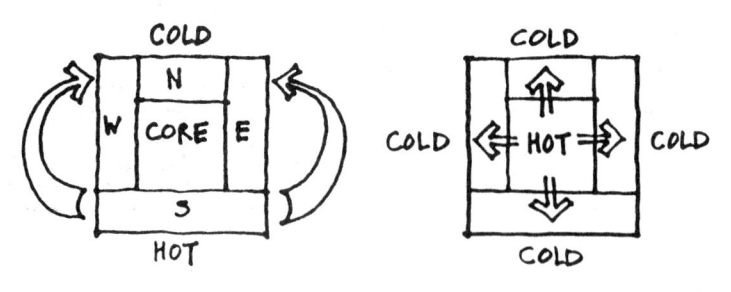

Move the load between zones

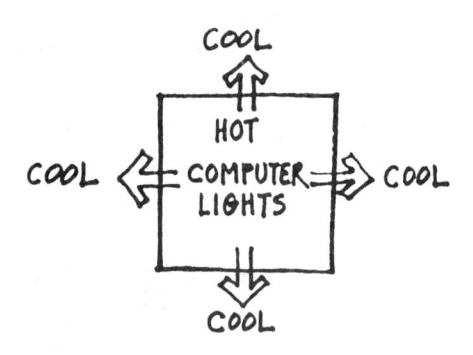

Move the load outside the building
- on spring day, outdoor air at 60 degrees (F.) is cool enough to help airconditioning load but not so cold as to impose a heating load

Move the Load Through Time (Thermal Storage)

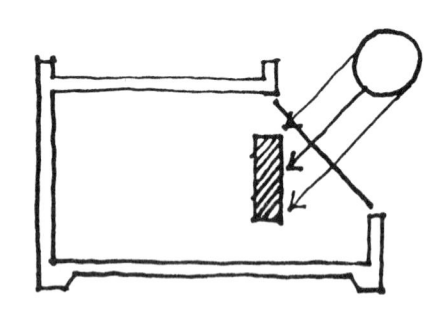

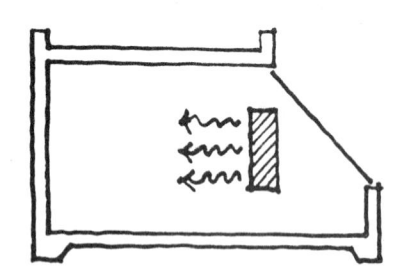

Move the load from day to night using thermal storage

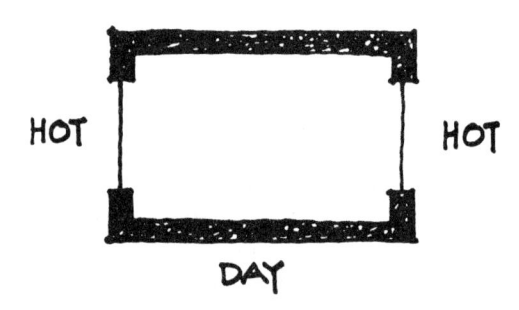

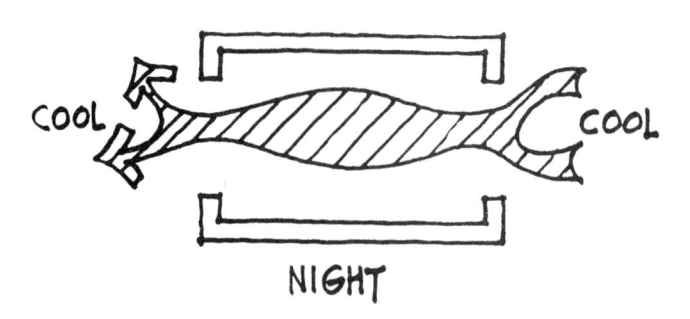

Move the load from summer to winter using thermal storage
- generate ice in winter to absorb heat over summer

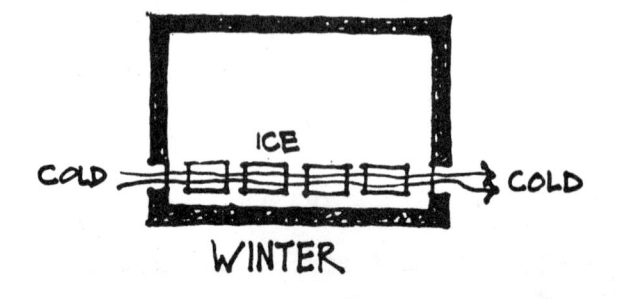

STEP 5: IMPROVE SYSTEMS

PRINCIPLES

FIRST CONSIDERATION: CONCENTRATE ON MOST IMPORTANT SYSTEM(S)

If HVAC*
**
(bars showing P, L, C, H)

If LIGHTING
(bars showing L, C, H)

SECOND CONSIDERATION: USE A PRIORITIZED APPROACH TO SYSTEM IMPROVEMENTS

EXAMPLES

Principle	Example
System Selection	- appropriate system for the job is most important
Controls	- controls have major impact
System Sizing	- avoid oversizing
System Zoning	- can have strong impact
Equipment Efficiency	- don't overlook this consideration
System Efficiency	- select HID, flourescent, or incandescent as appropriate for task
Illumination Level	- design for task
Controls	- control smallest practical area
Task Lighting	- allows lower ambient levels
Daylighting	- impact varies based on building type

* which end-uses are most important? (from STEP 1)
** P = Process, L = Lighting, C = Cooling, H = Heating

STEP 5: IMPROVE SYSTEMS

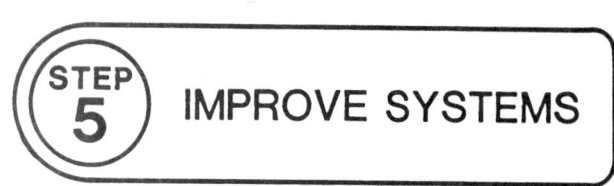

PRINCIPLES

FIRST CONSIDERATION: CONCENTRATE ON MOST IMPORTANT SYSTEM(S)

SECOND CONSIDERATION: USE A PRIORITIZED APPROACH TO SYSTEM IMPROVEMENTS

If SERVICE HOT WATER
- Quantity
- Set Temperature
- Point of Use Heating

If PROCESS
- Determine Efficient Process
- Technically Qualified Design

EXAMPLES

- tailor discharges to minimum practical
- lower to practical minimum
- consider for dispersed loads

- usually needs a specialized investigation
- impacts can be sizeable

STEP 6: INTEGRATE BUILDING SYSTEMS

#1 Principle: Major Energy Systems are Intergrated

Systems should be designed with integrated functioning in mind.

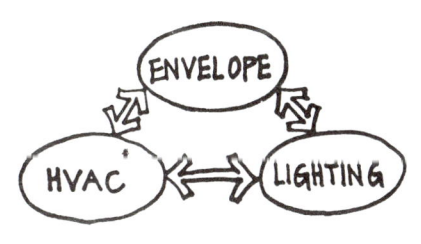

- objective is to optimize total building performance
- benefits from a design team approach
- synergistic effects often can save energy and energy cost, lower construction cost, and improve amenities

Example: consider downsizing cooling system based on lighting reduction

#2 Principle: Whenever You Change One System Look for Changes in Other Systems

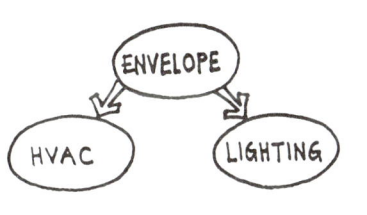

Example: Small windows = no daylight

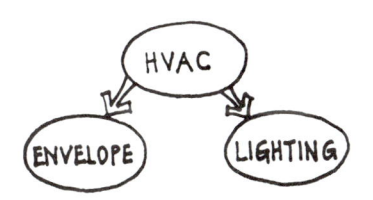

Example: Return Air plenum = lighting heat extraction

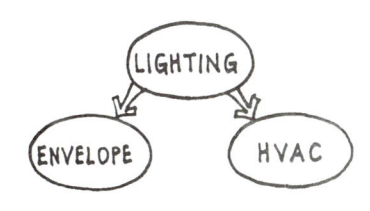

Example: more efficient lights = HVAC oversized

#3 Principle: Look for Trade-Offs and Compensating Effects

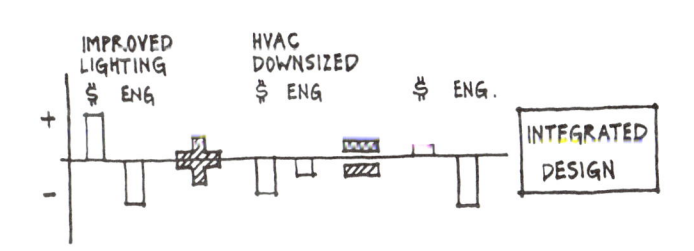

Example (POSITIVE): Improved lighting with HVAC downsized because cooling load is reduced

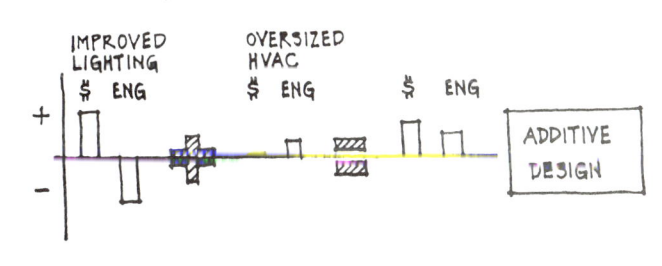

Example (NEGATIVE): Improved lighting with no HVAC change - reduced cooling load means HVAC system operates more at part-load and is thus inefficient

STEP 7: COMPARE RESULTS WITH GOALS

CONDUCT **ANALYSES** OF ENERGY CHARACTERISTICS OR BEHAVIOR OF BUILDING DESIGN, CONSISTENT WITH FORMAT OF GOALS SELECTED IN STEP 2 :

- COMPONENTS & SYSTEMS
- ENERGY TARGET
- DEMAND TARGET
- COST TARGET (ENERGY & DEMAND)
- QUALITY TARGETS

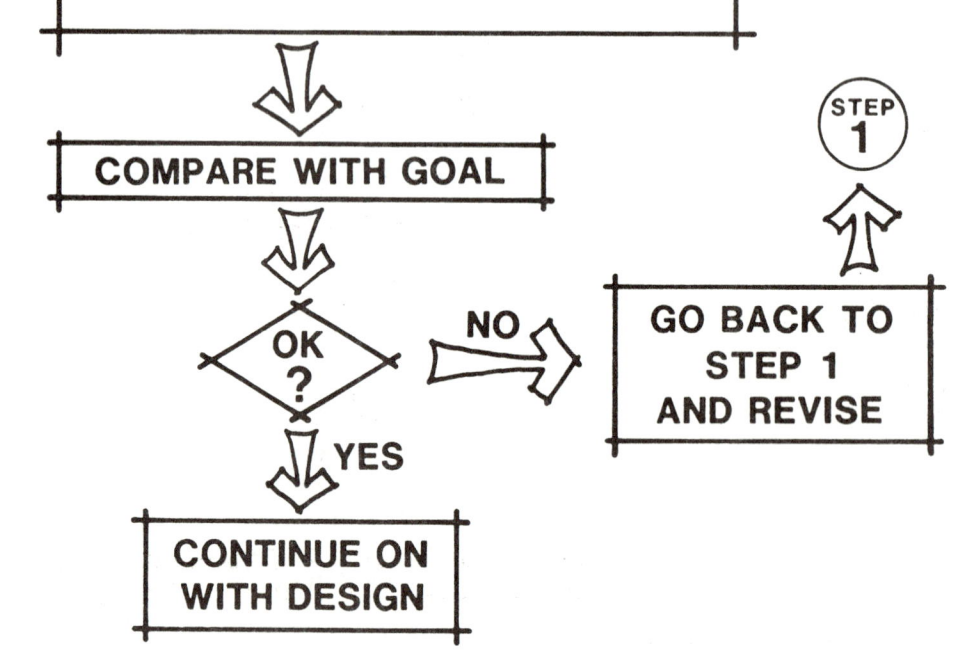

⬇

COMPARE WITH GOAL

⬇

OK? — NO → **GO BACK TO STEP 1 AND REVISE** ⬆ STEP 1

↓ YES

CONTINUE ON WITH DESIGN

2 ENERGY FUNDAMENTALS

2.1 ENERGY USE IN BUILDINGS

2.1.1 Thermodynamics

Thermodynamics describes heat movement. There is a certain order to the movement of heat energy: It flows in a specific manner; it can be manipulated through the use of materials; it can be stored, borrowed, bought and given away. To design with it, as opposed to against it, one needs to know its laws.

First Law of Thermodynamics

The first and second laws of thermodynamics are basic to any discussion of energy. The first law is: "Energy can neither be created nor destroyed." Energy can be transformed from one form, such as light, into equivalent quantities of another form, such as heat, but the total amount of energy in any transaction, and in the universe, remains constant. Energy can be converted, absorbed, stored, and distributed. Sunlight streaming through a window is absorbed by furniture, floor and walls as heat. Some is not absorbed--it is reflected as light back into the space. Electrical energy sent to a light bulb is converted into light and heat energy, illuminating and heating the space.

Ultimately, heat or light released or collected in a building either will be converted into work done (e.g., maintenance of satisfactory environmental conditions) or will be lost through the building skin.

Figure 2.1.1.1 - First Law of Thermodynamics: "Energy can be neither created nor destroyed."

Second Law of Thermodynamics

The second law of thermodynamics states that when free interchange of heat takes place, it is always the hotter of two bodies that loses energy and the colder that gains energy; (see Figure 2.1.1.2). A more general statement of this principle is that energy cannot spontaneously transform from a lower to a higher state. Work can only be done in passing from a higher energy state (such as light) to a lower energy state (such as heat). For energy to flow in the opposite direction, it must be forced: additional energy must be applied and, thus, work must be done on the system.

The second law of thermodynamics implies that all systems tend to achieve equilibrium. Thus, to establish a division between hot and cold in a substance that has reached a uniform temperature requires the use of either a heater to warm up part of the substance, or a cooling device to cool down part of it. Either action requires usage of additional energy.

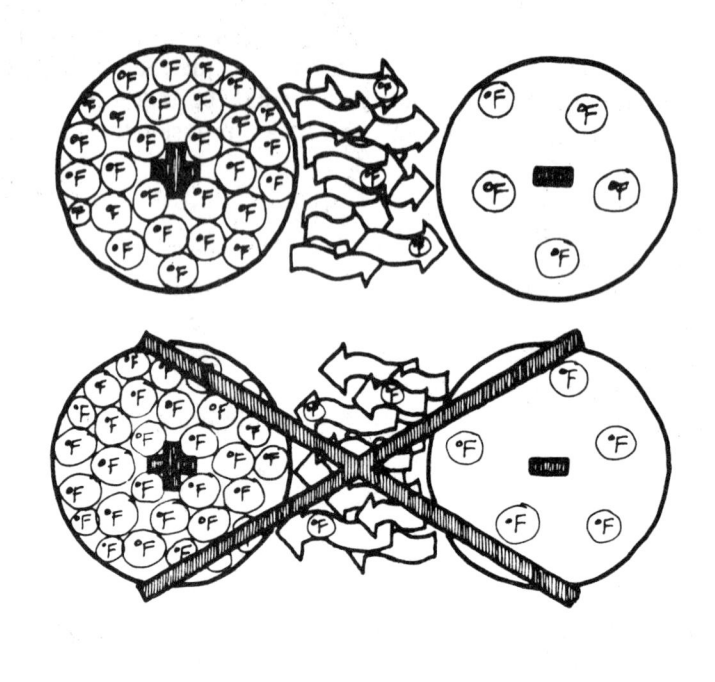

Figure 2.1.1.2 - Heat Flow

Heating a building is similar. Left alone, the cold air outside and the warm air inside will reach a state of equilibrium, with the warm molecules sharing their heat with the cold ones. This will happen even with a completely airtight building, because the warm air will heat the inside of the envelope and the cold air will cool the outside of the envelope until both bodies of air and the envelope are at the same temperature. To keep the inside air warm, then, requires an addition of energy, heat. Cooling a building is basically similar except that energy is required to extract unwanted heat from the building.

2.1.2 Heat Transfer

Heat flows or travels in different manners: conduction, convection, and radiation. Heat can also be absorbed or released in phase changes.

These types of heat transfer occur naturally outside the building, at the skin of the building, and within the building itself. The manipulation of these forces enables the design professional to provide suitable interior conditions without requiring the unnecessary expenditure of energy resources. An understanding of the laws of thermodynamics will help the designer to work in conjunction with these laws, creating and manipulating desired thermal transfers throughout a building.

Conduction

Conduction (Figure 2.1.2.1) is the heat flow between adjacent molecules, whether the molecules are within a single substance or in two separate bodies in direct contact, such as air molecules in contact with a warm substance. Conduction occurs when the warmer molecules, which are vibrating faster than the colder molecules, transfer part of their energy to the colder molecules.

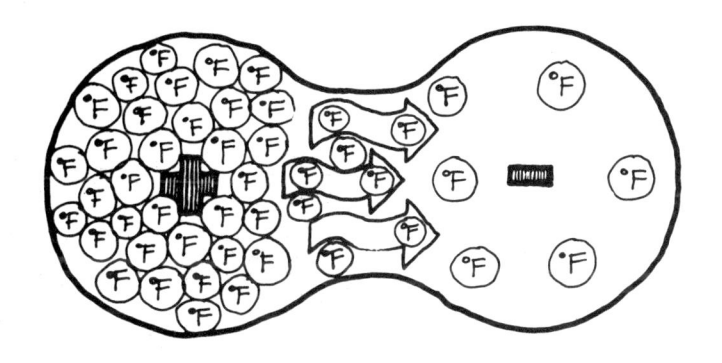

Figure 2.1.2.1 - Conduction

Convection

Convection (Figure 2.1.2.2) occurs when a fluid such as gas or liquid is involved. The fluid is heated (heat energy is added to the fluid) and then the fluid containing this heat moves from one place to another. This movement can be forced mechanically, such as by using a fan to move warm air from a furnace to a room, or more "naturally," without mechanical assistance, as when smoke rises up a chimney or when warm air in a room rises to the ceiling, allowing cool air to fall to the floor.

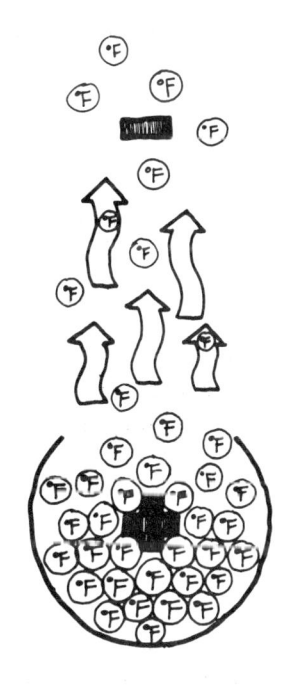

Figure 2.1.2.2 - Convection

Radiation

Radiation (Figure 2.1.2.3) is the transport of energy in the form of electromagnetic radiation. Sunlight, for instance, is one form of electromagnetic radiation. As sunlight passes through the air and a window pane to reach the interior of a room, very little of its energy is absorbed. When the light energy hits objects in the room, some of it is absorbed as heat, which is infrared energy. The portion of light energy that is not immediately absorbed when it hits objects in the room is reflected. Eventually this light energy is fully "used" or absorbed, either by objects in the room in the form of heat or by our eyes. Materials absorb, reflect and transmit radiation to varying degrees. For the same transmission level, high absorption means lower reflectance and vice versa.

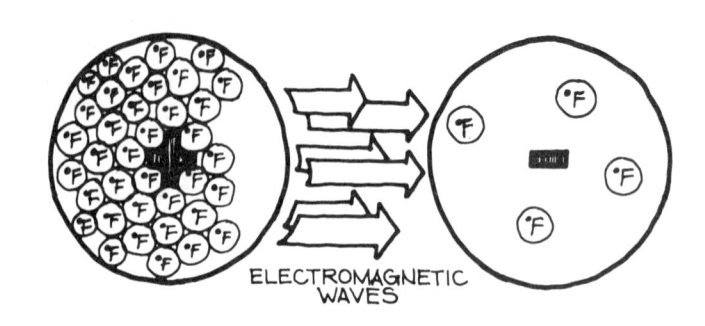

Figure 2.1.2.3 - Radiation

Polished aluminum is a good reflector of both light and heat radiation; asphalt paving is not.

2.1.3 Phase Changes

Phase changes (Figure 2.1.3.1) involve the relatively large amounts of energy needed to change the phase of substance (i.e., from solid to liquid and liquid to gas). The change of phase that occurs when water evaporates into water vapor, for example, requires almost a thousand times as much energy as it takes to raise water temperature one degree (F). This is the basis of evaporative cooling, which adds water to warm air; this process of evaporating water into air cools the air by the removing of heat required for evaporation.

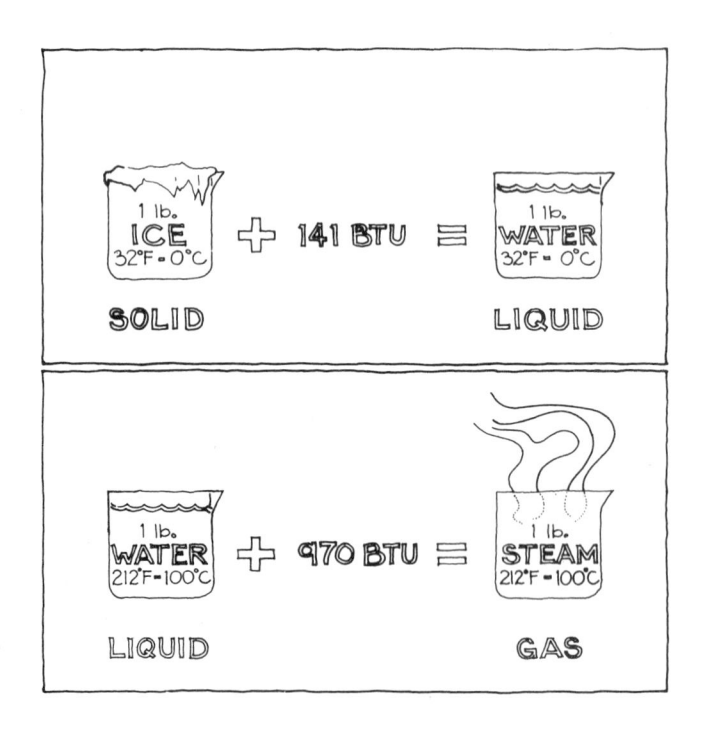

Figure 2.1.3.1 - Phase Change

2.1.4 Building Energy Flow

Energy flows into, within and out of a building according to the laws of thermodynamics. The energy transfer results from solar heat and light (sunshine), wind convection, pressure differences and temperature differences between inside and outside, as well as between conditioned and unconditioned spaces. It flows with people entering and leaving the building, their activity levels, the use of equipment in the space, and mechanical heating, cooling, ventilation, lighting, domestic hot water and conveyance systems.

An important element of energy flow is time. The quantity of energy (both natural and mechanical) that flows into and out of a building is ever-changing, as are the requirements for energy for various purposes. In many cases it may be as important to know *when* there is an energy problem as to know what the problem is. Solar energy is often abundantly available at a time when only a fraction of its total is needed. Many utilities offer power at a discount during off-hours when the energy is not needed or, conversely, charge a premium for power during peak times. Storing unneeded or relatively inexpensive energy at one time to use it at a later time can be an important energy-efficient design strategy.

The usefulness of energy depends in part on where it is located within the building. The waste heat from lighting may be a penalty in one part of the building, while other parts may use it instead of requiring the input of additional energy for heating. Heat can be transferred from one place to another either mechanically, such as by using a fan or pump to move warm air or water, or by heat exchange, in which a heated substance is used to heat a fluid, which is then used at that point or transported elsewhere. As an example of the first technique, an air-exhaust system located at the lights for the interior portion of a building can reduce the cooling load in this area due to the heat given off by the lights, while delivering the heated air to the perimeter of the building to satisfy heating loads there. This type of system generally requires the use of additional *mechanical* energy, but the *overall* efficiency of the system is improved. It is the efficiency of these and other building systems that will determine the size of the utility bill.

In most buildings some purchased energy will be required. Once this amount has been minimized by the use of on-site renewable energy, the next step is satisfaction of a building's remaining energy needs at the highest possible efficiency. Note that this efficiency is the ratio of energy purchased to service delivered, not simple mechanical efficiency. An example of the difference is the use of metal vapor lighting fixtures vs. fluorescents in an area that is ued only intermittently. The metal vapor lights give off more light per unit of electricity; however, because of their long warmup and restart times, these lights cannot readily be turned on and off. In this case, the fluorescents can require less energy to deliver the same light levels because they can be turned off when not needed.

Energy-Flow Diagram

To reduce the amount of purchased energy, the designer must develop strategies that reduce loads on consuming systems and/or their utility (delivery) systems. The energy-flow diagram (Figure 2.1.4.1) and accompanying definitions describe building energy flows and the load reduction concept. The diagram can be used to describe the complete energy-flow system of a building at a given instant in time.

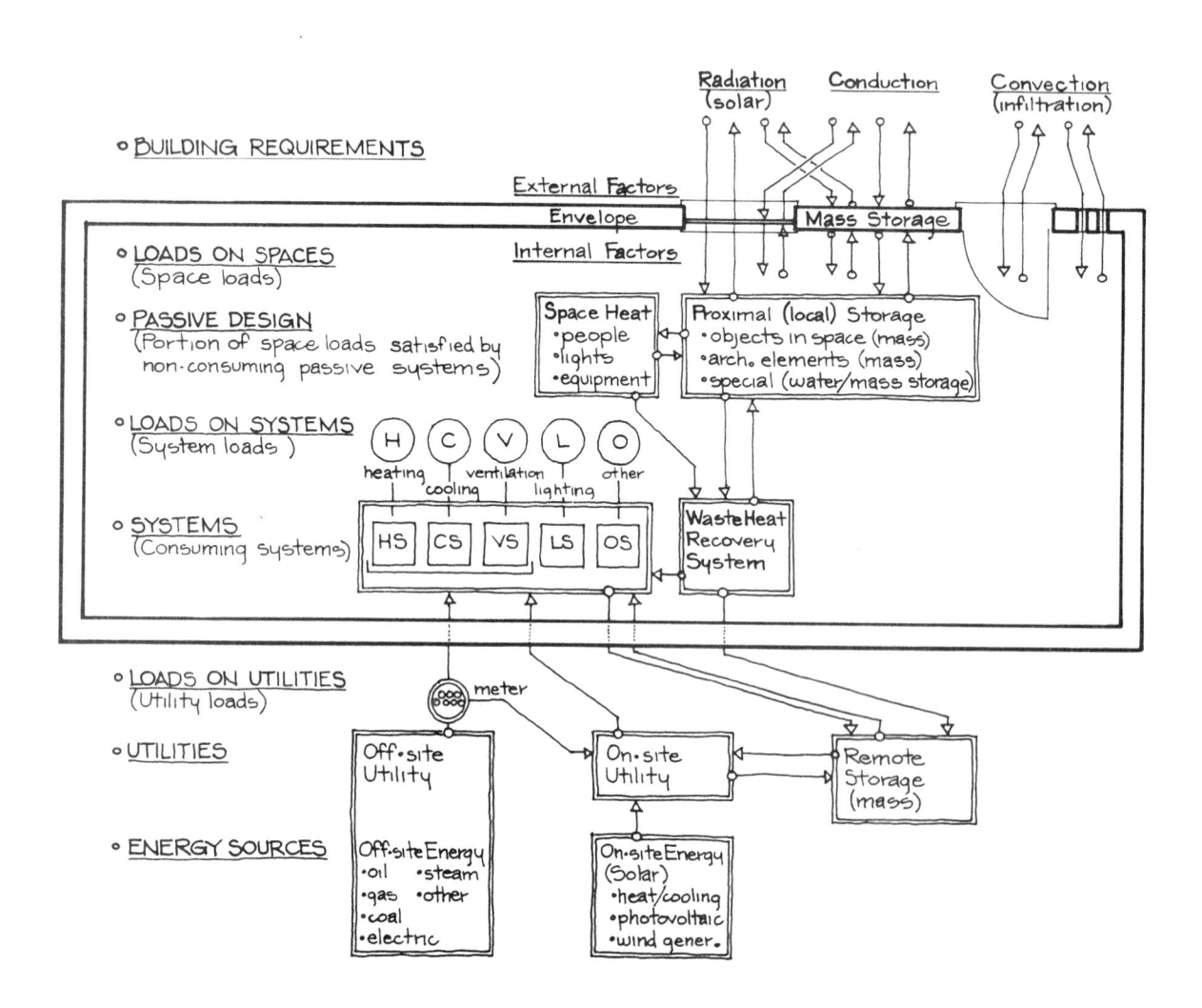

Figure 2.1.4.1 - Energy Flow Diagram

This instantaneous time can be used to describe any building design. However, actual energy use involves combining all these energy instants for a period of time. Like a motion picture, a series of these stop-action pictures must be put together sequentially to be useful.

Energy flow can be seen as a process in which building requirements (program factors) are translated into energy requirements (space loads) that are satisfied by passive (nonmechanical) and active (mechanical) systems. The active systems, depending on their efficiency, place loads on utility delivery systems (utility loads) that consume purchased energy resources.

The primary objective of energy-conscious design is to reduce utility bills by using cost-effective space and system design techniques.

The upper right of the energy-flow diagram shows passive energy flow into and out of the building or envelope system. The active energy flow appears at the lower left of the diagram. Passive flow consists of a direct solar radiation component through the glass envelope into internal spaces; a direct solar component absorbed by the opaque envelope and then conducted into internal space; a conduction component for the glass and opaque envelope; and convection components for infiltration, ventilation and air flow. Heat in the space can be stored and then released back into the space. Waste heat can be recovered from various sources. Recovered waste heat can be used directly to heat a space or as a heat source for heat-consuming systems, thus improving these systems' efficiency.

Storage systems can take advantage of waste heat by holding it until it is needed by the space or consuming systems. Storage can be used to collect unwanted heat, either solely to avoid overheating or to make it available for release back to the space later. Storage can be proximal--within the building or its structure--or remote. Storage can be coupled with and integral to the building structure or decoupled from the structure and located either inside or outside the building (e.g., in a hot water holding tank). Either type of storage can be used to keep heat from entering the internal spaces at an unwanted time by storing it during the day and releasing it at night.

Storage can fulfill other functions. It can collect energy from reclaimed waste heat, active heating and cooling systems, site utility systems, or some external source such as local industrial processes. Active systems (mechanical) can be used during hours when utility rates are low to heat or cool storage capacity, which then reduces the need to operate consuming systems when utility rates are higher.

Definitions for Building Energy Flow Diagram

Loads

Load: Demand for energy required at any given time to satisfy a need or needs.

Space Load: Energy demands resulting from program requirements, external factors, and internal factors.

Net Building Load: The demand for energy required to satisfy all space loads.

System Load: The demand for energy that must be provided by an active system in order to satisfy a space load. This is the <u>output</u> of systems such as the heating or cooling systems.

Utility Loads: The demand for energy that must be provided by a utility system (on-site or off-site) to satisfy system loads. This is the purchased energy <u>input</u> to a building. Also referred to as load "at the building boundary" or "at the meter."

Resource Load: The demand for an energy resource (fuel) that must be provided in order to satisfy utility loads.

Systems

Passive System: A system that uses natural, nonmechanical means to satisfy space loads.

Active System: A system that uses mechanical means to satisfy system loads.

Consuming System: A system that uses nonrenewable resources to satisfy loads.

On-and Off-Site Utility Systems: An off-site utility system is a local utility company, a district heating and cooling system, or an industrial cogenerator that makes excess energy available to others. An on-site utility is a system that satisfies utility loads from an energy supply located at the building site.

Storage

Stored Energy: Energy that is accumulated to satisfy a future imbalance between demand and system capacity.

Proximal Storage: Storage that is proximal to a space. It can either be coupled with the building structure or decoupled from the structure but within the building.

Remote Storage: Energy storage located outside the space and its envelope. Remote storage is normally used to improve heating- or cooling-system efficiency.

Cascading Energy

The concept of "cascading" energies considers changing energy quality as a hierarchial process in which recoverable waste heat is used repeatedly, each time on an application requiring a lower temperature or quality level, until the waste heat is no longer useful or needed.

Waste Heat: Heat that is unneeded at a current location or heat that is at too low a temperature or quality to do the work for which it was originally used.

Recoverable Waste Heat: The quantity of waste heat that is directly or indirectly available for use in some other purpose.

Energy

Energy is the capacity to do work. The units of energy most often used are the British thermal unit (Btu), which measures heat energy, and the kilowatt hour (kw-hr) or watt-hour (w-hr), which measure electric energy. The two units are inter-changeable: 3413 Btu = 1 kw/hr.

Power

Power is the <u>rate</u> at which energy is provided or used over a given <u>time</u> period. It is the ability to satisfy energy demand. Btu/hr (British thermal units per hour), kW (kiloWatt), and hp (horsepower) are units of power.

Usage

Usage is the total amount of energy used over a given period. Usage is often referred to as consumption. Since, by definition, energy can not be consumed, it is incorrect to describe energy use as consumption. Fossil fuels, however, can be consumed.

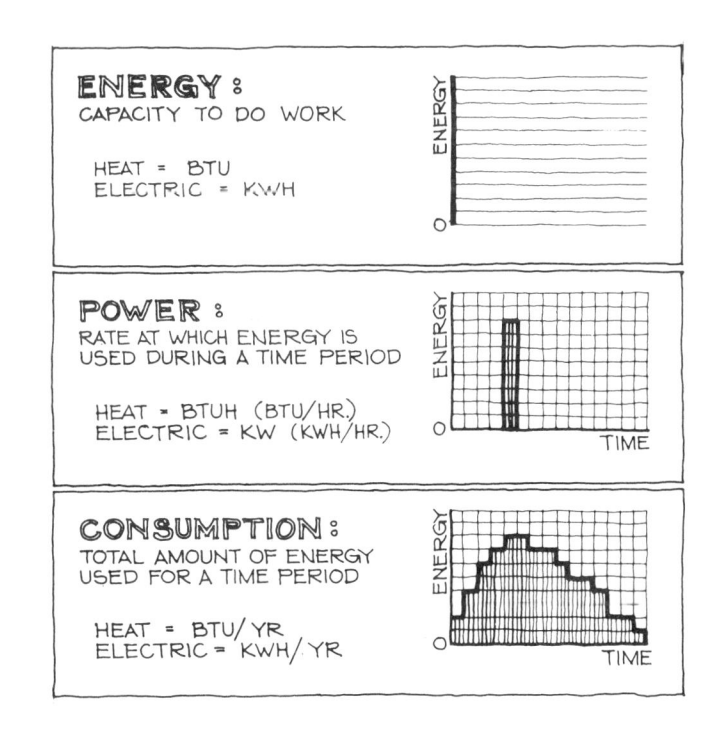

Figure 2.1.4.2 - Energy, Power and Usage

2.1.5 Heat Gain and Loss

In most buildings, heat gains and losses account for most energy use. The four basic components of heat gains and losses are:

- internal heat gain
- solar heat gain through glazing
- envelope heat gain and loss
- ventilation/infiltration heat gain and loss.

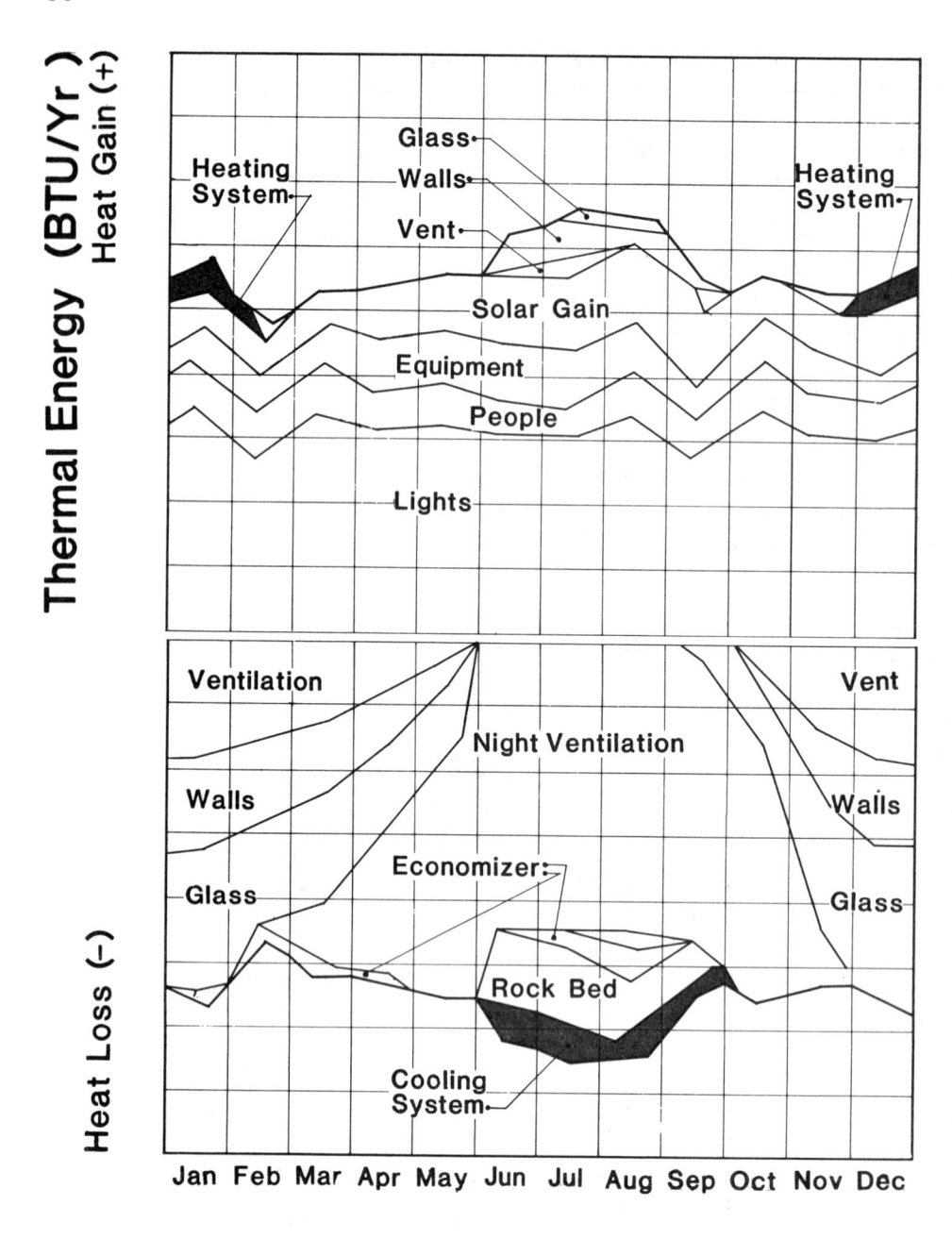

Figure 2.1.5.1 - Heat Gains and Losses

Internal heat gain is heat generated within a building space, and has three sources: occupants, lights and equipment. Internal heat gains are very regular and tend to follow occupancy patterns.

Solar heat gain through glazing is determined principally by the available insolation (both direct and diffuse sunlight), the exposed glazing area in each orientation and transmission through the glazed area of the envelope into the building.

Envelope heat gain and loss is the transmission of heat through the exterior envelope. The principal factors determining the rate and direction of heat flow are the temperature difference between the interior and exterior, the exposed envelope area (walls and roofs) and the heat transmission properties of the envelope.

Mechanical ventilation of a space also creates an opportunity for both heat gains and losses via the air being moved. The principal factors in ventilation heat gain and loss are the temperature difference between the interior and exterior and the ventilation rate.

Figure 2.1.5.1 above shows the full spectrum of gains and losses over a twelve-month period.

Infiltration heat gains and losses depend on the construction quality of the building. The rate of infiltration is associated with wind or stack effects on the building, and therefore tends to be high during winter months when winds are high.

Thermal balance analysis is a technique that adds up simultaneously occurring heat gains and heat losses to determine whether there is an overall loss or gain. Thermal balance calculations can be performed for rooms, zones, orientations, or entire buildings. They can also be performed for different times of day or year. The calculation compares the heat gain from lights, occupants, equipment, and solar to the losses and gains from envelope transmission and ventilation, including infiltration.

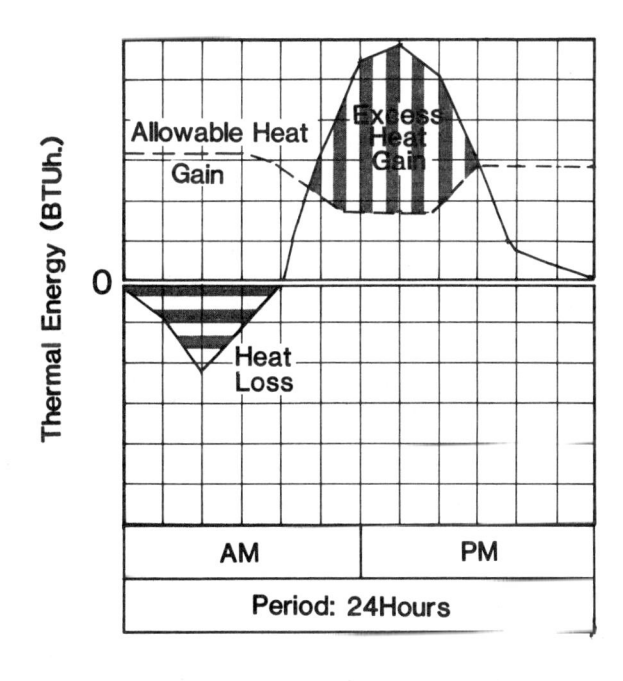

Figure 2.1.5.2 - Thermal Balance Analysis

The balance point is the theoretical condition where building gross heat gains equal gross heat losses. It has nothing to do with the action of an air-conditioning or heating system on building loads. It is affected by occupancy schedules, solar gain, and other factors that have time lag effects.

In the balance point model depicted in Figure 2.1.5.2, heat gains equal heat losses whenever the outdoor air temperature is at 52 degrees (F) without sunshine, and 41 degrees (F) with sunshine. Theoretically, this means that at these temperatures the buildings needs no heat addition or reduction. This analysis also shows the magnitude of the heat loss and gain components and their interrelations. This can provide an indication of potential tradeoffs among them.

Figure 2.1.5.2 shows a typical thermal balance analysis of a building. Figure 2.1.5.3 shows a thermal balance analysis for a single day.

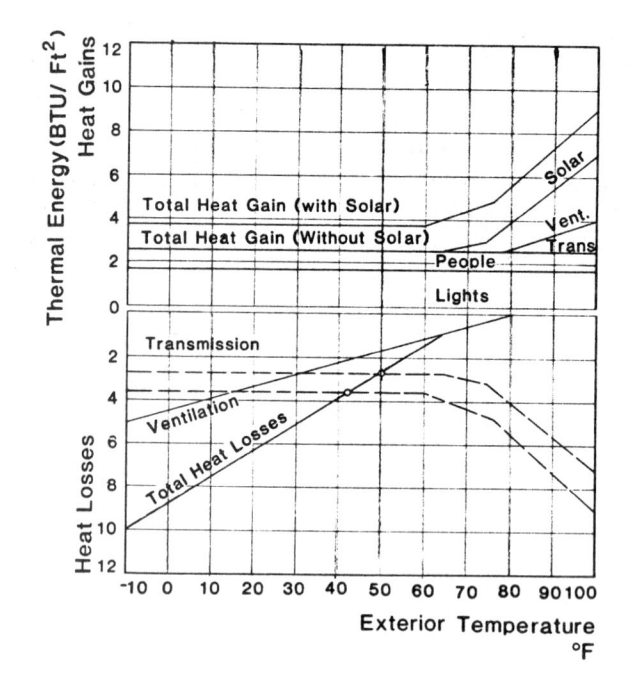

Figure 2.1.5.3. - Thermal Balance Analysis

2.1.6 Design Strategies

Introduction

Early design analysis should be directed toward balancing heat gains and heat losses. In this analysis, the heat-balance points are not as important as the magnitude of the heat losses or gains and their interrelation in order to assess the potential for energy efficiency. Thus, we can see the potential for trading heat gains for heat losses through proper design decisions. The thermal balance model allows the visualization of how different strategies increase or decrease certain heat gains or losses so that they approach equality.

Particular design strategies can be used to increase or decrease certain heat gains and losses to approach an equality between the heat gain/loss values on the thermal balance chart:

- increase/decrease internal heat gain;
- increase/decrease solar heat gain;
- increase/decrease envelope heat gain or loss;
- increase/decrease ventilation heat gain or loss;
- increase/decrease stored energy (heat or cold).

There are a number of available design options to accomplish each of these design strategies. When selecting these strategies, or options, heat gain or loss ramifications should be considered for each strategy. For instance, using daylighting to reduce the internal heat gains from artificial lighting will increase the solar heat gain if shading is not used.

Increase Internal Heat Gain	Decrease Internal Heat Gain
Concentrate Density of Heat Gains —Centralize spatial location of heat gain sources —Modify occupancy schedule —Use available heat sources	Reduce Lighting Use by Employing Daylighting —Increase window size —Locate windows high in the wall —Control glare with drapes, shutters —Eliminate direct sunlight, reflect into spaces —Slope walls to self-shade windows and reflect light —Use clear glazing —Use light colors on interior walls —Use automatic dimming controls on electric lighting Increase Exposure of High Heat Gain Areas —Increase local volumetric and/or ventilation loss —Isolate heat gain sources —Locate heat gain source in proximity to areas needing heat gain Capture Heat and Store or Transfer to Heat Loss Areas —Heat of light recovery —Heat recovery from condenser water —Water as equipment cooling medium Modify Occupancy Schedule to Shift or Disperse Internal Heat Gains Throughout Period —Shift heat gain operation to time when gain can be accommodated —Stagger operation of equipment to allow heat gain to dissipate —Use heat sinks if available.

Figure 2.1.6.1 - Internal Heat Gain (Design Strategies for Thermal Balance)

Increase/Decrease Internal Heat Gain

In commercial buildings, internal gains are generally dominant, with lighting usually the primary source of internal heat.

Although not an efficient method of heating, during the heating season, lighting will offset heat loss. In the cooling season, lighting can become the predominant internal heat gain. In fact, cooling the heat of light may account for as much as 50 percent of the airconditioning load, with ventilation, heat of occupancy, and equipment following as less dramatic but important sources of internal heat gain. Let us first consider the sources of internal load other than lighting.

Heat of occupancy or human use is affected by the schedule and intensity of use. These heat gains can be reduced by spreading the use of the building evenly over occupied periods to level loads and reducing the maximum size of mechanical conditioning equipment.

For a nonairconditioned building, it is important to match, as much as possible, the activities to the natural cycle of temperature fluctuation in the building.

Heat generated by equipment is an easily identifiable source of heat gain. In some cases, this heat may be exhausted directly to the outside. Unless it contributes to allowable heat gain, "throwing away" heated air as exhaust may be more energy-efficient than refrigerating and reusing it.

Equipment heat gains in general are small, and therefore, normally do not result in a serious energy use problem.

Lighting, the most significant internal heat gain, is also the one most easily modified. Electric light is created by the superheating of a filament or gas. In a typical office building, installation of fluorescent lighting fixtures, 20 to 30 percent of the energy used by lighting is converted to light. The remaining 70 to 80 percent is converted to heat and radiated from the fixture housing to the air in the occupied or ceiling space. Relative proportions depend on the type and design of the fixture. Therefore, electric lighting not only consumes energy to produce light, but produces space heat which must be offset with airconditioning when it doesn't contribute to allowable heat gain.

Any method of reducing the amount of electric lighting obviously reduces power use for both lighting and cooling. It is common knowledge that lighting standards tend to be general and, consequently, over-conservative, stressing quantity over quality. It is possible to reduce lighting levels significantly if good lighting design techniques are used for specific environments. This reduction can be quite dramatic, with a change from 3.0 to 1.0 watts/sq.ft.

More dramatic conservation may be achieved by maximum use of natural light. Not only does this further reduce the need for electric lighting, it also offers several distinct advantages. Natural light provides illumination equal to electric light, while producing less heat, as various glazings and shading techniques can be used to reduce the amount of infrared radiation transmitted to the space. Some form of shading must be provided for glass areas to prevent excessive direct solar gain if the use of daylighting is to be effective. Depending on the window-wall section, adequate lighting levels can be achieved from 18 to 28 feet from the window wall with no electrical lighting. Light can also be provided by skylights and light courts. In single-story buildings, inclusion of daylighting introduces minimal constraints on form, because skylights may be used. In multistory buildings, the building configuration must be relatively narrow to provide habitable space with natural light.

This configuration increases wall-surface area relative to floor area, and thus the potential for energy transfer through the building shell is similarly increased. In addition, it implies the use of larger glass areas with correspondingly low U values. In other words, maximum use of daylight may mean a corresponding increase in envelope heat gains/losses.

Increase Solar Gain	Decrease Solar Gain
Increase Exposure to Direct Solar Radiation —Provide reflectors to concentrate insolation —Avoid shading —Increase surface area to enclosed volume ratio —Slope roof toward south —Use clear glazing Reduce Reflectance —Use dark colors on walls/roof —Texture surfaces Consider Active Solar Heating —Hot water system —Hot air system	Decrease Surfaces Exposed to Radiation —Reduce surface area to enclosed volume ratio —Utilize site elements for shading —Orient building to minimize insolation —Configure building edge to provide self-shading —Provide shading devices Increase Reflectance —Use smooth surfaces —Use light colors —Use solar film on glazing Increase Thermal Transmission Resistance —Decrease U Increase Heat Capacity —Increase thermal mass Consider Solar Cooling —Absorption cooling for active systems —Long wave radiation for passive systems

Figure 2.1.6.2 - Solar Heat Gain   (Design Strategies for Thermal Balance)

Increase/Decrease Solar Heat Gain

Solar radiation is a major contributor to heat gain. Building configuration affects the amount of exterior wall area and therefore the available area exposed for solar heat gain. Exterior wall-to-floor-area ratios range from 1.5/1.0 in a residential-scale building, to 0.5/1.0 in a multistory building (30 floors). Building configuration is normally represented by the two variables of "length-to-width ratio" and "surface-area-to-volume ratio."

The impact of these two variables depends on both the amount of exterior wall and the percentage of wall area exposed to solar radiation (orientation). Percentage of east-west wall area are critical as these surfaces receive direct solar radiation, in some cases perpendicular to the surface. Consequently, for a given floor area, solar gains can be increased by increasing the external surface-area-to-volume ratio. In general, this means that taller buildings or buildings with a deep or wide floor areas receive less external gains. For two buildings with similar surface-area-to-volume ratio, the building with a smaller length-to-width ratio has less external gain. Another configuration often used for daylighting is the courtyard building. Its efficiency is roughly equivalent to that of an elongated rectangular building (length-to-width of 4:1). The reason this configuration is not more efficient is that shading advantages in the court can be offset by increased envelope heat loss/gain.

The enclosed-atrium building is similar to courtyard building, but differs in that it is enclosed. Unless the atrium is conditioned, its performance is superior to the courtyard, as external gains are only increased by the skylight area (as opposed to the internal courtyard wall area). This is just one way to use unconditioned space to buffer conditioned space.

If external factors are the dominant forces, configuration can dramatically affect heat gain by increasing the surface-area-to-volume ratio. The effect is most dramatic on small or residential buildings and is relatively true for both shaded and unshaded conditions.

Solar radiation is transferred through the building envelope directly through windows and skylights, as well as indirectly through wall and roof surfaces.

Like that transferred through opaque wall materials, the amount of solar radiation transferred through glass depends on orientation and the heat-transfer characteristics of the glass. The amount of radiation transfer can be affected by changing the transmission characteristics or size of the glazed opening and/or using shading. Reducing the area of the glass is the simplest method of reducing incoming radiation.

Shading can be provided in a variety of different ways (external films, reflective glass, etc.). For the same shading device, the actual shading factor will vary from location to location, depending on latitude and microclimate.

Increase/Decrease Envelope Heat Gain/Loss

Heat is transferred indirectly through the building envelope by conduction through building materials. The rate of transmission depends to a large extent on the mass and/or transmission characteristics of the material. Here, the difference between solar radiation and ambient air as a source of heat gain/loss needs to be re-emphasized. The mass (usually expressed as weight) of the exterior envelope affects heat transfer by acting as a heat "sink."

Heat energy is absorbed by the wall's "heating up" to the outside condition before energy is transferred to the interior. This is also true for internal heat. The stored heat is released to both the inside and the outside when either temperature drops below the wall temperature. Heat storage is obviously an unwanted characteristic when cooling loads occur, as the impact of both solar radiation and ambient air temperature is prolonged by storage. The heat-storage aspect of mass also affects its use as a mechanism to resist heat transfer or to insulate. This can be accomplished more effectively by insulation. It is important to note that placement of the insulation may be as important as the amount, especially in conjunction with thermal mass. In hot climates insulation should be placed on the exterior side of a high-mass envelope. In this way excess heat can be absorbed from internal sources during the day and released to the spaces during the night. The insulation will work to reduce heat gain from external sources.

Insulation affects the transfer of external heat by reducing the conductivity of the exterior wall. Its density is practically negligible, so it has none of the inherent heat storage problems of mass.

Envelope

Decrease Internal Heat Loss: (Winter)*

Decrease U, Increasing Thermal Resistance
—Increase insulation
—Use double roof with ventilation space in between
—Texture surface to increase film coefficient
—Protect insulation from moisture
—Use multiple-layer glazing
—Use operable thermal shutters
—Eliminate thermal bridges
—Use both horizontal and vertical insulation for slab on grade
—Use movable insulation

Decrease Exposure to cold outside air
—Reduce surface area to enclosed volume ratio
—Consider below grade location for part(s) of the building
—Consider compact configuration (low length/width aspect ratio)
—Reduce floor-to-floor dimension
—Avoid elevated buildings, large overhangs, parking garages or intermediate levels

Decrease Infiltration
—Minimize wind effects by orienting major axis into the wind
—Site near existing windbreaks
—Provide vestibules for entrances
—Locate entrances on downwind side of building
—Reduce building height
—Use impermeable exterior surface materials
—Seal all vertical shafts
—Vertically offset or stagger stairwells, elevator shafts, mechanical shafts to avoid chimney effect
—Articulate surface with fins, recesses

Decrease the Temperature Differential
—Consider below grade location
—Employ highly textured surface
—Plant deciduous trees adjacent to building to moderate surface temperatures

Envelope

Increase Internal Heat Loss: (Winter)*

Increase U, Decreasing Thermal Resistance
—Increase openings
—Provide thermal bridges
—Use single glazing
—Decrease film coefficient by using smooth surfaces
—Decrease movable insulation

Increase Exposure
—Increase surface area to enclosed volume ratio
—Elevate building, provide intermediate open spaces
—Consider loose (large amount of edge) configuration

Increase Temperature Differential Through Site Manipulation
—Shade during cold periods
—Absorb cold in mass around building

Decrease External Heat Gain. (Summer)*

Decrease U, Increasing Thermal Resistance
—Increase insulation
—Use double roof with exhausted air space in between
—Texture surface to increase film coefficient
—Protect insulation from moisture
—Use multiple-layer glazing
—Use operable thermal shutters
—Eliminate thermal bridges
—Use both horizontal and vertical insulation for slab on grade
—Use movable insulation

Decrease Exposure
—Reduce surface area to enclosed volume ratio
—Consider below-grade location for part(s) of the building
—Consider compact configuration (low length/width aspect ratio)
—Reduce floor-to-floor dimension
—Avoid elevated buildings, large overhangs, parking garages or intermediate levels

Decrease Infiltration
—Minimize wind effects by orienting major axis into the wind
—Site near existing windbreaks
—Provide vestibules
—Locate entrances on downwind side of building
—Reduce building height
—Use impermeable exterior surface materials
—Seal all vertical shafts
—Vertically offset or stagger stairwells, elevator shafts, mechanical shafts to avoid chimney effect
—Articulate surface with fins, recesses

Decrease the Temperature Differential
—Consider below-grade location
—Use water, fountains to decrease heat buildup
—Employ highly textured surface
—Reduce paved areas in vicinity of building
—Plant deciduous trees adjacent to building to moderate surface temperatures

Figure 2.1.6.3 - Envelope Heat Gain (Design Strategies for Thermal Balance)

Since radiant energy is the primary source of heat gain, shading may be the more effective overall heat-reduction strategy. If a shading coefficient cannot be achieved in a cooling-dominated building, an adequate barrier should be provided against incoming radiation. This could be a buffer (unconditioned) space or some form of thermal mass.

Nevertheless, there are important reasons why a relatively high insulation value can be desirable. The performance of the building during the entire year must be considered, along with issues outside the realm of straight heat gain and loss. Normally, the extent of insulation will depend on the need for reducing heat loss in the winter heating season. Insulation might also help reduce the discomfort caused by drafts or condensation that might occur in the wall during the heating season. In addition to insulation, a vapor barrier is normally provided to reduce vapor migration and unwanted condensation.

There is one final consideration regarding the optimal amount of insulation, and that is heat transfer *out* of the building envelope. In buildings with high internal loads and sufficiently moderate outdoor temperatures, it may be advantageous to allow heat to transfer from the inside to the outside. Obviously the amount of insulation would affect this flow rate. Reduced insulation may be beneficial.

In a passive cooling example, buildings may actually reradiate internal heat during cooler night periods. In this situation, insulation could hinder positive heat-flow to the outside.

Whereas air temperatures fluctuate dramatically on a seasonal and even diurnal basis, the temperature of the earth is relatively stable. In summer, the earth is generally cooler than the atmosphere; in winter, warmer. Therefore, it is possible to use the relatively warmer and cooler earth temperatures to heat and cool a building.

The most familiar method is to use earth-integrated or underground construction. These terms refer to a variety of building/earth configurations. The earth is used in two distinct ways: as an insulator, and as an alternate thermal environment, not subject to the same seasonal fluctuations as the outside air.

The efficiency of earth-integrated construction in reducing or eliminating external gains depends on two factors: the percentage of the building which is actually buried (or subterranean) and the depth of soil around this space. For the buried portion of the building, efficiency depends on the temperature of the surrounding soil.

The actual performance of an underground building can be roughly estimated by assuming that all normal external gains and losses (ambient air and solar) can be reduced or eliminated. This depends on the depth and exposure of the particular building. At an average floor depth of 10 feet, solar heat gain can be reduced by 100 percent and the conductive heat gain by about 50 percent, for a total reduction of about 75 percent. The effectiveness of underground construction in reducing solar loads makes this an especially appropriate cooling strategy for hot climates.

So far, only external gains and losses, which can demonstrably be reduced by underground construction, have been discussed. This would seemingly indicate the effectiveness of underground construction for residential and other externally dominated buildings. Unfortunately, underground construction has no effect on internal spaces. In general, the feasibility of this technique for a particular building depends on the importance of external factors. Since soil type, density and water content can differ from place to place, it would be well to check site soil conditions before choosing underground construction as a design strategy.

Ventilation	Ventilation
Decrease Internal Heat Loss: (Winter)*	**Increase Internal Heat Loss: (Winter)***
Decrease Rate, N	Increase Rate, N
—Cascade ventilation	—Use economizer cycle (check humidity level)
—Use recycled air and minimum fresh air for large requirements	—Increase ventilation rate subject to maximum tolerable level (limited by noise, air movement)
—Filter contaminated air for recycling	—Orient operable windows to windward and leeward sides of the building
—Periodically shut down the system for a short time if allowable	Increase Temperature Differential
—Credit infiltration toward general ventilation requirement	—Shade intake during cold periods
—Place operable windows on adjacent walls to reduce through-ventilation	—Consider evaporative cooling
Decrease the Temperature Differential	**Decrease External Gain: (Summer)***
—Increase solar radiation at air intakes during cold periods	Decrease Rate, N
—Transfer energy from exhaust air to incoming air	—Cascade ventilation
Increase External Gain: (Summer)*	—Use recycled air and minimum fresh air for large requirements
Increase Rate, N	—Filter contaminated air for recycling
—Increase ventilation rate subject to maximum tolerable level (limited by noise, air movement)	—Periodically shut down the system for a short time if allowable
—Orient operable windows to windward and leeward sides of the building	—Credit infiltration toward general ventilation requirement
Increase Temperature Differential	—Place operable windows on adjacent walls to reduce through-ventilation
—Reduce shade on intake during hot periods	Decrease the Temperature Differential
—Reduce evaporative cooling effects	—Shade air intakes during hot periods
	—Consider evaporative cooling

Figure 2.1.6.4 - Ventilation Heat Gain (Design Strategies for Thermal Balance)

Increase/Decrease Ventilation Heat Gain/Loss

The effectiveness of natural ventilation, whether induced by wind, thermally, or mechanically, depends on the total effect of air movement, temperature and humidity.

Any natural ventilation system operates by inducing the flow of large quantities of air through the building interior. The heat capacity of this air will usually be in excess of any internal gains generated by the building; that is, if ventilation is sufficient to satisfy occupancy cooling needs, it is sufficient to remove most internal heat gains. In fact, internal gains can actually be used to accelerate air movement. While it might appear that the same could be said of external gains, this may not be the case. The addition of an external source of gain can exceed the heat-extraction capacity of the air, especially at critical times when solar gain is at its peak.

Air movement is created by a pressure difference, i.e., air moves from a higher to a lower pressure area. That pressure difference can be created by climatic conditions (wind), temperature difference (thermosiphon), or mechanical means (fans). In general, the choice of a particular means of inducing air movement is related to the climate and the reliability required of the system. Wind-induced cross-ventilation requires a minimal commitment of resources, but at most locations is not highly reliable. At the other extreme, mechanical ventilation is reliable but involves a capital machinery cost and operating expense.

Besides wind, another method of inducing air movement is to utilize a pressure differential created by changing the density of air through heating. Heated air rises because it expands to a lower density per volume than cooler air.

Confined in a space, this creates air movement as unheated air is pulled in at the base of the air column to replace the rising, lighter air mass. This effect is identical to the draft caused in the flue of a fireplace, hence the name "chimney effect." Any source of heat (solar, waste, process, combustion) may be used.

Like wind, the "thermosiphon effect" can be used only to induce air movement, not to change the temperature or humidity of incoming air. The effectiveness of the system, or the effective temperature created, is a product of air temperature and humidity as well as velocity. Unlike natural ventilation, however, the system does not require an unobstructed wind flow or a certain building orientation. Depending on the source of heat, this system could be used in an urban area where the prevailing wind is obstructed or reduced.

Whereas using wind ventilation prescribes a diffuse organization of individual spaces in the plan (relative to prevailing breezes), the thermosiphon effect suggests a more centralized plan. Air enters the building in the area where it will be used to cool, but then must be routed to the vent stack(s) that will exhaust it. This means that the orientation of the building need not depend on prevailing winds.

While it may seem that the entire interior air volume of the building should be moved at ventilation speed, this would require an excessively large stack relative to the building area. When using thermosiphon, wind, or mechanical ventilation, the obvious goal is to derive the greatest benefit from the smallest air movement. The stack then is designed to control air movement.

> **Storage**
>
> **Use Heat from Storage**
> Actively:
> —Use hot water systems
> —Use hot air system with rock storage
> —Use eutectic salt storage system
>
> Passively:
> —Use Thermal Mass
>
> **Storage**
>
> **Store Heat for Later Use**
> Actively:
> —Use hot water systems
> —Use hot air system with rock storage
> —Use eutectic salt storage system
>
> Passively:
> —Use thermal mass to store heat
>
> **Store Cold for Later Use**
> Actively:
> —Use chilled water tanks (run chillers at coolest diurnal temperature)
>
> Passively:
> —Use thermal mass to store nighttime cold by use of night flushing

Figure 2.1.6.5 - Storage Heat Gain   (Design Strategies for Thermal Balance)

Increase/Decrease Stored Energy

Thermal Mass establishes the heat storage capacity of the materials of a building. The ability of a building to provide a predetermined thermal environment in the face of widely varying exterior and interior conditions is thus due in part to its thermal mass.

The distinction between thermal mass and thermal resistance (insulation) must be understood. It is entirely possible to have a building with high thermal resistance and low thermal mass.

There are various means on increasing thermal mass by introducing high-mass material into the building envelope or internally in the space (see Chapter 3.5 - Structure and Mass). Such materials can store heat for several hours, causing a time-barrier between the building's interior temperature and the outside temperature. This phenomenon, called thermal lag, allows for the storage of heat and its subsequent release into or out of the building.

Energy diffusion or decrement factor is the change of energy directly related to time lag. In summer during the day, the wall may have an average temperature cooler than the exterior surface and, therefore, absorbs thermal energy. At night, because the wall temperature is warmer than the outdoor air temperature, some of the heat is reradiated to the exterior and never affects the wall's interior surface temperature.

The thermal lag of a building is subject to manipulation through choices of structure, closure, and materials. The desirability of high or low thermal mass is a function of climatic conditions, site factors, design interior conditions, and operating patterns.

The most common method of utilizing thermal mass is to store sensible heat in solid materials. Internal storage mass systems, such as a Trombe wall, can be structural or nonstructural. The most common materials of solid mass storage include:

- poured and precast concrete;
- brick;
- steel or fiber tube containers;
- adobe blocks;
- concrete-masonry units.

Water, with the highest heat capacity per unit weight of any material, can also be used by the designer as thermal mass for heat storage. Water Trombe walls, familiar in passive residential construction, are an example of the concept.

Thermal mass storage can further be classified into direct (proximal) and remote systems.

In a direct system, the space itself is the collector of heat. Heat can be stored in the building structure (floors, walls, ceiling). Concrete, brick, stone, and containers of water are effective for direct thermal storage. Phase-change materials (i.e., eutectic salts) using heat of fusion are also becoming effective for thermal storage. For thermal storage to temper the interior temperature fluctuations effectively, it must be insulated on the exterior wall surface.

Movable insulation systems over the glazing are generally required to reduce night heat losses.

Rather than allowing incoming radiation to be distributed and stored evenly on the space surfaces, a storage-wall heating system places the thermal mass directly behind the glazing. The mass intercepts the sunlight on its outer surface and transmit this heat through the wall by conduction. By adding high and low vents to the interior wall, heat can be supplied or removed by convection. The exterior surface of a storage wall must be highly absorptive to maximize collected energy.

In addition, heat losses are increased because of the proximity of the thermal storage mass to the glazing.

The storage roof system is similar to a storage wall except the intercepting thermal mass is located in the roof of the building. The thermal mass is usually water in transparent plastic bags. Movable insulation is required to control thermal gains and losses. The system is equally suited to both heating and cooling.

Sunspaces are another form of direct gain system. Technically, a sunspace is a direct-gain heating space with a south-sloping aperture. It is generally added on to temper the south wall of a primary living space. In this mode, the temperature in the sunspace floats over a fairly wide range in winter;

overheating is partially controlled by venting in summer. If plants and vegetables are to be grown, thermal storage must be included in the sunspace to keep temperatures from dropping below freezing.

Remote storage simply means that storage mass is not adjacent to the area of heat collection. A fluid (usually air or water) is used to transfer heat from the collection place to the storage mass. Rock beds, radiant slabs and water storage systems are all examples of remote storage. Stored heat is then distributed to the space again by a fluid medium.

Design Concept Analysis

Although thermal balance is a major step towards understanding energy flow in a building, other factors are of equal, if not greater, importance in determining energy use.

To fully understand the energy implications of a design concept, the designer must understand not only thermal balance, but the utility loads and cost factors that can help identify an overall design strategy for the building.

The energy-flow discussion earlier in this chapter will reinforce the importance of seeing the complete energy-system picture before deciding on a major design strategy.

A thorough picture can be developed through the use of logical energy design process. The purpose of this process is to develop primary energy design strategies and evaluate their potential. In order to evaluate the potential of energy-conscious design strategies, their relative impact on energy use and costs should be considered. There is a logical sequence for such an evaluation:

- Determine energy problems/opportunities;
- Establish energy/cost goals;
- Convert building functional requirements into energy requirements;
- Identify the thermal imbalances;
- Optimize the impacts of these loads through proper design;
- Select and design proper systems to handle these load requirements;
- Integrate these systems to evaluate interactions and the end result;
- Compare this end result with the energy/cost goals.

2.2 COMFORT & HEALTH

2.2.1 Introduction

Comfort within a space is based on specific thermal, visual, acoustical, and air quality levels. While perceptions of human comfort vary between individuals, as well as within each individual, there are limits to the range of environmental factors within which human comfort can be maintained and beyond which the individual's physiological and psychological processes become hindered.

2.2.2 Thermal Comfort

The human body is, in its most fundamental mechanical behavior, a heat engine. The fuel for the engine is derived from food. But human bodies are only about 20-percent efficient in converting food energy into useful work. They therefore must give off four times as much heat as they use in order to maintain a stable internal temperature.

Continuous cooling of the body is accomplished primarily by the exhalation of warm breath, the vaporization of water from the lungs and breathing passage, and the convection and radiation of heat from the surface of the skin.

When the rate of cooling achieved by these mechanisms is not enough to meet our body's demands, we perspire. Water is exuded from the pores of the skin, and this water then evaporates, thus undergoing a phase change from liquid to vapor. As discussed in the previous chapter, large quantities of heat can be lost in this way, and perspiration is sufficient under most conditions to provide the cooling required.

The American Society of Heating, Refrigerating and Airconditioning Engineers has defined thermal comfort for a person as "that condition of mind which expressed satisfaction

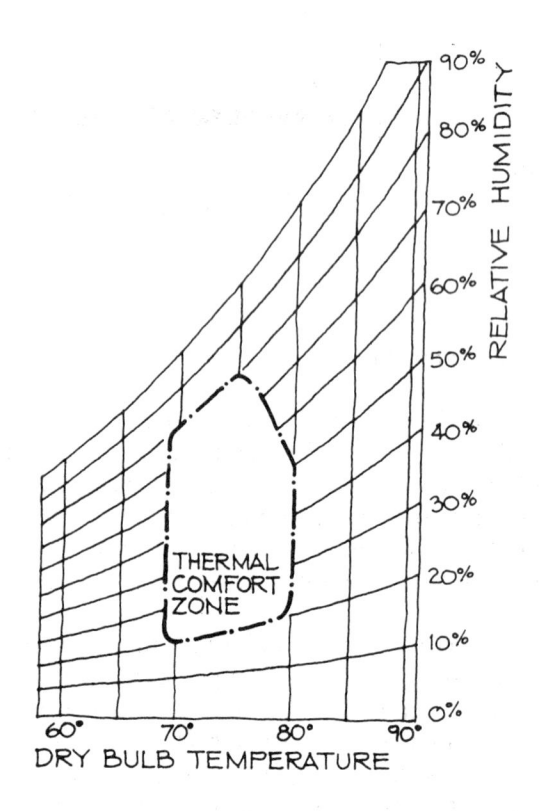

Figure 2.2.2.1 - Comfort Zone

with the thermal environment." It occurs within the "comfort zone" (see Figure 2.2.2.1), a physiological definition of a range of thermal conditions in which most of our bodily energy is freed for productivity and a minimal expenditure is required for adjustment to our surroundings.

Thermal comfort involves the following environmental factors:

- conductive heat transfer to and from surrounding surfaces
- radiant temperature
- ambient air temperature
- humidity
- air velocity.

Conductive Heat Transfer

Humans require, on the average, a normal deep body temperature of 98.6 degrees (F.), with the skin's surface around 92 degrees (F.). The human body radiates heat to anything at a cooler temperature and is heated by anything at a warmer temperature. Therefore, building surface temperature with which the human body comes into contact are important factors in achieving thermal comfort.

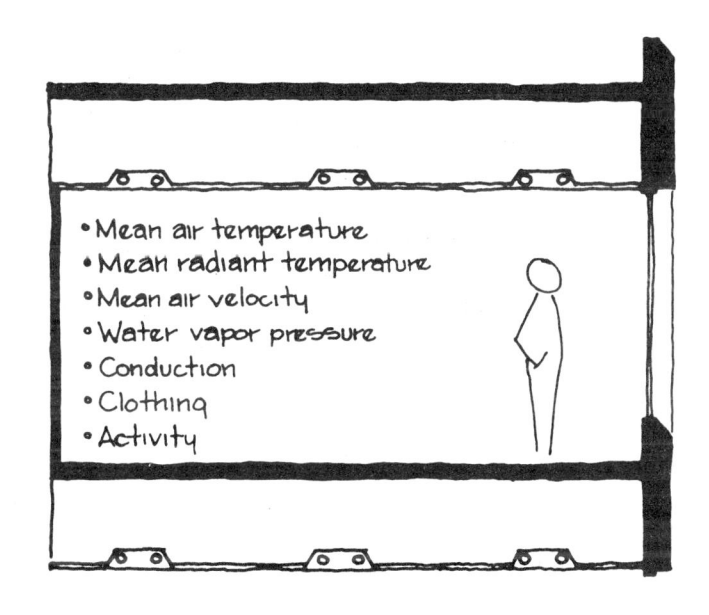

Figure 2.2.2.2 - Factors Affecting Human Comfort

Radiant and Ambient Temperatures

Mean radiant temperature (MRT) and ambient air temperature are two distinct but interrelated means of judging comfort. On a clear winter day, when a sheltered thermometer may read 25 degrees (F.), someone standing in the sunlight can feel quite comfortable, and perhaps even hot. The mean radiant heat from the sun is warming the body; the coldness of the ambient air is really not the final determinant of comfort.

The MRT has 40 percent more effect on comfort than air temperature. Thus, for every 1.4 degrees (F.) decrease in air temperature, only a 1 degree MRT increase is required to maintain the same comfort level. If the mass of a structure contains enough heat to register 75 degrees (F.), then the air temperature can be as low as 58 degrees (F.) and people will still feel comfortable. Conversely, with cold walls and floors and an air temperature of 75 degrees (F.), people will feel chilled.

Humidity

Human comfort also depends on the moisture content of the air, which is described by a relative humidity (RH) figure. This is the percentage of the maximum amount of water vapor that can exist in the air at a given temperature before condensation occurs. When RH is high, the atmosphere will accept little additional water vapor, and the body will have trouble cooling itself by the evaporation of perspiration. If the RH remains within the range of 20-80 percent, and the temperature is 69-78 degrees (F.), the body will remain comfortable. Figure 2.2.2.3 illustrates the impacts of temperature, humidity, and winds on human comfort.

Mean radiant temperature	65	66	67	68	69	70	71	72	73	74	75	76	77	78	79	80
Air temperature	77	75.6	74.2	72.8	71.4	70	68.6	67.2	65.8	64.4	63	61.6	60.2	58.8	57.4	56

Equivalent Mean-Radiant and Air Temperatures (for 70° F)

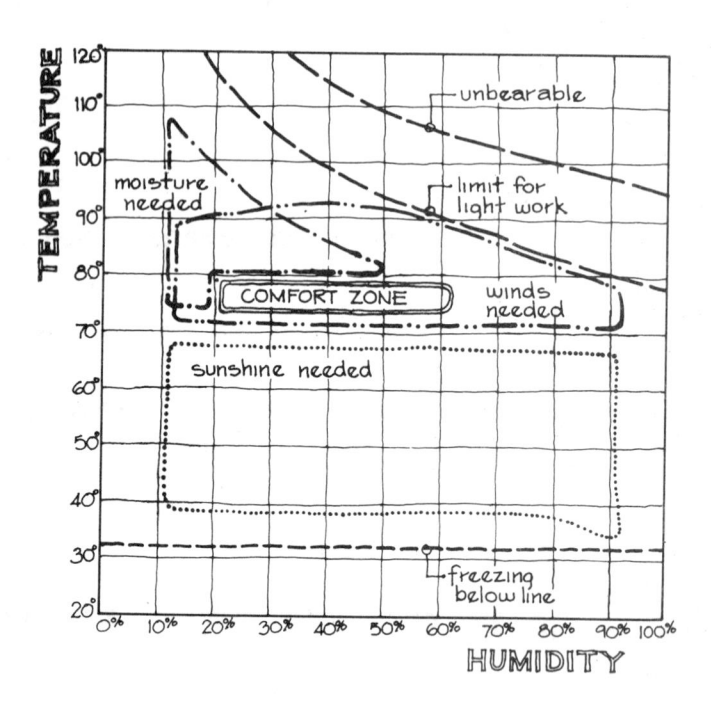

Figure 2.2.2.3 - Effect of Climate

Air Velocity

Ventilation is an important element of human comfort for three reasons:

- moving air removes heat that surrounds the body;
- moving air removes moisture and provides proper conditions under which the body can evaporatively cool itself by perspiration;
- moving air prevents buildup of pollutants, including cigarette smoke, combustion products, radon, bacteria and odor-producing organic materials given off by the human body, and organic compounds.

The amount of air movement needed to produce favorable thermal comfort conditions is 10-50 feet per minute (fpm). Lower levels will result in complaints about stagnant air. Higher levels (50-200 fpm) can be comfortable if air is above room-air temperature and introduced intermittently. Air movement above 200 fpm will be perceived by occupants as being too drafty and will disrupt tasks and activities.

Figure 2.2.3.1 - Psychrometric Chart

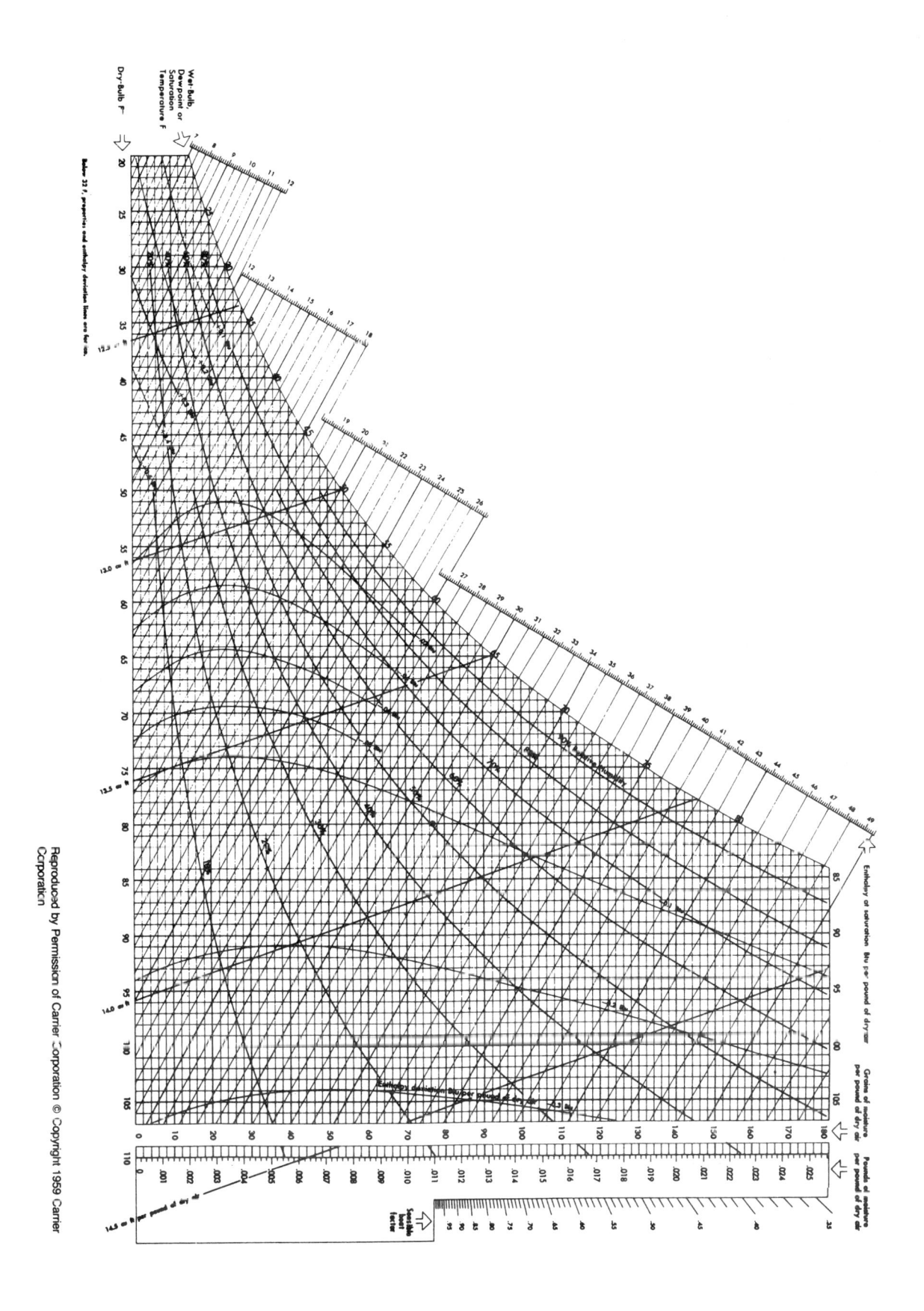

2.2.3 Psychrometric Chart

The psychrometric chart (Figure 2.2.3.1), which is a graphic representation of the relationship between air temperature and humidity, has been developed to enable the designer to understand more easily the interaction of the factors affecting thermal and indoor air quality, and human comfort. "Dry-bulb" temperature (degrees F.) is measured along the horizontal axis, and absolute humidity--moisture content of air regardless of temperature--along the vertical axis. The relative humidity (RH) is shown by the curved lines that climb from the lower left corner. The "wet-bulb" temperature is measured on the sloped left edge line of the psychrometric chart. Wet-bulb temperature (degrees F.) is that temperature indicated when a thermometer nose bulb is covered by a wet wick and exposed to air movement.

The dew-point temperature (DP), the temperature at which moisture from the air begins to condense, forms the upper curved boundary of the chart, the line of 100 percent humidity. Notice from the chart that, as the temperature falls, the maximum amount of moisture that the air can hold decreases. For example, if summer indoor conditions are 75 degrees (F.) and 68 percent RH, the dew-point temperature is 64 degrees (F.) (found by moving horizontally along the constant moisture line to the 100 percent RH curve). This means that in these conditions, condensation will occur on any surface colder than 64 degrees (F.), whether it is a glass of ice water, the coil of an airconditioning unit, or a foundation wall.

The parameters of human comfort can also be plotted on the psychrometric chart. The comfort zone is defined as those temperature and humidity conditions where 50 percent or more people feel comfortable. For most Americans, comfort falls between 69 and 80 degrees (F.) and from 20 to 80 percent RH. Conditions that fall outside this comfort zone indicate the need for some type of intervention. The area on the chart where conditions fall indicates which particular design strategies are needed to "shift" internal environments back into the comfort zone.

If climatological conditions are not too extreme, simple passive design strategies can usually reinstate thermal comfort. Design professionals can most easily change air temperature and velocity by design of the building envelope. Humidity, on the other hand, is practically impossible to modify architecturally without mechanical equipment, although its effect can be lessened by increasing air velocity. Radiant temperatures are also difficult for the designer alone to control, although in modern buildings radiant temperature differences seldom tend to track ambient air temperatures closely.

As the outdoor climatological conditions extend farther and farther from the comfort zone, or as other building considerations prevent passive design, mechanically assisted or "active" energy systems must be used. However, if the building is properly designed, the amount of purchased energy required can be minimized.

Unfortunately, there is probably no such thing as an optimal building, so these mechanical systems will always be needed, even if only to supplement the natural energy systems. Figure 2.2.3.2 displays design strategies suggested by the psychrometric chart.

A. Humidifying
B. Heating - Humidifying
C. Sensible Heating
D. Chemical Dehumidifying
E. Dehumidifying
F. Cooling - Dehumidifying
G. Sensible Cooling
H. Evaporative Cooling

Design Strategies

SOURCE: Reprinted from *Energy Conservation Through Building Design* by Donald Watson, AIA, ©1979, Architectural Record Books, McGraw-Hill, Inc.

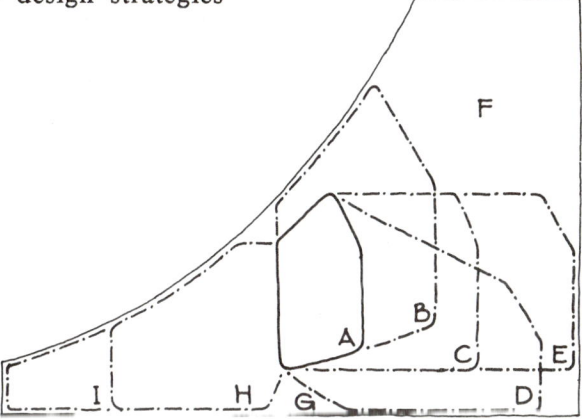

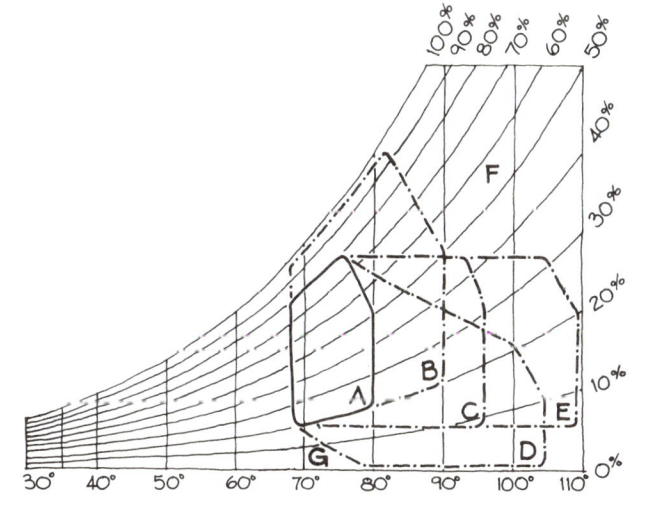

A. Comfort Zone
B. Natural/Mechanical Ventilation
C. High Thermal Mass
D. Evaporative Cooling
E. High Mass w/Nighttime Vent.
F. Conventional Air Conditioning
G. Humidification
H. Passive Solar Heating
I. Active Solar/Conventional Heating

Cooling and Heating Design Strategies

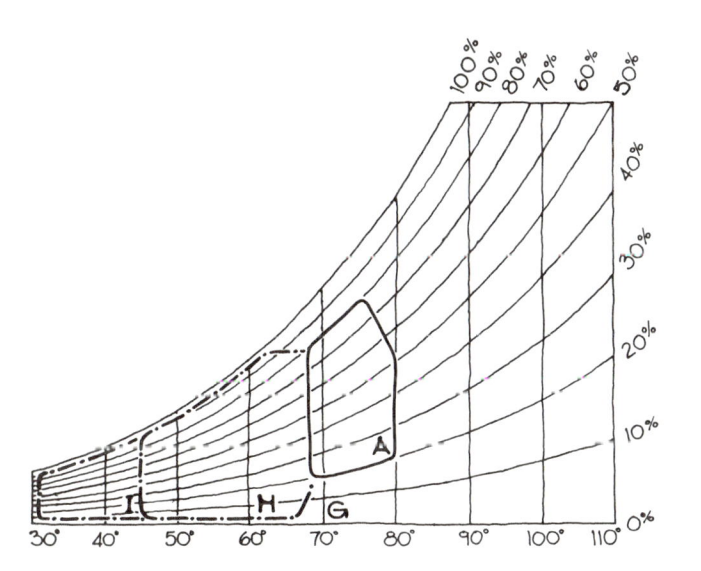

A. Comfort Zone
G. Humidification
H. Passive Solar Heating
I. Active Solar/Conventional Heating

Summary of Heating Design Strategies

SOURCE: Reprinted from *Energy Conservation Through Building Design* by Donald Watson, AIA, ©1979, Architectural Record Books, McGraw-Hill, Inc.

A. Comfort Zone
B. Natural/Mechanical Ventilation
C. High Thermal Mass
D. Evaporative Cooling
E. High Mass w/Nighttime Vent.
F. Conventional Air Conditioning
G. Humidification

Summary of Cooling Design Strategies

SOURCE: Reprinted from *Energy Conservation Through Building Design* by Donald Watson, AIA, ©1979, Architectural Record Books, McGraw-Hill, Inc.

Figure 2.2.3.2 - Cooling and Heating Design Strategies

2.2.4 Indoor Air Quality

The economic imperative of reducing building energy use has given prominence to the related issues of indoor air quality and building ventilation--which accounts for an estimated tenth of the nation's total energy consumption.

Typically, large buildings rely on mechanical ventilation rather than infiltration for air exchange, and, over the past several years, reductions in designed ventilation rates and the development of new ventilation strategies have combined to substantially reduce ventilation-- related energy consumption. In many case, though, these reductions of ventilation rates and infiltration have further increased existing levels of indoor air contamination. Substantial interest and research is being directed at this problem. The current ASHRAE Standard 62, "Standard on Ventilation for Acceptable Indoor Air Quality," is used by many building codes to address these problems.

The primary energy consideration for building designers concerned with indoor air quality today hinges on the simple recognition that an increase in ventilation rates is not the preferred solution to questions of indoor air quality. Alternative answers can often be drawn from the variety of design options including the use of heat recovery devices, the removal of pollutant sources, the adequate maintenance of system filters and moisture-producing components and the shifting of building ventilation to non-operational hours. Such measures may not be applicable in all instances, but from an energy standpoint they merit architectural consideration because they offer the potential to improve indoor air quality while minimizing energy consumption.

Problem Areas

Until recently, discussions of air quality focused almost exclusively on the air we breathe outdoors. Studies show, however, that most of us are actually outside only a small portion of our lives. Most people spend the vast majority of their time--perhaps 80 to 90 percent on a typical day-- indoors, moving from one controlled environment to another. Clearly, the quality of the air inside is as important, or perhaps more important, than the quality of the air outside.

While there are many indoor pollutants that have been found to be potentially harmful to human health, most fall into the following categories:
- radioactive radon gas and its byproducts, or progeny
- organic compounds, such as formaldehyde, which are present in many common building materials, insulating materials and furnishings
- asbestos and other fibers
- tobacco smoke
- odors
- indoor combustion byproducts, such as those produced by gas stoves and wood fires, and
- airborne microorganisms and allergens.

These pollutants are generated either by indoor activities, both mechanical and human, or the materials with which a building is constructed or furnished. They can also, to a lesser degree, be brought into the structure as airborne products, through ventilation and infiltration.

Each of the pollutants categorized above poses a different threat to health and emanates from a different source, which may be man-made or natural. Frequently the design of a building is responsible for exacerbating the dangers of the contaminants by allowing them to accumulate to levels that are threatening to health. On the other hand, careful building design can work to reduce these dangers and protect the health of occupants.

Generally, the two fundamental factors that render pollutants potentially harmful are the amount of time that is spent in their presence and their concentration in the air.

The concentrations of contaminants in a building are determined by:

- how quickly, and to what degree, pollutants are generated indoors
- the volume of indoor spaces
- the building's air-exchange rate
- the mixing efficiency of the indoor air
- the reactive decay rates of the contaminants
- to a lesser degree, how polluted the air is outside and how much of it enters the building.

The characteristics of a building's site can also influence the quality of its indoor air. Air flow around the building is a key consideration: Pollutants from street level or from neighboring stacks, parking garages, flues, vents and cooling towers can be swept over a building's facade, onto its roof and into makeup-air intakes.

All elements of building design--both interior and exterior--can affect indoor air quality as well. Open-plan office designs, for example, frequently result in incomplete air mixing and pollution dispersion (as well as being particularly susceptible to noise pollution due to limited acoustic control). The alteration or redesign of an open-plan office can also exacerbate indoor air quality problems if changes in existing ventilation systems and patterns are not considered when the renovation occurs.

Additionally, the choice of building materials can have an effect on the level of contamination. The materials used in walls, ceilings and floors often contain such potential pollutants as formaldehyde and fibers. The materials used in modern carpets, drapes and furnishings often contain organics that are significant pollutants.

A building's operations can have an effect on the quality of the indoor environment. The maintenance and operation of heating, ventilating and airconditioning systems; the care given to building services and repairs;

the condition of equipment and machines, and the efficiency with which hot water, lighting and power are distributed can all significantly affect the air in a building.

Finally, occupancy patterns, such as the type and intensity of human activity, the density of occupants within available space and the operating schedule of the building, can have a pronounced effect on indoor air quality.

Along with these factors, temperature and to a smaller extent humidity help determine the concentration of contaminants and their degree of chemical activity.

High relative humidity indoors is the product of many factors, including human breathing, indoor combustion, dish washing and bathroom functions, and decreased ventilation during heating seasons. High humidity has been shown to promote the growth of molds, algae and fungi, and to increase the release of formaldehyde from building materials.

Low humidity, on the other hand, may make odors, airborne particles and vapors like acrolein (found in cigarette smoke) more irritating.

Design Strategies

Workable and effective abatement strategies require understanding of several pertinent factors. First, contaminant characteristics--including the concentrations, chemical reactions and physical states involved--must be assessed.

Second, emission source configurations should be taken into account. Are discharges continuous or intermittent? Are they point or area releases? Do they originate primarily indoors or outdoors?

Third, the nature of exposure response relations must be considered. Are individuals to be protected from long-term exposures or peak concentrations?

Finally, the type of indoor enclosure being designed is important. Some measures are more appropriate for private residences than for large, nonresidential buildings, or for new rather than existing structures.

Pollution-abatement strategies associated with different types of pollutants and different building types generally use one or two primary principles:

- source control, in which several strategies may be used to remove the pollutant at its source or block its entry into the building, or
- concentration reduction, in which several strategies may be used to reduce pollutant concentrations either by the introduction of uncontaminated air or by the use of various air cleaning devices.

Source Control

In many cases, the sources of indoor air pollutants can be excluded or removed from a building or residence, isolated from the indoor air or modified so that the pollutant emission rate is decreased. Because source removal is usually a permanent, one-time measure that entails no maintenance or operating costs, it is the preferred control measure whenever practical. In some cases, however, source strategies are too costly, invite the use of substitute products that may also be sources of indoor pollution, or impose difficult demands on occupants--for example, giving up tobacco smoking or shifting to unfamiliar appliances. Specific pollutants particularly suited to source control are radon, formaldehyde and combustion products. Figure 2.2.4.1 illustrates entry paths for radon.

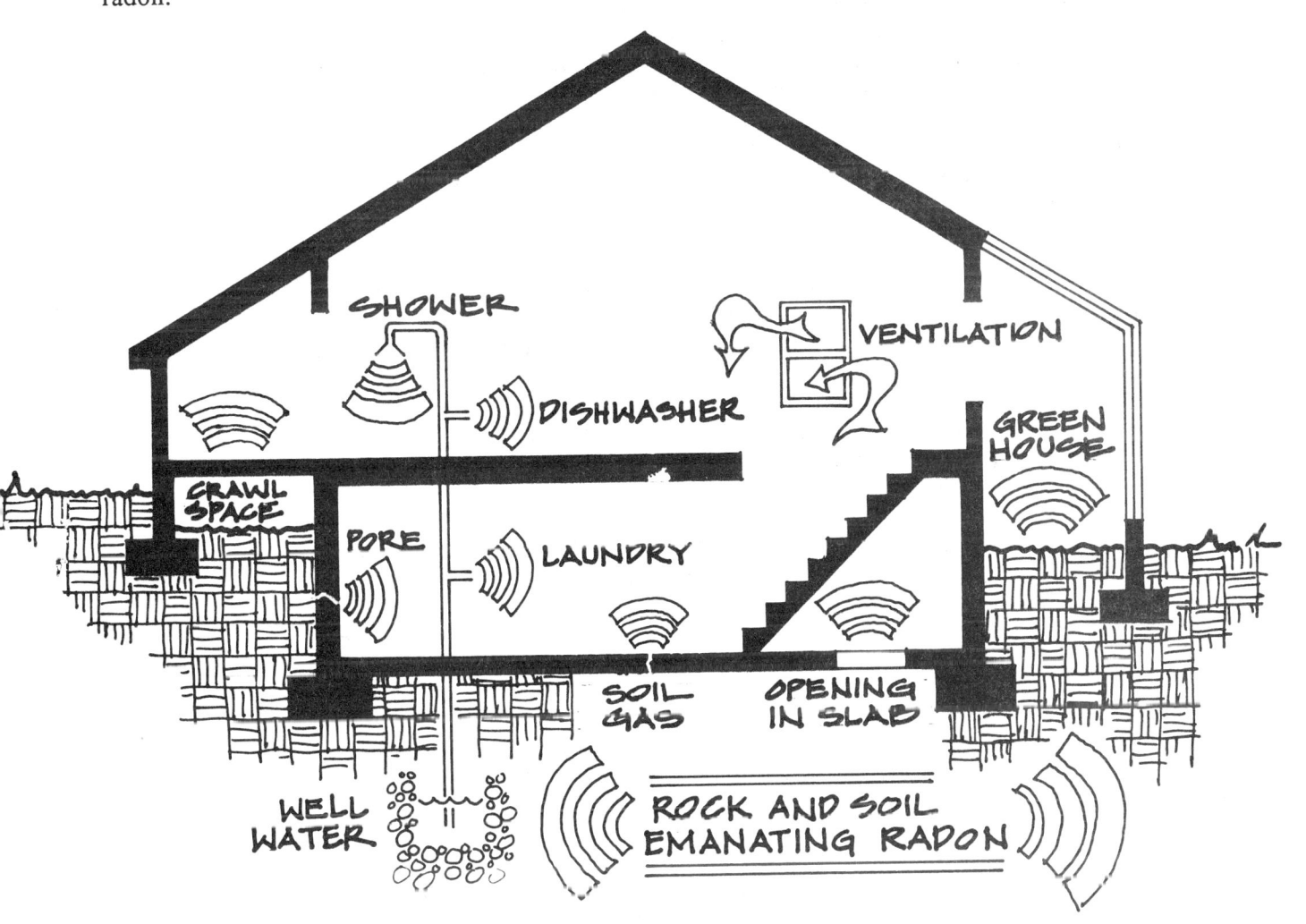

Figure 2.2.4.1 - Radon Entry Paths

The most common technique for controlling radon is to reduce its transport into the building from surrounding soil by plugging cracks or holes through which soil gas moves into the house.

Concrete walls and concrete slab floors can be sealed with commercially available polymeric and epoxy sealants. Cracks in foundation walls, gaps between walls and floors, and drain holes can be filled with nonporous materials, or covered and sealed with plastic sheets. The general applicability or effectiveness of these measures as long-term controls is not known, but in short-term studies these control measures have proved highly effective.

In laboratory studies, the application of various paints, lacquers, varnishes and vinyl papers to particleboard has significantly reduced the rate of formaldehyde emission, preventing its release into the surrounding air. The effectiveness of surface coatings applied to the exposed surfaces of particleboard once installed in the field is not known.

Two relatively simple procedures used effectively in individual houses having formaldehyde problems are ammonia fumigation and dehumidification, both of which reduce the rate of formaldehyde emission from building materials. Dehumidification, which may be the more feasible alternative, can be effected by using residential dehumidifiers, by placing ventilation devices near humidity sources (a bathroom fan exhausted to the outside) or by opening the house to outdoor air when the outdoor air is less humid than indoor air. Although no studies have been performed in actual homes to determine the effects of dehumidification on indoor formaldehyde concentrations, laboratory studies suggest that this procedure may be useful in obtaining moderate decreases.

Removing any unvented combustion appliance is an obvious technique--and an effective one--for eliminating the emission of combustion products into indoor air.

If even vented combustion appliances are poorly maintained (not receiving regular filter care and periodic burner adjustment) or are damaged or faulty (a furnace with a cracked heat exchanger, for example) they too can be a potential threat to indoor air quality.

Mechanical ventilation is widely used in industrial, institutional, commercial and transportation environments; it may require substantial energy for heating and cooling, or it may improve energy efficiency, depending on the control system. Local ventilation and the use of heat exchangers can be effective in either residential or larger structures. The efficiency of planned natural ventilation is not well documented and can be expected to vary considerably.

Source removal can be very effective, but it requires careful design consideration and planning; in a retrofit situation, it may be very costly. Source substitution has not been widely used or researched to date, but it may well be feasible if the substitute product is equally functional and does not pose similar hazards to indoor air quality.

Laboratory studies indicate that these techniques--other than basic design steps--need further development and research to define their effectiveness.

These strategies are very pollutant-dependent, and their effectiveness needs further documentation; contaminant control devices are also often large, expensive, noisy and maintenance-intensive.

Largely beyond the scope of informed architectural design, these techniques may be specified by clients or, in some instances, required by local codes and standards.

Concentration Reduction

Ventilation--the replacement of stale indoor air with fresh outdoor air-- is the most common technique for reducing levels of air pollutants generated indoors. Ventilation can be local or distributed, periodic or continuous, natural or mechanical, and it can be accomplished with or without heat recovery. A significant advantage of ventilation is that it reduces levels of almost all indoor air pollutants, assuming outdoor concentrations are less than the indoor concentrations. However, ventilation may be more effective for some pollutants than for others: Indoor air quality models indicate that an increase in ventilation causes a smaller decrease in the concentration of some air pollutants, such as formaldehyde, than in the concentration of others.

Natural Ventilation

The simplest ventilation technique is to bring in fresh outside air by opening windows and doors. Although this approach may work when the area is small and the need is short-term, it clearly adds to the heating (or cooling) load and, on any large or continuous scale, can be extremely energy-consuming. Natural ventilation is also an ineffective way to remove pollutants from a point source; that result can be better achieved through the kind of spot ventilation provided by exhaust fans in bathrooms and range fans in kitchens.

Local Ventilation

A significant source of concentrated, periodically released indoor air pollution is an operating gas stove. In one study, use of a range hood-fan effected 60 to 87 percent reductions in the amounts of carbon monoxide, carbon dioxide and all nitric oxides entering the occupied space of an experimental test house.

Although their performance depends somewhat on airflow rates and methods of installation, range hoods are generally quite effective in reducing the entry of combustion byproducts into occupied spaces. A key factor, however, is whether occupants use them when cooking.

Mechanical Ventilation With Air-to-Air Heat Exchangers

An alternative residential ventilation strategy is to tighten up the shell of the house and bring in a controlled supply of fresh air by means of mechanical ventilation. One way to accomplish this is to use an air-to-air heat exchanger to assure recovery of heat that would otherwise be a costly loss. The effectiveness of these devices, referred to simply as residential air-to-air heat exchangers, is limited by the initial concentrations of indoor pollutants. High initial concentrations will require excessive ventilation rates.

A second method of providing mechanical ventilation to residences involves using mechanical exhaust ventilation with or without heat recovery by a heat pump. In this technique a fan exhausts indoor air, thereby drawing outdoor air into the house through cracks or slots in the walls. The exhaust air is passed through a small heat pump, and the energy that would otherwise be lost is recovered. The heat pump generally transfers energy from the outgoing air to the domestic hot-water supply, although exhaust-air heat pumps that also transfer energy to the indoor air are also available.

Air Cleaning

The term air cleaning refers to methods of removing pollutants from indoor air without ventilation. Air cleaning techniques that may be suitable for controlling indoor pollution include filtration, electrostatic precipitation, ionization, absorption, and adsorption.

Air Filtration

Air filtration is accomplished by passing air through a filter (usually constructed from a woven fabric, paper or a fibrous mat) designed to remove particles (aerosols) rather than gaseous contaminants. Radon, for example, is an inert gas and will not be removed by filters, but radon progeny (i.e., the radioactive breakdown products of radon)--a large fraction of which attach to particles--will be effectively removed by filtration. Filters must be periodically cleaned or replaced, and significant tradeoffs exist between filter cost, collection efficiency, capacity and airflow resistance. Filters may be effective in removing aerosols from indoor air, but if the aerosols are volatile--as are tobacco smoke aerosols, which are primarily liquid--then gases and odors may be emitted into the indoor air from the collected aerosols.

Electrostatic Precipitators

Electrostatic precipitators can be highly effective in removing even submicron particles from indoor air, but are generally not effective in removing gaseous contaminants. Residential-size precipitators are readily available for installation in furnace ductwork and walls, and some are portable. Unlike filtration, precipitation can remove small particles without requiring fan power to overcome a large pressure drop in the airstream. Another advantage is that the collection surfaces of precipitators can usually be cleaned with soap and water or, in some models, in an automatic dishwasher. Some precipitators produce a small amount of ozone; many units are supplied with replaceable charcoal filters to remove the ozone.

Air Ionizers

Air ionizers produce large numbers of negative ions, which are thought to cause the attachment of air-borne particles to walls, floors and other surfaces that usually have a lower electrical potential. A criticism of negative-ion generators is that many models do not entirely remove offending particles, but instead remove them from the air and deposit them on surfaces around the room. The performance and utility of air ionizers is presently controversial.

Absorption

Absorption processes, generally used in industrial plants to remove gaseous contaminants, are not currently commercially available as a control strategy for residential indoor air quality. The terms scrubbing and air-washing are commonly used to describe absorption processes that work by passing contaminated air through a liquid spray or over wetted surfaces. Only pollutants that are soluble or chemically reactive to the liquid in use can be removed by absorption techniques. Absorption of nitrogen dioxide into water may be made possible if additives to the water are used, but at this time the process appears impractical for indoor use. Absorption processes appear least promising for radon, which is non-reactive and only slightly soluble in water.

Adsorption

Adsorbents, in contrast to liquid adsorbents, are porous solids that trap pollutants in the numerous pores on their surfaces. The most commonly used adsorbents are activated carbon (activated charcoal), activated alumina, silica gel and molecular sieves. Adsorbents become saturated after a period of use and must be regenerated or replaced.

The effectiveness of adsorption for removing radon and nitrogen dioxide from indoor air is currently unknown, and researchers have found that only materials impregnated with potassium permanganate show promise for controlling indoor formaldehyde.

2.3 COST OF ENERGY

2.3.1 Introduction

Energy costs in buildings generally involve electricity and fuels bought for heating and cooling the indoor environment and heating domestic hot water. (The energy required for the construction of the building and for manufacturing materials and equipment is usually not included.) For energy conservation, the emphasis is on reducing the use of nonrenewable fuels such as oil, natural gas and coal, whether these fuels are consumed in the building or at an electricity generating plant.

In residential buildings, the main energy costs are for heating and cooling, with lighting of secondary importance. In commercial buildings, electricity costs are proportionally larger because more cooling is required to handle heat from occupants, lighting and machinery. The cost of energy in commercial buildings can be a major factor in operating costs.

In existing buildings, it is relatively easy to analyze energy costs on the basis of fuel bills collected for several past years. For new buildings, estimating probable energy costs is more complicated, requiring computer-assisted computations to consider all variables, including the building envelope, heating and cooling systems, lighting and equipment, people, solar insolation, thermal mass, daylighting, and energy recovery.

The designer must then use available information and judgment in choosing appropriate energy systems, based on efficiency, so future availabilities and costs must be projected. With the certainty that nonrenewable energies will become scarce in the future, alternative renewable energy sources must be considered. These include solar, geothermal, wind, photovoltaic and other sources. Cogeneration with district heating and cooling increases the fuel efficiency of nonrenewable fuels and provides an opportunity for use of such renewable sources as biomass, wood and municipal and industrial waste.

2.3.2 Electricity

Most electrical utilities have many different rate schedules, depending on the type of service involved. In general, the rate schedules applicable to commercial and industrial buildings consist of the following: energy charges, demand charges, fuel adjustment charges, and low-power factor load penalties.

<u>Energy charges</u> are assessed on the basis of actual usage. Also, there is generally a <u>fixed customer charge</u>, a flat amount per customer.

Customer cost generally decreases per kWh with increased use; this is referred to as a "declining block" rate, and is designed to encourage usage during <u>off-peak demand periods</u> to increase the utility's power load factor. Utilities also use an "inverted block" rate, which increases the cost per kilowatt-hour in increments similar to those used in a declining block rate. This is designed to give the customer an incentive to reduce usage <u>during peak demand periods</u>. Inverted block rates are used in conjunction with higher overall energy charges during peak periods.

Load Factor	Demand Cost per kWh
30% — $5.00/kW = $5.00 = 2.283c/kWh 30% x 730 hrs = 219 kWh	
40% — $5.00/kW = $5.00 = 1.712c/kWh 40% x 730 hrs = 292 kWh	
50% — $5.00/kW = $5.00 = 1.370c/kWh 50% x 730 hrs = 315 kWh	

Figure 2.3.2.1 - Demand Cost Computation

Depending on the load factor for the commercial class of customers, the rates may vary above and below the average load. For example, if the customer-related charge is $4.00 per customer per month and the energy-related charge is 2.5 cents per kWh delivered to the customer, the demand charge may be based on $5.00 per month per kW supplied at the delivery point. Considering 30-percent, 40-percent and 50-percent load factors, the demand costs are calculated as shown in Figure 2.3.2.1 (based on hypothetical costs). The monthly costs can be computed for each load factor as shown in Figure 2.3.2.2 (using, for this example, the 30-percent load factor).

TOTAL MONTHLY COST

	50 kWh	100 kWh	250 kWh	500 kWh	1M kWh	2M kWh
Customer Cost	4.00	4.00	4.00	4.00	4.00	4.00
Demand Cost	1.14	2.25	5.71	11.42	22.83	45.66
Energy Cost at 2.5c/kWh	1.25	2.50	6.25	12.50	25.00	50.00

AVERAGE COST PER kWh (CENTS)

Customer Cost	8.000	4.000	1.600	0.800	0.400	0.200
Demand Cost	2.283	2.283	2.283	2.283	2.283	2.283
Energy Cost	2.500	2.500	2.500	2.500	2.500	2.500
TOTAL	12.783	8.783	6.383	5.583	5.183	4.983

Figure 2.3.2.2 - Total Monthly Cost Factors

When using the other load factors, the higher the factor, the lower the overall cost. The chart in Figure 2.3.2.3 illustrates costs for 30 and 50 percent load factors.

About a fourth of the nation's electric utilities also offer special-purpose incentives for customer participation in a variety of specific conservation programs.

Electricity Cost Curves

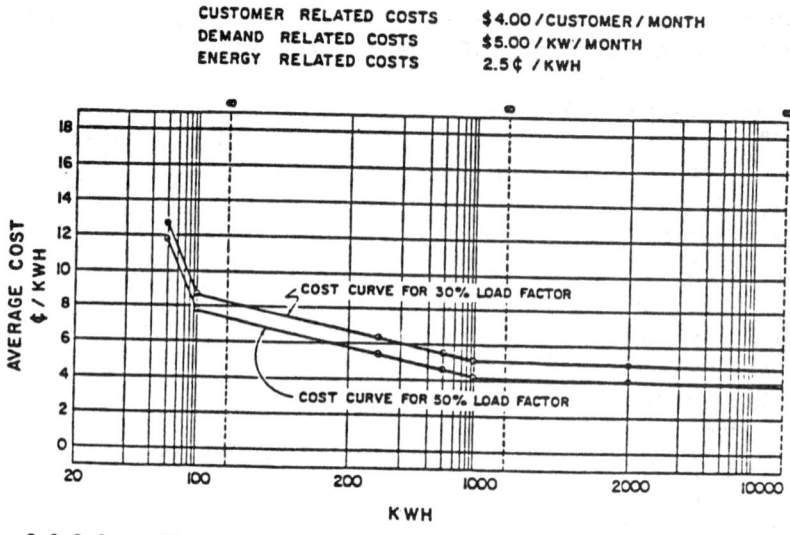

CUSTOMER RELATED COSTS $4.00/CUSTOMER/MONTH
DEMAND RELATED COSTS $5.00/KW/MONTH
ENERGY RELATED COSTS 2.5¢/KWH

Figure 2.3.2.3 - 30 and 50 Percent Load Factors

Demand charges are designed to assess the customer for its share of the utility's fixed investment in production, transmission and distribution equipment. A demand charge is based on the utility's need to increase its generating capacity to meet peak demand. If, hypothetically, a customer uses an insignificant amount of power throughout the year, but does so all at once, during periods of peak demand from other customers, the fact that the customer's annual usage is small does not reduce the utility's need to add capacity.

Demand has commonly been measured over 15-minute intervals over the day. The maximum demand recorded is used to compute the demand charge.

Many utilities now use new devices--pulse initiated meters--to eliminate fixed demand intervals. These meters enable the utility to identify the highest demand interval (again, a consecutive 15-minute interval) during the day, no matter when during an hour the highest demand interval begins. This is termed sliding window demand billing.

Demand-control or load-shedding equipment can be used to lower peak demand. It is connected to current transformers through a demand pulse relay on incoming lines or to a kilowatt-hour meter with a demand attachment. The equipment is generally attached to "secondary load," which are loads that can be turned off and on periodically without disrupting building or production operations. Demand-control equipment monitors usage and sheds secondary loads when a present demand level has been reached.

Demand control can become particularly important when a utility's demand rate structure includes a ratchet clause. Ratchet clauses state that the minimum amount of demand a customer is billed for will be based on the customer's highest recorded demand interval. A typical ratchet clause says that the minimum winter demand charge will be based on 80 percent of the maximum summer demand; if the maximum summer demand is 1,000 kW, the minimum winter demand bill will be for 800 kW, even though actual winter demand may never exceed 400 kW.

Partly as a result of ratchet charges, demand charges often account for 40 to 45 percent of a commercial building's annual electricity cost. Figures 2.3.2.4 and 2.3.2.5 show examples of Monthly Charge Rates for Energy and Demand, respectively.

Design-based load-reduction efforts can also be important. Demand reduction efforts need not be limited to after-the-fact techniques such as load shedding. Designers should make an effort to take advantage of daylighting and other means of reducing the basic need for electricity at peak load levels.

	Block (kWh)	$/kWh
First	6,000	$ 0.02789
Next	14,000	0.01829
Next	100,000	0.01509
Next	180,000	0.01499
Next	220,000	0.01316
Next	500,000	0.01267

Figure 2.3.2.4 - Monthly Energy Charge: Example Rate

Purchased energy cost estimates usually require calculations of energy consumption and peak demands on a month-to-month basis. The most reliable energy and demand estimating procedures require hourly integration of calculated energy use of each building component as a function of weather, internal loads, building heat gains and losses, ventilation and infiltration, energy recovery results and other factors.

First	25 kW of billing demand or less	$85.50
Next	75 kW of billing demand/kW	2.82
Next	200 kW of billing demand/kW	2.68
Next	200 kW of billing demand/kw	2.56
All Over	500 kW of billing demand/kW	2.26

Figure 2.3.2.5 - Monthly Demand Charge: Example Rate

Applicable utility rates are then applied, resulting in an estimate of highest incidental demands and monthly and annual operating costs. Separate estimates of energy consumption, demand and resulting costs should be determined for each alternative building design under consideration.

Low power factor load penalties are designed to assess a customer for the added costs to the utility for the necessary increased capital investment to supply low power factor loads. This penalty also gives plants an incentive to improve their power factor.

Many electrical utilities define low power factor as anything less than 0.90. That is, the customer pays for the difference between 0.90 and the actual power factor. The difference can be computed on the basis of kWh and kVah consumption, kW demand and kVa or kVAR demand.

<u>Fuel adjustment charges</u> are adjustments that increasing numbers of public services commissions have allowed their utilities to assess customers for increased fuel costs.

2.3.3 Natural Gas

Natural gas rates are generally structured the way electricity rates are. Usually the utility allocates customer costs, demand costs and energy costs, with adjustments for fuel price fluctuations, interruptibility and the availability of gas from deregulated versus regulated sources. Residential rates are generally based on customer costs and energy costs, metered at the customer's premises. Commercial rates take into consideration the peak demand, purchased gas adjustments, availability and interruptibility of service. Commercial energy uses are often assigned the lowest priority for fuel service during shortages, leading many large users to install equipment that can be converted to use light oil or other fuels when natural gas is in scarce supply because of residential or priority commercial needs. This can results in a reduced rate for the large user.

Graduated rates are common for large users. For example, a commercial gas user may be charged at one rate for the first 400 cu.ft., with gradually reduced rates at 1,600 cu.ft., 6,000 cu.ft., 12,000 cu.ft., and 20,000 cu.ft., etc.

Utilities also use seasonal and seasonal limit rates to further stabilize gas demand. An on-peak demand surcharge is levied for peak-period use of the maximum daily gas contracted for. The fuel rate adjustment again may be of linear type, such as $0.055/100 cu.ft. for gas.

2.3.4 Delivered Fuel

Delivered fuels include bottled gas and several grades of fuel oil. The lighter oils, No. 1 and No. 2, ignite and burn at lower temperatures and are more satisfactory than heavier oils for intermittent, automatically controlled heating systems. The lighter fuels are also more expensive, and as prices have risen, burners have been developed to make use of the heavier, No. 5 and No. 6 oils (or No. 4 oil, which is generally a mixture of light and heavy oil). These oils must be preheated and atomized by being forced under pressure through a nozzle.

Light oil is often used as an alternative in a system designed for interruptible natural gas. Bottle gas can also be used in interruptible natural gas. Bottle gas can also be used in interruptible systems, as long as the burning chamber is made suitable for the higher temperature of burning bottle gas. Oil tanks can be placed in storage rooms or buried underground.

The price of fuel oil fluctuates depending on market forces. It is not usually available under long-term contracts, so that in analyzing the use of fuel oil one must consider future price developments. In some areas, fuel oil is competitive with natural gas. Oil can have more sulphur in it than the natural gas, so environmental effects may need to be considered. Bottle gas is manufactured to contain low amounts of sulphur.

2.3.5 Cogeneration, District Heating and Cooling

Cogeneration is the use of waste heat from large-scale energy users, generally electricity-generating plants, for other loads that can use relatively low-quality heat. Total energy plants producing both electricity and heat can be constructed specifically for medium and large commercial projects. A portion of the steam generated for electricity production is directed by extraction turbines to heat exchangers to produce either suitable lower-temperature steam or hot water for heating and cooling.

Hospitals that use steam in autoclaves and laundries, as well as projects with multiple buildings with sufficient densities to make district heating economical, provide opportunities for those strategies. (Large plants also can more easily use municipal and industrial waste for fuel by mixing it with coal or other fuels.)

Price structures for steam and hot water from a utility company are similar to those for other energy types: user fee, demand charge, and energy cost. Steam and hot and chilled water supply contracts are usually for an extended term, up to 30 years in some cities, primarily because of the initial major cost of the facility and the distribution piping system.

2.4 CLIMATE

2.4.1 Introduction

Climate is one of the major external forces at work on any building. It is crucial that the designer consider the effects of climatological factors--both the negative and positive aspects--when trying to achieve energy-conscious design.

Four major climatic elements--temperature, humidity, sun and wind--account for virtually all of a building's thermal behavior.

Temperature often elicits an almost automatic response: If winter climate is severely cold, maximize insulation. Unfortunately, this oversimplifies the problem and disregards the fact that wind, humidity, and solar radiation also affect indoor temperature. Considering temperature alone misses the positive and negative effects that the other elements, in combination with temperature, have on the building's internal living conditions.

Each of the climatic elements, and their combinations, should be analyzed early in the design process using regional climatic data as a guide to building design strategies that work <u>with</u> climatic forces and not against them.

2.4.2 Climatic Analysis

Climatic Zones and Regions

Most sources agree that there are four major climatic regions in the United States:
- cool
- temperate
- hot-arid
- hot-humid.

Figure 2.4.2.1 shows these climate zones. In actuality the boundary between regions is not clear or sharp; each region merges gradually into the next.

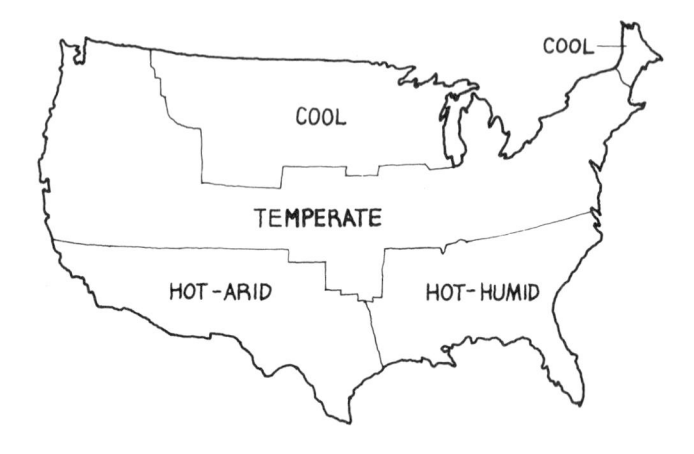

Figure 2.4.2.1 - Climatic Regions in U.S.

Figure 2.4.2.2 illustrates the pyschrometric implications of these climate regions.

Regional-specific architecture inevitably results from the application of climatic factors to energy-conscious design. Before mechanical HVAC systems made it easy to conquer hostile weather conditions the built environment had to be responsive to local climatic conditions. History preserves rich examples of regionally specific architecture, from the New England saltbox, to the Louisiana plantation house, to the southwestern adobe pueblo. These historical precedents, coupled with today's technology, suggest many design opportunities for achieving comfort and delaying the point when the mechanical system has to be switched on.

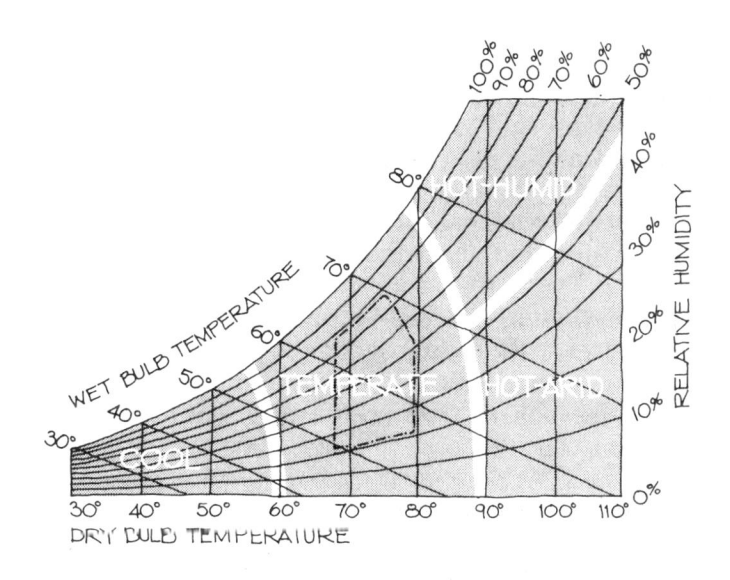

Figure 2.4.2.2 - Psychrometric Chart

While the distinction between the four climate zones above is drawn on the basis of just two variables--temperature and humidity--the United States can be separated into many zones based on more complex climatic systems. These classifications are "composite" climates that come closer to approximating actual annual patterns. During research for the BEPS (Building Energy Performance Standards), the federal government considered adopting over 100 climate zones. One study identified 13 distinct U.S. macroclimates (see Figure 2.4.2.3), each presented with a reference city as an example:

1A.	Hartford, Conn.
1B.	Madison, Wisc.
2.	Indianapolis, Ind.
3.	Salt Lake City, Utah
4.	Ely, Neb.
5.	Medford, Ore.
6.	Fresno, Calif.
7A.	Charleston, S.C.
7B.	Little Rock, Ark.
8.	Knoxville, Tenn.
9.	Phoenix, Ariz.
10A.	Midland, Texas
10B.	Fort Worth, Texas
11.	New Orleans, La.
12.	Houston, Texas
13.	Miami, Fla.

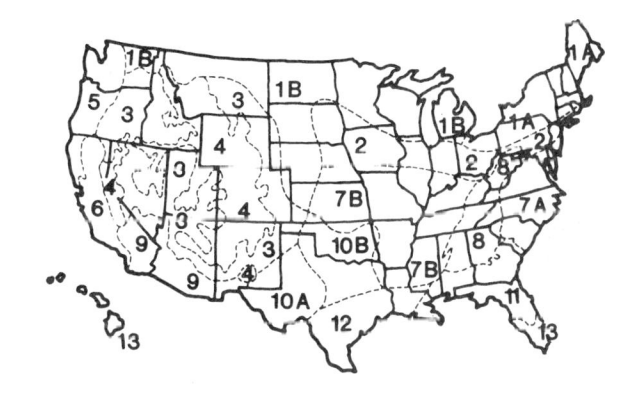

Figure 2.4.2.3 - MacroClimatic Regions

Temperature

Temperature is the most common gauge of human comfort and the foundation on which designers can begin to manipulate the interaction of humidity, solar radiation and wind.

To predict the effect of outdoor temperatures on building design, the designer needs to understand diurnal temperature patterns for all 12 months of the year. The diurnal temperature swing is the difference between the day (maximum) and night (minimum) temperatures. A wide diurnal range (hot days, cold nights) occurs in areas when clear night skies allow reradiation from the earth to escape through the atmosphere. This is why some dry, high-altitude deserts experience temperature swings of 35-45 degrees (F.).

A wide diurnal swing can be a great advantage from the designer's point of view, because it means that usable "free" energy is likely to be available at some point during those 24 hours. Many passive energy conserving strategies, such as thermal mass storage and night ventilation, depend on wide diurnal swings. Diurnal temperature swings can be as great as 40 degrees (F.) in some areas of the country, allowing design strategies that let summer heat accumulated in the daytime be released during the cool night. A diurnal swing of 20 degrees (F.) or higher indicates that thermal mass storage or night ventilation could be an effective strategy.

All sources of climatic data present monthly temperatures in three categories:
- monthly mean temperature
- average daily maxima and minima
- record high and low temperatures.

These numbers can be used to draw a set of annual curves of temperature conditions (see Figure 2.4.2.4) to give a picture of this aspect of the local climate.

The designer also needs to know the most likely <u>extreme</u> temperatures the building will experience. The American Society of Heating, Refrigerating

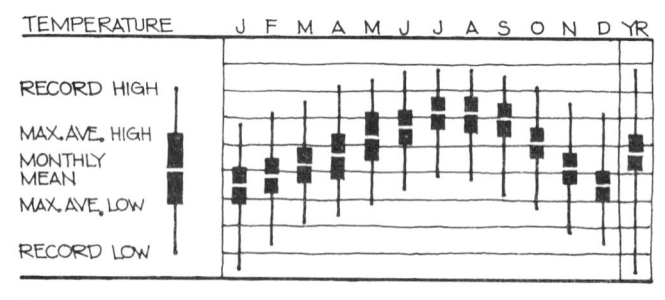

Temperature Ranges

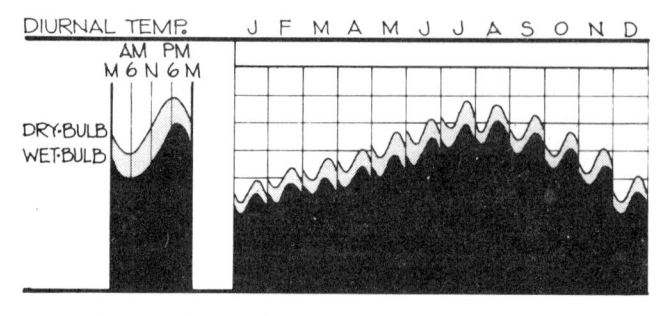

Diurnal Temperature Cycle

Figure 2.4.2.4 - Temperature Patterns

and Air-Conditioning Engineers (ASHRAE) publishes a winter and summer design temperature for many cities. It is usually not economically effective to design for the actual extreme high and low temperatures, especially when using natural conservation strategies. It is better to design for the high summer and low winter temperatures that occur 95 percent or 97.5 percent of the time. Cutting off the extreme tips of the recorded temperature curve in this way is a generally accepted trade-off between system cost and performance. ASHRAE's <u>Fundamentals</u> handbook lists high summer temperatures as 1 percent, 2.5 percent and 5 percent, and low winter temperatures for 95 percent and 97.5 percent, for almost 800 locations across the United States.

"Degree days" are based on a selected indoor design temperature, usually 65 degrees (F.). Degree days offer a measure of the amount of heating or cooling needed in an area. Heating degree days are determined by subtracting the actual outside temperature each day from the 65-degree design temperature. If the average temperture for a day is 64 degrees, that day would represent one degree day. Minneapolis has a total of about 8,400 degree days a year; Jackson, Miss., 2,300. ASHRAE's <u>Systems</u> handbook lists degree days for some 250 U.S. cities. Cooling degree days are calculated by the same procedure.

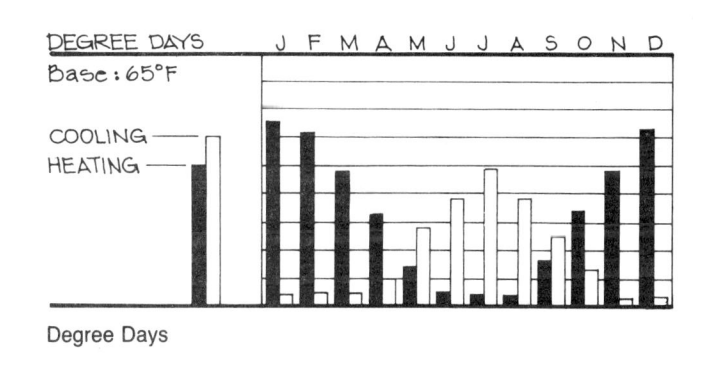

Figure 2.4.2.4 - Temperature Patterns

Degree hours are computed in the same way, but they provide a more detailed picture of temperature differentials throughout the day. They are generally used for computer simulations; this procedure is usually too lengthy for hand calculations.

Humidity and Precipitation

Humidity, the amount of moisture in the air, is measured in two somewhat similar ways. <u>Absolute humidity</u> is the amount of water held in the air. It is measured in pounds of water per pound of dry air and in various other units. <u>Relative humidity</u> (RH) is the percentage of water in the air compared

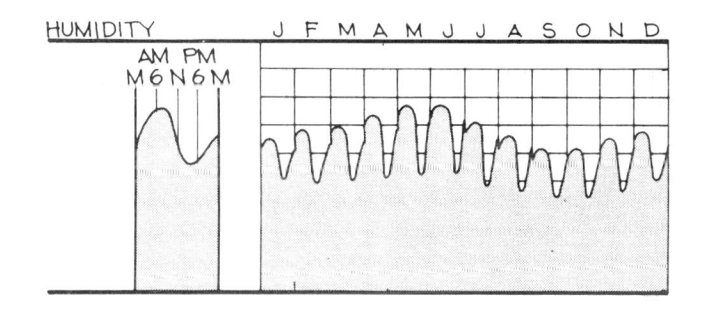

Figure 2.4.2.5 - Relative Humidity

to the maximum amount of water it can hold at any given temperature (see Figure 2.4.2.5). Warmer air can hold more moisture than colder air. At 100-percent relative humidity, the air is totally saturated at the given temperature; it cannot accept or hold any additional moisture. If the air cools, this moisture must precipitate as rain, snow, fog, dew or other condensation.

Comfort is directly affected by humidity. Wetness in the air intensifies feelings of both hot and cold. Low humidity causes dryness. High humidity allows perspiration to accumulate on the skin, and encourages growth of fungus and mildew in equipment and on building surfaces.

The amount of precipitation (rain, fog, snow) seldom influences the energy implications of design decisions. A rare instance is the use of snow to insulate or reduce surface emissivity. But understanding precipitation patterns is important because of their indirect effect on air temperature. For example, some regions get all their rain during a few winter months (Los Angeles), while others have wet summers and relatively dry winters (Houston). These seasonal shifts in precipitation patterns account for most of the differences between various composite climates. Knowing the annual precipitation cycles, along with the daily weather patterns and anomalies, will generally be sufficient to enable the designer understand the local climate.

Unfortunately, designers have very few options for dealing with humidity. Increasing natural ventilation will make humid environments more comfortable, but the only other possibilities are fan-forced ventilation and mechanical dehumidifiers. In dry environments, pools and fountains, or mechanical humidifiers are the best choices to increase humidity levels.

Sun

The sun affects a building and its site in two separate ways--the energy falling on the site (solar radiation) and its "motion" across the site (solar path). Solar radiation, or "insolation," is composed of three different components: direct radiation from the sun; diffuse radiation from the sky-vault (due to atmospheric scattering of direct sunlight); and reflected radiation from the ground and nearby buildings.

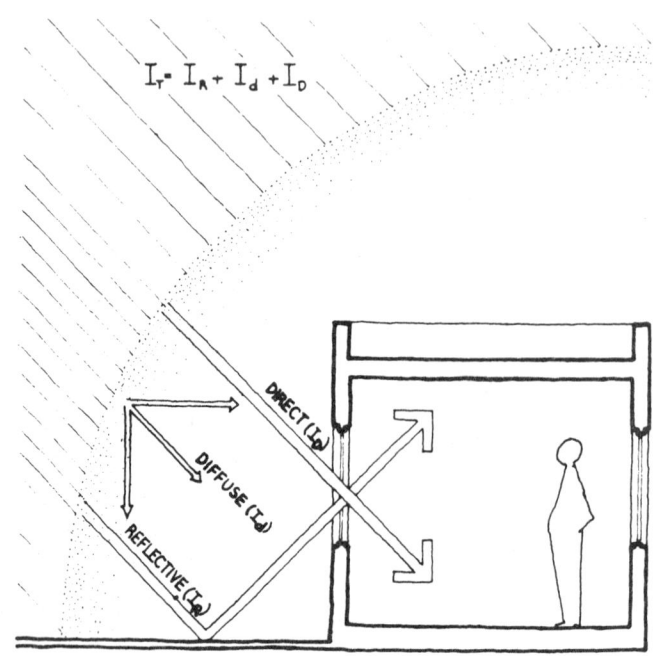

$I_T = I_R + I_d + I_D$

Figure 2.4.2.6 - Solar Radiation

The amount of solar radiation at a given location provides an indication of the energy available for solar heating systems and natural daylighting. Site-specific analysis of the availability of incoming solar radiation will also require consideration of the shading effects of surrounding buildings, both existing and future.

Wind

Wind can have both a negative and positive effect in terms of energy conservation. In winter, it infiltrates and overchills. In hot climates it reduces discomfort by spurring evaporation. The extent to which a designer can use wind to modify and control human comfort is determined by seasonal patterns of wind direction, speed and frequency.

The predominant westerly breezes in the United States are deflected by regional high-pressure centers. In summer, the regional highs tend to remain fairly fixed, but in the fall and winter, some tropical storms and Arctic cold fronts overpower the highs, sweeping in from the south and north. Studying the local climatological data will often reveal radical shifts in wind direction during the winter months. This allows the designer to design a building that is open in the direction of summer winds and shielded from the direction of winter winds.

To be usable for ventilation, wind speeds need to be at least five miles per hour. Through the design of the site and building, low-speed breezes can be boosted to usable velocities.

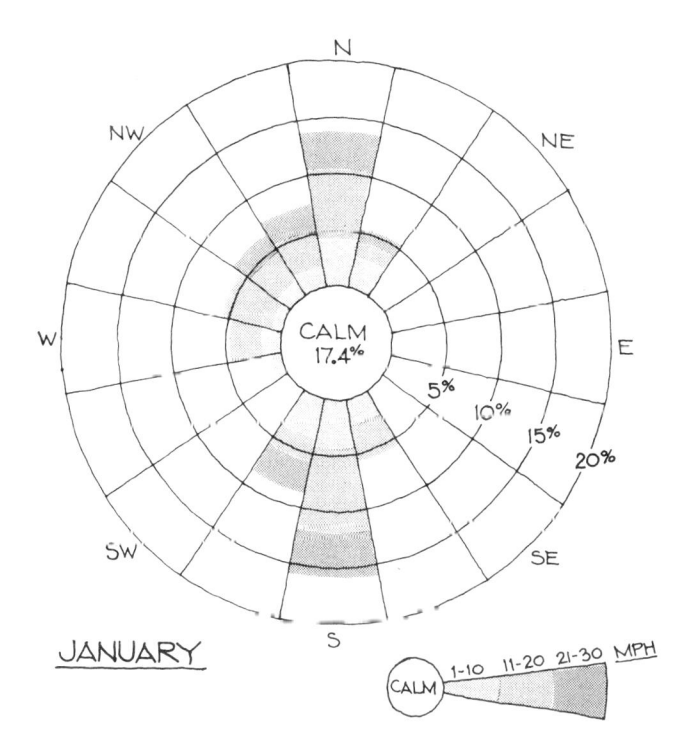

Figure 2.4.2.7 - Wind Rose

The frequency of the occurrence of winds from each direction can be represented graphically, making it easy to identify the most likely wind directions. "Wind roses" are a common graphic method for presenting wind data (see Figure 2.4.2.7). The rose indicates frequency of occurrence, in percent of different wind speeds, for 16 directions. The size of the middle circle indicates the percent of time the wind is calm.

Recurrent Weather Events and Anomalies

Many climate regions experience distinctive patterns that tend to be masked by overall statistics. Los Angeles architects are aware of night and morning low clouds and fog along the coast in the summer, and extremely hot, dry Santa Ana winds from the nearby deserts in the fall. Farmers across the country become particularly adept at predicting weather patterns that will affect their crops.

The descriptive summaries that accompany the local weather data issued by the National Oceanographic and Atmospheric Administration (see below) provide information on the intensity and frequency of weather anomalies such as these, as well as on the predictability of recurrent weather patterns.

Weather anomalies, though they may rarely occur, often have a great influence on building design, especially in connection with hazard mitigation. In South Florida, a major determinant of form is protection from high winds and flooding caused by hurricanes.

Limitations of Climatic Data

Climatic data are useful for developing general design strategies for a specific region, but present a serious potential danger when used by a designer for more than that purpose. Site-specific factors form a small-scale pattern of microclimates in any given climatic zone. Microclimatic modifications play an important part in site planning and, ultimately, in energy-conscious design. Microclimatic analysis is discussed in Section 3.1.4, Microclimate.

2.4.3 General Design Considerations in Relation to Climatic Data

While regional climatic factors are always tempered at the local level by the physical composition of on the site, climatic data _can_ suggest design strategies that give the designer a starting point.

All climatic regions offer opportunities for taking advantage of natural daylighting. Using the four climatic zones' characteristics, a number of other general, very basic, design guidelines can be developed:

<u>Hot-Humid Climates</u>
- Maximize natural ventilation: Use large openings, cross ventilation, high ceilings, narrow spaces, single-loaded corridors
- Minimize thermal mass: Diurnal temperature swings are too low to be a benefit, high humidity will cause mildew

- Shade all openings
- Provide outdoor shaded spaces for daytime activities.

Hot-Arid Climates
- Minimize natural ventilation
- Use small air flow openings
- Maximize thermal mass: usually high diurnal temperatures are available
- Shade openings
- Use compact forms and light exterior colors.

Temperate Climates
- Make dual use of radiation and wind effects, cross ventilation
- Use southern openings
- Use forms elongated on east-west axis
- Use medium colors.

Cool Climates
- Use southern windows; small openings on other exposures
- Use high interior thermal mass
- Use summer shading
- Use compact forms and medium-to-dark colors.

2.4.4 Sources of Climatic Data

Climatic data can be obtained from many sources. Included in the following list are publications that contain raw data, and tabulated data in formats usable by designers. Most design tools require only simple summary data. The most complex computerized analysis tools require actual readings for all 8,760 hours of the year.

The National Oceanic and Atmospheric Administration (NOAA)

NOAA, the national weather service, collects a huge amount of data from hundreds of stations across the country. NOAA weather stations are located in major cities and sometimes in more than one location within the same metropolitan area. Each local weather station provides data in a variety of formats and for a variety of time periods. A comprehensive guide to their publications giving sample data is available from NOAA.

NOAA's Local Climatological Data presents on one sheet a narrative description plus a statistical summary of average data for any weather station in the United States. Also available are 12-month, hour-by-hour summaries. Sheets on the 13 typical locations listed earlier in this section are available at the local NOAA facility, or postpaid from Asheville, N.C., for a minimal fee.

The total amount of sunlight--direct, diffuse and reflected--that hits a horizontal surface, called "incident solar radiation" or insolation, is measured in terms of Btu/sq.ft./hour (or month or day) or Langleys/hour. This number does not appear in NOAA's LCDs, but is available in ASHRAE's Applications handbook and the Climatic Atlas (see below), as well as in many solar handbooks.

The LCDs provide data on the number of hours the sun is up every day and, based on historical measurements, the "percent [of] possible sunshine" likely to be actually available. Percent possible sunshine in LCDs is averaged over each month. This percentage, multiplied by the solar radiation figure, will yield a monthly average of available insolation.

For daylighting analyses, the distribution of sun from day to day can be seen from a plotting of data on clear and cloudy days, also available from LCDs and from <u>Daylight Availability Data for Selected Cities in the United States</u>, C.I. Robbins and K.C. Hunter (Golden, Colo.: Solar Energy Research Institute, 1982).

Climate of States

The two-volume <u>Climate of States</u> contains chapters for every state including the local climatological data summary for each NOAA station in the state plus a narrative summary describing the climatological features of a state as a whole.

Architectural Graphics Standards

The AIA's <u>Architectural Graphics Standards</u>, published by John Wiley & Son, Inc., provides solar path diagrams that allow designers to compute the sun's position in the sky as a function of specific geographic location, season, and time of day.

Weather Tapes

Weather data also exist on magnetic tapes for use with computerized load calculations or energy analysis programs, including the Test Reference Year (TRY) tapes, the Typical Meteorological Year (TMY) tapes and The California Energy Commission's (CEC) tapes.

Air Force Data

The U.S. Air Force also collects weather data at each Air Force base, available in printed tabular format.

Universities and State Energy Commissions

Departments of meteorology, energy laboratories and university extension services may also be a source of local weather data. In some states where energy codes have been implemented, weather data have been collected.

The Tennessee Valley Authority (TVA) has prepared an excellent series of booklets giving all climatic data for all the major metropolitan areas within its jurisdiction.

AIA Research Corporation's Regional Guidelines

This publication is a comprehensive source of climatological analyses for 13 regions in the United States.

2.5 THE BUILDING DESIGN PROCESS

2.5.1 Introduction

When approaching an energy design problem, design professionals can be overwhelmed by the number of available options. The designer may be tempted to select design based on familiarity with only a limited set of possibilities. This approach can be dangerous. Buildings have different uses, sizes, occupancy patterns, sites, and other variables. Successful energy design responds to a different set of variables for each given building. Therefore, understanding the key energy issues related to the design of different building types and knowing the variety of available options is of the utmost importance.

The goals for designing energy-conserving buildings should be: 1) to ensure that the decision-making process related to energy concerns is accurate, and 2) to make the resulting design responsive to other architectural concerns, such as cost, schedule, function, and form. The goal should not be to provide the "perfect" architectural solution in response to a need for energy conservation. Such an unattainable goal creates only frustration. The solution should use both the building form and the mechanical system to conserve energy. The architectural design should respond to the energy requirements first form, climate and available energy sources. The appropriate mechanical systems should be integrated into the design.

Designers unfamiliar with energy-conscious design often approach the problem through the "add-on" approach, in which specific measures are grafted onto a preexisting design concept. Energy can often be saved with this approach through modifications to building form, envelope and other building systems.

Once the basic framework of energy-conscious design is understood, the design of successful energy-efficient buildings often becomes intuitive. True energy-conscious design always takes energy into account early in the design process. Designers are urged to understand fully the energy problem for each project and the range of possible solutions before beginning the design. Experience with the use of the various design strategies enables design professionals to produce buildings that use less energy while maintaining the integrity of other design criteria.

2.5.2 Predesign

In addition to establishing all of the conventional architectural and engineering program factors for new buildings, a predesign energy analysis should be conducted. The basic steps for the predesign energy analysis include:

1. Problem Definition
    a. collect data
    b. establish decision making criteria

c. prepare "base case" analysis
d. identify energy types

2. Identification of Design Strategies
   a. assess opportunities
   b. match energy types to various strategies
   c. set priorities

3. Programming
   a. establish energy performance targets
   b. establish energy-related goals and program requirements

Problem Definition

Energy problems need to be defined thoroughly to characterize the potential energy needs of the proposed building. Basic facts regarding the energy requirements for the building that must be collected include construction costs and operating cost expectations, utility rate structures, site constraints, building form and envelope factors, climatic data, thermal and luminous comfort considerations, and so forth. Decision-making criteria for the energy design features should also be established. This information should include quantitative as well as qualitative energy-related criteria. Figures 2.5.2.1 and 2.5.2.2 show typical breakdowns for the various building elements.

			BTU/sf/yr
A.	Building Envelope	11.0%	7,150
B.	Building Contents	39.0%	25,675
C.	Lighting Systems	50.0%	32,500
D.	Total Energy Budget	100.0%	65,000

Figures 2.5.2.1 - Energy Budget

			BTU/sf/yr
A.	Building Envelope	10.5%	6,825
	1. Walls + Windows	9.0%	5,850
	2. Roof, Floor + Skylights	1.5%	975
B.	Building Contents	39.5%	25,675
	3. Occupants	2.5%	1,625
	4. Ventilation	12.0%	7,800
	5. Appliances	5.0%	3,250
	6. Elevators, Motors, Fans + Misc.	15.0%	9,750
	7. Water Heating	5.0%	3,250
C.	Lighting Systems	50.0%	32,500
	8. Task + General Illumination	48.0%	31,200
	9. Outdoor + Special	2.0%	1,300
D.	Total Energy Budget	100.0%	65,000

Figures 2.5.2.1 - Energy Budget

A.	Building Envelope	10.5%
	1. Walls + Windows	9.0%
	2. Roof, Floor + Skylights	1.5%
B.	Building Contents	39.5%
	3. Occupants	2.5%
	4. Ventilation	12.0%
	5. Appliances	5.0%
	6. Elevators, Motors, Fans + Misc.	15.0%
	7. Water Heating	5.0%
C.	Lighting Systems	50.0%
	8. Task + General Illumination	48.0%
	9. Outdoor + Special	2.0%
D.	Total Energy Budget	100.0%

Figures 2.5.2.2 - Energy Use

Factors that affect energy use in buildings include:
- Functional Factors
    - Building location
    - Building size and function
    - Floor area per person
    - Size of processing equipment and appliances
    - Building operating schedules
- Environmental Factors
    - Lighting comfort levels
    - Thermal comfort levels
    - Need for view
- Envelope Factors
    - Orientation of building
    - Shape of building
    - Mass of building
    - Wall and roof insulation value (U-value)
    - Glass area and location
    - Reflectivity of skin (walls, roof, glass)
    - Skin shading or screening
- Airconditioning System Factors
    - System controls
    - Airconditioning system design characteristics
    - Airconditioning equipment selection and efficiency
    - Heat recovery and recycling
    - Natural (outside air) ventilation provisions
- Energy Source Factors
    - Availability of reclaimable waste heat
    - Energy-source selection
- Electrical System Factors
    - Electrical power utilization efficiencies
    - Lighting system design characteristics
- Additional Considerations
    - What alternative energy sources are available?
    - How will the utility rate structure affect energy use?
    - How will building operation schedules affect energy use?

Since the energy-use requirements for most buildings are not intuitively obvious to

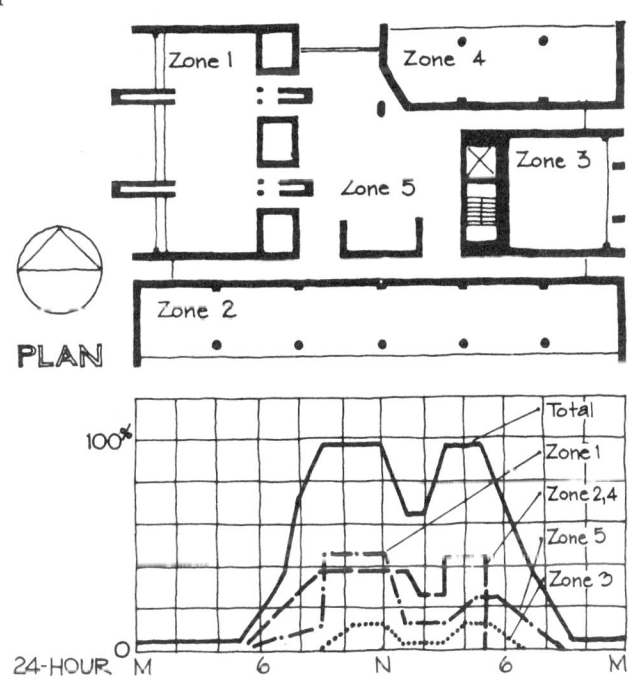

Figure 2.5.2.3 - Energy Profiles

the generation of a "base case" building energy analysis is recommended. A "base case" building is one of similar type and size which can be used as a prototypical model in the effort to understand the nature of the energy problem. This base case building can help the architect understand the energy use and energy cost for a specific building using typical construction techniques and modern design standards in a specified location.

Preliminary architectural and engineering assumptions must be made to establish a base case analysis. The profiles shown in Figure 2.5.2.3 will be useful in the process of establishing the "base case" building. Just as the design team will establish general building characteristics to determine the construction cost budgets for a project, they must make general assumptions to determine the energy requirements for the building. These assumptions can be based on minimum requirements to meet the local building codes or common design practices. Evaluation techniques for conducting the predesign energy analysis of the base case building are presented in Section 4.2, "Analytical Techniques."

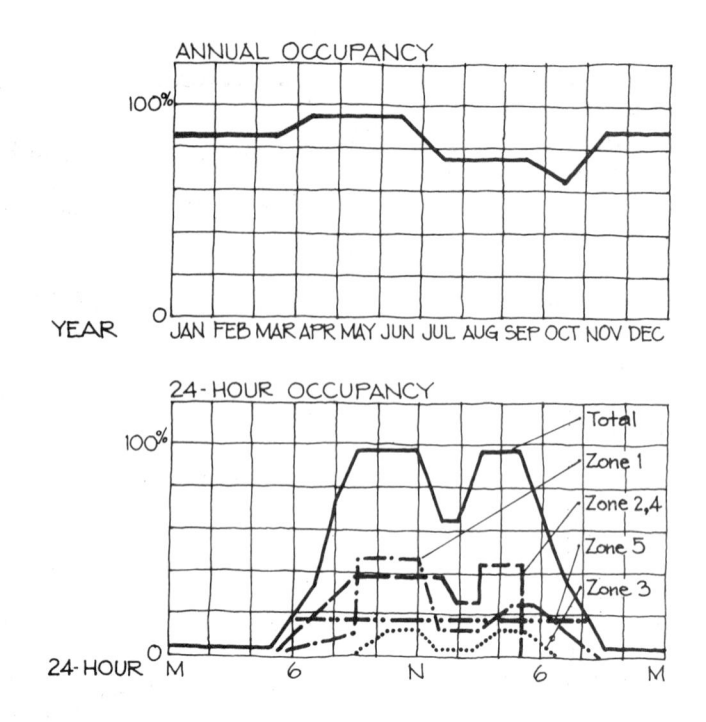

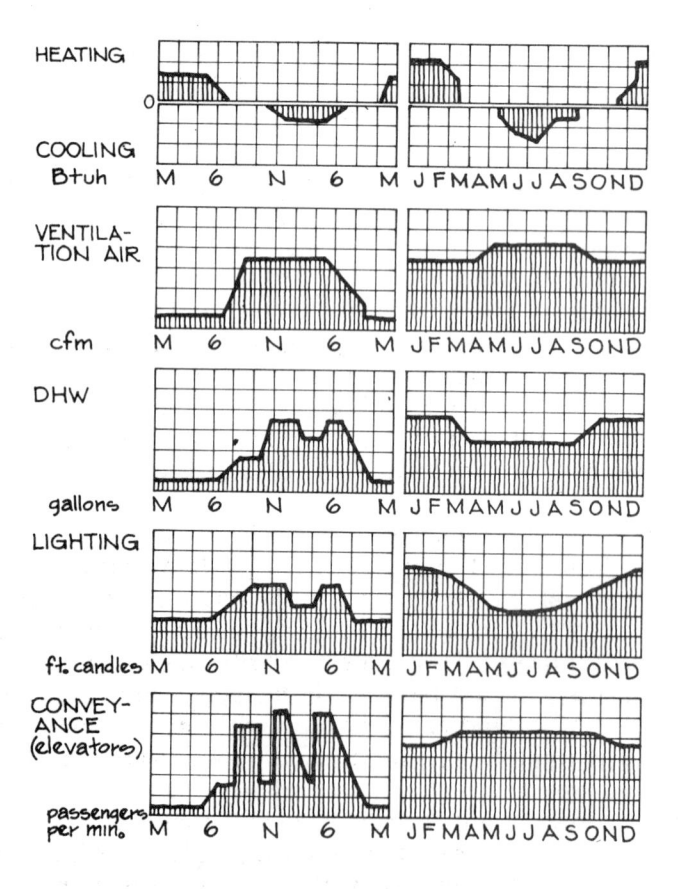

Figure 2.5.2.3 - Energy Profiles

The types of energy
sources available at the
site of the proposed
building should also be
identified.
Conventional energy
sources and their costs
(see Section 2.3, Cost
of Energy) should be
thoroughly understood so
that their consequences
can be evaluated.
Natural energy
considerations such as
solar availability,
daylighting conditions,
wind applications, and
others also need to be
documented. An "energy
profile" of the "base
case" building (see
Figure 2.5.2.4) can
greatly help the
architect to understand
the full nature of the
design problem.

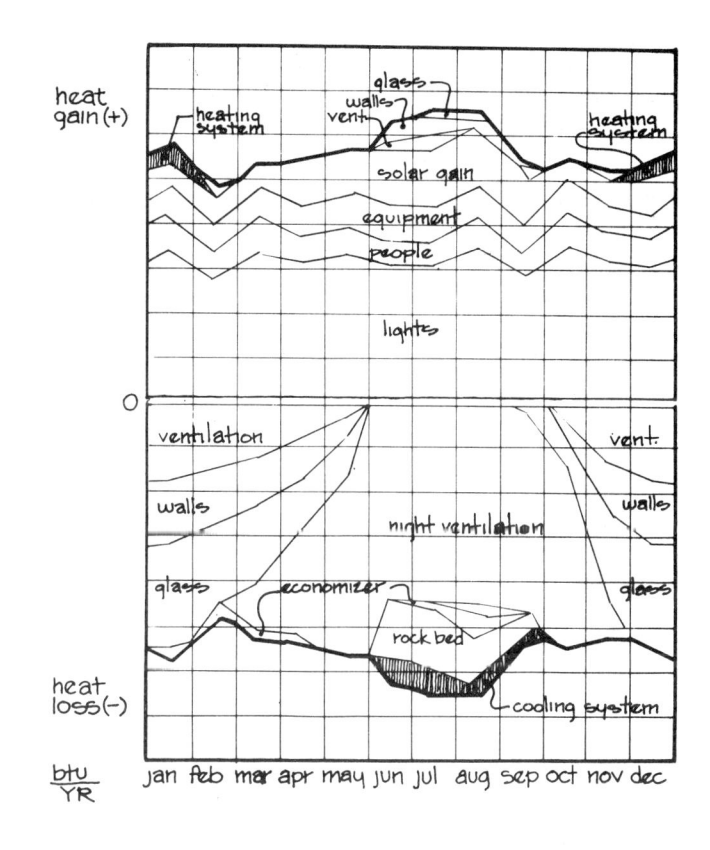

Figure 2.5.2.4 - Energy Profile

Design Strategies

The range of design strategies for energy conservation should be
identified and understood by the design team. Energy needs should be
matched with appropriate design solutions. This information will enable
the design professionals to select the proper solutions. At this point,
the key opportunities for energy conservation should become apparent, and
priorities for design strategies can be established.

The design strategies thus established will help determine the envelope
and form of the building. For example, if a building has a potentially
high lighting requirement, daylighting would likely be an effective design
strategy to reduce both the energy requirements for electric lighting and
the cooling load it creates. This strategy would indicate that spaces
needing much lighting should be close to daylight openings. The strategy
may result in narrower buildings, buildings with interior courtyards, or
buildings with a high building-surface-area-to-floor-area ratio.

Such a solution, however, should not be looked at as a singular strategy.
All of the energy needs of the building must be considered; decreasing the
energy requirement for one end use will change the energy requirements for

other energy uses as well. For example, the use of daylight in place of artificial lighting may increase or decrease heating or cooling requirements depending on how the daylighting is achieved.

The design strategies for building systems should also be identified during this phase. For example, for some climates and buildings, evaporative cooling might be an effective design strategy, while for other buildings, active solar systems might be effective. Whatever the system used in the building, it is best to understand the architectural and system consequences early in the design process.

	Form	Function	Economy	Time	Energy
GOALS Decide	• Site • Environment • Quality • Site elements • Psychological environment • Quality space • Neighbors • Projected image	• People • Activities • Relationship • Human values • Relationships • Efficiency • Identity • Relationship	• Initial budget • Operating • Long term • Limit of funds • Quality • Time • Limits	• Present • Future • Growth • Occupancy • Change • Limits	• Energy budget • Efficiency • Resources • Building prototypes • Comfort • Cost
FACTS Organize Analyze	• Site analysis • Codes • Psychological implications	• Activities • Statistical data • User characteristics • Community considerations • Area parameters • Space limits	• Economic data • Budget • Market analysis • Feasibility	• Schedule • Economic projections	• Analysis techniques • Codes and standards • External factors • Internal factors • Program factors
CONCEPT Uncover Develop	• Orientation • Place concept • Psychological influence	• Priority • Flow • Affinities • Security	• Multifunction • Flexibility	• Convertibility • Expansibility • Phasing	• Program analysis • Form and Envelope • External dominant • Internal dominant • Passive or active
NEEDS Determine	• Environment • Site • Cost influence • Form-giving image	• Area requirement • Parking • Efficiency ratio • Alternatives • Performance requirements	• Budget analysis • Initial cost	• Phasing growth • Escalation • Change implications	• Loads • Systems • Utilities use and demand • Energy cost

Figure 2.5.2.5 - Architectural Program Factors

Factors That Affect the Building Concept
- Is the building going to be internally or externally dominated? In other words, are primary loads due to outside weather conditions or to such internal factors as heat produced by lights, occupants, and machines?
- How will climate affect building energy use?
- Is the primary problem energy demand or consumption?
- Are there sources of reclaimable waste heat available?
- What energy concepts enhance the project's non-energy priorities?
- Is there a process within the building that has special energy features or energy effects?

Programming

The third component of the predesign phase is to establish the program factors related to the energy considerations. Energy performance targets or goals should be established. These targets should be established using the base of information collected during the first two steps in the predesign process. These energy targets will help determine the appropriate response to the energy concerns in the building design process. Figure 2.5.2.5 provides an overview of architectural programming factors.

Energy-budget levels developed from the Building Energy Performance Standards (BEPS) by the federal government may serve as one set of energy targets. These were developed to establish minimum levels of energy consumption for different types of buildings in different climatic regions (see Figure 2.5.2.6).

To use the energy budget effectively as a goal, the designer needs an understanding of the energy used by the major elements of the building. A simple breakdown might include allotments for the building envelope, HVAC systems and equipment, lighting and electrical distribution, domestic hot water system, conveyance systems and energy-intensive processes such as cooking. A more detailed allotment might break these categories down further. These breakdowns can be shown numerically or graphically as pie charts. Once the allotments have been made, the designer can use them to guide energy design decisions and evaluate those decisions after they have been applied.

The final task of the programming stage is to identify the best energy-related goals and opportunities for the project. These goals and opportunities should be a list of optimal solutions rather than a selection of components or design concepts. These program statements should deal with approximate sizes, shapes, and relationships, as well as the quantitative information (i.e., Btu and footcandle needs). This information should be clearly and concisely stated for good communication among all of the design team members. The actual means for accomplishing the desired results will be evaluated during the design phase that follows.

State	SMSA	Clinic	Community Center	Gymnasium	Hospital	Hotel/Motel	Multifamily Highrise	Multifamily Lowrise	Nursing Home	Office Large	Office Small	School Elementary	School Secondary	Shopping Center	Store	Theater/Auditorium	Warehouse
Alabama	Birmingham	48	42	49	140	65	45	43	63	44	39	35	46	71	56	54	21
	Mobile	48	44	50	140	65	43	45	63	45	39	33	45	71	56	55	16
Arizona	Phoenix	50	45	52	140	67	44	46	64	46	41	34	46	72	58	57	17
California	Bakersfield	47	42	49	140	64	43	43	62	44	39	33	45	70	55	54	18
	Fresno	47	41	48	140	64	44	42	62	43	38	33	45	69	54	53	20
	Los Angeles	43	38	43	140	59	39	39	57	40	34	28	40	65	50	48	16
	Sacramento	46	40	47	140	63	43	41	61	42	37	33	44	68	53	51	20
	San Diego	43	39	44	140	60	39	40	58	41	35	28	41	65	51	49	15
	San Francisco	42	36	42	140	59	40	37	57	39	34	30	40	64	49	46	20
Colorado	Denver	50	40	50	140	66	49	41	64	45	41	39	48	72	56	55	29
Connecticut	Bridgeport	50	41	51	140	66	48	41	65	45	41	39	48	73	56	55	28
	Hartford	52	42	53	140	68	50	43	67	46	43	41	50	75	58	58	30
D.C.	Washington	50	42	51	140	66	47	43	64	45	41	37	47	72	56	56	24
Florida	Jacksonville	49	44	51	140	66	44	45	63	45	40	33	46	71	57	56	16
	Miami	52	48	55	140	69	45	50	66	48	43	35	48	74	61	60	14
Florida	Tampa	49	46	52	140	67	44	47	64	46	41	33	46	72	58	57	15
Georgia	Atlanta	48	41	49	140	64	44	42	62	44	39	34	45	70	55	54	21
Idaho	Boise City	51	41	51	140	67	49	41	65	45	41	40	49	73	57	56	29
Illinois	Chicago	52	42	53	140	68	51	42	67	46	43	42	50	75	58	58	31
	Glenview	52	42	53	140	69	51	43	67	47	43	42	51	75	59	58	31
Indiana	Indianapolis	52	42	53	140	68	50	43	67	46	43	42	50	75	58	58	30
Kansas	Dodge City	49	44	51	140	66	45	45	64	45	40	35	46	72	57	56	19
Kentucky	Louisville	50	42	51	140	67	48	42	65	45	41	38	48	73	57	56	26
Louisiana	Baton Rouge	48	44	50	140	65	43	45	63	45	39	33	45	71	57	55	16
	New Orleans	49	44	51	140	66	44	45	64	45	40	34	46	71	57	56	18
Maine	Portland	54	41	54	140	69	53	42	68	47	44	45	52	76	59	59	35
Massachusetts	Boston	51	41	52	140	67	50	42	66	45	42	41	49	74	57	57	30
Michigan	Detroit	53	42	53	140	69	51	42	67	47	43	43	51	75	59	58	32

Figure 2.5.2.6 - Energy Targets (MBtu/SqFt/Year)

Minnesota	Minneapolis	58	45	59	140	74	58	45	73	51	48	50	57	82	64	65	38
Mississippi	Jackson	49	43	51	140	66	45	45	64	45	40	35	46	72	57	56	19
Missouri	Columbia	52	42	53	140	68	49	43	66	46	42	40	50	74	58	58	28
	Kansas City	52	43	53	140	68	50	44	67	46	43	40	50	75	59	58	27
Missouri	St. Louis	52	43	53	140	68	50	44	67	47	43	41	50	75	59	58	28
Montana	Great Falls	54	42	54	140	70	53	42	68	47	44	45	52	77	59	59	35
Nebraska	Omaha	53	43	54	140	69	52	43	68	47	44	43	51	76	59	59	31
Nevada	Las Vegas	50	45	52	140	67	46	46	65	46	41	36	47	73	58	57	19
New Jersey	Newark	50	42	51	140	67	48	42	65	45	41	39	48	73	57	56	27
New Mexico	Albuquerque	50	42	51	140	66	47	42	64	45	41	38	48	72	56	56	25
New York	Albany	54	42	54	140	70	53	43	68	47	44	45	52	77	59	60	34
	Buffalo	53	41	53	140	69	52	42	67	46	43	43	51	75	58	58	33
	New York	49	41	50	140	66	47	42	64	44	40	38	47	72	56	55	26
No. Carolina	Raleigh	49	41	50	140	65	46	42	63	44	40	36	46	71	56	54	23
North Dakota	Bismarck	60	45	61	140	76	60	46	75	52	50	53	59	83	65	66	42
Ohio	Akron	52	42	53	140	68	51	42	67	46	43	42	50	75	58	58	31
	Cincinnati	51	42	52	140	67	49	43	65	46	42	39	49	73	57	57	27
	Cleveland	53	42	53	140	69	52	42	67	47	43	43	51	76	59	58	32
	Columbus	52	42	53	140	69	51	43	67	46	43	42	51	75	58	58	31
Oklahoma	Oklahoma City	50	43	52	140	67	47	44	65	46	41	38	48	73	58	57	24
	Tulsa	50	43	51	140	66	47	43	64	45	41	37	47	72	57	56	23
Oregon	Medford	47	39	47	140	63	45	39	62	43	38	35	45	69	53	52	25
	Portland	47	38	47	140	63	45	39	61	42	38	35	45	69	53	51	26
Pennsylvania	Allentown	51	41	51	140	67	49	42	65	45	41	40	49	73	57	56	29
	Philadelphia	51	42	52	140	67	49	43	66	46	42	40	49	74	57	57	28
	Pittsburgh	51	41	52	140	67	50	42	66	46	42	41	49	74	57	57	29
So. Carolina	Charleston	48	43	50	140	65	44	44	63	44	39	34	45	70	56	55	19
Tennessee	Memphis	49	43	51	140	66	46	44	64	45	40	36	47	72	57	56	22
	Nashville	49	42	50	140	65	46	43	64	44	40	36	47	71	56	55	23
Texas	Amarillo	49	41	50	140	66	47	42	64	45	40	37	47	72	56	55	25
	Dallas	51	45	52	140	67	46	46	65	46	41	36	48	73	58	56	19
	El Paso	49	43	50	140	65	45	43	63	44	40	35	46	71	56	55	20
	Houston	49	44	51	140	66	44	46	64	45	40	34	46	72	57	56	17

Figure 2.5.2.6 - **Energy Targets continued** (MBtu/SqFt/Year)

Texas	Lubbock	49	42	50	140	66	46	43	64	45	40	36	47	72	56	55	23
	San Antonio	50	44	51	140	67	45	46	64	46	41	35	47	72	58	57	18
Utah	Salt Lake City	53	42	53	140	69	51	43	67	47	43	43	51	75	59	59	31
Vermont	Burlington	55	42	56	140	71	55	43	70	48	45	47	54	78	60	61	37
Virginia	Norfolk	48	41	49	140	65	45	42	63	44	39	35	46	70	55	54	22
	Richmond	50	42	51	140	67	48	43	65	45	41	38	48	73	57	56	26
Washington	Seattle	46	37	46	140	62	45	38	61	42	38	36	45	69	52	51	27
	Spokane	51	40	52	140	67	51	41	66	45	42	42	50	74	57	56	32
West Virginia	Charleston	50	41	51	140	66	48	42	65	45	41	39	48	73	57	56	27
Wisconsin	Madison	54	42	54	140	70	53	42	69	47	44	45	53	77	59	60	35
	Milwaukee	54	42	54	140	70	53	42	69	47	44	45	53	77	59	60	35
Wyoming	Cheyenne	52	41	52	140	68	52	41	67	46	43	44	51	75	58	57	34

Figure 2.5.2.6 - Energy Targets continued (MBtu/SqFt/Year)

2.5.3 Design

Schematic Design

Maximum energy savings can occur in the schematic design phase. The objective for energy-conscious design schematics, as with any design schematics, is to identify the most appropriate concepts to respond to the time, quality, cost, and energy constraints that were identified during the programming phase. Ideally, several schematic designs would be developed for each project.

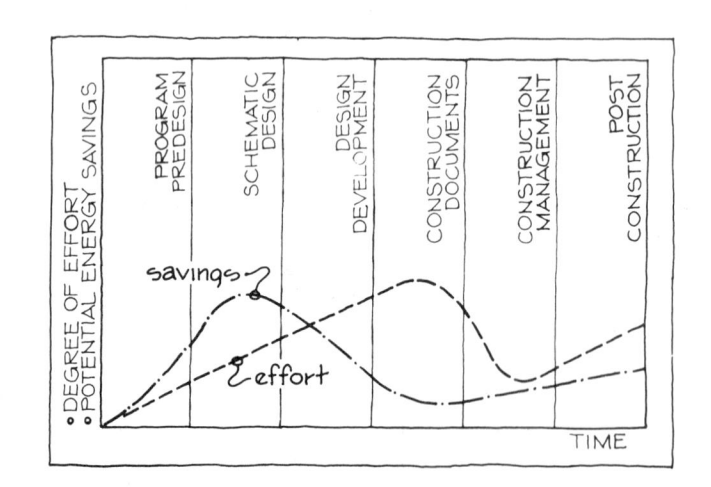

Figure 2.5.3.1 - Energy Savings at Design Stage

The design team must now establish a preliminary evaluation of the program requirements in terms of function, budget, schedule, envelope, and form consequences. The design team should review the alternative approaches to design and construction of the proposed building. These approaches should be evaluated on a preliminary basis to assess the affect of each on the

proposed design costs and energy-related performance. The objective of
this process is to establish relationships and identify opportunities
among various architectural forms, envelopes, and building systems.

An energy analysis for each schematic design option should be conducted to
assess both the energy performance and the economic effects of initial
construction and operating costs.

Design Development

As with the traditional design process, the next step is to define the
architectural, structural, mechanical, and electrical systems for the
proposed building. These include the amount and type of glazing, the
thermal characteristics of building envelope, shading devices (such as
overhangs or wingwalls), and building configuration and form issues.

The design development process completes the synthesis of the building's
energy components. At the end of this phase, an energy analysis should be
prepared to assess the building design and to assure that the resulting
energy performance and cost considerations are within the established
range.

Construction Documents

Construction documents establish all details for both architectural and
systems components. A more accurate estimate of the energy requirements
as well as the construction costs will be prepared at this stage. A
refinement of the life-cycle cost/benefit analysis should be prepared as
the basis for any final decisions on the architectural and system design.

Specifications, performance requirements and working drawings for energy-
conservation products will require most of the work at this stage. The
designer will also prepare any documentation needed to demonstrate
compliance with building energy regulations. The State of California is
developing a manual to enable designers there to demonstrate compliance
with prescriptive codes. The Portland Cement Association's <u>Simplified
Thermal Design of Building Envelopes</u> is designed to determine compliance
with ASHRAE Standard 90, Energy Conservation in New Building Design, which
is used extensively in various codes.

The designer should ascertain that the energy analysis method chosen is
certified by the local jurisdiction as acceptable documentation. Some
firms have developed in-house computer programs that not only perform the
necessary calculations but also print out completed forms that can be
submitted directly to building officials.

Two areas require special consideration for code compliance. If the
designer wishes to reduce the quantities of circulated air, a variance may
be required from code officials. See Section **2.2.4**, Indoor Air Quality.
Second, the energy-conscious designer may wish to use new products or
materials that have not met code approval. Normally, the supplier or
contractor obtains such approval.

Design of Energy-Responsive Commercial Buildings, a Solar Energy Research Institute publication, presents a more detailed discussion of the design process issues.

2.5.4 Construction Management and Commissioning

Construction management and, subsequently, proper operation, maintenance and use of the building's energy-related systems can determine the building's success or failure. See Section 3.10, Construction and Commissioning.

2.5.5 Redesign

Several valid approaches, all containing similar elements, are currently being used for energy design analysis of existing buildings. The essential elements are as follows.

Pertinent energy analysis data, including operational schedules and occupant loads, must be collected. There should also be a physical survey of installed equipment and existing construction.

The present energy use of the building should be analyzed. The major energy uses and requirements should be calculated and compared with actual utility bills.

The primary design opportunities and strategies should be identified on the basis of the foregoing analysis. This should result in specific design options for mechanical systems, electrical systems and building modifications. This is analogous to the schematic design phase discussed above.

For a detailed discussion of energy analysis and design for retrofit applications, the reader is referred to Energy Conservation in Existing Buildings, a U.S. Department of Energy publication.

2.6 CODES, STANDARDS, AND REGULATORY ISSUES

2.6.1 Introduction

A variety of codes and standards have been developed for the purpose of mandating energy-conserving design or providing guidelines to ensure that energy-conserving design elements function as intended. While codes generally have the force of law, standards are usually voluntary except when they are incorporated into the mandatory codes. Figure 2.6.1.1 depicts the full spectrum of issues which go into energy codes and standards.

Codes and standards are generally considered as providing only minimum requirements for energy conservation. Designers should strive for maximum energy savings.

Codes and standards fall into two basic categories-- "prescriptive" and "performance." Prescriptive codes and standards specify basic requirements for specific materials and components. The American Society of Heating, Refrigerating and Air-Conditioning Engineers (ASHRAE) Standard 90 has in the past been a "prescriptive" standard, although efforts are being made to broaden its approach. In contrast, a performance code or standard specifies the overall energy performance of a whole building, based on an energy analysis of similar buildings. An example of a "performance standard" is the Building Energy Performance Standard (BEPS), mandated in 1977 for all buildings. Since then the BEPS has been made mandatory for federal buildings only, with building energy performance targets made voluntary for nonfederal buildings.

2.6.2 Model Building Codes

Building codes are by tradition established for the protection of "public health, safety and welfare." They are issued as legal requirements by a city, state, or national authority. Codes are generally based on "model" codes developed by national or regional code organizations. Model codes often incorporate standards developed by organizations such as ASHRAE, the Illuminating Engineering Society of North America (IES), and the ASTM (formerly the American Society for Testing and Materials). Model codes are sometimes amended to meet local and regional requirements and practices. Architects and engineers are responsible for knowing about and following all mandatory codes and standards, including those related to energy, and may be liable for negligence, errors and omissions.

The three major model codes that deal in part with energy conservation and energy-conscious design are:

- Basic Building Code -- Building Officials and Code Administrators International, Inc. (BOCA)
- Southern Building Code -- Southern Building Code Congress International, Inc. (SBCCI)
- Uniform Building Code -- International Conference of Building Officials (ICBO)

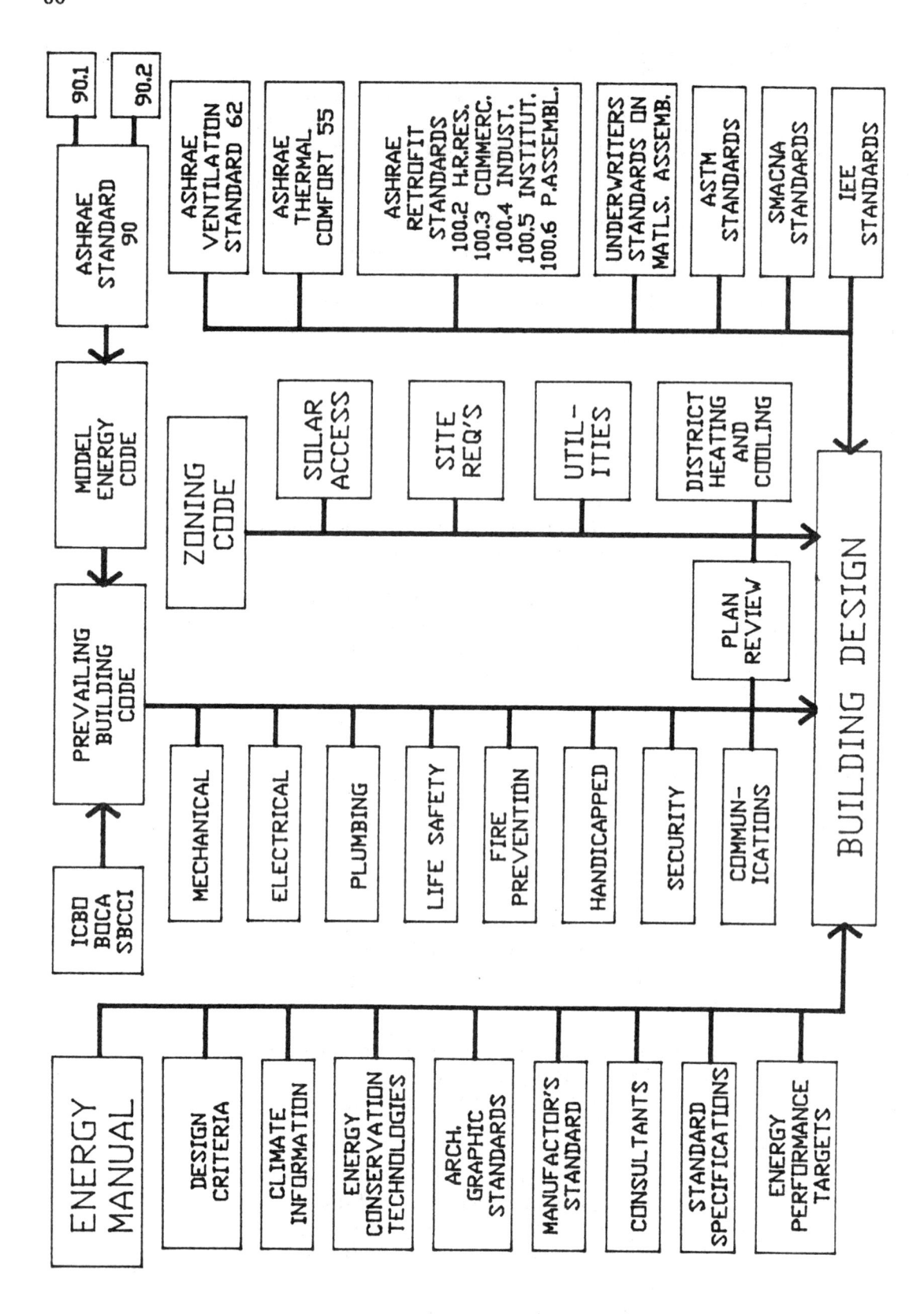

Figure 2.6.1.1 - Energy Codes and Standards (Eino Kainlauri, PhD, AIA)

2.6.3 Model Energy Code

The organizations that develop the three above codes, together with the National Conference of States on Building Codes and Standards (NCSBCS) and the Council of American Building Officials (CABO), have prepared the Model Energy Code.

The Model Energy Code is primarily based on ASHRAE'S Standard 90 (see below) and sets mandatory requirements for minimum energy conservation in new buildings. The code describes, in detail, requirements for maximum allowable U-values for various building components, particularly for the building envelope, and minimum coefficients of performance for various systems and equipment.

The code provides three alternative "paths":
- systems analysis
- component performance
- acceptable practice.

Systems Analysis. This method is perhaps the most important to a creative designer. It requires an energy analysis, which for other than the most simple buildings calls for the use of a computer or at least a programmable calculator. While this option may mean more labor on the part of the designer, it provides a better assessment of alternatives available and tradeoffs between design options, and more accurate estimates of the actual energy use of the proposed building.

The results are expressed as Btu input per sq.ft. of gross floor area per year at the building site. These are compared with a similar design based on the component performance method, which incorporates building components (floor, wall, ceiling) with allowable U-values, as well as applicable equipment and system coefficients of performance, to arrive at an annual energy budget. This annual energy budget allows the designer to make trade-offs as long as the final result is within the budget.

Buildings with major internal energy generation should, in most cases, be subjected to an energy analysis. The systems analysis method also provides for buildings using renewable energy sources, such as solar, wind, geothermal, biomass and photovoltaic energy.

Component Performance. Component performance is perhaps the most common method used by architects and engineers in designing buildings, particularly if the building envelope is a dominating factor in the design.

The building envelope requirements call for maximum allowable U-values based on the annual heating degree days for walls, roof/ceilings, floors over unheated spaces, and slab-on-grade floors (perimeter insulations); (see Figure 2.6.3.1).

TABLE NO. 5-1[1]

ELEMENT	MODE	TYPE A-1 BUILDINGS U_o	TYPE A-2 BUILDINGS U_o
Walls[2]	Heating or cooling		
Roof/Ceiling[3]	Heating or cooling		
Floors over unheated spaces	Heating or cooling		
Heated slab on grade[4]	Heating	R Value	R Value
Unheated slab on grade[5]	Heating	R Value	R Value

[1] Values shall be determined by using the graphs (Figures Nos. 1, 2, 3 and 6) contained in Chapter 7 (based on Standard RS-9) using heating degree days as specified in Section 302.

[2] Walls. The requirements for locations with less than 500 heating degree days shall be:
 (a) No maximum U_o if building is heated only.
 (b) If the building is to be mechanically cooled when built or if provision is made for the future addition of mechanical cooling, the maximum U_o for walls in Type A-1 buildings shall be 0.30 Btu/h ft.²°F. and in Type A-2 buildings shall be 0.38 Btu/h ft.²°F.

[3] There are no insulation requirements for heated slabs in locations having less than 500 Fahrenheit heating degree days.

[4] There are no insulation requirements for unheated slabs in locations having less than 2,500 Fahrenheit heating degree days.

TABLE NO. 5-2[1]

ELEMENT		MODE	VALUE
Walls	3 stories or less	Heating	$U_o =$
		Cooling	$OTTV_W =$
		Cooling	SF* =
	Over 3 stories	Heating	$U_o =$
		Cooling	$OTTV_W =$
		Cooling	SF* =
Roof/Ceiling[2]		Heating or cooling	$U_o =$
		Cooling	$OTTV_R =$
Floors over unheated spaces		Heating or cooling	$U_o =$
Heated[3] slab on grade		Heating or cooling	R value =
Unheated[4] slab on grade		Heating or cooling	R value =

*SF = solar factor

[1] Values shall be determined by using the graphs (Figures Nos. 3, 4, 5, 6 and 7) contained in Chapter 7 (based on Standard RS-9) using heating degree days as specified in Section 302.

[2] The overall thermal transfer value $OTTV_R$ for roof/ceilings of buildings that are mechanically cooled shall not exceed 8.5 Btu/h ft.².

[3] There are no insulation requirements for heated slabs in locations having less than 500 heating degree days.

[4] There are no insulation requirements for unheated slabs in locations having less than 2500 heating degree days.

Figure 2.6.3.1 - Model Energy Code Criteria

For cooling, values are selected from diagrams related to Overall Thermal Transfer Values for Walls and Solar Factor (both based on degrees north latitude), and Temperature Difference TD_{EQ}) Walls and (TD_{EQ}) for Roofs.

Air leakage for all buildings is covered by "Allowable Air Filtration Rates" for windows and doors. Building mechanical systems are covered, and minimum coefficients of performance (COP) or energy efficiency ratios (EER) are given for various equipment and systems.

Electrical power and lighting are also covered in the code. A lighting power budget (Unit Power Density in watts per square feet) needs to be developed, using criteria given by the code. Levels of illumination are to be determined with energy conservation in mind, with trade-offs made between general and task lighting. Luminaire coefficients of utilization (CU), reflectances and light losses are given.

Acceptable Practice. Under the acceptable-practice method, the requirements for building envelope, building mechanical systems, service water heating, and electrical power and lighting are described briefly in relatively simple terms for buildings less than 5000 square feet in gross floor area and three stories or less in height. Two diagrams are shown for U_w-values for opaque walls as related to single- or double-glazed windows, respectively. Figure 2.6.3.2 shows charts 6-A and 6-B from the code.

The 1986 version of the Model Energy Code is available from the Council of American Building Officials, 5205 Leesburg Pike, Falls Church, VA 22401, and from many AIA state chapters and components.

2.6.4 Standards-Developing Organizations

ASHRAE. The American Society of Heating, Refrigerating and Air-Conditioning Engineers has been actively involved in developing building energy standards. Chief among these is ASHRAE's Standard 90, Energy Conservation in New Building Design, which is used extensively in various codes, including the Model Energy Code.

Standard 90 is being updated and expanded, with current drafts proposing the inclusion of a combination on compliance paths, including system/component prescriptive and performance methods and an energy budget method.

Since 1981, the 100-series ASHRAE standard for energy conservation in existing buildings has been available for building retrofit purposes. The ASHRAE 100-series has the same energy conservation target as ASHRAE 90 Standard, but since existing buildings can be difficult to bring up to the same physical conditions as new buildings, additional means are recommended: energy auditing and provisions for operations and maintenance. This series can also be helpful for new buildings; these latter provisions can be used by designers to provide owners guidelines on how to maintain energy conservation benefits.

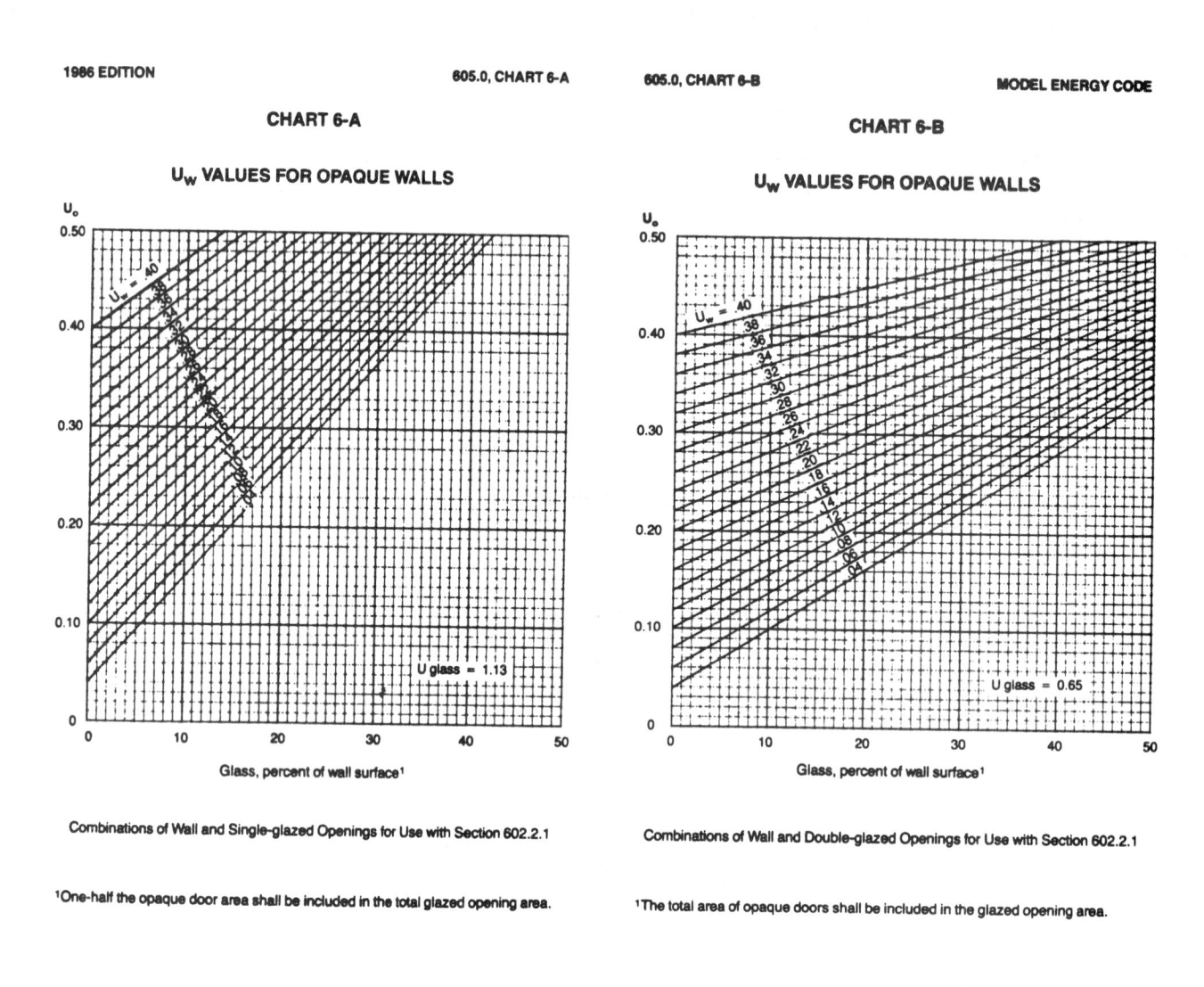

1986 EDITION   605.0, CHART 6-A   605.0, CHART 6-B   MODEL ENERGY CODE

CHART 6-A

U_w VALUES FOR OPAQUE WALLS

(U glass = 1.13)

Combinations of Wall and Single-glazed Openings for Use with Section 602.2.1

[1] One-half the opaque door area shall be included in the total glazed opening area.

CHART 6-B

U_w VALUES FOR OPAQUE WALLS

(U glass = 0.65)

Combinations of Wall and Double-glazed Openings for Use with Section 602.2.1

[1] The total area of opaque doors shall be included in the glazed opening area.

Figure 2.6.3.2 - Model Energy Code U-Values

SMACNA. The Sheet Metal and Air Conditioning Contractor's National Association, Inc., has published several particularly useful guides and standards:
- energy conservation guidelines
- energy recovery equipment and systems
- installation standards for heating, air conditioning and solar systems
- retrofit of building energy systems and processes.

ASTM. ASTM, formerly the American Society for Testing and Materials, publishes a 56-volume set of standards covering a wide range of materials, equipment and systems.

The two-volume ASTM Standards in Building Codes contains more than 500 standards specifically incorporated into building codes. Those most closely associated with energy issues are to be found in the following categories:
- bituminous roofing, waterproofing, and related building (specifications)
- building constructions (rate of air leakage, and water penetration)
-     sealants
- thermal and cryogenic insulating materials (cellulosic fiber-loose fill)
- thermal insulating materials.

Manufacturers. Manufacturers generally follow certified standards issued by professional organizations and government agencies. In addition, they produce standards for their own products. For energy-conserving design, it is important to become familiar with manufacturers' standards in order to make appropriate choices for materials and equipment for buildings, especially items that affect building envelope insulation and infiltration values.

IES. The Illuminating Engineering Society's Lighting Handbook and other standards for lighting attempt to balance lighting quality and energy efficiency.

ARI. The Air Conditioning and Refrigeration Institute issues standards for a variety of air-conditioning components and heat pumps.

NWMA. The National Woodwork Manufacturers Association provides industry standards for Wood Window Units (NWMA IS-2) and Wood Sliding Patio Doors (NWMA IS-3) among others.

Uniform Solar Energy Code. This code, developed by the International Association of Plumbing and Mechanical Officials provides minimum requirements and standards for active solar systems.

Another solar standard is the U.S. Department of Housing and Urban Development's Intermediate Minimum Property Standards Supplement, "Solar Heating and Domestic Hot Water Systems."

3 DESIGN ELEMENTS

3.1 SITING

3.1.1 Introduction

Although many commercial buildings are influenced predominantly by their internal loads, the design can take advantage of natural features of the site to reduce energy consumption.

General climatic data, i.e., insolation, temperature, humidity and wind patterns, must be analyzed in conjunction with particular site elements--topography, vegetation, water conditions on site and built forms--all of which can affect the site's microclimate. The climatic data and site elements should be considered in the selection of the building orientation, form, envelope construction, and size and location of apertures and controls.

The designer may want to map individual site elements on overlays to get a composite view of their effects. Energy-conscious site analysis uses basically the same tools and methods as traditional site analysis--only the interpretation and emphasis change. Design solutions are generally more successful if internal functions and external influences are identified concurrently. However, the climatic and site analysis presented here determine only the external factors affecting building design. As the building's form and envelope evolve, and its internal factors are understood, the balance of these two factors can be approached.

3.1.2 Orientation and Configuration

During the winter months approximately 90 percent of the sun's energy output is received between the hours of 9 AM and 3 PM (sun time). Buildings with heating loads should therefore be oriented to the sun's position between these hours to make direct use of the sun's energy.

Building configuration determines in large part the amount of energy the building will use. Variations in configuration greatly affect the amount of exterior surface area for a given enclosed volume and, hence, the relative amount of thermal transfer through the envelope.

A tall, narrow building has a relatively high surface-to-volume ratio. It has a small roof area and is affected less by solar gain on this surface during the summer months. On the other hand, tall buildings are generally subjected to higher wind velocities, and thus have greater infiltration rates and heat losses.

Low buildings have a greater roof area in proportion to wall area, so special attention must be given to the roof's thermal characteristics.

Of all rectangular shaped buildings, a cube-shaped building has the smallest amount of exterior surface area for a given volume.

Other things being equal, the optimal shape for a building is one that loses a minimum of heat in the winter and gains a minimum of heat in the summer. Victor Olgyay, in <u>Design With Climate</u>, investigated the thermal effects (sun and air temperature) of different shapes in different U.S. climates (see Figure 3.1.2.1). He drew the following conclusions:

- The square is not the optimal form in any location.
- All shapes elongated on the north-south axis work both in winter and summer with less efficiency than the square one.
- The optimal shape in all climates is a form elongated along the east-west direction.
- In most commercial buildings, in most climates, the principal penalty of a north-south axis is increased operational costs due to higher peak cooling loads; however, penalties can be reduced by using a saw-toothed east-west envelope.
- At all latitudes, although buildings elongated along the east-west axis are the most efficient, optimal elongation depends on the climate.
- Some general principles can be stated for different climates. In cool (Minneapolis) and hot-dry (Phoenix) climates, a compact building form, exposing a minimum of surface area to a harsh environment, is desirable. In temperate (New York City) climates, there is more freedom of building shape without severe penalty (excessive heat gain or loss).
- In addition to elongating the building, the plan may open to a courtyard, allowing a more central solar penetration. Although additional perimeter wall is required in buildings with totally enclosed courtyards or atriums, the additional wall is exposed to less severe exterior conditions. Since there would be relatively little energy loss through the windows or openings on the courtyard side, there can be considerably more glass or openings here. The courtyard itself could be naturally lit with skylights, wall glazing or a well-insulated clerestory. If solar heat gain is required, passive collection from south-facing windows is possible.

It is important to avoid sharp lighting contrast at walls and floors adjacent to openings. The high contrast of the natural light, either direct or diffuse, will cause uncomfortable glare problems.

As a building is <u>elongated</u> in the east-west direction, and the section becomes more complex, its surface area increases with respect to its volume, allowing the potential for more solar gain as well as daylight to be admitted.

The building form and configuration can be manipulated using architectural elements (cantilevering floors, horizontal platforms and shelves, projecting rooms and wing walls, or selective wall openings and finishes) to control sun and wind.

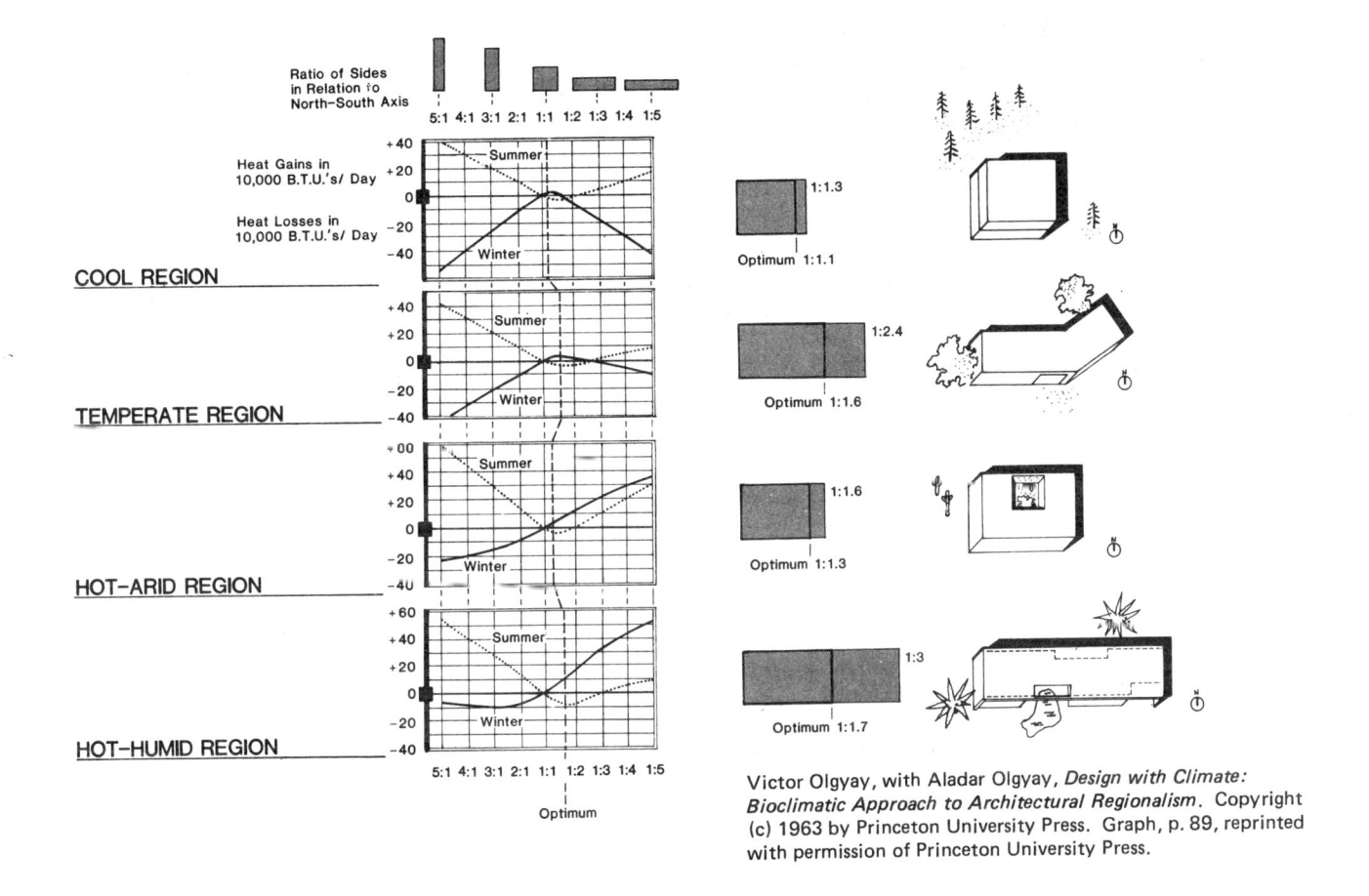

Victor Olgyay, with Aladar Olgyay, *Design with Climate: Bioclimatic Approach to Architectural Regionalism*. Copyright (c) 1963 by Princeton University Press. Graph, p. 89, reprinted with permission of Princeton University Press.

Figure 3.1.2.1 - Building Shapes in Different Regions

3.1.3 Underground Design

Underground Characteristics

In climates with severe winter or summer temperatures, underground construction offers a more hospitable outside design temperature as well as reduced wind exposure. Temperatures underground, below the frost line, remain stable at approximately 56 degrees (F.). The overall range of temperatures 2-26 feet down (corresponding to the wall of a two-story underground building) varies only about 8 degrees (F.) over the course of a year. Figure 3.1.3.1 shows annual underground temperature variation for Minneapolis. For a 2-12 foot profile (corresponding to a typical single-story underground building), the range is about 18 degrees (F.), still no more than a 9-degree (F.) change over the course of a three-month season.

Annual fluctuations of a few degrees occur in depths of 16-32 feet, depending on soil conditions. In most parts of the United States, ground temperature below 20 feet is regarded as stable for building purposes.

Temperature in the soil also lags behind the surface temperature in linear relation to depth. This lag amounts to about one week per foot in most soils. For example, if it is December at the surface, it is "September" at a depth of 12 feet. Therefore, the two maximum heating loads (from the slight cooling of the ground and from cold intake air) are separated in time. This reduces overall peaks in both heating and cooling.

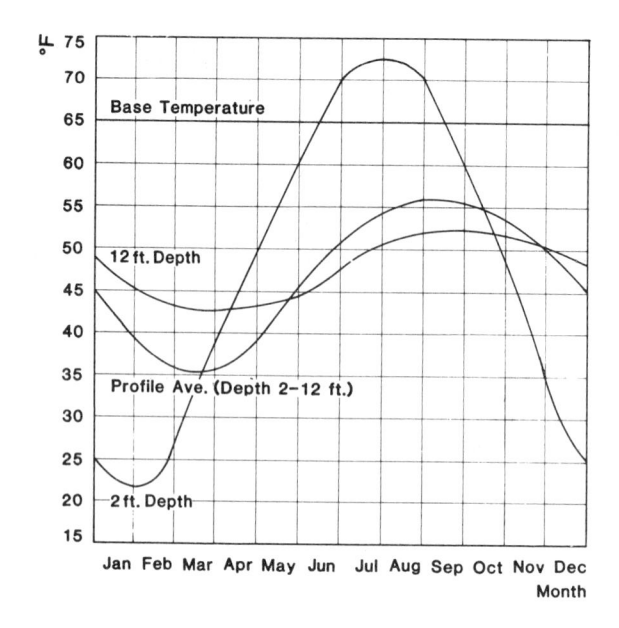

Figure 3.1.3.1 - Underground Degree Day Lag

Degree days for heating and cooling are significantly reduced in an underground building. Temperature profiles in Minneapolis indicate that the need for cooling is eliminated and the heating degree days, at base 65 degrees (F.) are reduced by 26 percent. Identical profiles in Temple, Texas, show that the 2-12 feet profile eliminated heating degree days entirely and reduced the cooling degree days by 21 percent. Underground structures also eliminate most of the heat exchange caused by infiltration.

Underground Construction

In cool and cold climates it is necessary to add exterior insulation to underground walls to keep heat from flowing out into the "heat sink" of the ground. Most heat transfer from shallow underground walls occurs between the wall and the surface, rather than horizontally to the subsoil, as indicated by Figure 3.1.3.2.

Care should be taken when building on clay;

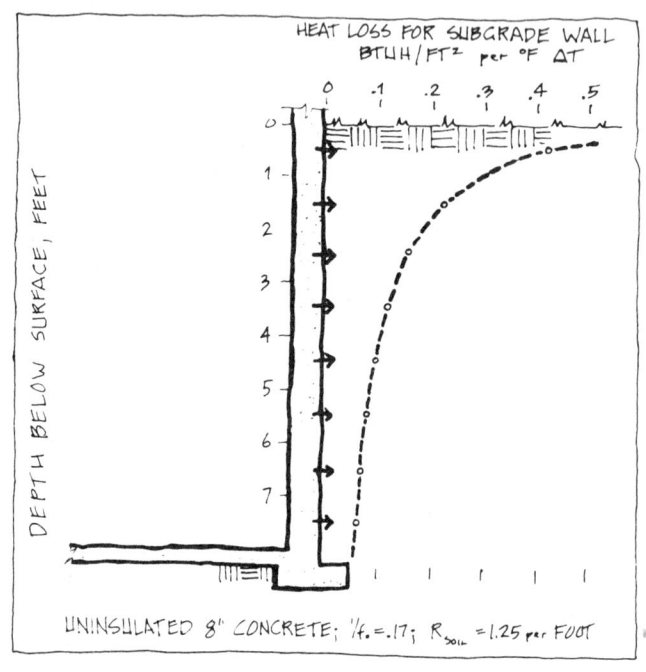

Figure 3.1.3.2 - Heat Loss for Subgrade Wall

shoring should be provided against erosion in slopes.

In humid climates, care should be taken to prevent the accumulation of excess humidity, moisture and mildew in underground structures.

Roof insulation for underground buildings is critical; as much as 50 percent of heat losses can occur through the roof.

In an underground structure, "perimeter zones" are virtually eliminated, creating, in effect, a total "internal zone." For most underground buildings, a single all-air ventilation system is appropriate. Supplemental perimeter heating would be necessary only at interfaces with above-ground.

The reduction in equipment capacity also implies the suitability of interface with relatively low-level energy sources (such as solar). Heat reclamation strategies are readily adaptable to most underground structures.

The placement of skylights and window openings must be carefully designed to minimize breaks in the earth's sheltering thermal mass.

Berming

If berming, rather than underground construction, is chosen, the grade should be carried horizontally from the building as far as possible before the surface is pitched downward.

3.1.4 Microclimate

Macroclimatic data required in the design analysis include solar insolation temperature, humidity, wind and precipitation. The analysis of this information and sources for macroclimatic data for different U.S. regions and climates are discussed earlier, in Section 2.4, Climate.

There is a danger in using macroclimatic data for anything other than regional design guidelines. Weather data are usually collected at places where "undisturbed" weather conditions prevailed, such as airports or mountaintops. Climate can vary perceptibly within a few feet of elevation or within the distance of a mile. This principle is clearly shown by vegetation differences and snow melting patterns on southern vs. northern slopes. Water bodies and changes in vegetation induce further variations in macroclimatic zone.

Site-specific factors combine to form a small-scale pattern of microclimates in any given climatic zone. Each site and each slope, valley and exposed hill of a particular site have precise microclimates that greatly affect the ability to use various portions of the site for architectural or landscape purposes. Microclimatic modifications play an important part in site planning and, ultimately, in energy-conscious design.

Future changes such as new construction adjacent to the site and the growth of vegetation should be considered. The degree of exposure of various slopes and areas of the site, as well as the existence of natural sun pockets, should also be determined during this stage of the analysis. The precipitation reaching the site--amount, type and seasonal variations--should be reviewed. The designer also needs to know about site-mediated temperature extremes, temperature differences between day and night (diurnal range), humidity, direction and force of air movements, snowfall and its distribution, sky conditions, and special conditions such as pollution levels and temperature inversions.

The sun is the deciding factor for many energy-conserving strategies. The sun's position relative to the site is defined by the "altitude," which is the angle of the sun above the horizon, and "azimuth," which is the angle between the sun's position and true south. Solar path diagrams (see Figure 3.1.4.1), available in <u>Architectural Graphics Standards</u>, project the relationship of sun to the site on a horizontal plane. The sun's position (altitude and azimuth) at any date and hour can be discerned from the chart for a given latitude. The months are vertical concentric curves, ranging from 6 A.M. on the east side to 6 P.M. on the west side. The sun's position is found by locating the point at which the chosen month and hour coincide. The

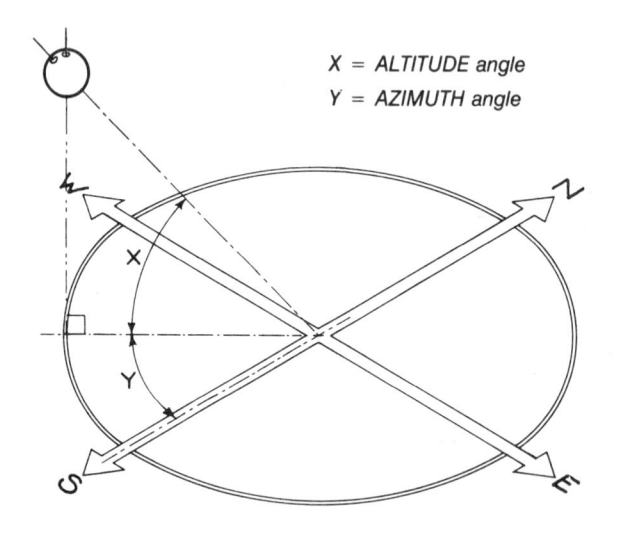

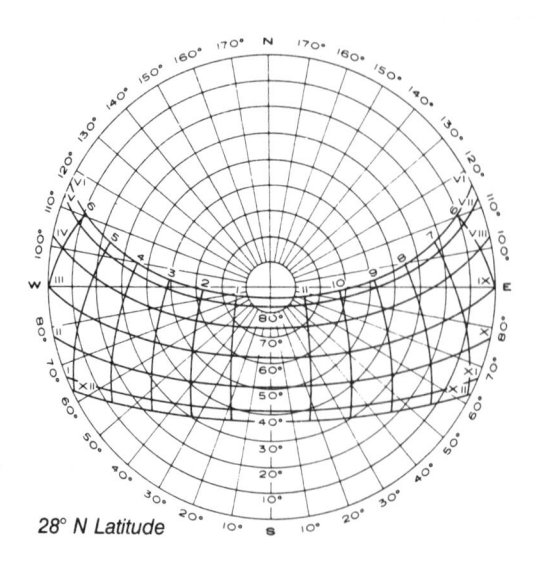

X = ALTITUDE angle
Y = AZIMUTH angle

28° N Latitude

Figure 3.1.4.1 - Solar Geometry

altitude is the concentric circle nearest to this point. The azimuth is
read from the nearest radial line. Sun path diagrams can aid the designer
for daylighting, active and passive solar systems,
and shading studies.

For cooling:
- activities can be placed to the north and east of a building, and
  activity areas on the south side can be shaded
- advantage can be taken of downhill airflow
- vegetation can be placed to divert winds and breezes throughout the site
- activities can be located to the leeward side of water bodies
- pools, fountains, spray devices and irrigation can be provided
  throughout the site.

For heating:
- large paved areas can be exposed to solar radiation, especially on
  south-facing slopes and surfaces
- "Sunpockets" can be created by exposing south-facing areas protected
  from north and west winds
- walls and roofs of buildings can be exposed to maximize solar radiation
- the use of water can be reduced by minimizing the number and size of
  pools, fountains, and irrigation
- the building can be located on the windward side; windbreaks and
  diverters can be used to minimize cooling winds
- obstructions can be placed in valley floors or on side slopes to act as
  dams that keep cold air pockets away from the building.

Topography

Natural Forms. Landforms are excellent microclimate modifiers. Just as
mountains affect the macroclimate, small differences in terrain can create
large modifications in the microclimate. Cool air is heavier than warm,
and at night the outgoing radiation causes a cold air layer to form near
the ground surface. The cold air behaves like any liquid, flowing toward
the lowest points. This "flood of cold air" causes "cold islands" or
"cold puddles." Accordingly, elevations that impede the flow of air
affect the distribution of the nocturnal temperatures by dam action, and
concave terrain formations become cold air lakes at night.

Temperature in the atmosphere decreases with altitude. The temperature
drop in the mountains is approximately one degree (F.) for each 330-foot
rise in summer, and for each 400-foot rise in winter.

Bodies of water also affect the microclimate. Water, having a higher
specific heat than land, is normally warmer in winter and cooler in
summer, and usually cooler during the day and warmer at night, than the
terrain. Accordingly, the proximity of bodies of water moderates extreme
temperature variations, raising the minimum temperatures in winter and
lowering the heat peaks in summer. In large bodies of water like the
Great Lakes, this effect raises the average January temperature about 5
degrees (F.), the absolute minimum temperature about 10 degrees (F.), and

the annual minimum about 15 degrees (F.). Average July temperature is decreased about 3 degrees (F.), and the annual absolute maximum is depressed about 5 degrees (F.). Diurnal temperature variations cause land and sea breezes. When the land is warmer than the water, low cool air moves over the land to replace the heated updraft (see Figure 3.1.4.2). During the day, such offshore breezes may have a cooling effect of up to 10 degrees (F.). At night the direction of the breeze is reversed.

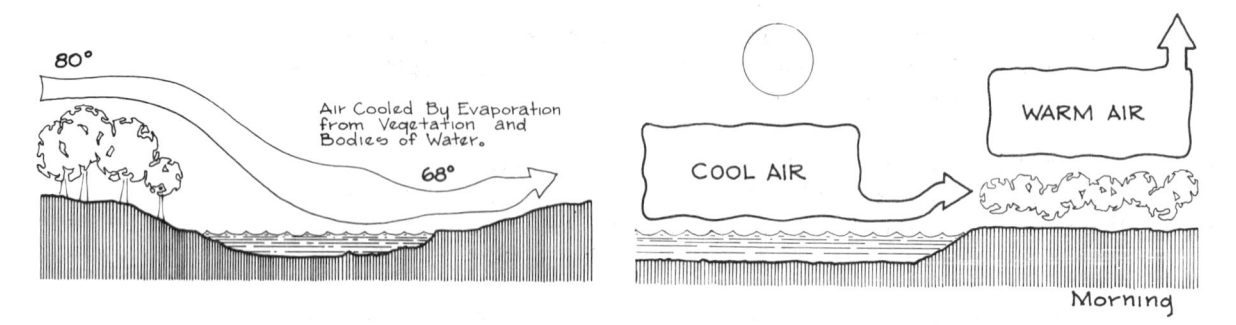

Figure 3.1.4.2 - Effects of Water Bodies

The effects depend on the size of the water body and are more effective along the lee side.

<u>Vegetation.</u> Vegetation also affects the microclimate. The natural cover of the terrain tends to moderate extreme temperatures and stabilize conditions through the reflective qualities of various surfaces. Plant and grassy covers reduce temperatures both by the absorption of insolation and the cooling of evaporation. This reduction can amount to 1,500 Btu/sq.ft./season. It is generally found that temperatures over grass surfaces on sunny summer days are about 10-14 degrees (F.) cooler than overexposed soil.

The effectiveness of specific plant materials in climate control depends on:
- the form and character of the plant
- the climate of the region
- the specific requirements of the site.

Vegetation can absorb 90 percent of the light falling on it, can reduce wind speeds by 90 percent, and reduce daytime temperatures by as much as 15 degrees (F.). In certain situations vegetation can raise nighttime temperatures. Basically, vegetation controls the sun's effect by filtration of the direct solar radiation.
The seasonal variations of trees and plants can be useful to the designer. Deciduous trees should be used near portions of structure that the designer wants exposed winter sun. Buildings and outdoor areas can also be shaded in summer by deciduous trees. Existing or planned trees should be evaluated for their usefulness in providing desired shade.

The twigs and branches of barren decicuous trees obstruct more sun than is generally perceived from discernable shadow patterns (10-15 percent). They can obstruct as much as 50 percent of the light. This should be taken into account if maximum solar gain is desired during the winter. Likewise, even trees in full bloom allow some light penetration. Young trees have only a 0.60 to 0.50 shading coefficient, while mature trees have a 0.25 to 0.20 coefficient .

Nut-bearing trees, including hickory and oak, tend to hold their leaves well into the winter. They make good shading devices but should not be used for both summer shading and winter solar gain.

Built Forms. Built forms affecting the microclimate range from groups of buildings to manmade surface conditions. Horizontal surfaces, such as pavings and decks, affect the microclimate through the properties of absorption and reflectivity.

The microclimate of a site can also be modified by built forms that affect wind patterns.

Built forms have an effect opposite to vegetation, as their materials tend to be absorptive; for example, asphalt surfaces can reach 124 degrees (F.) when the air temperature is 98 degrees (F.). The temperature distribution on a bright summer day in Washington, D.C., varies 8 degrees (F.) within horizontal distances of a few miles. At night the differences in temperature are even larger; some suburban territories have temperatures 11 degrees (F.) lower than those downtown.

When maximum solar gain is desired, built forms should not be located within the "winter solar cone" delineated by the sunrise and sunset azimuths around the winter solstice. The solar cone varies with latitude. Conversely, built forms can be placed in the "solar cone" if solar gain is unwanted.

3.1.5 Sun Control

Shading Patterns

Solid obstructions--hills, vegetation, buildings, etc.--adjacent to or near a site can either obstruct and minimize available daylight or reflect light into a space or onto the site.

Shading patterns caused by nearby buildings should be examined for both summer and winter conditions. Simple shading diagrams can be drawn for a site using the sun angle chart appropriate for the site's latitude. The variety of solar angles in different seasons should be mapped.

Reflection

Light reflected from ground surfaces represents a considerable percent of the total daylight transmitted through a window. This percentage can be up to 40 percent of the interior light when the reflecting surfaces are light in color.

Heating and cooling needs should be considered in conjunction with lighting needs when choosing exterior surfaces. Increased light is accompanied by heat. This can be a disadvantage during the cooling season and an advantage during the heating season.

Asphalt can be used to increase heat gain. It has a high mass and relatively unreflective surface and becomes warm in sunlight. A window radiates less heat in winter when adjacent ground surfaces are warm. Grass can be used to reduce heat gain. It has a cool surface because of evaporative cooling for plant transpiration and lack of heat storage due to minimal mass. Figure 3.1.5.1 compares the temperature and reflectance of various covers.

Material	Surface Temp.	Dev. from Air
Dark Asphalt	124	+40
Light Asphalt (dirty)	112	+28
Concrete	108	+24
Short grass (1–2 inches)	104	+20
Bare ground	100	+16
Tall grass (36 inches)	96	+12

Surface	Reflectance %
Fresh snow cover	75–95
Dense cloud cover	60–90
Old snow cover	40–70
Clean firm snow	50–65
Light sand dunes, surf	30–60
Clean glacier ice	30–46
Dirty firm snow	20–50
Dirty glacier ice	20–30
Sandy soil	15–40
Meadows and fields	12–30
Densely built-up areas	15–25
Woods	5–20
Dark cultivated soil	7–10
Water surfaces, sea	3–10

Figure 3.1.5.1 - Material Temperature and Reflectance

Skyvault

An area's overall climate will affect the available daylight. In a predominantly cloudy climate there may be 500-10,000 footcandles of light available for most of the year. Larger windows or alternative lighting systems such as skylights, monitors, and clerestories can be used to take advantage of this condition.

The daylighting available from an overcast sky provides relatively uniform illumination. However, illumination on the window can vary from 100 to several thousand footcandles. When skies are generally bright and clear, glare and direct sun can be avoided by using diffusers or shading devices.

An overcast sky is brighter overhead (as much as three times) than at the horizon. This gives a designer flexibility in terms of lighting source direction (top lighting, high windows).

A clear sky is brighter at the horizon (except near the sun). This also gives the designer flexibility in terms of location of lighting source (sidelighting).

3.1.6 Wind Control

When a stream of air is interrupted by built forms or vegetation, the wind must flow either around or through the structure and eventually return to the original flow pattern. Airflow slows as it approaches the obstruction, creating a positive pressure zone on the windward face. The wind speeds up as it is deflected around the corners of the mass, creating negative pressure zones on the end walls and on the leeward side (see Figure 3.1.6.1).

Wind Patterns

Air movement patterns created by nearby buildings offers the potential for beneficial ventilation as well as problems from infiltration.

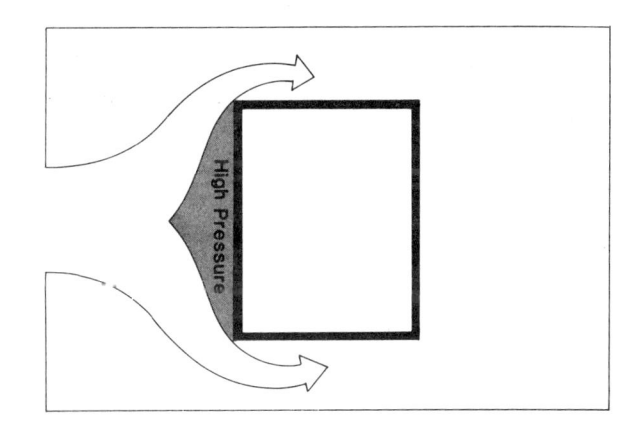

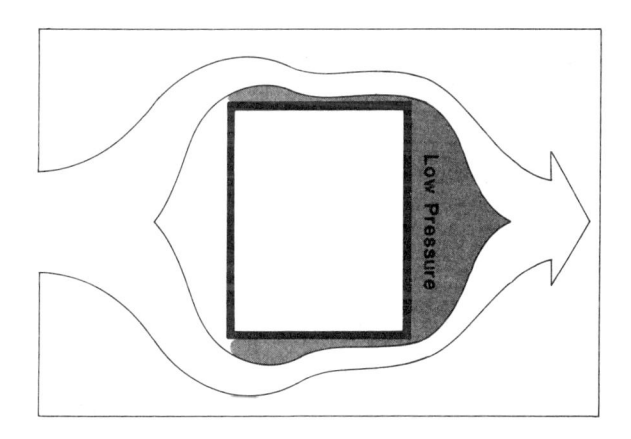

Figure 3.1.6.1 - Wind Effects

Airflow can be directed into a building, providing evaporative and convective cooling.

Secondary winds can often be directed into particular interior zones with simple adjustments in orientation.

Wind exerts the greatest pressure when it is angled 90 degrees to the surface of the building. When it is at 45 degrees, the pressure is reduced about 50 percent. Yet, it can still provide effective ventilation when a building is anywhere between these two angles.

Windbreaks

Barriers (both vegetation and built forms) can be designed and sized to direct wind into or around buildings. As mentioned, wind can be effective at angles between 45 degrees and 90 degrees with the building surface. Increasing the "roughness" of a building will cause an air film to form around it, protecting the surface from wind and reducing heating needs.

The following rules of thumb provide the designer with varying shapes, heights, depths and lengths from which to determine windbreak dimensions and orientation.

In general, eddy air flow speed can be reduced significantly by using <u>perforated</u> windbreaks.

As the height of a windbreak increases, the depth and height of the eddy zones increases; the wind is "thrown" farther upward and back before it approaches the ground level. Higher windbreak height can be used for upper level ventilation and/or to provide larger wind-protected zones. For vegetation windbreaks, density is also a consideration, as shown in Figure 3.1.6.2 and 3.1.6.3.

PERCENT WIND SPEED REDUCTION				
Density of Belt	Avg: Over First 50 Yds	Avg: Over First 100 Yds	Avg. Over First 150 Yds	Avg. Over First 300 Yds
Very Open	18	24	25	18
Open	54	46	37	20
Medium	60	56	48	28
Dense	66	55	44	25
Very Dense	66	48	37	20

As the length of the windbreak increases, the depth as well as the length of the eddy zone increases. For ventilation purposes the windbreak should be located so that the building doesn't fall in the no-wind zone. For sheltering purposes it should be located so that the building does fall in the eddy zone.

Figure 3.1.6.2 - Wind Speed Reduction

The depth of a windbreak has little or no effect on the wind pattern if it is less than twice the height. If the windbreak depth is twice the height or more, the arc of the wind is dampened and the eddy zone depth varies.

Windbreaks should be placed at different distances from the building and at different heights above the ground depending on the desired through-building airflow. Secondary currents at the understory, when trees are situated at the proper distance, can be directed through the building and used for ventilation.

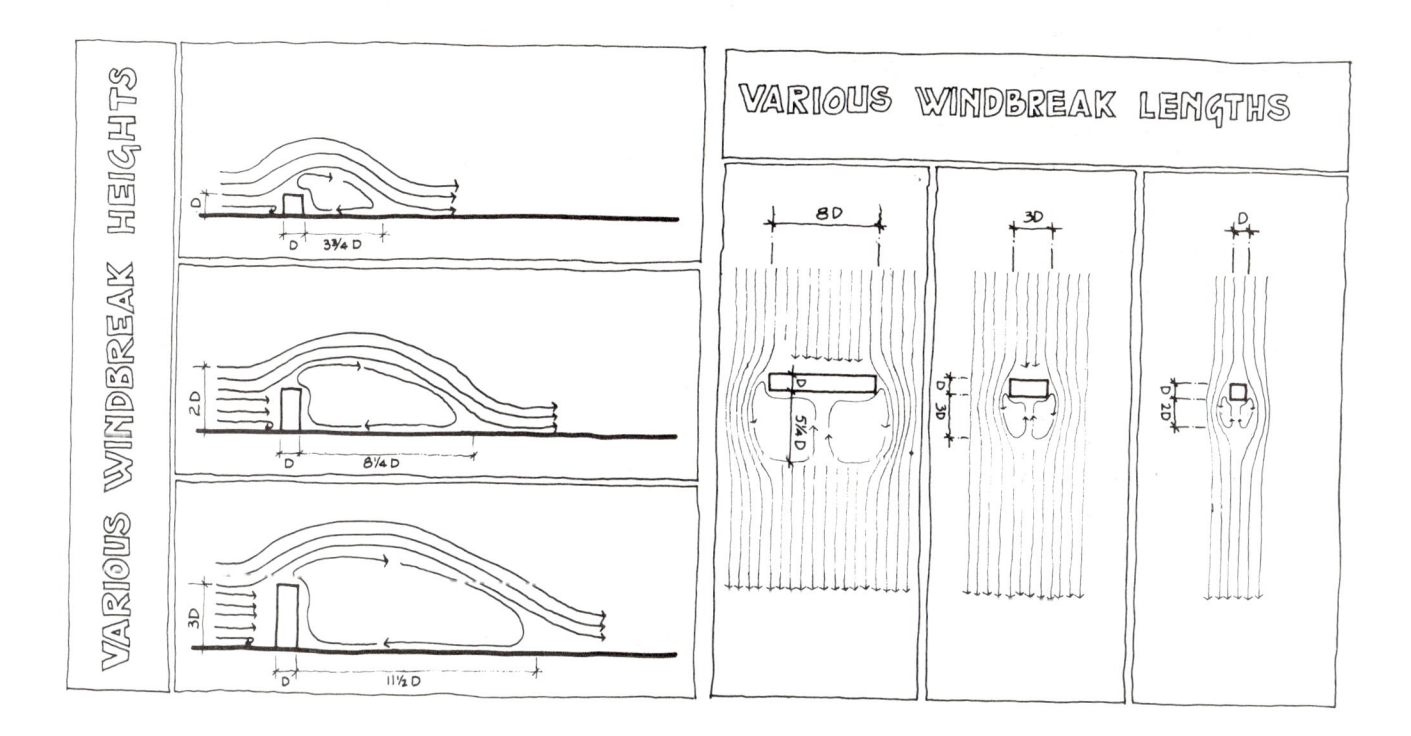

A vegetation windbreak should contain a variety of sized of trees and bushes. A dense tree mass will direct the winds without creating the secondary currents at the understory.

Wind flow tests should be made at the preliminary design stage as well as at the later design stages.

Figure 3.1.6.3 - Windbreak Effects

3.2 SPACE PLANNING

3.2.1 Introduction

The planning of the internal factors for buildings can significantly affect the building's energy use. Key planning issues include internal heat gain, solar heat gain and zoning.

The hours of operation of a building and its energy-consuming systems also play a major role in energy use. Developing use profiles of internal factors--occupancy, lighting, equipment, process, and domestic hot water--will help the designer to understand the energy needs of the building.

3.2.2 Internal Heat Gain

Internal heat gain is heat added to a space as a byproduct of another activity. Heat gain can be beneficial, when used to reduce the heating load on the mechanical system, or detrimental, when it adds to the cooling load of an airconditioning system.

The major internal heat gains to be considered (see Figure 3.2.2.1) are caused by:
- occupants
- lighting
- equipment and process loads.

Figure 3.2.2.1 - Heat Gain Sources

Occupants

The human body releases both heat and moisture as a byproduct of its metabolism of food. Food is used by the body with approximately 20-percent efficiency; the remaining 80 percent is given off as heat. Metabolic rates vary with each activity level. The first step in determining the internal heat gain from

Building Type	Typical Sq. Ft./Person
Office	200–300
Educational.	
Classrooms	50–100
Dormitories	100–150
Hospital	100–150
Assembly	30–45
Restaurant	25
Mercantile	100–150
Highrise Apartments	300–400

Figure 3.2.2.2 - Space Requirements

occupants is to identify the number of occupants and the type of activity they are engaged in. If the number of occupants is unknown, Figure 3.2.2.2 can be used as a guide.

Occupant effects should be considered over a 24-hour period for:
- a typical work day
- a typical non-work day
- any special conditions.

Figure 3.2.2.3 shows the heat gain per occupant, which can be used in the following equation:
Occupant Heat Gain (Btu/hr) = Number of Occupants X Heat Gain (Btu/hr/person)

This can then be used to determine the annual heat gain from occupants:
Annual Occupancy Heat Gain = Number of Occupants x Number of Occupied Hours/Day x Occupied Days/Year x Heat Gain/Occupant (Btu/hour)

Building Type	Sensible BTU/Hr.	Latent BTU/Hr.
Office	250	200
Educational:		
Elementary	250	204
Secondary	250	204
College	250	204
Hospital	250	175
Clinic	250	200
Assembly:		
Theater	230	120
Arena	250	250
Restaurant	275	275
Mercantile	250	250
Warehouse	340	450
Residential:		
Hotel	250	200
Nursing	250	175
Highrise Apartment	250	200

Figure 3.2.2.3 - Heat Gain per Occupant

The designer can make use of occupant heat gain to supplement heating systems, or, by means of internal layout and space planning, can help minimize its effect if the main load on the building is cooling.

Electric Lighting

The designer should be concerned with two major aspects of the lighting system: the amount of electrical energy needed to operate the lights and the energy that the lights give off as heat. Commercial buildings can use more than 60 percent of their electricity for lighting.

To calculate the energy needed to operate the lighting system, the designer must know the optimal levels of illumination needed for the various tasks to be performed.

Designing to light levels for specific spaces or tasks can save more energy than a uniform lighting plan. Figure 3.2.2.4 offers guidelines for lighting levels in task-specific spaces. The designer should keep in mind that quality of lighting rather than higher intensity illumination should be the goal. Some general rules are:

- Task Areas: The lighting level should provide proper illumination for the task to be performed.
- Nontask Areas: General non-task areas need an average lighting of approximately one-third the level of task areas.
- Noncritical Lighting: In areas where casual visual tasks occur, a lighting level of approximately one-third the level of general lighting is needed.
- Reflectivity: The efficiency of any lighting system is directly affected by the reflectivity of interior surfaces, such as walls, ceilings, floors and furniture. In general, the designer can select light colors that reflect and contribute to the general visual comfort of a space. Figure 3.2.2.5 below recommends reflectance values related to lighting efficiency.

It can be in the designer's best interest to consult with a professional experienced with lighting design early

Area/Activity	Illuminance (footcandles)
Auditoriums	
Assembly	10 to 20
Social Activity	5 to 10
Banks	
General	10 to 20
Writing Area	20 to 50
Conference Rooms	20 to 50
Drafting Area	
High Contrast	50 to 100
Low Contrast	100 to 200
Educational Facilities	
General	20 to 50
Science Laboratories	50 to 100
Lecture Rooms	100 to 200
Exhibition Halls	10 to 20
Food Service Facilities	
Dining	5 to 10
Kitchen	50 to 100
Hotels (Motels)	
Rooms	20 to 50
Corridors	10 to 20
Lobby	10 to 20
Front Desk	50 to 100
Libraries	
Reading Areas	20 to 50
Book Stacks (active)	20 to 50
Merchandising Spaces	
Stock Rooms	20 to 50
Packaging	20 to 50
Sales	50 to 100
Municipal Buildings	
Police Records	100 to 200
Police Cells	20 to 50
Fire Station	20 to 50
Museums	
Non-sensitive Displays	20 to 50
Lobbies	10 to 20
Offices	
Lobbies	10 to 20
Offices	20 to 50
Residences	
General	5 to 10
Dining	10 to 20
Grooming	20 to 50
Kitchen	20 to 50
Service Spaces	
Stairways, Corridors	10 to 20
Elevators	10 to 20
Toilets, Wash rooms	10 to 20

Figure 3.2.2.4 - Illuminance Values

in the design process to ensure the development of lighting schemes that deliver maximum effectiveness for minimum electrical power use.

Commercial buildings present many opportunities for the use of daylighting. Since commercial building design and retrofit decisions are ultimately concerned with economics, it is important to establish the basis for significant cost savings possible with daylighting. Since most commercial buildings have high occupancies and high lighting levels during daylight hours daylighting should be considered as a prime energy-efficient strategy.

One of the most powerful reasons for incorporating daylight design in buildings is that, when properly used, daylight provides a lighting quality in architectural spaces rarely equaled by artificial systems. Daylight through windows can enhance modeling effects, reduce ceiling reflections and provide time orientation by contact with outdoor conditions. Window openings also can provide visual relief to occupants. Lighting and daylighting design issues

Elements	Reflectance
Ceilings	80% to 90%
Walls	40% to 60%
Furniture	25% to 45%
Floors	20% to 40%

Figure 3.2.2.5 - Reflectance Values

Fluorescent			
Lamp Watts	Length	No. of Lamps	Total Watts
20	24"	1	25
20	24"	2	51
40	48"	1	53
40	48"	2	92
40	48"	3	145
40	48"	4	184
60/HO	48"	1	95
110/HO	96"	2	264
115/SHO	48"	1	138
215/SHO	96"	2	440
39/Slimline	48"	2	95
75/Slimline	96"	2	172
Metal Halide			
400	—	—	440
1000	—	—	1080
1500	—	—	1620
Mercury Vapor			
	Ballast Loss		
40	10	—	50
50	15	—	65
75	15	—	90
100	35	—	135
175	35	—	210
250	42	—	292
400	65	—	465
700	65	—	765
1000	100	—	1100
High Pressure Sodium			
150	—	—	180
250	—	—	300
400	—	—	400
1000	—	—	1200

For types and sizes of fixtures not listed, see manufacturer's data.
Incandescent lamps have same wattage input as rating on lamp.

Figure 3.2.2.6 - Light Source Comparison

are discussed further in Section 3.4 and 3.6. Figure 3.2.2.6 gives lamp wattages for common light sources.

The designer must know the specifics of the lights to be provided in the space, such as: type of fixtures, number of fixtures/type, watts per fixture and hours of use.

The designer can use these data to develop a lighting use profile similar to the one developed for occupancy loads. Working day and nonworking-day profiles should be developed.

From the use profile, the annual operating load for the lighting system can be determined using the following equation:
Annual Lighting Operating Load (W/hr) = Total Watts x Lighted Hours per Day x Lighted Hours per Year x Utilization Factor (percent)

The following equation can be used to compute the heat gain from lights:

Heat Gain (Btu/hr) = Footcandles/sq.ft. x Area (sq.ft.) x .06 Watts/Footcandle x 3.41 Btu/hr/Watt

The rules of thumb for footcandles in Figure 3.2.2.7 can be used prior to more definitive decisions and analysis.

From the use profile developed for the building, the annual heat gain from the lighting system can be found by the following formula:

Annual Lighting Heat Gain (Btu/hr) = Total Watts x Lighted Hours per Day x Lighted Days per Year x Utilization Factor (percent) x 3.41 Btu/Watt x Cooling Load Factor

Type Of Activity	Illuminance Range (Footcandles)		
	Low	Mean	High
General Lighting Public spaces with dark surroundings	2	3	5
Simple orientation for temporary visits	5	7.5	10
Working spaces where visual tasks are only occasionally performed	10	15	20
Illuminance on Task Performance of visual tasks of high contrast or large size	20	30	50
Performance of visual tasks of medium contrast or small size	50	75	100
Performance of visual tasks of low contrast or very small size	100	150	200

Figure 3.2.2.7 - Illuminance Values

Utilization factor is the ratio of wattage in use to the total installed wattage (in commercial buildings this ratio is usually 1.0). The cooling load factor (based on the number of hours per day that the lights are on) can be applied to achieve a more accurate calculation. The cooling load factor equals 1.0 if the cooling system is operated only when the lights are on, or if the lights are on more than 16 hours per day. Cooling load factor tables are available from the American Society of Heating, Refrigerating and Air-Conditioning Engineers (ASHRAE). For fluorescent lights, the cooling load factor is 1.25.

One of the most efficient ways to make use of internal heat gains is to recover heat from the lighting systems and use it to supplement mechanical heating systems. One example of a heat recovery system, proven effective for large applications, is the removal of lighting heat by circulation of nonrefrigerated water through jacketed fixtures. Several new federal offices in Canada use the piped water in the fire protection sprinkler system to circulate through luminaires (see Figure 3.2.2.8).

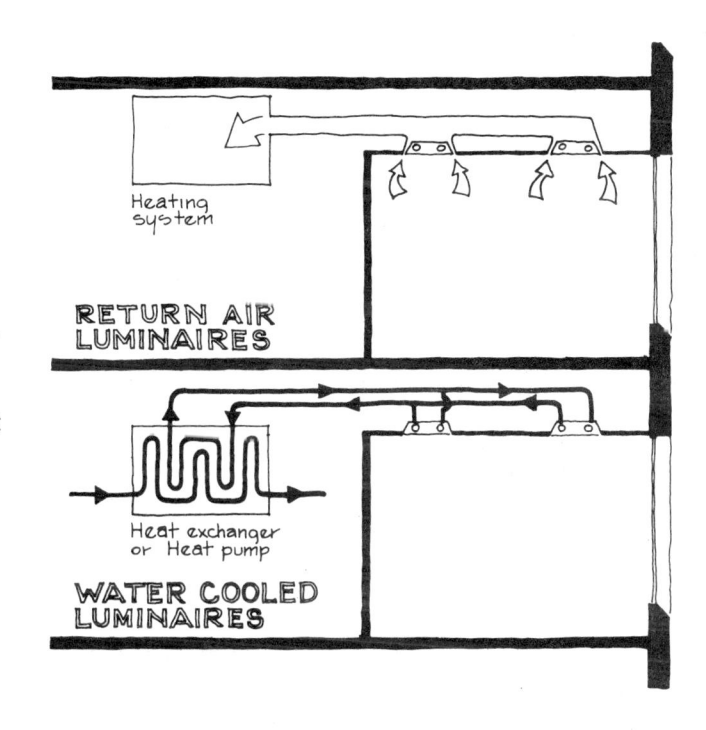

Figure 3.2.2.8 - Heat Recovery

System controls for lighting--photoelectric controls and automatic timers, for example--can also help save energy.

Equipment and Process Loads

Proper location of computer rooms and mechanical spaces can permit use of their waste process heat to heat other spaces.
The following formula can be used to calculate the heat gain resulting from operation of building equipment (such as computers, copiers, etc.):
   Annual equipment heat gain (Btu/hr) = equipment heat gain (Btu/hr) x operating hours per day x operating days per year
where:
   Equipment heat gain (Btu/hr) = heat gain (Btu/hr/sq.ft.) x area (sq.ft.)

3.2.3 Solar Heat Gain

Solar heat gain is another factor to consider when space planning. Solar heat gain results when insolation (direct and diffuse sunlight) is converted into heat inside a space. Building elements can be designed so that solar gains are minimized during periods of net heat gain and maximized during periods of net heat loss. Three variables determine the amount of solar heat that actually reaches the interior of a building:

- the amount of insolation available
- the area of glass exposed to insolation
- the proportion of incident heat transported from outside to the inside.

Month 1																		
Orientation	Hourly Solar Radiation BTU/Hr./Sq.Ft.																	Daily Total Radiation BTU/Hr./Sq.Ft.
	4	5	6	7	8	9	10	11	12	13	14	15	16	17	18	19	20	
South	0.	0.	0.	0.	39.	130.	185.	216.	227.	216.	185.	130.	39.	0.	0.	0.	0.	1366
Southwest	0.	0.	0.	0.	5.	20.	71.	124.	169.	198.	203.	172.	63.	0.	0.	0.	0.	1025.
West	0.	0.	0.	0.	5.	14.	22.	27.	29.	79.	116.	122.	53.	0.	0.	0.	0.	467.
Northwest	0.	0.	0.	0.	5.	14.	22.	27.	29.	27.	22.	14.	15.	0.	0.	0.	0.	175.
North	0.	0.	0.	0.	5.	14.	22.	27.	29.	27.	22.	14.	5.	0.	0.	0.	0.	165.
Northeast	0.	0.	0.	0.	15.	14.	22.	27.	29.	27.	22.	14.	5.	0.	0.	0.	0.	175.
East	0.	0.	0.	0.	53.	122.	116.	79.	29.	27.	22.	14.	5.	0.	0.	0.	0.	467.
Southeast	0.	0.	0.	0.	63.	172.	203.	198.	169.	124.	71.	20.	5.	0.	0.	0.	0.	1025.
Horiz.	0.	0.	0.	0.	12.	54.	91.	115.	124.	115.	91.	54.	12.	0.	0.	0.	0.	668.

24 Deg N									
	N	NNE/ NNW	NE/ NW	ENE/ WNW	E/ W	ESE/ WSW	SE/ SW	SSE/ SSW	S	HOR
Jan.	27	27	41	128	190	240	253	241	227	214
Feb.	30	30	80	165	220	244	243	213	192	249
Mar.	34	45	124	195	234	237	214	168	137	275
Apr.	37	88	159	209	228	212	169	107	75	283
May	43	117	178	214	218	190	132	67	46	282
June	55	127	184	214	212	179	117	55	43	279
July	45	116	176	210	213	185	129	65	46	278
Aug.	38	87	156	203	220	204	162	103	72	277
Sep.	35	42	119	185	222	225	206	163	134	266
Oct.	31	31	79	159	211	237	235	207	187	244
Nov.	27	27	42	126	187	236	249	237	224	213
Dec.	26	26	29	112	180	234	247	247	237	199

40 Deg N									
	N (shade)	NNE/ NNW	NE/ NW	ENE/ WNW	E/ W	ESE/ WSW	SE/ SW	SSE/ SSW	S	HOR
Jan.	20	20	20	74	154	205	241	252	254	133
Feb.	24	24	50	129	186	234	246	244	241	180
Mar.	29	29	93	169	218	238	236	216	206	223
Apr.	34	71	140	190	224	223	203	170	154	252
May	37	102	165	202	220	208	175	133	113	265
June	48	113	172	205	216	199	161	116	95	267
July	38	102	163	198	216	203	170	129	109	262
Aug.	35	71	135	185	216	214	196	165	149	247
Sep.	30	30	87	160	203	227	226	209	200	215
Oct.	25	25	49	123	180	225	238	236	234	177
Nov.	20	20	20	73	151	201	237	248	250	132
Dec.	18	18	18	60	135	188	232	249	253	113

Figure 3.2.3.1 - Solar Radiation

The following formula can be used to compute the solar heat gain (see Figure 3.2.3.1) for each orientation (N, S, E, W, Horizontal):
Solar Heat Gain (Btu/hr) = Insolation (Btu/hr/sq.ft.) x Exposed Area (sq.ft.) x Transmission (percent)

This calculation can be made for all major exposures, and corrected for the tilt of the surface (vertical vs. horizontal).

The exposed area is the number of square feet in a particular orientation and is a function of a building's geometry. It is possible, by manipulating a building's geometry, to increase the ratio of surface area in a particular orientation. Exposed areas can be eliminated to some degree or altogether by burying the building or a portion of it.

The third factor, transmission of the incident heat from the exterior to the interior, depends on qualities of the material the heat is passing through. For purposes of simple analysis, it can be assumed that 80 percent of the heat on single-pane glass can be transmitted to the interior.

Description	Thickness	U-Value (Winter)	U-Value (Summer)	Visible	Solar	S.C.
Single, Clear	⅛"	1.16	1.04	.90	.84	1.00
	¼"	1.13	1.04	.89	.78	.95
	⅜"	1.11	1.03	.88	.72	.90
	½"	1.09	1.03	.86	.67	.86
Single, heat absorbing	¼"	1.13	1.10	.52	.96	.71
Double	3/16" air space	.62	.65		.71	.88
	¼" air space	.58	.61			
	½" air space	.49	.57	.80		.82
	½" air space Low e Coating e = .20	.32	.38			
	e = .40	.42	.49	.14		.25
	e = .60	.43	.51			
Triple	¼" air space	.39	.44			.71
Acrylic, single glazed	¼" air space	.96	.89	.92	.85	.98
Acrylic, w/reflecting coating	¼" air space	.88	.83	.14	.12	.21

Figure 3.2 3.2. - Glazing Characteristics

The transmission of the heat through the glass is often referred to as the shading coefficient. It is given as a percentage of heat being transferred through the glass and takes into account the physical characteristics of the glass. Examples of various glass types and their shading coefficients are shown in Figure 3.2.3.1. Additional discussion of glazing types is included in section 3.4 Fenestration.

The transmission of heat through the glass by conduction is discussed in section 3.3 Building Envelope. The selection of glass is always based on a comparison of the heat radiated through the glass, the heat conducted through the glass, and the amount of visible light allowed through the glass. Solar heat gain can be calculated for each orientation by using the following formula:

Annual Solar Heat Gain (Btu/hr) = Insolation (Btu/day/sq.ft.) x Exposed Area (sq.ft.) x Transmission (percent) x Days per Year.

3.2.4 Zoning

Classifying and organizing spaces according to their different heating/cooling, lighting and ventilation needs can facilitate substantial energy savings (see Figure 3.2.4.1).

During the winter, the microclimate conditions along outside walls of a building are the key to the location of indoor spaces. The north side of a building remains the coolest during the winter because it receives no direct

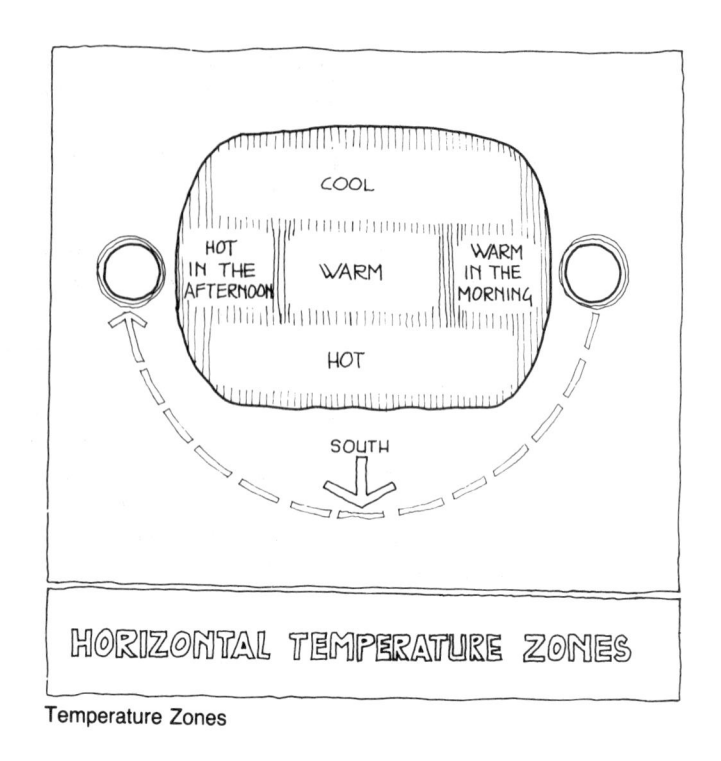

Temperature Zones

Vertical Zoning

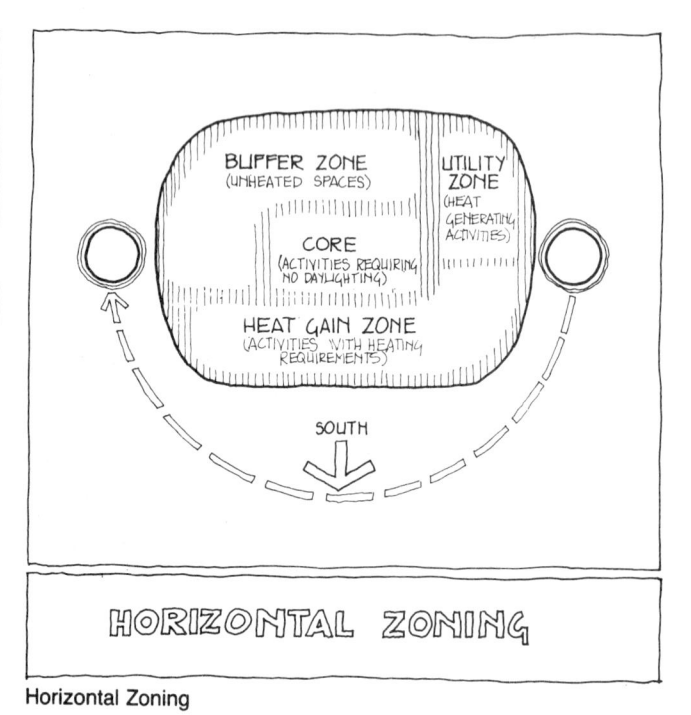

Horizontal Zoning

Figure 3.2.4.1 - Zone Planning

sunlight. The east and west sides of a building receive equal amounts of direct sunlight for half a day each, but over the period of a day, the west side will be slightly warmer than the east side because of the combination of solar radiation and higher afternoon air temperatures. The south side of a building will be the warmest and sunniest during the winter because it receives sunlight throughout the day.
- Interior spaces can be supplied with much of their heating and lighting requirements by placing them along the south side of the building to capture the sun's energy during the day. Spaces that need the most heat and light should be located near good solar exposure on south walls, or upper levels for roof apertures.
- Spaces placed along the north face of the building can serve as a buffer between the colder north face and spaces with high heating requirements.
- Spaces that are ventilated naturally can be zoned vertically according to their heat-generation potential to promote nonmechanical passive internal heating and cooling. For example, to heat the building, those spaces that generate the greatest internal heat load due to people, processes or lighting might be located at the lowest level of the building, and the warmed air allowed to rise through the building to heat the spaces above. For cooling, the vertical organization could be reversed so that the warmest spaces are near the roof (for ease of ventilation), and the cooler spaces located below. Code requirements can affect use of vertical zoning strategies.
- Spaces can also be zoned according to frequency of use and the amount of energy necessary to keep the space comfortable. If a space is used infrequently, it might best be placed to serve as a minimally conditioned buffer space.
- Careful organization of mixed-use spaces can produce a more efficient distribution of internally generated heat than would be possible if each space had to function as an isolated unit. For example, excess heat energy generated in one space can be cascaded through other spaces that need supplementary heat in order to maintain a comfortable temperature level. Aggregation of diverse spaces has the additional benefit of minimizing energy distribution routes and reducing overall surface exposures to temperature extremes.

Zoning is also applicable to the selection and placement of heating, ventilating and airconditioning systems. The space conditioning requirements of specific spaces or zones within a building often differ widely. Zoning design strategies that organize the appropriate HVAC systems with groups of spaces having similar conditioning needs can have significant energy and cost savings potential. Such zoning strategies also reinforce coherent and well-integrated distribution system design.

Space conditioning requirements that should be considered when developing zones and HVAC systems are:
- Often environmental quality standards vary between spaces. Zoning strategies that organize spaces according to quality standards avoid unnecessary ventilation losses or simultaneous heating and cooling.
- Climate and occupancy characteristics often cause varia- tions in the required heating, cooling and ventilation for specific spaces or zones.
- Internal spaces are very often zoned separately from peripheral zones

because internal spaces require only cooling.
- HVAC systems are zoned according to orientation in perimeter spaces (spaces with exterior wall or roof) because thermal-load variations between these orientations exceeds the efficient "flexibility" of the system. If it is not possible for a centralized HVAC system to provide for thermal-load variations efficiently, decentralized HVAC systems should be considered.
- In developing occupancy schedules, individual spaces with similar occupancy characteristics can be grouped together and considered a "zone" (see Figure 3.2.4.2). HVAC systems can then be organized so that zones with differing occupancy can be separately controlled, enabling variations in the system loads of these spaces to be handled more economically. Occupancy characteristics can be the primary determinants of whether a centralized system or decentralized unitary HVAC systems are more efficient for a particular application.

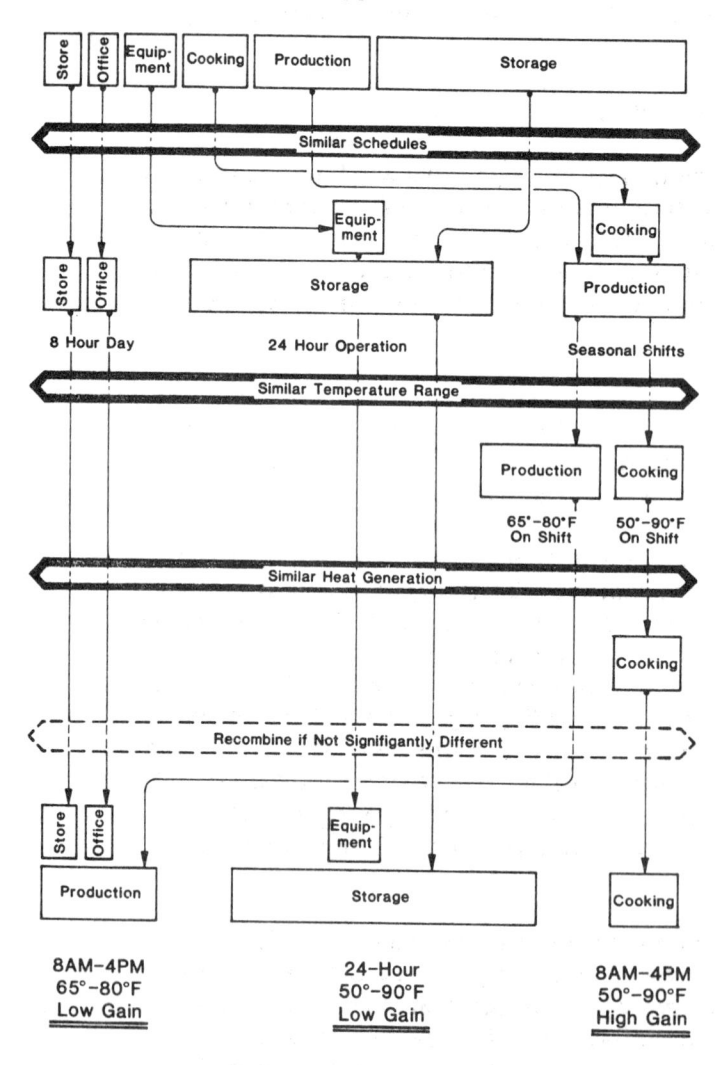

Figure 3.2.4.2 - Energy Use Groups

3.3 BUILDING ENVELOPE

3.3.1 Introduction

The building envelope is an integrated part of the building's energy system, interfacing with the HVAC and lighting systems. The building envelope has mass that serves as thermal energy storage and helps control temperature by resisting heat losses during the cold season and heat gain during the summer. Windows and openings in the building envelope provide for daylighting and ventilation and give the occupants a view to the outside.

With careful design the building envelope can be made energy efficient almost to the point where it starts "producing" energy. There are trade-offs available, for instance for using more or less glass at the exterior, but each choice has certain implications for the total energy efficiency of the building.

3.3.2 Surface Area-to-Volume Ratio

Building configuration determines in large part the amount of energy the building will use, because variations in building configuration greatly affect the amount of exterior surface area for a given enclosed volume and, hence, the relative amount of thermal transfer through the envelope. See Section 3.1.2, Orientation and Configuration, for further discussion.

3.3.3 U Values

The fundamentals of energy transfer through the envelope involve the ability of heat to travel through material, called a C- or U-factor, or the resistance to that movement, called an R-factor.

The C, U, and R coefficients are expressed in terms of Btu/sq ft x hr x degree (F.). The coefficient C indicates the ability of material to transfer heat through a one-inch thickness of it. The U-value indicates the thermal transmittance (air-to-air) through the total thickness of material involved or a combination of materials. The U-value of a section of a building element is obtained by adding together the R-values of various materials and air films inside and out. As heat flow ability and resistance are opposite terms, the U-value is a reciprocal of the total R-value, the sum of the component R-values, or $1/(R_1 + R_2 + ... R_n)$. A U-value cannot be obtained by adding together the C coefficients of various materials.

The U-value of the total area of an element is expressed as U_o or Overall U-value. Multiplying the area by U_o produces the total heat loss or gain through the element per hour per one-degree difference between inside and outside temperatures. The U-value is thus the time rate of heat flow per unit of area and unit temperature difference between the inside and outside, and the U_o of the total area of a building element.

Insulation materials are usually rated by their R-value, which is often expressed for the total thickness of the material used. Engineering handbooks provide both C, U, and R-values for specific materials and combinations of materials in a section of wall, floor or floor/ceiling. Figure 3.3.3.1 shows R-values for various building materials. There can be more than one kind of a section present in a wall, and a portion of it may be of wood frame, another faced with brick, or concrete, and containing windows and doors; thus the overall U_o-value must be calculated by adding together the U-values x areas of each kind, and dividing the total by the total area of the element:

Building Insulations	Density (LB/CU FT)	Resistance (R) (HR/SQ FT °F BTU PER 1 IN. THICKNESS)
Fiberglass	0.6–1.0	3.16
Rock or slag wool	1.5–2.5	3.2–3.7
Cellulose	2.2–3.0	3.2–3.7
Molded polystyrene	0.8–2.0	3.8–4.4
Extruded polystyrene	0.8–2.0	3.8–4.4
Polyurethane	2.0	5.8–6.2
Polyisocyanurate	2.0	5.8–6.2
UREA Formaldehyde	0.6–0.9	4.2
Perlite (loose fill)	2–11	2.5–3.7
Vermiculite (loose fill)	4–10	2.4–3.0

Figure 3.3.3.1 - Insulation R-Values

$$Uo_{wall} = \frac{SumU_{opaque\ wall} \times area + SumU_{windows} \times area + SumU_{doors} \times area}{Total\ wall\ area}$$

Each U-value of an opaque wall, windows and doors must include all different kinds of sections involved in the total component or element. Computation of a U-value of a section must include air films both inside and outside, in addition to the actual materials. Figure 3.3.3.2 shows examples of various kinds of sections.

Wall Section	Wall Description	Weight Pounds Per Sq. Ft.	U-Value (Winter)	Heat Gain BTU/Hr/Sq.Ft. (Dark Color) Orientation Average	West	Time Lag (Hours)	Amplitude Decrement Factor
	Metal panel curtain wall 2-layers 18-gauge steel, 2" polyurethane insulation (between steel layers)	4.5	0.066	3.17	5.73	1	0.99
	Metal panel curtain wall 2-layers 18-gauge aluminum, 2" polyurethane insulation (between aluminum layers)	2.0	0.066	3.20	5.78	1	0.99
	½" Plywood siding, ½" insulation board sheathing, wood studs, full batt (R–11) insulation, ½" gypsumboard	5.0	0.076	3.05	4.60	2	0.75

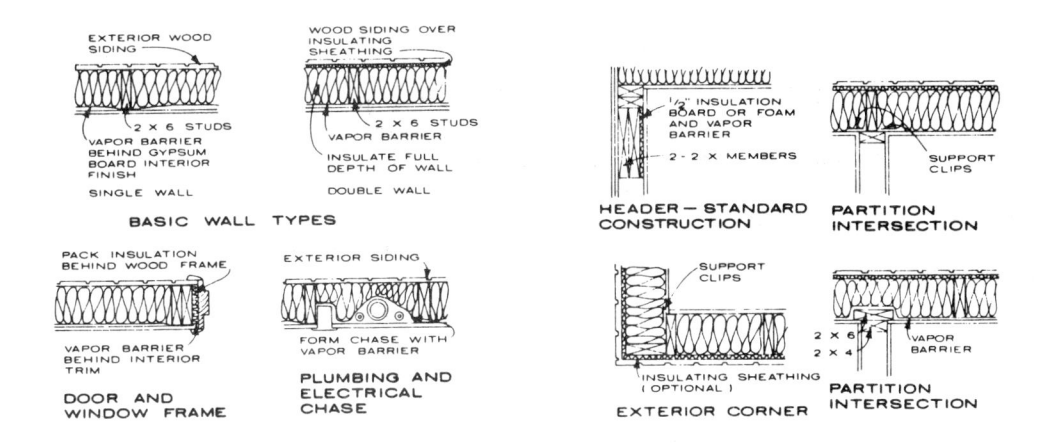

Figure 3.3.3.2 - Wall Sections

Human thermal comfort can be affected in winter by the radiation of body heat to cold indoor surfaces (floors, walls or ceilings) and, conversely, by body heat gain from warm surfaces in summer. In winter, surface temperatures about 5 degrees (F.) or less below indoor air temperature will generally provide satisfactory radiant comfort conditions.

In a temperate region, the walls of a motel with an indoor design temperature of 75 degrees (F.) will require a U-value of 0.10 Btu/hr/sq ft/degrees (F.) or less. A U-value of 0.06 or less is often preferred in cool and temperate climate regions.

If uninsulated construction has a U-value of 0.40, the addition of 2-inch thick insulation will result in an improved U-value of 0.10 Btu/hr/sq ft/degrees (F.).

Surface-to-surface heat flow across an air cavity is caused by convection, radiation and conduction. Conduction occurs if heat bridges (metal or wood trim) are present. Convection occurs if the airspace is poorly sized (if too wide, convection currents negate the air's insulating property). Radiation will transfer heat in both directions, including the direction the insulation is designed to prevent. These types of heat flow can be avoided by insulating joints and trim, sizing the cavity width properly and using a foil surface on one side.

3.3.4 Exterior Walls

As the above examples indicate, the overall U-values of the various wall sections affect the total heat flow through the building envelope. In residential buildings of frame construction, the amount of insulation becomes a major factor, as well as the type of windows, single or double glazed. When a part or all of the exterior wall is of masonry construction, the U-value is increased for the cooling season, reducing the need for airconditioning.

In commercial and highrise residential buildings, the structure may be of steel or concrete framing. Steel is usually covered by sprayed on, rigid or blanket insulation. Concrete is a poor insulator and needs to be covered. Before energy conservation was a concern it was relatively common to have the concrete floor supporting beams and columns exposed to the outside, reflecting the true nature of the structure. However, this produced not only cold areas next to outside walls but also condensation within the wall structure, causing water damage. In new buildings, a separation of the floor and exterior structure should be provided (see Figure 3.3.4.1).

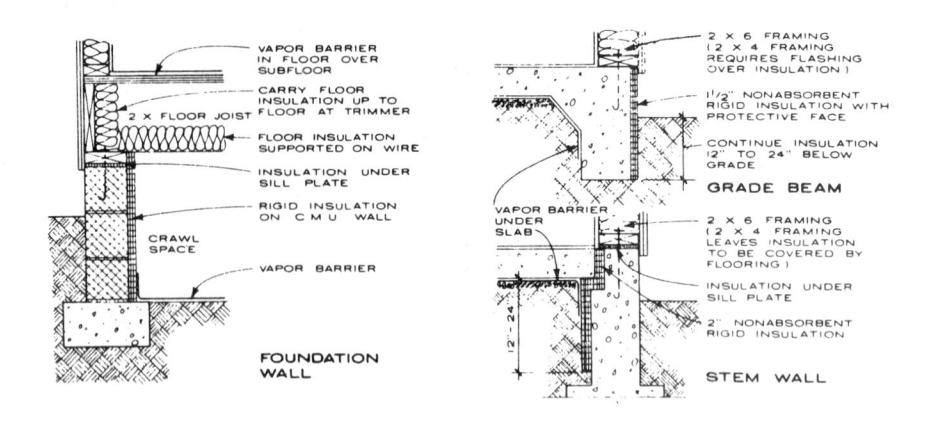

Source: The American Institute of Architects, *Architectural Graphic Standards*, Seventh Edition, © 1981. Reprinted by permission of John Wiley & Son, Inc., New York, New York.

Figure 3.3.4.1 - Insulation Detail

To reduce the condensation within a residential wall structure, a vapor barrier is usually provided at the inside face of the exterior wall. This can be produced by a polyethylene film or aluminum foil at the inside face of the insulation, a plastic wallpaper or by several coats of oil-base paint. A vapor barrier is especially important in areas of high humidity such as bathrooms and kitchens. In very cold climates, it is also installed in ceilings.

A vapor barrier is more accurately called a vapor "retarder," as few materials eliminate totally the flow of water vapor. The flow of vapor within building structures is being researched in order to create better wall systems. Preventing rain water from entering the exterior wall is also important. When water leaks or condensation occurs, the material becomes wet, loses its value as an insulator, and can deteriorate.

Insulation comes in many different forms: rigid boards of various materials, blankets, and loose fill. Loose fill of cellulose, expanded perlite, vermiculite, of mineral fiber (rock, slag, glass), or chemical products (polystyrene, polyurethane) can be used to fill wall cavities. Loose fill insulation is often used in retrofitting buildings for greater energy conservation. Fiberglass blankets are used both in wood framing, between studs and around openings and, in steel framed buildings, around columns and beams and inside wall paneling and curtain walls. The R-value of various insulation materials varies. Figure 3.3.4.2 shows the R-values of several common insulation types.

Selection of insulation depends on performance, cost and availability. Where limited space restricts the allowable thickness of insulation, insulation with higher R-value per inch can be selected. The newest type

Material	Description	Thickness	R-Value
Poured Concrete	Foundation & Roof 140 pcf Sand & Gravel or Stone Agg. (Not Oven Dried)	6" 8" 12"	.48 .64 .96
Lightweight Concrete	Lightweight Agg. Incl. Expanded Shale, Slag Vermiculite & Cinders 120 pcf	6" 8" 12"	1.14 1.52 2.28
Very Lightweight Concrete	60 pcf	10"	5.90
Concrete Hollow Core Deck	85 pcf	8"	2.70
Concrete Block (Uninsulated)	3-Hole Load Bearing 100 pcf	4" 8" 12"	1.40 1.75 2.14
Concrete Block (Insulated)	3-Hole Load Bearing 100 pcf, With Loose Fill Vermiculite	4" 8" 12"	2.33 4.85 6.80
Lightweight Concrete Block (Uninsulated)	3-Hole Non-Load Bearing 60 pcf	4" 8" 12"	2.07 2.30 3.29
Lightweight Concrete Block (Insulated)	3-Hole Non-Load Bearing 60 pcf, With Loose Fill Vermiculite	4" 8" 12"	3.36 7.46 10.98
Face Brick	Standard Face Brick 130 pcf	4"	.44
Stone Panel	Marble Granite Sandstone Limestone	1"	.08

Design Guide For Insulated Buildings, © 1981. Used with the permission of Owens-Corning Fiberglas Corporation, Toledo, Ohio.

Figure 3.3.4.2 - R-Values of Materials

contains phenyl and is said to provide more than R-value 8 per inch of thickness. Some rigid insulation boards are used as "removable" insulation, and are left exposed indoors. Polystyrene boards must be covered with 5/8-inch plasterboard or other fireproofing. Polystyrene, polyurethane and phenyl containing boards are often used to add R-value to walls that already contain other insulation.

The previous examples show how the overall U-values are calculated. ASHRAE Standard 90 indicates recommended limits for U_o values in various climate zones. These values have been made mandatory in building codes and are generally the same as in the Model Energy Code (see Section 2.6, Codes, Standards and Regulatory Issues). As the ASHRAE Standard 90 is further modified, these recommendations may change.

The overall U_o value of the exterior wall depends on the amount of <u>windows area</u> and other openings in it. In lowrise residential buildings, the ratio of windows to the total wall area can be 10-20 percent.

Material	Description	Thickness	R-Value
Gypsum Wallboard	Drywall	3/8" 1/2" 5/8"	.32 .45 .56
Gypsum Roof Deck	Gypsum Fiber Concrete 87.5% Gypsum, 12.5% Wd. Chips 51 pcf	1"	.60
Plywood	Douglas Fir, 34 pcf	1/4" 1/2" 3/4"	.31 .62 .93
Fiberboard Sheathing	18 pcf	1/2"	1.32
Wood Decking	Fir, Pine, Softwoods	1-1/2" 2-1/2" 3-1/2"	1.89 3.12 4.35
Wood Siding	Plywood Wood Bevel 1/2" × 8" Lapped Wood Shingles (16 in., 7.5 Exposure)	3/8" 1/2"	.59 .81 .87
Prefab Sheet Metal Roof Deck	Uninsulated Panel No Backing	26 ga.	NEGL.
Vapor Retarder	Plastic Membrane 2-Ply Kraft Paper With Asphaltic Adhesive	.006	NEGL. .06
Air Space	Non-Reflective, 50°F. Mean 10°F. Temperature Difference	3/4"-4"	.96 45° Slope .93 Horizontal 1.01 Vertical
Air Film	Exterior Wall (15 m.p.h. Wind) Interior Wall (Still Air) Exterior Roof (15 m.p.h. Wind) Interior Roof—45° (Still Air) Interior Roof—Level (Still Air)		.17 .68 .17 .62 .61
Shingles	Asphalt, 70 pcf Slate	 1/2"	.44 .05
Built-up Roof	3-Ply, 70 pcf	3/8"	.33

Design Guide For Insulated Buildings, © 1981. Used with the permission of Owens-Corning Fiberglas Corporation, Toledo, Ohio.

Figure 3.3.4.2 (continued) - R-Values of Materials

The Model Energy Code is used as the only design criterion. Passive solar systems and daylighting offer the opportunity to provide more window area.

The U-value of windows is important for buildings that have skin-dominated heating or cooling loads. This value can be increased by adding a reflecting film to the inside (to reduce cooling load) or by additional storm windows and shutters. Recessing the window from the exterior wall face can reduce the wind factor. For design purposes, the wind speed is usually taken as 15 mph in winter and 7.5 mph in summer.

Glass is an important factor in commercial buildings with large internal loads. These buildings may generate enough heat from the equipment and occupants for the heating season, but are vulnerable during the cooling season. Reflective glass and glare- and heat-reducing glass are available. Note that doors should be analyzed as a part of the overall fenestration.

The color of exterior materials affects heat penetration into the building. Light, reflective colors reduce cooling loads, while dark colors increase the sun's effect. In New Mexico, the orientation of colors around the building is part of the building code, particularly in regard to adobe-faced buildings, whose structure acts as thermal storage mass. Orienting windows to maximize the benefits from passive solar systems and daylighting serves the same purpose. Shading is another means which can be used to improve the efficiency of the building envelope.

Three basic types of heat penetration occur during the cooling season: through the opaque wall, through the windows, and by the difference between outside and inside temperatures. The Overall Thermal Transfer Value (OTTV) equals:

$$\frac{U_{wall} \times A_{wall} \times TD_{eq} + A_f \times SF \times SC + U_f \times A_f \times (t_o - t_i)}{A_o}$$

where--Figure 3.3.4.3 defines terms

The OTTV allowed by Model Energy Code depends on the latitude of the building. Generally, buildings with little clear glass have a smaller OTTV. The use of shading helps to keep the OTTV within code requirements.

"Super-insulation" refers to a method of providing more insulation than is

WHERE:
$OTTV_w$ = the overall thermal transfer value—walls
A_o = gross wall area above grade
U_w = the thermal transmittance of all elements of the opaque wall area
A_w = opaque wall area
U_f = the thermal transmittance of the fenestration area
A_f = fenestration area
TD_{EQ} = temperature difference value
SC = shading coefficient of the fenestration
Δt = temperature difference between exterior and interior design conditions, °F.
SF = solar factor value

Figure 3.3.4.3 - OTTV Terms from Model Energy Code

either required by codes or recommended by life-cycle cost/benefit analysis, i.e., R-values of 40 or more for walls. In wood frame walls it can be accomplished by staggering two layers of 2x4 studs and placing continuous insulation between to end up with a nominal eight inch wall.

3.3.5 Roof-Ceilings

Roofs are often more heavily insulated than walls, because of the availability of space above the ceilings and the fact that heat rises. R-values of 30 or 40 are now being used in single-family homes and other low residential buildings. In multistory buildings, the ratio of the roof to the outside wall becomes smaller. A light-color roof is also effective, particularly during the cooling season. Code requirements for the roof U-values are also gradually tightening.

Light roof structures generally have a wood or metal deck with insulation above the ceiling, or rigid or sprayed insulation under the roofing. A number of different systems of insulation and roofing have been developed. In order to obtain an acceptable U-value for the roof system, insulation with high R-values per inch are often required. For flat roof deck systems insulation is manufactured with varying thickness to also provide slope for drainage of rain water into roof sumps. Figure 3.3.5.1 shows examples of roof sections with different insulations.

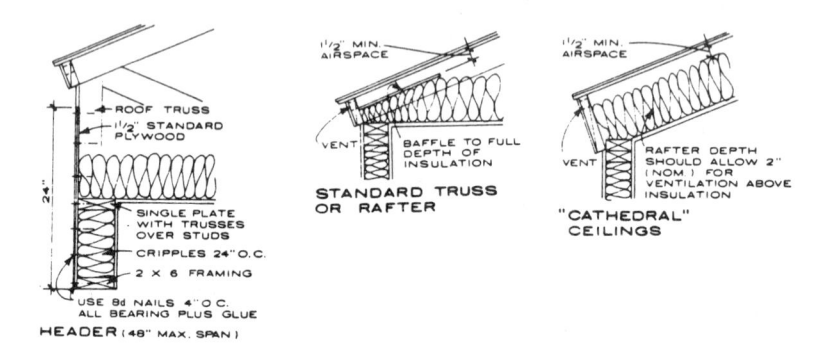

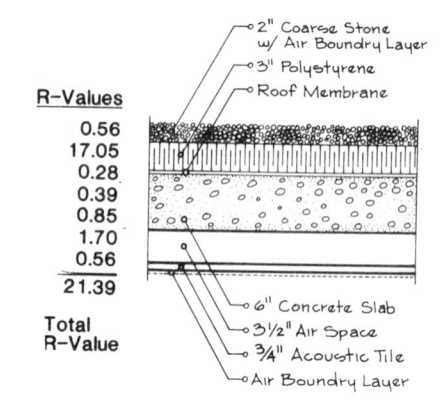

Figure 3.3.5.1 - Roof Sections

Buildings with attic spaces are usually easy to insulate by placing insulation in the rafter space above the ceiling. When the ceiling combines with the roof, space may be limited, but insulation can be placed above the roof deck. For "cathedral" ceilings, the insulation value can be increased by using higher R-value insulation in rafter spaces.

When roof insulation is inadequate or has been damaged by leaks, additional insulation can be placed under a new membrane. The new insulation can be either rigid boards or sprayed-on foam. If feasible, the old membrane can be removed. Loose aggregate should be removed if the old membrane is left in place. Blisters and ridges should be repaired before a new membrane is installed. Mechanical fastening or ballasts are needed to ensure that the roof withstands uplifting winds.

Pipes and ducts in unheated attic spaces must be adequately insulated. Ducts placed above the ceiling are considered to be within the conditioned space and are required to have the same insulation U-value as the roof/ceiling itself. Water pipes must also be protected from freezing.

The U_o values for a roof are calculated in a manner similar to walls. The effects of skylights and clerestory windows should be included. Calculations are generally simple as there seldom is more than one type of roof involved. The effect of slope, structural supports, rafters and purlins must all be considered. Figure 3.3.5.2 shows samples of roof structures and calculations of U-values.

18. Shingle or Slate on Wood Deck

Materials	R	U
Exterior Air Film	.17	
Asphalt Shingles	.44	
Building Paper	.06	
3" Wood Deck	3.75	
Interior Air Film (Still Air)	.62	
Basic Roof	5.04	.198
Retrofit Option: Asphalt Shingles, Building Paper, ½" Plywood Sheathing	1.12	
Insulation Option: ½" Plywood Sheathing	.62	
Optional ½" Gypsum Wallboard Finish	.45	

19. Shingle or Slate on Sheathed Rafter

Materials	R	U
Exterior Air Film	.17	
Asphalt Shingles	.44	
Building Paper	.06	
½" Plywood Sheathing	.62	
Air Space	.96	
½" Gypsum Wallboard Finish	45	
Interior Air Film (Still Air)	.62	
Basic Roof	3.32	.301

26. Sheet Metal on Wood Deck

Materials	R	U
Exterior Air Film	.17	
Sheet Metal Roofing	NEGL.	
Building Paper	.06	
3" Wood Deck	3.75	
Interior Air Film (Still Air)	.62	
Basic Roof	4.60	.217
Retrofit Option: Metal, Building Paper, ½" Plywood Sheathing	.68	
Insulation Option: ½" Plywood Sheathing "B"	.62	
Optional ½" Gypsum Wallboard Finish	.45	

27. Sheet Metal on Purlin

Materials	R	U
Exterior Air Film	.17	
Metal Roof Panel	NEGL.	
Interior Air Film (Still Air)	.61	
Basic Roof	78	1.282
Optional ½" Gypsum Wallboard Ceiling	.45	

Figure 3.3.5.2 - Roof System Descriptions

20. Built-up or Single-Ply on Metal Deck

Materials	R	U
Exterior Air Film	.17	
Stone	NEGL.	
3-ply Built-Up Roof	.33	
¾" Glass Fiber	2.78	
Metal Deck	NEGL.	
Interior Air Film (Still Air)	.61	
Basic Roof	3.89	.257
Optional ½" Gypsum Wallboard Ceiling	.45	

21. Built-up or Single-Ply on Poured Concrete Slab

Materials	R	U
Exterior Air Film	.17	
Stone	NEGL.	
3-ply Built-Up Roof	.33	
4" Concrete Slab (140 pcf)	.32	
Interior Air Film (Still Air)	.61	
Basic Roof	1.43	.699
Optional ½" Gypsum Wallboard Ceiling	.45	

22. Built-up or Single-Ply on Precast Concrete Slab

Materials	R	U
Exterior Air Film	.17	
Stone	NEGL.	
3-ply Built-Up Roof	.33	
8" Hollow Core Slab (85 pcf)	2.70	
Interior Air Film (Still Air)	.61	
Basic Roof	3.81	.262
Optional ½" Gypsum Wallboard Ceiling	.45	

23. Built-up or Single-Ply on Wood Deck

Materials	R	U
Exterior Air Film	.17	
Stone	NEGL.	
3-ply Built-Up Roof	.33	
3" Wood Deck	3.75	
Interior Air Film (Still Air)	.61	
Basic Roof	4.86	.206
Optional ½" Gypsum Wallboard Ceiling	.45	

24. Built-up or Single-Ply on Gypsum Deck

Materials	R	U
Exterior Air Film	.17	
Stone	NEGL.	
3-ply Built-Up Roof	.33	
2" Gypsum Deck (51 pcf)	1.20	
1" Formboard	4.17	
Interior Air Film (Still Air)	.61	
Basic Roof	6.48	.154

25. Metal Panel on Sheathed Rafter

Materials	R	U
Exterior Air Film	.17	
Sheet Metal Roofing	NEGL.	
Building Paper	.06	
½" Plywood Sheathing	.62	
Air Space	.96	
½" Gypsum Wallboard Finish	.45	
Interior Air Film (Still Air)	.62	
Basic Roof	2.88	.347

Figure 3.3.5.2 (continued) - Roof System Descriptions

The OTTV of the roof is also limited by the Model Energy Code. It becomes somewhat harder to calculate, as the mass is less but is made up of insulation, roofing, and structure. The ASHRAE 90 methods of calculation are repeated by the Model Energy Code.

$$8.5 \Rightarrow OTTV_{roof} = \frac{U_{roof} \times A_{roof} \times TD_{eqr} + 138 \, A_s \times SC_s + U_s \times A_s \times (t_o - t_i)_s}{A_o}$$

$$26.8 \Rightarrow OTTV_{roof} = \frac{U_{roof} \times A_{roof} \times TD_{eqr} + 434.7 \, A_s \times SC_s + U_s \times A_s \times (t_o - t_i)_s}{A_o}$$

Figure 3.3.5.3 shows the TD_{eqr} diagram provided in the Model Energy Code.

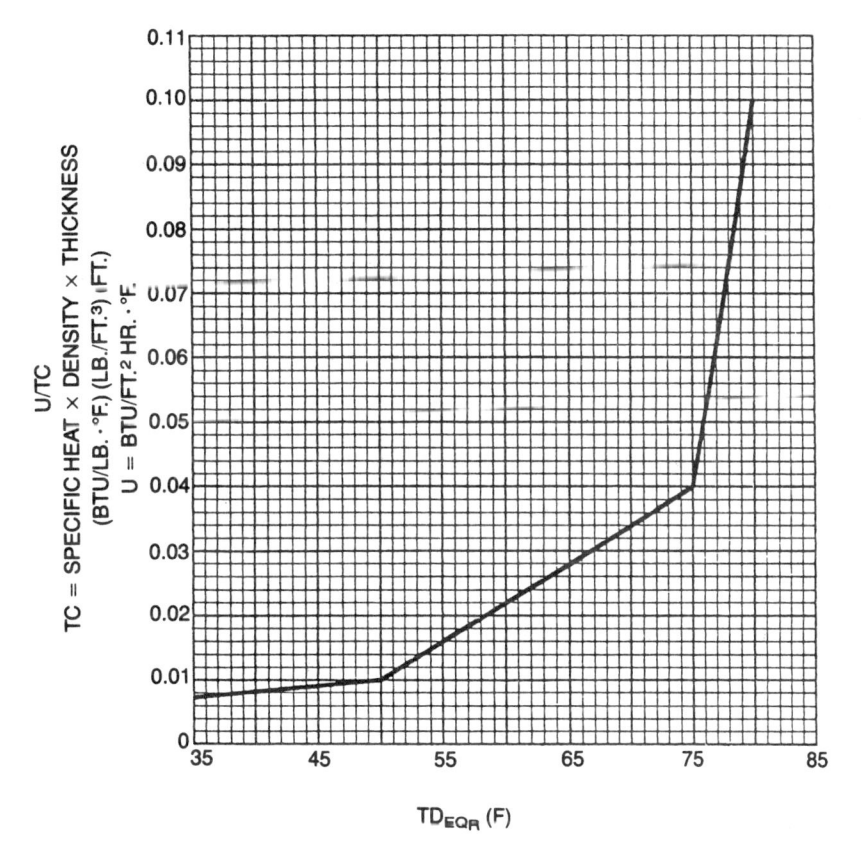

Note: TC is calculated as the sum of the TC's for each layer in the roof construction.

Figure 3.3.5.3 - TD_{EQR} from Model Energy Code

3.3.6 Floors and Slabs

Floors

Floors over unheated spaces should be designed with insulation values similar to roofs. Floors may be extended over drive-ways, open garages, or crawl spaces. It is particularly important to protect any mechanical pipes and ducts that are placed in or below the floor structure. Crawl spaces can be insulated with the floor structure or at the perimeter of the space. A vapor retarder should be placed on ground below crawl spaces where moisture problems may be present.

Floors can be constructed of wood, steel framing, or concrete. Insulation in wood framing is placed between joists. Code requirements are that overall U-value includes the insulation value of joists. Over unheated basements where basement walls are insulated, the rim joist space also needs to be covered. Figure 3.3.4.1 shows details of an insulated floor.

Floors with steel joist framing usually have enough space for insulation. However, the bottom chord needs to be isolated to prevent condensation. Concrete flat slab floors are more difficult to insulate but rigid insulation can be placed below, and covered with appropriate facing. Edges of exposed concrete floor structures need to be insulated at the perimeter of finish floor.

Perimeter insulation is also required for floors placed on fill dirt. Vapor retarders should be continuous under floors. Perimeter insulation can be horizontal or vertical, but most codes require that insulation be a minimum of 2 feet wide, running from the finished floor surface directly down on inside of the foundation wall, or turning horizontally under the floor. R-values depend on climate conditions and are shown by code. Figure 3.3.6.1 shows perimeter insulation.

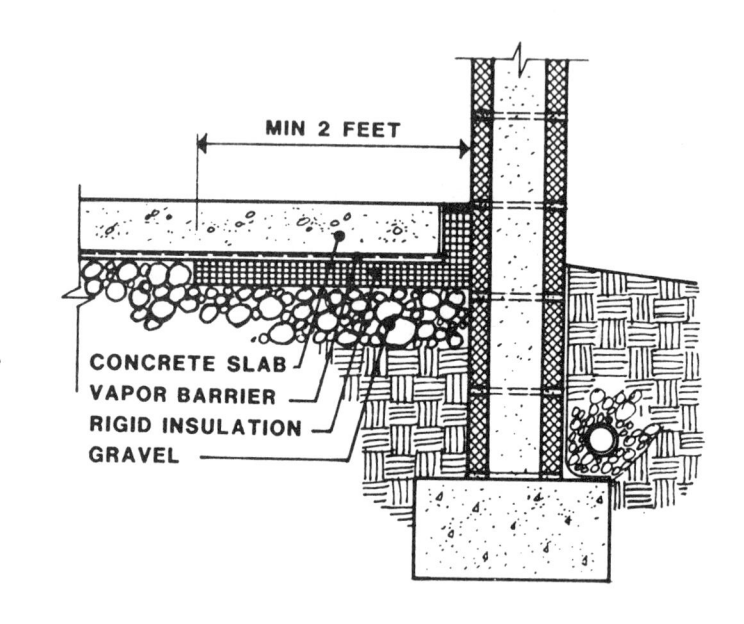

Figure 3.3.6.1 - Perimeter Insulation

Slabs

Floor slabs on fill can be heated or unheated. To qualify as a "heated" slab for code purposes, the heating element must be within the floor slab. Perimeter insulation R-values differ for heated and unheated floors.

Pipes and ducts within and below floor structures need to be insulated-- cold water pipes to prevent freezing and hot water pipes and ducts to save energy. Access to pipes and ducts is necessary.

Insulation is sometimes designed under slabs when the temperature of the floor surface is to be maintained higher than the approximately 56 degrees (F.) temperature of the earth below.

Slab insulation is usually of rigid polystyrene, polyurethane, or phenyl-containing boards. Insulation placed outside of the foundation wall should be waterproofed, usually by a membrane.

Berming of foundation and basement walls provides additional protection and should be considered for floor slabs above grade level. Temperatures above the frost line reflect above-ground temperatures in winter.

3.3.7 Infiltration

Infiltration is uncontrolled air leakage through cracks and holes in any building element, particularly around windows and doors. Infiltration air can flow in or out, depending on pressure effects of wind and/or differences in the indoor and outdoor air density. (The effects of wind and ways to moderate them are discussed in Section 3.1.6.) Infiltration has energy implications because outdoor air needs to be heated or cooled. Infiltration is increased when windows and doors are left partially open.

The building envelope interfaces with the HVAC system in several ways and plays an integral role in infiltration and ventilation. Openings in the building envelope are provided for ventilation intakes and exhaust. Combustion air is provided to boilers and furnaces. Humidity control also depends on the quality of the building envelope.

ASHRAE Standard 90 sets criteria for curtain walls. Windows and doors are required by manufacturing standards and codes to have a certain limit of air leakage when closed. ASHRAE 90 specifies:

> Compliance with the criteria for air leakage shall be determined by ANSI/ASTM E283-(83) Standard method of Test of Air Leakage through Exterior Windows, Curtain Walls and Doors, at a pressure differential of 1.57 lb/sq ft (75 Pa) which is equivalent to the effect of a 25 mph wind.

For windows, this means a maximum infiltration rate of 0.5 cu. ft./min per foot of sash crack.

Infiltration can often be reduced by pressurizing the building. Occupants can be educated to reduce unnecessary opening of windows or not allowed to do so.

Caulking and sealants help to limit infiltration. Exterior joints in the building envelope, such as around window and door frames, between walls, foundation, and roof should be caulked, gasketed, weatherstripped or sealed.

If the building is sealed so tightly that there is little or no infiltration, indoor air quality must be maintained by ventilation. See Section 2.2.4, Indoor Air Quality. Infiltration is discussed further in Section 3.4.1.

3.3.8 Double Envelope

"Double envelope" structures are both innovative and controversial: The occupied space is surrounded on four of its six sides (north and south walls, roof and floor) by an airspace. The airspace is, in turn, enclosed by an outer shell consisting of the roof, north and south wall, and exposed earth underneath the floor. East and west walls are single walls.
- The double envelope concept is that the occupied space is heated with a "convective loop" of air that circles in the airspace between the two shells. Air heated in the sunspace rises through the inner space over the roof and falls down the north wall and under the house, where it gives up excess heat to the earth. The air is then pulled into a greenhouse to be heated again for nighttime use.

3.3.9 Total Envelope Performance

Whole building energy performance has in recent years become the subject of intensive research. Whole building energy performance is a synergistic concept based on the notion that optimum energy performance is not a simple addition of parts. It is instead a complex, dynamic integration of parts, a balancing of tradeoffs which can turn negatives into positives. The interface between building envelope, HVAC system, solar and daylighting aspects are being investigated. The balance between the external loads acting on the building envelope and the internal loads needs to be understood. For example, energy audits in existing buildings show that infiltration and ventilation make major demands on the total energy requirements, amounting to one third of the total energy used. Other factors, such as the seasonal efficiency of boilers and HVAC systems, lighting, and occupants, also contribute significantly. Heat losses or gains can be large or small depending on the mix of factors above. When a building is being designed it is difficult to anticipate all the various conditions that may take place during the building's useful life. Modeling and simulation can be used to analyze alternative conditions and corresponding energy demands for the building. Section 4.2, Analytical Techniques, discusses modeling and simulation issues.

3.4 FENESTRATION AND OTHER APERTURES

3.4.1 Introduction

Fenestration, clerestories, roof monitors, and other apertures can be used to control transmission of daylight, solar heat, and air flow and to provide views. For an aperture to perform any or all of these functions well, it must maximize benefits (e.g., daylighting, cooling air flow in summer, and solar heating in winter) and minimize the liabilities (e.g., overheating, winter air leaks, glare). This generally suggests the use of some carefully designed controls either outside or inside the building or as part of the aperture glazing.

Apertures can consist of a single pane of glass or large panels of glass or plastic in metal, wood, or plastic frame consisting of a large percentage of the building surface. They can come in the form of vertical clerestories above the roof and skylights in the roof, either horizontal or sloped.

Window types include:

Fixed (nonoperable)	Horizontal Awning
Vertical Hung	Horizontal Sliding
Vertical Pivoted	Horizontal Pivoting
Vertical Casement	Horizontal Projected
	Horizontal Jalousie

Solar Heat Gain

Solar heat gain results when insolation (direct, diffuse and reflected solar radiation) is converted into heat after passing through an aperture. Heat gain can be controlled through the geometry of the building, through the use of architectural controls (e.g., overhangs, louvers, light shelves, blinds, screens) and through light-controlling glazing (e.g., selectively transmitting glass).

Three variables determine the amount of solar heat that enters the interior of a building through glazing: (1) the amount of insolation available at the aperture, (2) the area of glass exposed to radiation, and (3) the proportion of available insolation transmitted.

Available insolation on a given site can be determined from a variety of sources, as discussed in Section 2.4.4.

The area exposed to insolation is the number of square feet of glazing or a particular orientation. The amount of insolation exposure can be partially optimized with building orientation.

Solar heat gain through glazing can be calculated (for each orientation) using the following formula:

Annual solar heat gain (Btu/hr) = insolation (Btu/day/sq ft) x exposed area (sq ft) x transmissivity of glazing (percent) x days per year.

The transmissivity of glazing can be determined from manufacturers' literature.

Condensation

Condensation on glazing occurs when the temperature of the glazing surface reaches the dew point. This generally occurs on the inside surface of the glazing in the winter and on the outside in the summer. The graph in Figure 3.4.1.1 can be used to predict the glazing U-value necessary to prevent condensation based on the inside and outside air temperature and relative humidity.

To use the graph: (1) Find the point where the inside temperature and the design outdoor temperature coincide. Carry this line across horizontally to the right side of the chart. (2) Find the relative humidity (percent) and draw a vertical line to meet the temperature line. The point where the two lines intersect indicates the minimum U-value of glazing necessary to avoid condensation.

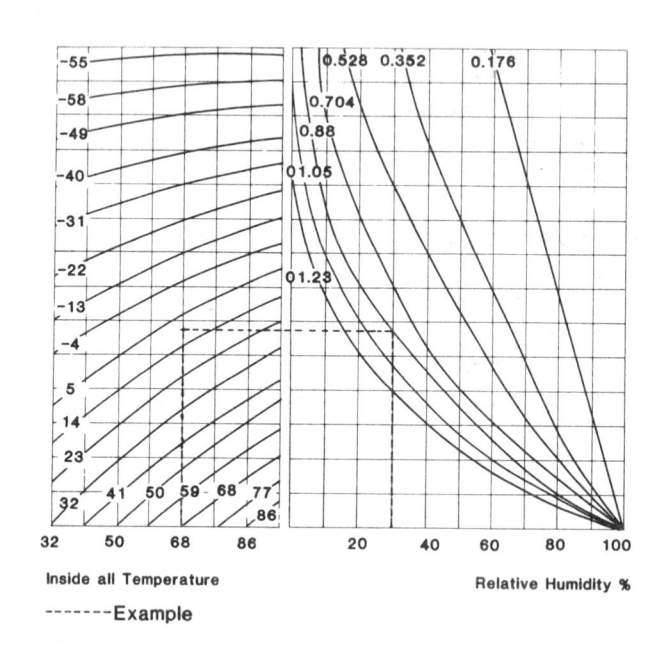

Figure 3.4.1.1 - Condensation Prediction

3.4.2 Ventilation and Natural Air Flow

Throughout major portions of the United States, there are periods of the year when no interior cooling would be necessary if buildings did not retain and store heat generated by interior electrical lighting, mechanical equipment, office equipment, human bodies, etc. If buildings under such conditions could be opened to the natural flow of air (see Figure 3.4.2.1), this heat could be carried away by fresh breezes, and the interior would be comfortable. Ventilating buildings with cool nighttime air is one useful technique for disposing of unwanted heat.

Under mild exterior conditions, interior discomfort can be considerably reduced by inducing air movement through buildings. Unfortunately, most buildings are not designed to allow interior through-air movement. Windows are seldom operable, interior spaces are partitioned to prevent the cross flow of air, and buildings are improperly oriented or spaced to take advantage of natural breezes.

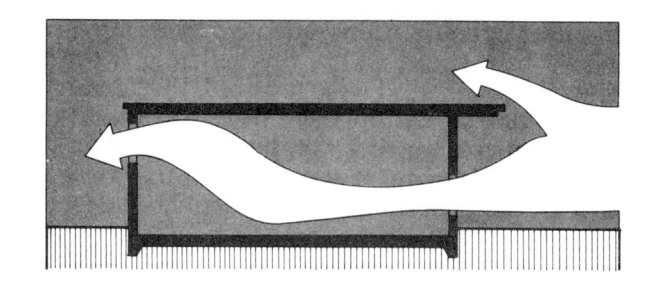

Figure 3.4.2.1 - Natural Ventilation

Air is moved by pressure differences, from higher pressure areas to lower pressure areas. Orienting buildings with the long axis perpendicular to the prevailing warm-weather breezes produces the greatest pressure differentials. Adjacent buildings should be located far enough away to avoid blocking the oncoming wind. Windbreaks and other site elements that affect wind are discussed further in Section 3.1.6, Wind Control.

Air flow through a building (cross ventilation) requires both inlets and outlets. For best results, the inlets should be placed in areas of maximum outdoor pressure (windward side of the building) and outlets placed in areas of minimum outdoor pressure (leeward side). For maximum air speed, outlets should be greater in size than inlets (total open area). For practical purposes, it is usually sufficient for outlets to be of equal size to inlets.

The type of window chosen is also important. Incoming air generally follows the direction it is given by the vanes of the window. Horizontal jalousies and venetian blinds can be adjusted to produce a downward flow of air into the interior space where it can cool occupants. Projected windows, on the other hand, usually direct incoming air toward the ceiling where the cooling effect of the air is mostly lost for the occupants.

A more complex technology, based on the that cause wind itself,

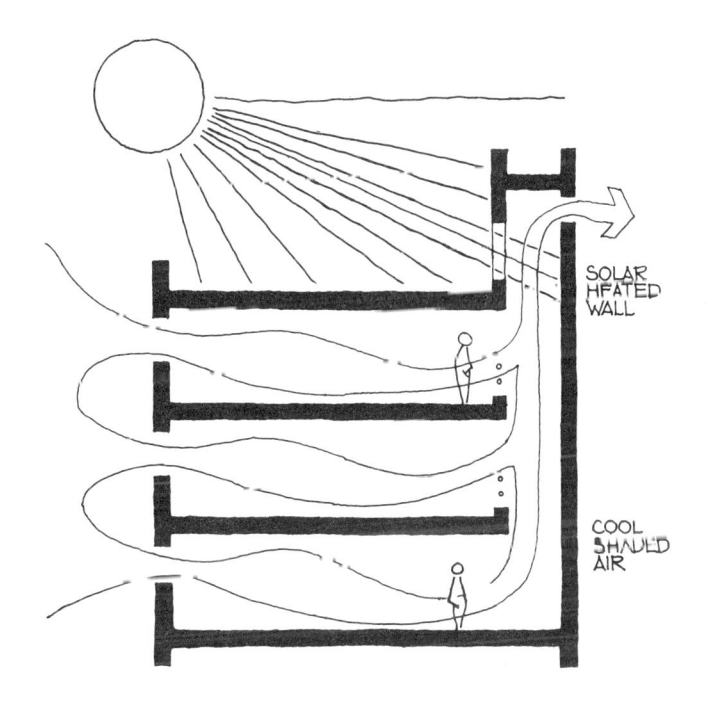

Figure 3.4.2.2 - Thermosiphon Effect

is an induced ventilation cooling system. It uses sunshine to heat a pocket of air inside a building to a temperature greater than ambient. The heated air to searches for a way up and out drawing replacement air from a cool outdoor space. This "thermal chimney" can create continuous air circulation through a building (see Figure 3.4.2.2), providing significant cooling. It is not sufficient to handle sizable internal loads such as heat from machinery or numerous occupants. The amount of pressure induced by thermal differences in a building is directly proportional to the height of the "stack."

In lowrise buildings, thermal forces are rarely sufficient to create sufficient air movement for thermal comfort in overheated periods. They are usually only enough to provide fresh air ventilation. In highrise, pressurized buildings with sealed windows and revolving doors, on the other hand, stack effect can cause heat loss/gain through elevator shafts and stair towers.

The prediction of air movements for anything beyond simple characteristics, is very difficult, and wind tunnel studies using scale models are recommended for many design projects where precise predictions are desired.

Inlet and Outlet Location

- In spaces where the only outlet is through the roof, oblique or perpendicular air flow will give acceptable ventilation.
- The vertical placement of the inlet has a major effect on the direction of flow of air through a space. The placement of the inlet high on the wall diverts airflow upward, decreasing cooling effect.
- The placement of an inlet a few feet off the floor results in an ideal pattern.
- The placement of an inlet on the floor causes the flow to sweep across the floor surface.
- The placement of an inlet in one corner of a room may result in asymmetrical airflow.
- However, placement of the outlet--high, midway or low on a wall--has little effect on airflow patterns. The horizontal placement of the outlet also has a minimal effect on air distribution.

Aperture Size

The inlet primarily determines the distribution of air. To maximize velocity, the outlet should be larger than the inlet. The greater the relative area of the outlet, the greater the airflow velocity through a room.

Partitions
- The shape of the room and the location of inlets and outlets are important when trying to achieve maximum ventilation. A rectangular room with a single outlet and inlet on a long wall is not nearly as effective as a rectangular room with openings on a short wall.

- Double-loaded corridors allow good ventilation to windward spaces, but poor ventilation to leeward spaces.
- Single-loaded corridors with small openings are good in high-wind conditions but less effective in quieter conditions.
- Partitions located within the flow of wind will tend to dissipate it.
- The closer a partition can be to an outlet, the more satisfactory the ventilation will be.
- Corridors can also be used to direct air, but since the air will continue to flow along the path defined by the corridor, it will be necessary to deflect the air into the spaces off the corridor.
- Closed partitions tend to hinder airflow and may create the need for more vents and mechanical ductwork. Variations on the floor-to-ceiling partition (e.g., half-height, glass partitions with openings, or sliding doors) can be effective.

3.4.3 Infiltration

Heating and cooling loads due to infiltration of unconditioned air can account for as much as one-third of the load in externally-load dominated buildings.

Infiltration results when there are air leaks around aperture openings and pressure differences exist between the interior and exterior. Winds impinge on a building, causing higher pressure on the windward side and lower pressure on the leeward side. Infiltration air enters the building through cracks around apertures on the windward side, travels through the building and exits (exfiltrates) through cracks on the lower pressure or leeward side.

Infiltration can also be caused by temperature differences inside the building--the "stack effect" discussed in Section 3.4.2, (see Figure 3.4.3.1). As the warm air rises, it draws cooler exterior air in through cracks and openings in the lower part of the building, causing air to move vertically up the building. These thermal currents, however, are generally not sufficient to overcome interior air flow currents caused by pressure differences on the exterior of the building.

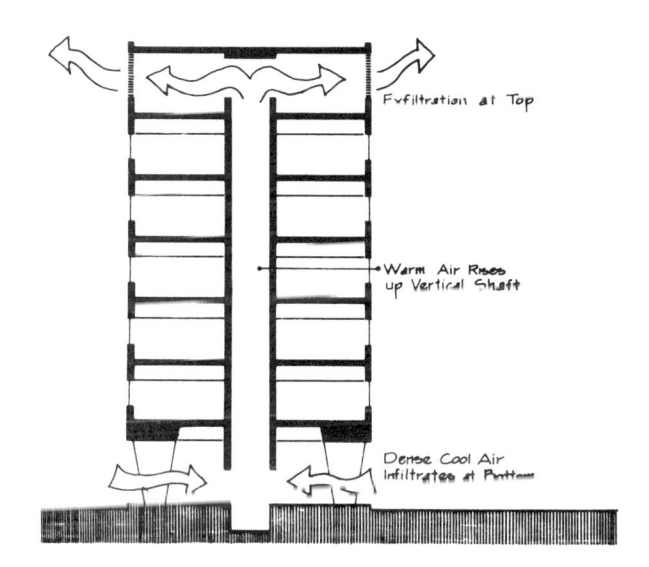

Figure 3.4.3.1 - Stack Effect

- Infiltration occurs at three joints in window openings: the joint between the frame and wall, the joint between the sash and frame, and the joint between the glass and the sash. Infiltration control requires proper joint sealings.
- Infiltration is of greatest concern in buildings with operable windows. It can account for 30 percent of all heat losses and gains in both low and highrise housing. Weatherstripping can reduce heat losses and gains by about 40 percent.
- Infiltration can be reduced by reducing the perimeter of glazed areas. One method is to use fewer larger windows rather than more smaller ones.
- The entrance of the building can be designed as an enclosed space that provides an airlock or double entry.
- The entrance can be oriented away from the prevailing winter wind or protected by a windbreak.
- Minimizing the surface-to-volume ratio, diminishes from the effects of infiltration and exfiltration. Building shape can also increase low-pressure areas: for example, an L- or U-shaped building with the center space oriented to the leeward side will offer increased protection.
- Air density varies with temperature. In cold weather with warmer lower density inside a building, air rises and is replaced by outside air infiltration at its base. In summer the infiltration will occur at the top of a tall building and exfiltration at the bottom.
- In extremely tall buildings (exceeding about 35 stories), serious consideration should be given to providing a relatively airtight horizontal separation at the building's midpoint. This can be done by using vestibule airlocks in the stair shafts at the midpoint or at elevator transfer floor(s). Air movement can be controlled in elevator shafts by using airlocks at transfer floors.

Window Frames and Seals

Window frames, particularly those made of metal, can be responsible for considerable heat loss by conduction through the frames. Providing a thermal break in the path of heat flow can save significant energy. The effectiveness of the thermal break depends on the insulating value and thickness of the thermal-break material. Figure 3.4.3.2 shows thermal break detail. An aluminum frame with a good thermal break

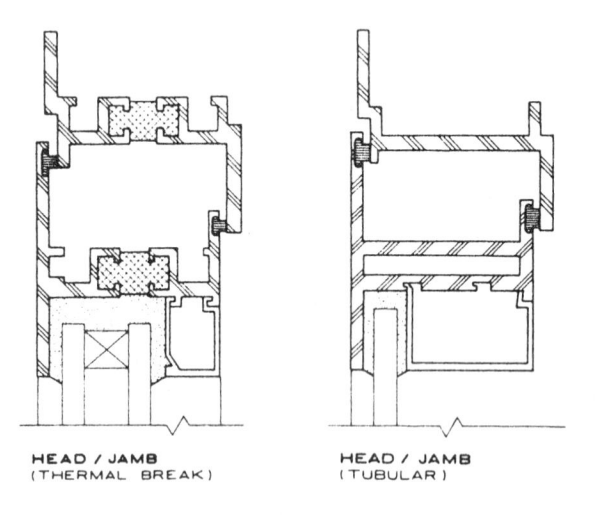

Figure 3.4.3.2 - Thermal Break Detail

has a U-value (0.85) similar to that of insulating glass. Tight fits and proper gasketing are essential.

Weatherstripping around the perimeter joints of an operable sash also effectively reduces air infiltration.

3.4.4 Multiple Glazing

Glass conducts heat quite well--nine times better than plywood. Heat flows easily through glass, escaping outdoors in winter and penetrating indoors in summer. Figure 3.4.4.1 shows conduction heat losses through glass. Air spaces between the layers of glass interrupt the path of conduction, and significantly reduce the rate of heat flow. To move through air spaces, heat must be transferred by radiation and convection.

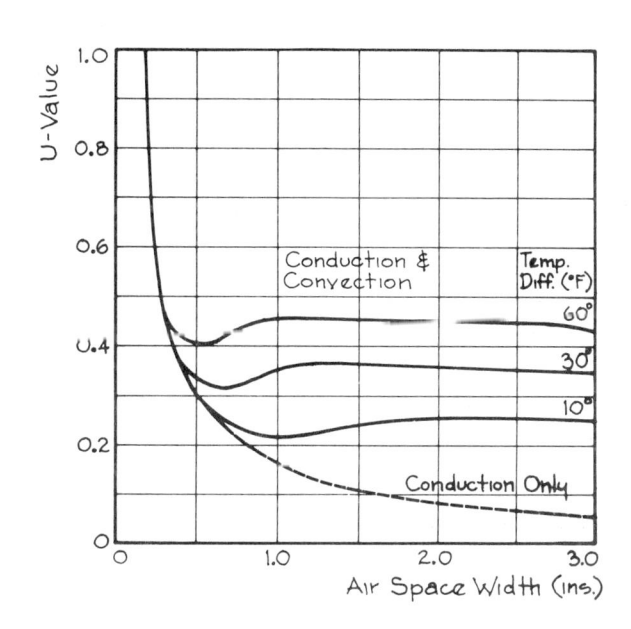

Figure 3.4.4.1 - Air Space U-Values

- The width of the air space does affect its thermal performance, but not in a linear fashion. An air space narrower than 3/16 inch begins to be ineffective. Up to approximately 5/8 inch, the wider the air space, the greater the reduction in heat flow. Increasing the air space beyond 5/8 inch does not substantially improve its U value. Figure 3.4.4.2 shows U-values for different air space widths.

- Because the heat flow across multiple glazing is substantially reduced, the temperature of the glazing surface facing the room is much closer to room temperature than is the case with single glass. This alleviates discomfort near windows and reduces both ice formation and condensation.

- Three layers of glass enclosing two air layers are more effective than two layers of glass enclosing the same overall width. Triple glazing with two 1/4-inch air spaces has a U-value of 0.47, compared to 0.58 for double glazing with a single 1/2 inch air space.

Description	Thickness	U-Value (Winter)	U-Value (Summer)	Visible	Solar	S.C.
Single, Clear	⅛"	1.16	1.04	.90	.84	1.00
	¼"	1.13	1.04	.89	.78	.95
	⅜"	1.11	1.03	.88	.72	.90
	½"	1.09	1.03	.86	.67	.86
Single, heat absorbing	¼"	1.13	1.10	.52	.96	.71
Double	3⁄16" air space	.62	.65		.71	.88
	¼" air space	.58	.61			
	½" air space	.49	.57	.80		.82
	½" air space Low e Coating e = .20	.32	.38			
	e = .40	.42	.49	.14		.25
	e = .60	.43	.51			
Triple	¼" air space	.39	.44			.71
Acrylic, single glazed	¼" air space	.96	.89	.92	.85	.98
Acrylic, w/reflecting coating	¼" air space	.88	.83	.14	.12	.21

Figure 3.4.4.2 - Glazing Performance

- The heat-absorbing and radiating properties (characterized by the terms "absorptances" and "emittance") of the two glass surfaces facing toward the air space will affect the rate at which heat is radiated across the cavity. A coated film such as tin oxide or indium oxide, or a pure metal such as gold, silver, or copper, applied to either of the glass surfaces facing the cavity will reduce heat transfer by radiation. Figure 3.4.4.3 gives examples of the effectiveness of such coatings.

Glass Type	Glass Width	% Visible Transmission	% Total Solar Transmission	Shading Coefficient
Clear single glazed	¼"	89	78	0.95
Gray reflective single	¼"	34	25	0.60
Clear insulating (double-glazed)	1"	80	59	0.82
Gray reflective insulating	1"	30	29	0.47

Figure 3.4.4.3 - Glazing Performance

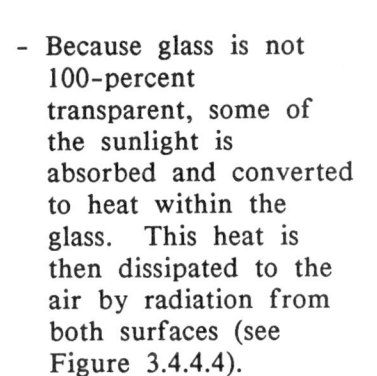

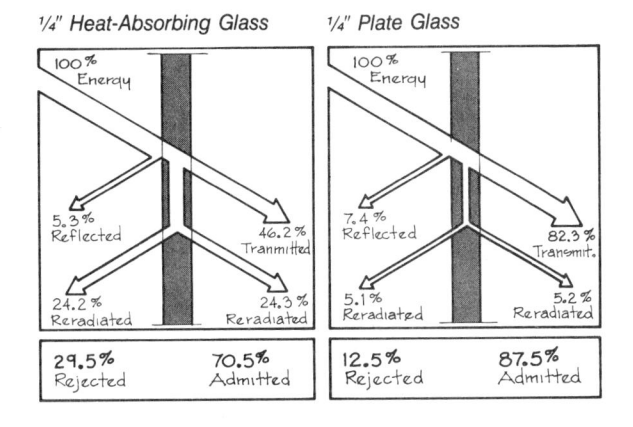

- Because glass is not 100-percent transparent, some of the sunlight is absorbed and converted to heat within the glass. This heat is then dissipated to the air by radiation from both surfaces (see Figure 3.4.4.4).

Figure 3.4.4.4 - Solar Transmission

Air-Flow Windows

Air-flow windows offer a variation on standard multiple glazing. Air-flow windows (see Figure 3.4.4.5) usually have a double-pane, insulated glass on the outside, an air space sufficient for installation of venetian blinds and air flow through the space at the middle, and an inside glass pane. Clear glass is suitable for air-flow windows.

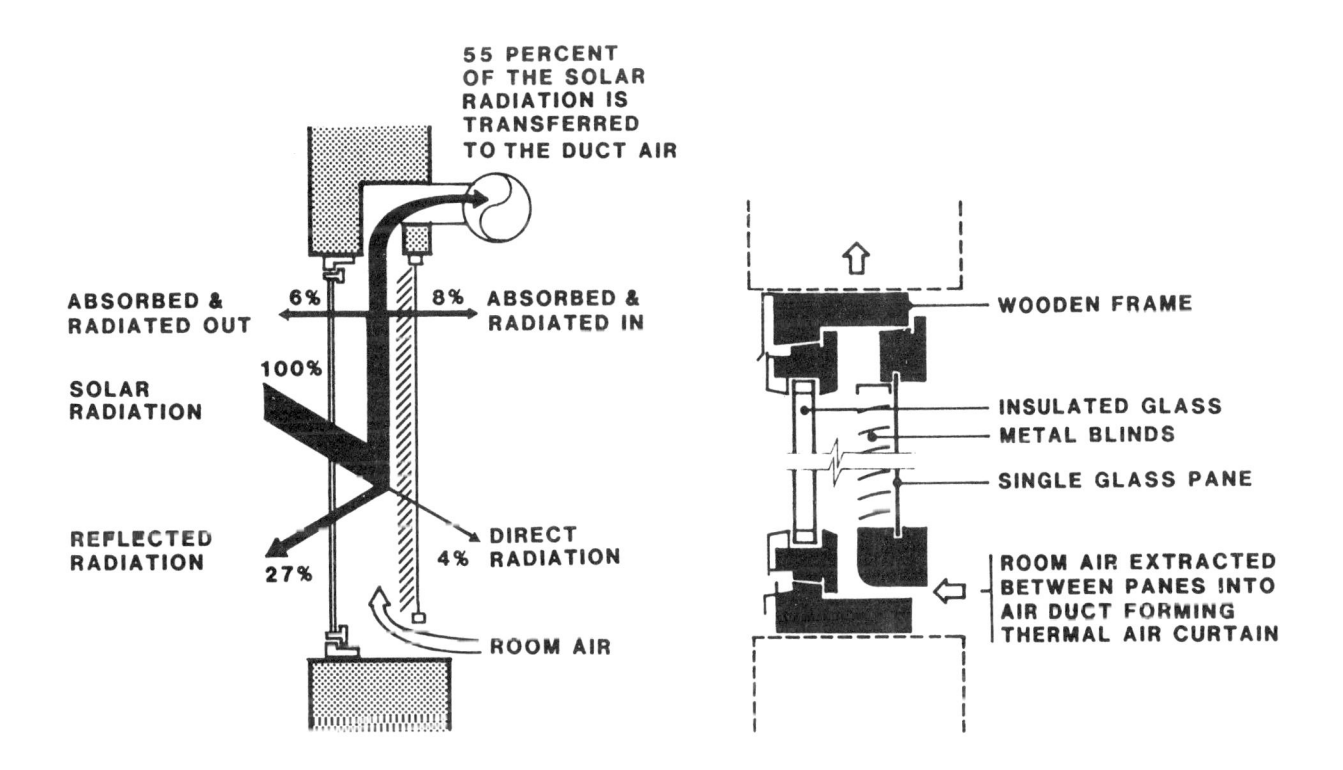

Figure 3.4.4.5 - Air Flow Window Details

Air flows through the middle space from the sill to the window head, and from there is either exhausted to the outside (in the cooling mode) or (in the heating mode) sent to the HVAC system for distribution to other parts of the building or, potentially, to thermal storage for later use.

Air-flow windows are typically installed in institutional and office buildings that have concrete or other building materials that can serve as thermal storage. In the heating mode, venetian blinds serve as solar collectors. Because most of the direct solar energy is transported to the mechanical system, no overheating occurs. This is also true in the cooling mode, and the inside pane remains at a comfortable, controlled room temperature.

3.4.5 Glazing Materials

Glazing materials commonly used in buildings include clear glass (single or multiple layers), glass block, heat-absorbing glass, heat-reflecting glass, selectively transmitting glass, and plastic sheets and panels that have good light transmittance. The heat and light transmission characteristics of each of these types of glazing are described in manufacturers' literature. When selecting glazing materials consideration should be given to trade-offs between reducing solar heat gain and increasing daylight availability.

The 1980's have seen the introduction of a wide variety of new glass products that attempt to meet the different needs for light and heat in different building types and climates. These products use new glass coatings to deal selectively with four bands of energy (three from sunlight and one from objects struck by sunlight:

Components of Sunlight
- ultraviolet radiation (wavelength less than 0.4 microns--fades furniture and other furnishings)
- visible light (0.4-0.8 microns--"daylight"; accounts for less than half the heat gain from sunlight)
- shortwave infrared radiation (0.8-2.5 microns--accounts for over half the heat gain from sunlight).

Heat Radiated by Objects Struck by Sunlight
- longwave infrared radiation (2.5-50 microns--cannot penetrate glass).

Figure 3.4.5.1 shows how an ideal selective transmitter differs for large office buildings, where internal cooling loads dominate and solar heat gain is unwanted,

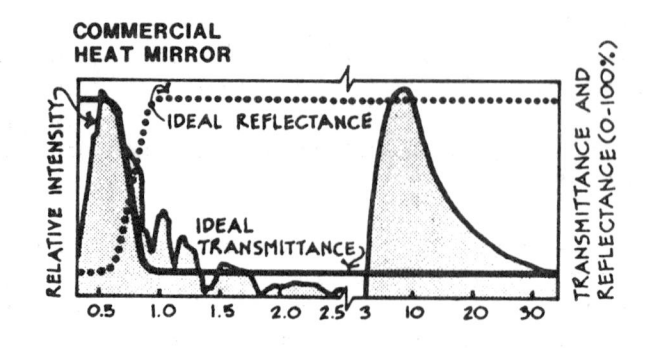

Figure 3.4.5.1 - Selective Transmittance Spectrum

and for skin-dominated homes and light commercial buildings in cold climates, where solar gain is desirable in the heating season. (Both ideals would block ultraviolet radiation.)

For the offices, an ideal glazing would admit a high portion of visible light and reflect both the shortwave infrared component of sunlight and longwave infrared reradiated from outdoor surfaces.

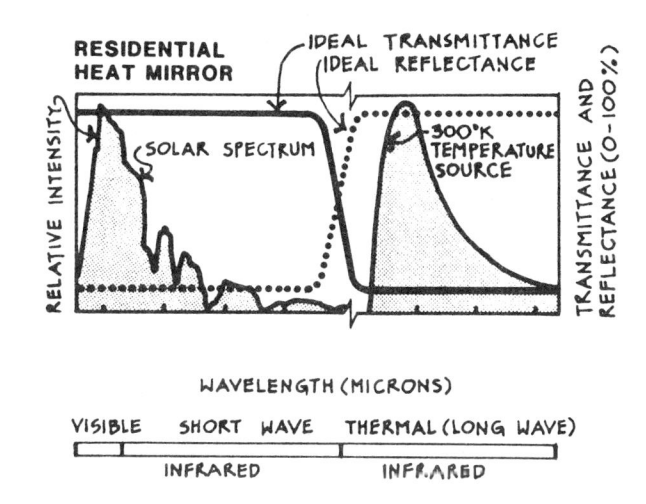

Figure 3.4.5.1 - Selective Transmittance Spectrum

In homes and light commercial buildings in cold climates, the ideal glazing would admit both light and the shortwave infrared component of sunlight and reflect reradiated longwave infrared back into the space.

These ideal characteristics are the goals of the recently developed anti-reflective and "low-e" (low-emissivity) coatings discussed later in this section. While more familiar glazing technologies such as glass blocks, heat-absorbing glass and reflective glass all attempt to meet some or all of these goals and often still have advantages over the newer technologies in terms of cost, appearance, ease of handling or other characteristics, anti-reflective and low-e coatings are rapidly evolving technologies that have proved effective in recent designs. At present, however, no single glazing is best in all situations.

Glass Block

Glass blocks, usually hollow but sometimes solid, are useful in transmitting daylight and have good insulating value. They come in clear, diffuse, patterned, and light-directing varieties.
- Glass block admits sunlight and daylight. Building heat loss is lowered because U-value is low. Heat gain is partially reduced because only 50-60 percent of incident solar energy is admitted. Daylighting is not significantly reduced: up to 80 percent of visible light is admitted.
- Larger-sized blocks offer more thermal resistance than smaller ones, because the percentage edge area is reduced.

Light-directing (directional) glass block were developed primarily for use in exterior walls above a vision strip. Light from both the sky and is directed, through prisms built into the interior of the block, toward the ceiling of the interior space. Daylight is sufficiently redirected so that the block is not excessively bright when viewed from the inside.

Heat-Absorbing Glass

Solar energy at sea level is composed of approximately 3 percent ultraviolet radiation, 44 percent visible light and 53 percent thermal (infrared) radiation. Light is converted to heat whenever it strikes an opaque surface. Therefore, the amount of total solar energy transmitted determines the amount of heat gain. Adding a metallic oxide to the ingredients of glass increases the absorptivity of ultraviolet, visible, and near-infrared solar energy, especially the latter. Figure 3.4.5.2 indicates characteristics of glass coating materials. This distinguishes heat-absorbing glass from glass that is merely tinted.

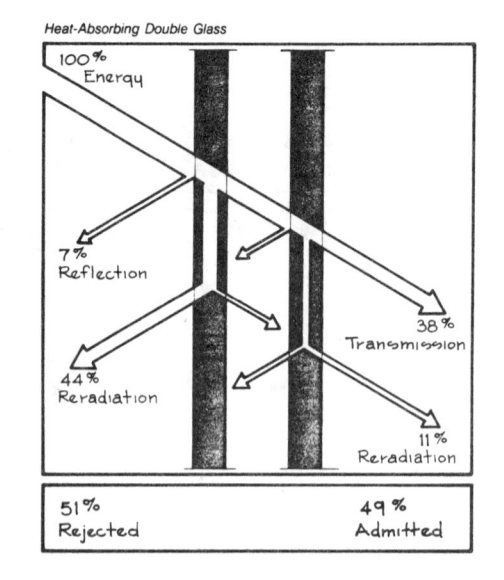

Figure 3.4.5.2 - Solar Transmission

- The solar energy absorbed by heat-absorbing glass (or any glass) is converted to heat, which is subsequently radiated and convected from both sides of the glass. The rate of heat loss is proportional to the temperature differentials, air movements and the surface characteristics of either side of the glass. On a summer day more heat is dissipated indoors because the interior of an airconditioned building is cooler. But in winter more heat is dissipated to the outdoors because the outside temperature is lower. Heat-absorbing glass is an improvement over single glass plate but still admits much heat from the summer sun.
- Heat-absorbing glass reduces fading of interior fabrics more than clear glass because it absorbs more ultraviolet solar radiation. At the same time, heat-absorbing glass radiates more heat than clear glass creating discomfort for occupants near windows.
- Heat-absorbing glass used as the outer sheet of glass in double glazing performs much better than it does as a single glazing. The trapped air space between the two layers of glass acts as insulation, impeding the inward flow of heat and providing more opportunity for dissipation to the outside air.

Reflective Glass

Reflective glass, which has a coating of metallic oxide or other material, increases the amount of solar energy reflected at the window, thus reducing the cooling load within the building while still admitting useful (although reduced) amounts of daylight (see Figure 3.4.5.3).

- Reflective glass used as the outer sheet of double glazing is more effective in keeping out the sun's heat than reflective glass used as single glazing. The trapped air space between the two layers of glass acts as insulation, impeding the inward flow of heat and providing more opportunity for dissipation to the outside air.

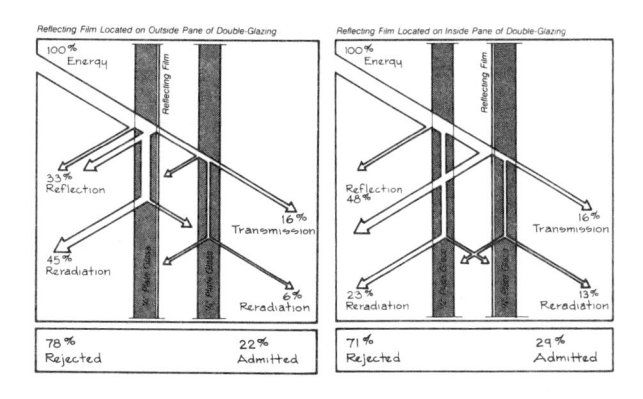

Figure 3.4.5.3 - Location of Reflective Film

- If the reflective coating or film is placed on the outer sheet of double glazing, not on the inner sheet, heat admitted through glass can be reduced. This is because reflective glass absorbs more sunlight--and heat--than clear glass. When this heat is concentrated in the outer sheet of insulating glass it is more easily dissipated to the outside air, especially when there is a breeze.
- The winter U-value of clear double glazing with 1/2-inch air space is only 0.58, as opposed to as low as 0.28 for double glazing with an outer sheet of reflective glass.
- Proper adhesives should be used in single glazing to ensure stable bonding of reflective coating to the glass.
- Proper detailing of reflective glass is important to avoid glass breakage because of the higher solar absorptivity. If the glass is installed in a high-mass material such as concrete, the lag in time it takes the concrete to heat up in comparison to the glass will result in extreme center-to-edge temperature differences and edge stresses in the glass.
- Distortion of reflected images is a problem with some reflective glass. Mock-ups on the site are worthwhile to study the visual appearance of reflective glass and distortion effects.
- Reflective glass can create a glare for the occupants of adjacent buildings, pedestrians and drivers.
- Reduced light transmission with reflective glass darkens the view out. Bronze or other tinted reflective glasses can also distort colors.

Anti-Reflective Coatings

Recently developed anti-reflective coatings increase both daylight and solar heat gain in a space by cutting down the amount of solar energy (visible and short-wave infrared) reflected from the glazing. They also block ultraviolet light better than other coatings (see Figure 3.4.5.4).

Tiny needle-like protruberances on the coated surface eliminate surface reflection losses, increasing both light and energy transmission (98 to 99 percent of visible light and 93 to 96 percent of the solar energy). They let in more energy, but do little to stop heat loss. Anti-reflective glazing is typically combined with either two or three panes of clear glass separated with air spaces to increase the R-value.

GLAZING TYPE	Ultraviolet Transmittance (%)	Solar Transmittance (%)
Single, clear	78	.85
Insulated, clear	64	.74
Triple, clear	51	.61
Low-E, triple	43	.46
Quad, clear	41	.50
Low-E, insulated	29	.52
Anti-reflective, insulated	6	.68
Anti-reflective, triple	2	.63

Figure 3.4.5.4 - Reflective Properties: Blocking Ultraviolet
(BEST to worst)

Low-e Coatings

Recently developed low-e (low-emissivity) coatings reflect most longwave radiation back into a space, for winter heating, and reflect longwave radiation from outside surfaces back for summer cooling. The glass absorbs what longwave radiation it does not reflect. As with anti-reflective coatings, the R-value of the windows can be raised by combining the low-e surface with multiple layers of insulated glass, tinted or not. Low-e coatings also block ultraviolet light. Figure 3.4.5.5 shows the various properties of low-e glazings compared to clear glazing units.

One manufacturer offers three varieties of low-e coatings: one for cold-climate buildings with large heating loads, a second, with lower relative heat gain, for cooling dominating buildings, and a third for moderate climates where daylighting is desired but heat gain is not.

There are two types of low-e coatings, referred to as hard- and soft-coat. Soft-coat is vacuum-deposited and is generally applied to a thin film material. Lower U-values can be achieved with soft-coat, but the material is extremely fragile to both moisture and touch; it cannot be handled, cut or stored like ordinary glass. Hard-coat low emissivity glazings are manufactured in a pyrolitic process in which a hot, thin, metallic oxide coating is sprayed onto a ribbon of hot glass coming off the basic float production line. A hard coat will not dull with age, has an unlimited shelf life, and is unaffected by being touched. It can be handled, washed, and cut like normal glass. Some sealants are incompatible with the hard coat, however.

GLAZING	Air Space	Transmittance (Visible Range)	Shading Coefficient	U-Values Winter	U-Values Summer
SINGLE					
1/8	—	.90	1.00	1.16	1.05
1/4	—	.89	.95	1.13	1.04
DOUBLE					
1/8	1/4	.82	.90	.55	.60
1/4	1/2	.79	.82	.42	.55
TRIPLE					
1/8	1/4	.74	.85	.39	.49
1/4	1/2	.79	.78	.34	.40
QUAD					
1/4	1/2	.63	.74	.25	.34
DOUBLE WITH LOW-E SOFT COAT ON SURFACE 3					
1/8	1/4	.76	.74	.44	.48
1/4	1/2	.73	.70	.32	.32
DOUBLE WITH LOW-E HARD COAT ON SURFACE 3					
1/8	1/4	.74	.23	.52	.54
1/4	1/2	.72	.78	.40	.44
TRIPLE WITH LOW-E SOFT COAT ON SURFACE 5					
1/8	1/4	.70	.67	.32	.37
3/16	1/2	.68	.64	.23	.37
TRIPLE WITH LOW-E SUSPENDED FILM					
1/8	3/8	.63	.62	.25	.28
1/4	1/4	.66	.52	.31	.35
1/4	1/2	.66	.58	.23	.25

Data from the Sealed Insulated Glass Manufacturers Association

Figure 3.4.5.5 - Glazing Properties

Plastic Sheets

Plastic sheets enclosing a thickness of insulating materials diffuse incoming light with limited daylight transmission but have good thermal insulating properties (U-value).

Caution should be exercised in using any diffusing (translucent) glazing material where it will be exposed to direct sun. The diffusing properties of such materials can cause them to be exceedingly bright when viewed from the interior. Small apertures with high-transmission translucent glazing are especially inappropriate. However, if the diffusing material has a low transmission factor (e.g., 10-20 percent) and is used in a relatively large area (e.g., atrium skylight), its brightness can be tolerable.

3.4.6 Shading Devices

Large glass areas to admit daylight and solar heat gain in winter will also admit these elements in summer, when solar heat gain is not wanted. Although the intensity of solar radiation striking vertical glass directly in the summer is less than in the winter (because the radiation is coming from a higher angle), it can still cause overheating.

The transmission of unwanted solar radiation can be controlled by shading devices. The overall effectiveness of a shading device depends not only on its ability in the summer to shade an aperture from direct solar radiation, but on its ability to admit daylight throughout the year and proper quantities of solar radiation in the winter. The appropriate type of shading device will depend on the orientation of the fenestration or other aperture relative to the sun at critical times.

Exterior Shading Devices

Using exterior shading devices to interrupt solar radiation <u>before</u> it reaches an aperture or its glazing is the most effective way to prevent interior heat gain from solar radiation. Apertures can be shaded on the exterior with overhangs, louvers, light shelves, awnings, shutters, shrubbery, etc. Figure 3.4.6.1 indicates the range of exterior shading devices.

Interior shading devices are also useful, but less effective in shading solar radiation; some incoming radiation is reflected back to the exterior through the glazing but the rest is absorbed by the interior shading device, converted to heat, and then transmitted to the building air system by convection.

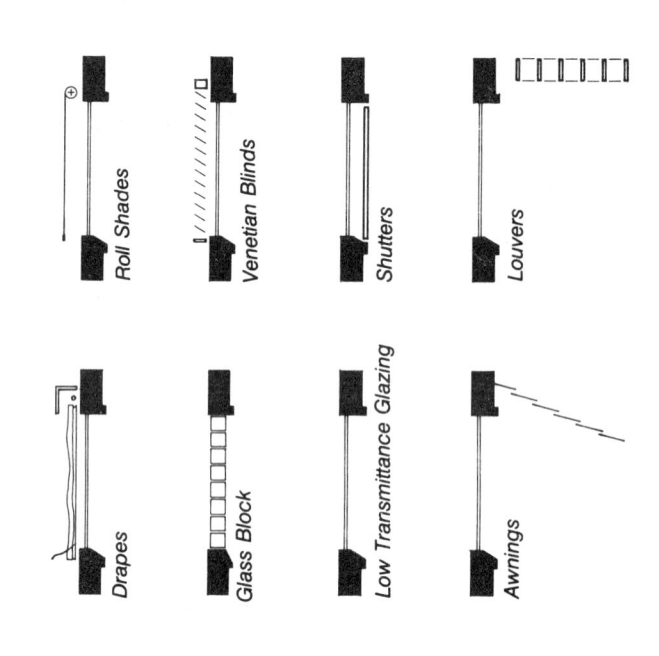

Figure 3.4.6.1 - Shading Options

For east and west orientations the critical times for shading are normally early in the morning and late in the afternoon. During these periods, the sun is at a low angle relative to the facade.

Horizontal louvers on east and west orientations provide very little shading until the sun gets higher in the sky. Vertical louvers, while effectively shading the sun, have an obstructing effect on vision to the outside. Vertical louvers that can be opened fully when the sun is no longer impinging on the aperture will provide improved view and daylighting.

For south orientations, when the sun is relatively high in the sky for most of the day, horizontal louvers, overhangs, or light shelves provide the most effective shading. The necessary dimensions for shading devices can be determined through the use of a sun-angle calculator or sun-angle tables from <u>Architectural Graphic Standards</u> and solar design references.

The introduction of daylighting when exterior shading devices are used depends somewhat on the reflectivity of the shading device surfaces. Light-colored surfaces are usually helpful. Darker surfaces can be necessary to avoid causing excessive brightness when they are illuminated by direct sun and visible from the interior.

Horizontal shading devices can be slatted (i.e., divided into small horizontal louvers) to allow additional daylight while still providing shading. In such cases, the reflective surfaces will be more productive if they are of a light-colored finish.

Metal or plastic sun screens consisting of very small (1/8-1/4 inch) louvers can provide adequate summer shading while still allowing a reasonable view to the exterior, similar to common fly screen. Such screens are available that roll up during periods when shading is not needed.

Operable exterior shutters of the louvered variety can provide excellent shading according to need. If the shutters are closed at night, especially if they have a tight fit on all edges, they can also be useful as insulation against convective heat losses.

Interior Shading Devices

Interior shading devices include venetian blinds, roller shades, draperies, and a wide variety of specially made panels and louvers. Being on the inside they are not as effective as comparable exterior devices, which intercept solar heat <u>before</u> it gets into the building interior. Figure 3.4.6.1 also shows several interior shading devices.

Generally, interior shades are operable. Interior shades are less subject than exterior ones to dirt accumulation and weather wear and more accessible for cleaning and maintenance.

Horizontal or vertical venetian-type blinds can be tilted to respond to changing sun conditions. These blinds can effectively reduce excessive exterior brightness (glare).

A commonly experienced limitation on the effectiveness of interior shades is that occupants fail to adjust blinds to account for sun movement throughout the day. Automatic adjustable blinds, activated by a light-sensitive photocell, are available.

- Horizontal or vertical blinds can be tilted to provide maximum reflection of sunlight either back out the window or deeper into the room.
- Louvers also provide shading that will help somewhat to reduce the cooling load of a space.
- Draperies should be sealed against the wall or window frame at the sides and window sill to insulate the window in the winter.
- When room air comes into contact with the cold glass behind an unsealed drapery, it is cooled and flows back into the room at the bottom of the drapery. Under such conditions, the winter U-value of a single-glazed window is only slightly reduced (1.06). By contrast, the U-value of a tight-fitting, tight-weave closed drapery and a single-glazed window can be as low as .81.
- Double draperies (two layers of draperies separated by an air space) can further improve the U-value of a single-glazing system (.65-.57).
- Drawn draperies are more comfortable than uncovered windows because draperies are closer to room temperature than cold glass.
- Transparent film shades-- clear or coated, singly or in multiple layers separated by a layer of air--can be even more effective for thermal control. They can limit daylighting benefits. They should be sealed at the sides and bottom to provide insulation. The U-value will be reduced to .55 with one shade, .31 with two shades, and .18 with three shades.
- Low-emissivity film can reduce window absorption of heat radiated from interior wall surfaces, furniture and people. Heat loss is reduced 57-64 percent compared to a single-glazed window.
- Reflective film shade will reflect as much as 60 percent of incoming sunlight; 60 percent of available daylight will also be lost.
- Selective-transmissivity films can transmit 75 percent of the visible light, but only 55 percent of the total solar radiation.
- Opaque or translucent wall shades can be used for reflecting sun back out to the exterior during the summer. If the shade is reversible with one dark side, it can be turned around in the winter to absorb

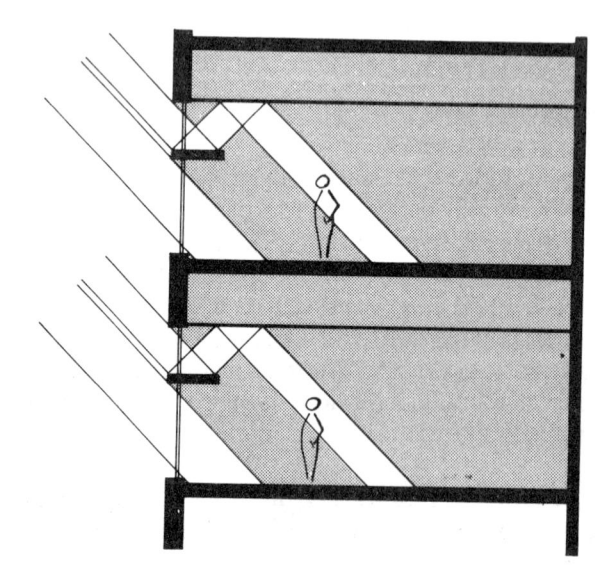

Figure 3.4.7.1 - Light Shelves

solar heat. U-values of opaque shades/single glazing vary from .59 for dark colors to .25 for white shades.

3.4.7 Light Shelves

Light shelves (i.e., horizontal planes in the aperture opening) can be placed on the exterior, the interior, or both. Such shelves (see Figure 3.4.7.1) gather daylight and reflect it into the building while shading the direct sun. Light shelves are often overrated, however. To be effective daylight collectors/reflectors, they must be exposed to direct sunshine. Use of highly reflective surfaces on the top of the shelves (e.g., white paint, mirrors, aluminum foil) will increase the quantity of daylight, but probably will not be cost effective. Use of light shelves with diffuse skylights (such as on a north facade) produce only minimal improvements in interior daylighting.

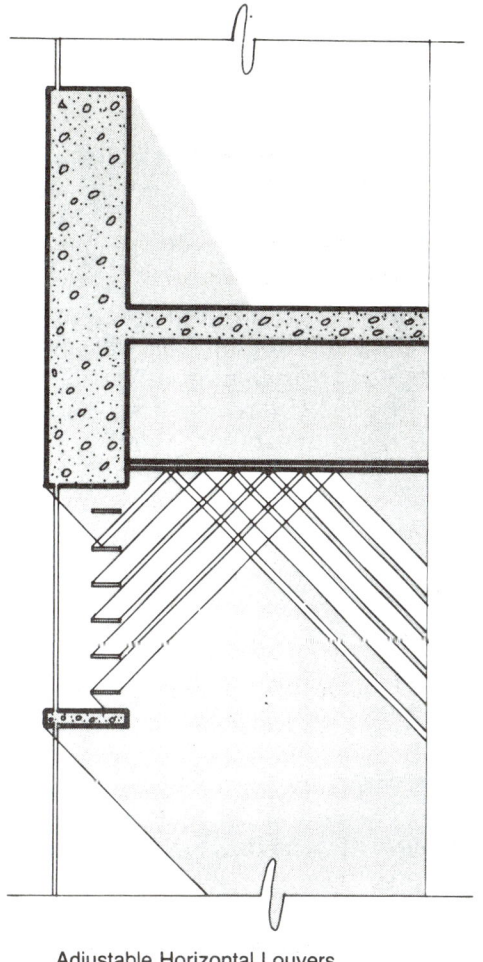

Adjustable Horizontal Louvers

Figure 3.4.7.1 - Light Shelves

3.4.8 Daylighting

Great architecture throughout history has benefited from the sensitive treatment of natural lighting. The availability of daylight in interior spaces has well-known benefits: visual connection to the out-of-doors and to outdoor weather conditions, the sense of well being associated with "natural" as opposed to "artificial" light, avoidance of monotony and stress, and the esthetic qualities from the play of daylight in interior spaces.

Daylighting offers major economic and energy benefits. It can reduce the need for electric lighting, which accounts for 35-60 percent of a commercial building's energy use.

Daylighting can only fulfill part of a building's lighting needs and must be designed to complement rather than replace the electric lighting system. Ensuring that daylighting and the electric lighting system perform their respective roles optimally requires carefully designed control systems for the electric lighting, as discussed in Section 3.6.

Functional Objectives

Functional objectives in daylighting a building are to (1) get significant quantities of daylight as deep into the building as possible (see Figure 3.4.8.1), (2) maintain a uniform distribution of daylight from one area to another, with no dark spots, and (3) avoid visual discomfort (excessive brightness differences) or visual disability (glare).

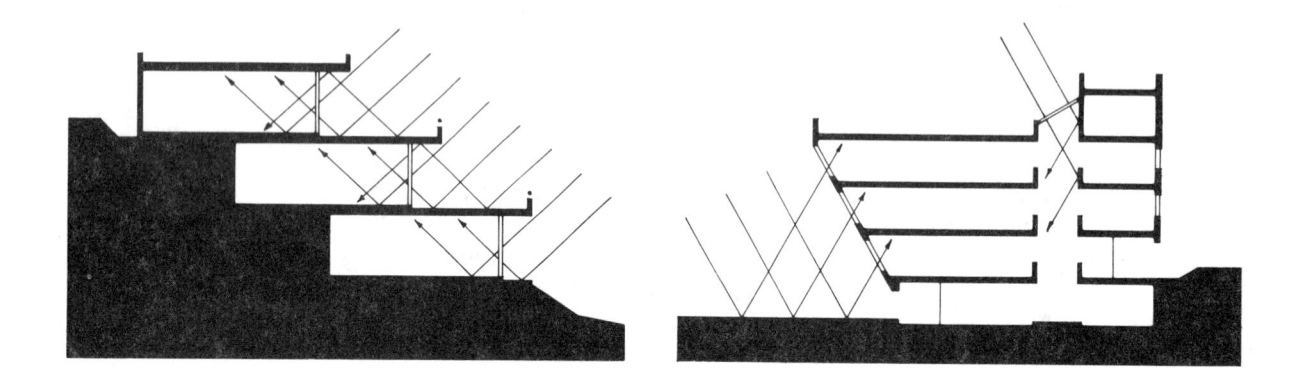

Figure 3.4.8.1 - Daylighting Configurations

Daylight Availability

"Daylight design" involves three types of skies, each with different opportunities and problems. The clear blue sky provides a relatively steady source of low-intensity light (e.g., 2,000-3,000 footcandles on the ground), penetrated by direct sun of high intensity (e.g., 6,000-7,000 footcandles). The overcast sky can be very dark, providing only a few hundred footcandles on the ground, or it can be very bright, producing several thousand footcandles. The partly cloudy sky is characterized by a blue background with bright, white clouds (often passing and changing shape very rapidly) and direct sunshine penetrating off and on. Intensities on the ground can change rapidly from 2,000-3,000 to 8,000-10,000 footcandles. These clouds when viewed from the interior of a building can be exceedingly bright, causing excessive contrasts and visual discomfort.

During the day there is almost always enough light available from the sun and sky--several thousand footcandles--to provide illumination for most human visual tasks. Various reference handbooks provide reasonably accurate data on anticipated daylight at particular locations based on time of year and time of day. However, daylight data must be modified by data on historical cloud cover, which is generally not as predictable.

Because the amount of daylight available from the sun and sky tends to change almost constantly, it is impossible to predict with any precision what the interior daylighting conditions in any building will be at any moment. However, it is not necessary that precise conditions be predictable. The building designer should establish a set of goals to be achieved within a reasonable range of expected exterior daylight conditions and then attempt to make the most of that available daylight, while providing a supplemental electric lighting system to contribute the necessary lighting when sky conditions are inadequate.

Site Criteria

Site criteria for daylighting include several issues:
- Can a new building be placed on the site so that daylight can, in fact, reach the apertures? That is, is the property surrounded by tall buildings, mountains, trees, or other obstructions that cannot be eliminated?
- Are there highly reflective surfaces near the site, such as glass-covered buildings, that could cause excessive glare on the site?
- Are there trees and shrubs on the site that might be used to reduce the possibility of interior discomfort glare caused by the bright sky or other nearby bright surfaces?
- Ground surfaces (e.g., white concrete illuminated by bright sunlight), often must be shielded from view but can also contribute considerable daylight. As much as 40 percent of interior daylighting can come from reflected ground surfaces.

None of these features need necessarily prohibit the use of daylight in a new building, but their implications for the design should be considered carefully.

Building Configuration

Generally speaking, daylighting in multistory buildings will be most effective if the buildings are long and narrow so that daylight will have a chance to penetrate to the deep interior of both sides. A rule of thumb is that useful daylighting can be achieved with reasonably sized fenestration openings to a depth of about 25 feet. In single-story buildings, skylights can be used, permitting the building to assume a more square shape.

Courtyards, light wells, and atriums can be used effectively to admit daylight interior building spaces. Such wells, however, are not as effective as apertures open to the unobstructed outdoors. Light wells can be improved by using highly reflective finishes (white paint, concrete) on the well surfaces. However, if any direct sun illuminates these surfaces, they can become excessively bright. The effectiveness of wells can only be determined through testing of physical scale models.

Building Orientation

Usable daylight can be effectively admitted into apertures in walls of any orientation. The amount of daylight available will differ with each orientation. The _essential_ difference in both quality and quantity of daylighting received on different orientations has to do with direct sunlight. There is some difference in the brightness of the sky in different quadrants caused by the location of the sun at a particular moment, but this difference is of minor importance to the designer.

Apertures facing north will receive sky-contributed illumination only (assuming no direct sun) and will require larger glass areas than other orientations to achieve similar results. There are advantages to the north orientation (e.g., no sun control is necessary; illumination tends to be soft and diffuse), but sky glare-control can still be required.

East and west facades offer abundant useful daylight. These facades require controls to avoid excessive brightness and overheating from the early morning and late afternoon sun. This low-altitude sun, moving rapidly from east to west, is best controlled by some type of vertical louver. Horizontal louvers are of little help until the sun is relatively high in the sky; generally on the south facade.
Vertical louvers that can be adjusted (preferably automatically) will best respond to the sun's changing location on east and west facades. When opened fully (perpendicular to the window), vertical louvers obstruct vision to the exterior to only a minor degree. If movable vertical louvers are not feasible, static louvers can be used although vision to the exterior will be significantly limited. A combination of vertical and horizontal louvers can sometimes provide satisfactory control.

The south facade generally provides the best opportunity for daylighting since this orientation receives the maximum quantity and duration of daylight. Horizontal controls (e.g., overhangs, louvers, venetian blinds) can be effective controls. An advantage with the south orientation is that the sun, is high in the sky in the summer, but can easily be shaded by a horizontal device which allows some low-altitude sun penetration during the cold winter months.

If direct winter sun is allowed, care should be taken to ensure that it will not create excessive brightness in the occupant's field of view, thereby causing visual discomfort or disability.

Daylight Apertures

The amount of daylight entering an aperture is directly proportional to the size of the opening. At any point in the interior, the amount of daylight present is related to the area and brightness of both the exterior sources of daylight and interior daylighted surfaces that are "seen" from that particular point. A point close to the aperture sees a larger portion of the sky and has a higher footcandle level than a point farther away from the aperture. Interior brightness is influenced not only by direct light from the sky but by light reflected from other surfaces, particularly the ground. Horizontal overhangs pick up ground-reflected daylight and bounce it into interior spaces.

To maximize daylighting results, interior surfaces should be kept light in color (high reflectivity)--especially the ceiling, which is the most important light-reflecting surface.

If tasks at work-table height (i.e., 30 inches above the floor) are the
prime target for daylighting, glazing in apertures below work-table height
is essentially ineffective in lighting those tasks, even though it may
provide illumination to the floor surface. The higher the aperture above
the work-table task, the more daylight the task will receive, as the point
in question "sees" a brighter portion of the sky.

The height of the ceiling must permit the use of windows above the
work-task which are large enough to provide the desired daylight. Often
this suggests putting the top of the apertures at ceiling level.
Increasing the height of the ceiling while keeping the top of the
apertures at the former ceiling level will increase neither the quantity
nor the distribution of daylighting.

A horizontal aperture of given size will provide daylight over a wider
portion of a room than the same size opening placed vertically. The
vertical opening will produce a higher intensity of light over a smaller
area.

A clerestory high over a work-table will generally contribute a greater
quantity of daylight at that point than a vertical window because of the
greater brightness of the sky "seen." Likewise, a horizontal skylight
will allow a point to see a greater portion of the sky than a vertical
aperture of the same size.

Clerestory
L = 1.5H

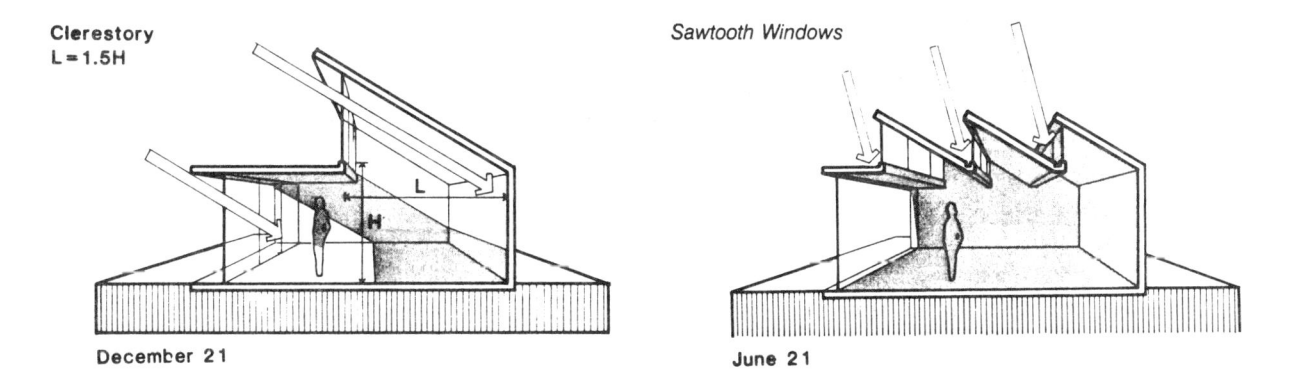

December 21

Sawtooth Windows

June 21

Figure 3.4.8.2 - Daylighting Clerestories

Clerestories (Figure 3.4.8.2) in single-story buildings are useful for
introducing and distributing daylight deep into interiors. They are also
high in the ceiling, out of the normal field of vision so that sky
brightness may not be a concern. Clerestories oriented to the east, west,
and south will probably need control of direct sun. Light-colored roof
materials such as white rock reflect daylight into the interior,
increasing the effectiveness of the aperture.

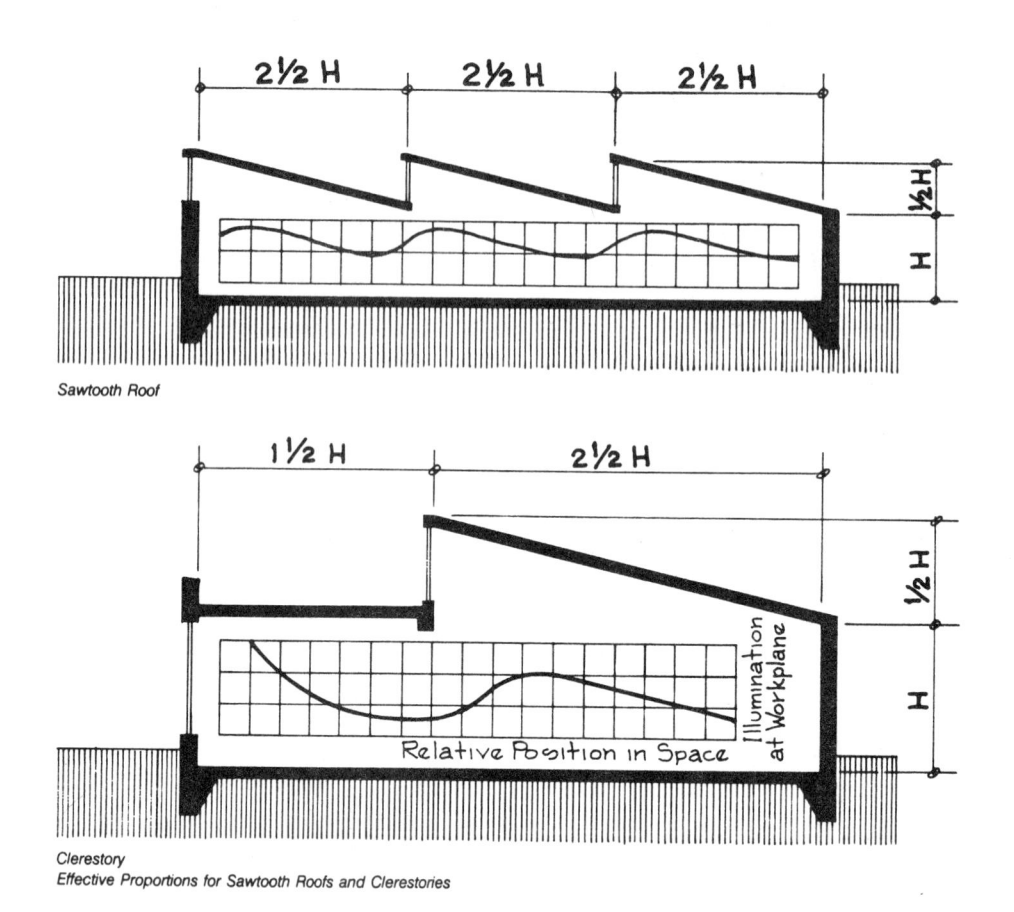

Figure 3.4.8.3 - Daylighting Sections

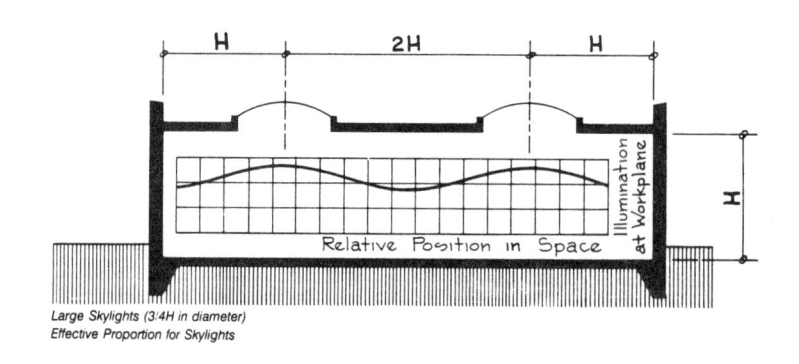

Figure 3.4.8.4 - Skylight Configurations

Skylights (Figure 3.4.8.3) are also effective, but controls are necessary for handling direct sun, thermal gains and losses, and visual brightness. Diffusing ceiling panels of translucent material, when illuminated by daylight, particularly direct sun, create glare and veiling reflections on work tasks similar to electric luminaires.

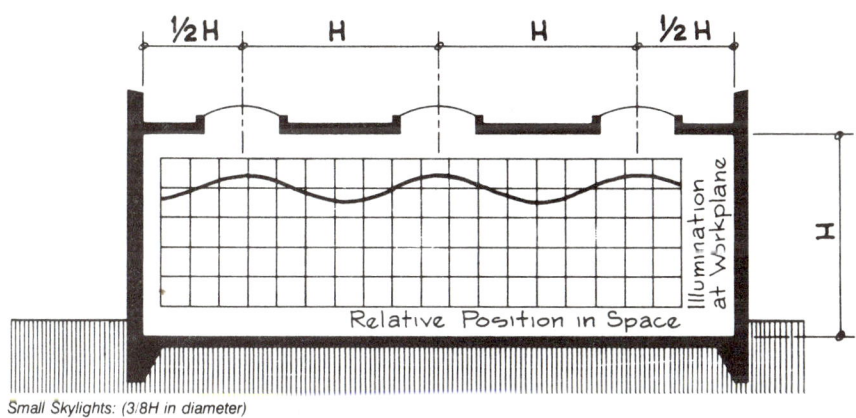

Small Skylights: (3/8H in diameter)

Figure 3.4.8.4 (continued) - Skylight Configurations

Horizontal roof skylights can also collect solar energy for heating and lighting in the winter, but be detrimental in warm weather. Shading devices above the skylight (on the roof) are most effective in keeping out excess solar radiation.

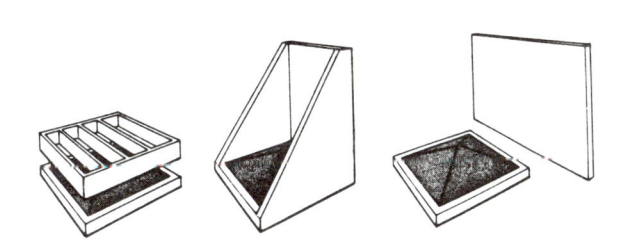

Figure 3.4.8.5 - Skylight Shading Devices

Skylights can loose considerable energy by exfiltration through cracks and by nighttime radiation. Shades and movable insulation should be considered. Double glazing is recommended in colder climates, and triple glazing for severely cold climates.

The "vision strip" (i.e., fenestration that provides a view from a normal sitting or standing position) will contribute a smaller portion of the daylight than the aperture higher in the wall. Glare control can be achieved by treating the vision strip differently from higher glazing areas.

Location of the aperture is an important element in the quantity and distribution of daylight received, but for purposes of preliminary thermal analysis the amount of heat exchange between exterior and interior is essentially a function of aperture size and transmission characteristics (see Section 3.4.2). Aperture size and the selection of transmission characteristics involve trade-offs among heat gain, heat loss, and daylighting needs. The location of the aperture is relatively unimportant to this thermal exchange.

Glare Control

Glare is a potential problem with any source of light. Exterior surfaces illuminated by the sun can be excessively bright when compared to interior surfaces illuminated by reflected daylight. The human eye has difficulty distinguishing detail when the field of view contains a wide range of brightnesses. Glare may cause only minor discomfort (which can still cause fatigue) or may create significant difficulty in seeing task surfaces properly.

Glare from direct sun can be eliminated by preventing visual contact with apertures, e.g., by orienting work stations so that occupants do not face toward the apertures while performing visual tasks. This is not always feasible, however. Trees can be planted outside the aperture so as to block the occupant's direct view of the bright sky and other outside surfaces. Overhangs and louvers, (on the exterior or interior) can be effective. Venetian blinds provide glare control and are movable to accommodate different sky conditions and user needs. Drapes and curtains can be effective. Care should be exercised in the selection of materials, sheer curtains can become excessively bright when illuminated by direct sun. Tinted glazing can be used to reduce the apparent brightness of exterior surfaces.

All of these techniques for reducing glare also reduce the amount of daylighting reaching the interior. Achieving a balance between glare control, aperture size, and glazing transmittance is a key element in daylighting design.

3.4.9 Physical Models

Procedures for evaluating daylighting designs should reflect the nature of information available at each phase of design. As the design proceeds, and decisions become more refined, so should the means of evaluating these decisions.

Scale models are useful in making the qualitative assessment that is the final arbiter of any design (see Figure 3.4.9.1). Light behaves in scale models exactly as it does in full-sized buildings. Because accurate data on available daylight are not available in all locations in the United States, scale models can be a necessary means of evaluating a design for daylighting. Models are particularly useful in "observing" the effects of daylight in a space, either with the naked eye or with a camera. An additional reason for using models is that there is no predictive technique that can evaluate the amount of illumination on a work surface when direct sun shines into a space.

During the <u>schematic phase</u> of design, a rough scale model, with openings cut for daylighting, can provide a rough estimate of the amount of illumination (footcandles) available on a work surface. Since these models can be constructed relatively quickly, several different concepts, as well as the same concept with windows in different places, can be prepared.

In the <u>development phase</u> of design, a more detailed scale model can help determine window sizes and locations. The model measures the amount of illumination on the work surface with an accuracy sufficient for this design stage.

Finally, a <u>full-scale mock-up</u> of key sections of the design can be made to evaluate final daylighting decisions.

Model Geometry
- In any daylighting model the size of the openings should be accurate, as should window frames, mullions, sills, jambs and skylight wells. Louvers must be represented if they block or reflect light.

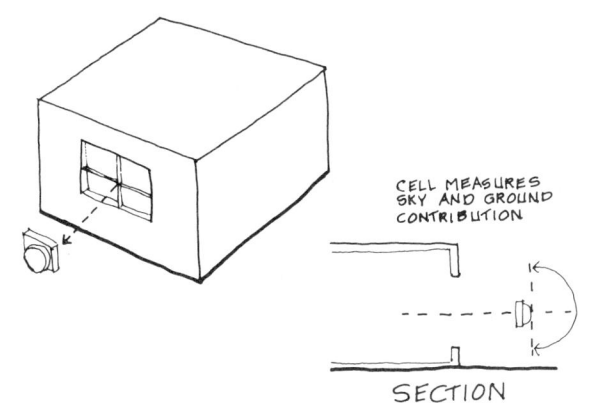

Measurement of Illumination on Vertical Surfaces

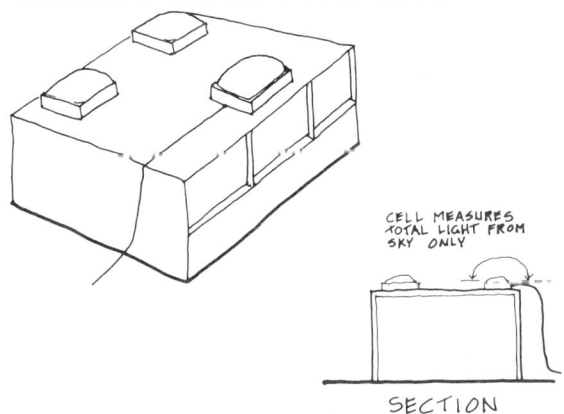

Measurement of Illumination on Horizontal Surfaces
SOURCE: Evans, Benjamin H., *Daylight in Architecture*, © 1981. Reprinted by permission of McGraw-Hill Book Co., New York

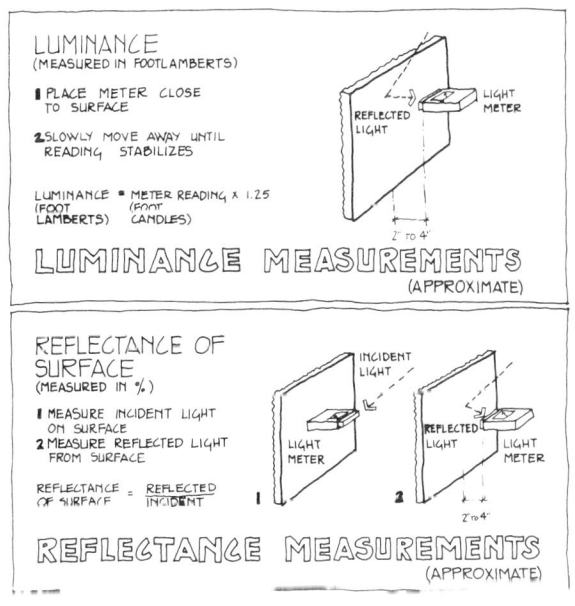

Measurement of Luminance and Reflectance
Note: Do not allow body to block any light when taking measurements.

Figure 3.4.9.1 - Daylighting Measurements

- Depth and reflectivity of window sills must be accurately represented.

Materials
- Materials used in the model should have the same opacity, transparency, reflectance and texture as those to be used in the building. Paint can be used to simulate most wall surfaces.
- Glass can be simulated with real glass of float glass quality.
- For overcast skies, plastic domes and skylights can be simulated with a flat covering of translucent or transparent material approximating the transmission properties of the dome material.

Scale
- Models can be constructed at any convenient scale; however, models should be large enough to reproduce details accurately and to accommodate an illumination meter probe without causing excessive reflection.
- A scale of 3/4 inches to one foot is convenient for daylighting studies of a room, but a 1/2- or 3/8-inch scale can be used if care is exercised in construction and measurement.

Instrumentation
- Many kinds of photometers (light meters) and photocells are available for daylighting studies.
- Most suitable photometers use a photovoltaic power cell; battery-operated photometers are also available.
- For measuring actual illumination levels, the photocell should be adapted with a color corrector (a "Viscor Filter") to screen out portions of the spectrum other than visible light.
- Because photocells are not as sensitive to light striking them from a low angle (as opposed to direct or high angles), they must also be fitted with a cosine correction device.
- A photometer should provide a range in measurement 1-12,000 footcandles.
- Caps can be made to adjust the percentage of light admitted to a photocell, making it possible, for example, to simulate the measurement of a lighting level of 2,000 footcandles with a photocell that has a maximum range of 1,000 footcandles.

Model Testing
- The outdoor location should approximate the sky and ground conditions for the proposed building.
- Ground conditions can make a significant difference in interior illumination levels and distribution because much of the light entering the building can be reflected from the ground.
- Exterior sky conditions must be measured at the beginning, during and at the end of model daylight tests to give a basis for test comparison and to indicate changing sky conditions. This is especially important if alternative design schemes are being compared.

Measurement of Ev and Eh

- Ev = illumination from the sky on the plane of the vertical fenestration or window wall and parallel to the wall (a few inches immediately outside the window but beyond any obstructing parts of the building, such as overhangs and louvers. This measurement is made by placing a photocell on the center of the vertical window wall of the model if there are no protruding building parts to restrict the light reaching the cell. This measurement provides an indication of the total light from the sky, plus the light reflected from the ground and surrounding objects near window openings. If the ground surface is to be altered in any way, the Ev reference measurement should include only the light from the sky; this can be accomplished by attaching a horizontal black shield to the light cell.

- Eh = total hemispheric illumination on the unobstructed plane of the ground from both the sun and sky (any distance from the ground up to several hundred feet is effective; usually the model roof is appropriate). This measurement is necessary when the model has horizontal openings. The measurement is made by placing the light cell on a flat surface, such as the model roof, where light from the sky will not be obstructed.

3.4.10 Daylighting Analysis by the Lumen Method

The Lumen Method, which is the method most widely used daylighting analysis tool in the United States, was developed by J. W. Griffith for Libbey-Owens-Ford Co. In this method, many different variables are taken into account, including sky conditions, position of sun, room size, glazing area and transmission characteristics such as overhangs, shades and blinds. The calculation technique is limited to predicting the amount of illumination (see Figure 3.4.10.1) on a centerline five feet from the window, five feet from the back wall, and at a point midway between, but can be modified by combining with area source comparative calculations to give reasonable values anywhere on a horizontal work plane.

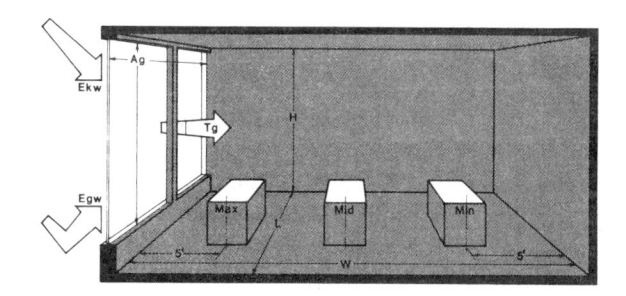

Figure 3.4.10.1 - Lumen Method Factors

The Lumen Method is as follows:

1. Determine solar altitude from a solar handbook or with a sun-angle calculator.

2. Choose sky conditions. Determine illumination on window (Ekw) and illumination on horizontal surfaces (Ekg) from Figure 3.4.10.2.

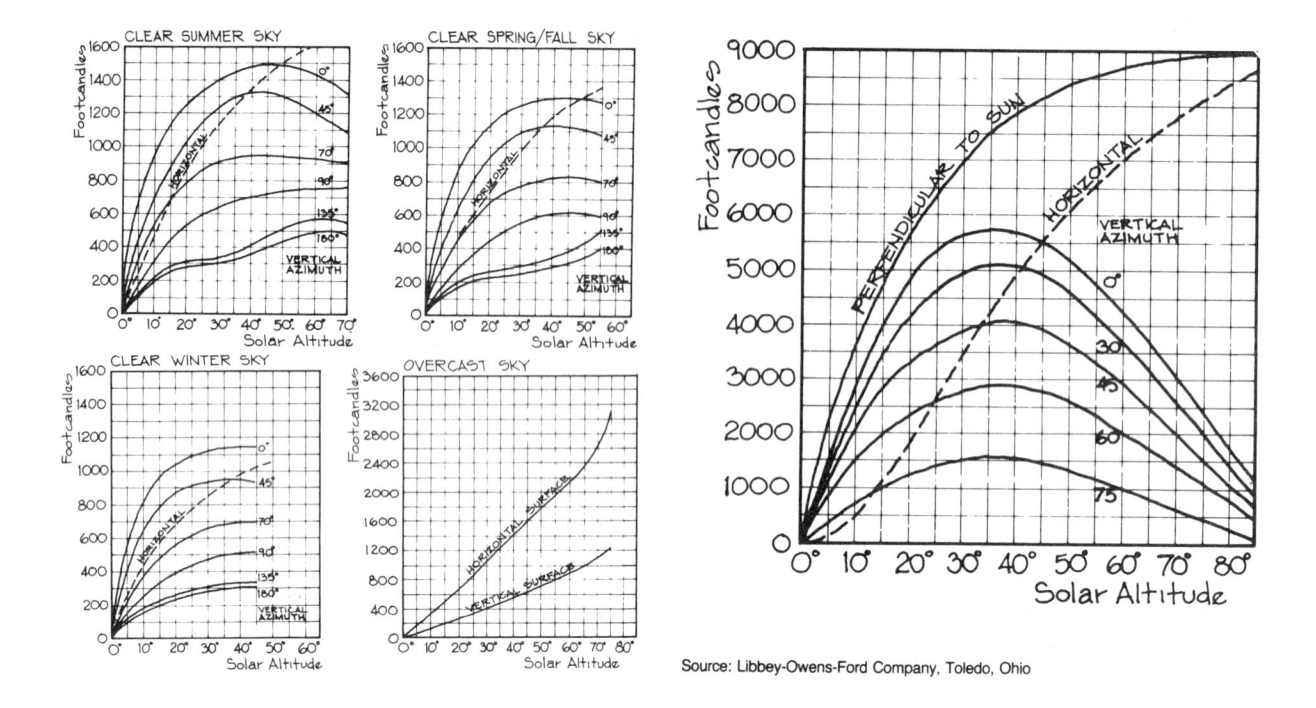

Figure 3.4.10.2 - Lumen Method

Figure 3.4.10.3 - Lumen Method

Source: Libbey-Owens-Ford Company, Toledo, Ohio

3. Determine solar illumination value (Euw and Eug) from Figure 3.4.10.3. Add to illumination on window (Ekw) and illumination on horizontal surfaces (Ekg).

<u>Illumination on ground (Ekug)</u> = illumination from sky on ground (Ekg) + illumination from sun on ground (Eug).

<u>Illumination on Window (Ekuw)</u> = illumination from sky on window (Ekw) + illumination from sun on window (Euw).

4. Multiply the illumination on the ground by the reflectance factor of the ground (rg) and the field proportion factor 0.5 to obtain the illumination on the window from the ground (Egw).

<u>Illumination from ground on window (Egw)</u> = illumination on ground (Ekug) x reflectance of ground surface (Rg) x 0.5.

5. Determine the total transmitting area (Ag) of the window, taking into account the metal frame. From manufacturers' product data, find the transmittance factor of the glass itself (Tg).

6. Determine room dimensions and reflectances of wall surfaces. Determine coefficients of utilization (C and K) from Figures 3.4.10.4 and 5. For diffusing shades use 1/2 total incident illumination from sun, sky and ground on window, or 1/2 x (Ekuw + Egw).

Coefficient of Utilization (C)
Overcast Sky

	Room Length	20'		30'		40'	
	Wall Reflectance	70%	30%	70%	30%	70%	30%
	Room Width						
Max	20'	.0276	.0251	.0191	.0173	.0143	.0137
	30'	.0272	.0248	.0188	.0172	.0137	.0131
	40'	.0269	.0246	.0182	.0171	.0133	.0130
Mid	20'	.0159	.0117	.0101	.0087	.0081	.0071
	30'	.0058	.0050	.0054	.0040	.0034	.0033
	40'	.0039	.0027	.0030	.0023	.0022	.0019
Min	20'	.0087	.0053	.0063	.0043	.0050	.0037
	30'	.0032	.0019	.0029	.0017	.0020	.0014
	40'	.0019	.0009	.0016	.0009	.0012	.0008

C_{os} Coefficients of utilization (C) for room length and width, illuminated by overcast sky.
Lumen Method: Table 5
Source: Libbey-Owens-Ford Company, Toledo, Ohio

Coefficient of Utilization (C)
Clear Sky

	Room Length	20'		30'		40'	
	Wall Reflectance	70%	30%	70%	30%	70%	30%
	Room Width						
Max	20'	.0206	.0173	.0143	.0123	.0110	.0098
	30'	.0203	.0173	.0137	.0120	.0098	.0092
	40'	.0200	.0168	.0131	.0119	.0096	.0091
Mid	20'	.0153	.0104	.0100	.0079	.0083	.0067
	30'	.0082	.0054	.0062	.0043	.0046	.0037
	40'	.0052	.0032	.0040	.0028	.0029	.0023
Min	20'	.0106	.0060	.0079	.0049	.0067	.0043
	30'	.0054	.0028	.0047	.0023	.0032	.0021
	40'	.0031	.0014	.0027	.0013	.0021	.0012

C_{cs} Coefficients of utilization (C) for room length and width, illuminated by clear sky (with or without direct sun).
Lumen Method: Table 5
Source: Libbey-Owens-Ford Company, Toledo, Ohio

Coefficient of Utilization (C)
Ground

	Room Length	20'		30'		40'	
	Wall Reflectance	70%	30%	70%	30%	70%	30%
	Room Width						
Max	20'	.0147	.0112	.0102	.0088	.0081	.0071
	30'	.0141	.0112	.0098	.0088	.0077	.0070
	40'	.0137	.0112	.0093	.0086	.0072	.0069
Mid	20'	.0128	.0090	.0094	.0071	.0073	.0060
	30'	.0083	.0057	.0062	.0048	.0050	.0041
	40'	.0055	.0037	.0044	.0033	.0042	.0026
Min	20'	.0106	.0071	.0082	.0054	.0067	.0044
	30'	.0061	.0026	.0041	.0023	.0033	.0021
	40'	.0029	.0018	.0026	.0012	.0022	.0011

C_{ug} Cofficients of utilization (C) for room length and width, illuminated by uniform ground light.
Lumen Method: Table 5
Source: Libbey-Owens-Ford Company, Toledo, Ohio

Figure 3.4.10.4 - Lumen Method

Ground

Room Length	20'		30'		40'	
Wall Reflectance	70%	30%	70%	30%	70%	30%
	Room Width					
Max 20'	.0556	.0556	.0392	.0426	.0303	.0348
Max 30'	.0528	.0539	.0370	.0433	.0289	.0337
Max 40'	.0506	.0544	.0359	.0426	.0278	.0344
Mid 20'	.0556	.0556	.0414	.0459	.0320	.0381
Mid 30'	.0367	.0356	.0274	.0308	.0217	.0270
Mid 40'	.0239	.0233	.0192	.0222	.0153	.0181
Min 20'	.0556	.0556	.0430	.0486	.0328	.0398
Min 30'	.0261	.0228	.0217	.0211	.0170	.0192
Min 40'	.0128	.0108	.0119	.0107	.0098	.0097

C_{gv} Coefficients of utilization for room length and width, illuminated by ground light through horizontal louvers.
Lumen Method: Table 5
Source: Libbey-Owens-Ford Company, Toledo, Ohio

Figure 3.4.10.4 (continued) - Lumen Method

Coefficient of Utilization (K)
Overcast Sky

Ceiling Ht.	8'		10'		12'		14'	
Wall Reflectance	70%	30%	70%	30%	70%	30%	70%	30%
	Room Width							
Max 20'	.1250	.1290	.1210	.1230	.1110	.1110	.0991	.0973
Max 30'	.1220	.1310	.1220	.1210	.1110	.1110	.0945	.0973
Max 40'	.1450	.1330	.1310	.1260	.1110	.1110	.0973	.0982
Mid 20'	.0908	.0982	.1070	.1150	.1110	.1110	.1050	.1220
Mid 30'	.1560	.1020	.0939	.1130	.1110	.1110	.1210	.1340
Mid 40'	.1060	.0948	.1230	.1070	.1110"	.1110	.1350	.1270
Min 20'	.0908	.1020	.0951	.1140	.1110	.1110	.1180	.1340
Min 30'	.0924	.1190	.1010	.1140	.1110	.1110	.1250	.1260
Min 40'	.1110	.0926	.1250	.1090	.1110	.1110	.1330	.1300

Ceiling Ht.	8'		10'		12'		14'	
Wall Reflectance	70%	30%	70%	30%	70%	30%	70%	30%
	Room Width							
Max 20'	.1450	.1550	.1290	.1320	.1110	.1110	.1010	.0982
Max 30'	.1410	.1490	.1250	.1300	.1110	.1110	.0954	.1010
Max 40'	.1570	.1570	.1350	.1340	.1110	.1110	.0964	.0991
Mid 20'	.1100	.1280	.1160	.1260	.1110	.1110	.1030	.1080
Mid 30'	.1060	.1250	.1110	.1290	.1110	.1110	.1120	.1200
Mid 40'	.1170	.1180	.1220	.1180	.1110	.1110	.1230	.1220
Min 20'	.1050	.1290	.1120	.1300	.1110	.1110	.1110	.1160
Min 30'	.0994	.1440	.1070	.1260	.1110	.1110	.1070	.1240
Min 40'	.1190	.1160	.1300	.1180	.1110	.1110	.1200	.1180

K_{cs} Coefficients of utilization (K) for ceiling height and room width, illuminated by clear sky (with or without direct sun).
Lumen Method: Table 6
Source: Libbey-Owens-Ford Company, Toledo, Ohio

Figure 3.4.10.5 - Lumen Method

Coefficient of Utilization (K)
Ground

Ceiling Ht.		8'		10'		12'		14'	
Wall Reflectance		70%	30%	70%	30%	70%	30%	70%	30%
	Room Width								
Max	20'	.1240	.2060	.1400	.1350	.1110	.1110	.0909	.0859
	30'	.1820	.1880	.1400	.1430	.1110	.1110	.0918	.0878
	40'	.1240	.1820	.1400	.1420	.1110	.1110	.0936	.0879
Mid	20'	.1230	.1450	.1220	.1290	.1110	.1110	.1000	.0945
	30'	.0966	.1040	.1070	.1120	.1110	.1110	.1100	.1050
	40'	.0790	.0786	.0999	.1060	.1110	.1110	.1180	.1180
Min	20'	.0994	.1080	.1100	.1140	.1110	1110	.1070	.1040
	30'	.0816	.0822	.0984	.1050	.1110	.1110	.1210	.1160
	40'	.0700	.0656	.0946	.0986	.1110	.1110	.1250	.1320

K_{ug} Coefficients of utilization (K) for ceiling height and room width, illuminated by uniform ground light.
Lumen Method: Table 6

Source: Libbey-Owens-Ford Company, Toledo, Ohio

Coefficient of Utilization (K)
Diffuse Shade
Sky

Ceiling Ht.		8'		10'		12'		14'	
Wall Reflectance		70%	30%	70%	30%	70%	30%	70%	30%
	Room Width								
Max	20'	.1450	.1540	.1230	.1280	.1110	.1110	.0991	.0964
	30'	.1410	.1510	.1260	.1280	.1110	.1110	.0945	.0964
	40'	.1590	.1570	.1370	.1270	.1110	.1110	.0973	.0964
Mid	20'	.1010	.1160	.1150	.1250	.1110	.1110	.1010	.1100
	30'	.0952	.1130	.1050	.1220	.1110	.1110	.1100	.1220
	40'	.1110	.1050	.1240	.1070	.1110	.1110	.1300	.1240
Min	20'	.0974	.1110	.1070	.1210	.1110	.1110	.1120	.1190
	30'	.0956	.1250	.1030	.1170	.1110	.1110	.1150	.1250
	40'	.1110	.1050	.1250	.1110	.1110	.1110	.1330	.1240

K_{us} Coefficients of utilization (K) for ceiling height and room width, illuminated by uniform sky light through diffuse window shade.
Lumen Method: Table 6

Source: Libbey-Owens-Ford Company, Toledo, Ohio

Coefficient of Utilization (K)
Diffuse Shade
Ground

Ceiling Ht.		8'		10'		12'		14'	
Wall Reflectance		70%	30%	70%	30%	70%	30%	70%	30%
	Room Width								
MAX	20'	.1240	.2060	.1400	.1350	.111	.111	.0909	.0859
	30'	.1820	.1880	.1400	.1430	.111	.111	.0918	.0878
	40'	.1240	.1820	.1400	.1420	.111	.111	.0936	.0879
MID	20'	.1230	.1450	.1220	.1290	.111	.111	.1000	.0945
	30'	.0966	.1040	.1070	.1120	.111	.111	.1100	.1050
	40'	.0790	.0786	.0999	.1060	.111	.111	.1180	
MIN	20'	.0994	.1080	.1100	.1140	.111	.111	.1070	.1040
	30'	.0816	.0822	.0984	.1050	.111	.111	.1210	.1160
	40'	.0700	.0656	.0946	.0986	.111	.111	.1250	.1320

K_{ug} Coefficients of utilization (K) for ceiling height and room width, illuminated by uniform ground light through diffuse window shade.
Lumen Method: Table 6

Source: Libbey-Owens-Ford Company, Toledo, Ohio.

Figure 3.4.10.5 (continued) – Lumen Method

7. Multiply the values of illumination on the window by the window factors and the coefficients of utilization, separately for light from the ground and light from the sky (Ekwp and Egwp).

Illumination from sky on work plane (Ekwp) = illumination on window (Ekuw) x window area of transmittance (Ag) x transmittance of glass for average daylight (Tg) x coefficient of utilization (C) x coefficient of utilization (K).

Illumination from ground on work plane (Egwp) = illumination from ground on window (Egw) x area of transmittance (Ag) x transmittance of glass for average daylight (Tg) x coefficient of utilization (C) x coefficient of utilization (K).

8. Add the values found in step 7 in order to obtain the total illumination of the work plane in footcandles.

Total Illumination on Work Plane = illumination from sky on work plane (Ekwp) + illumination from ground on work plane (Egwp).

3.5 STRUCTURE AND MASS

3.5.1 Introduction

Heat losses or gains through a building envelope can be relatively large or small. Heat gain can be attributed to lights, occupants, equipment and solar. Heat losses and sometimes gains are attributable to envelope transmission and ventilation, including infiltration. A relatively large heat loss or gain will require substantial energy consumption to maintain a reasonably constant indoor temperature. Ideally, such a thermal balance--in which a building's gross heat gains equal its heat losses-- would be achievable with only minimal expenditures for purchased energy. The characteristics of the building envelope determine the nature of the energy flow. However, the building's thermal mass determines the rate and therefore timing of this energy flow. Mass can be manipulated to reduce purchased energy costs by balancing heat loss and gain.

In temperate climates, thermal mass can play a major role in a tight envelope-dominant building. For load-dominant buildings, a relatively loose envelope may offer less restriction to energy flow, while the structural mass maintains a thermal inertia cycle. This delay is sometimes referred to as a thermal flywheel. When heat energy enters or is generated within a building, a portion of it is absorbed by the building's mass and stored there for delayed, or future, use. For example, the heat stored in thermal mass in the daytime may not be released until nighttime, counteracting the exterior diurnal temperature swing. This can result in significant energy savings.

3.5.2 Storage Strategies

Heat storage can be either "controlled" or "uncontrolled." In controlled storage, heat is manipulated and moved by fans, movable insulation or other mechanical means. In uncontrolled heat storage, a mass storage medium accepts, stores, radiates heat and distributes convective heat on the basis of the physical properties of the material, not mechanical controls. The selection of controlled or uncontrolled storage depends on the opportunities and constraints of the project.

Thermal mass storage determines the magnitude of temperature swings that will be experienced in a building. The average daily temperature can be within the comfort range but, if there is inadequate thermal mass, temperature swings will be large, resulting in the building being uncomfortably warm in the afternoon and uncomfortably cold at night. As shown in Figure 3.5.2.1, the difference between the average inside and outside temperatures is affected primarily by the building load and the amount of solar gain, while the magnitude of temperature swing is governed principally by the amount and the effectiveness of thermal storage. It is generally desirable to provide high thermal mass when outside temperatures swing above and below the interior design temperature. Generally, low-thermal mass buildings will perform better when the outside temperature is consistently above or below the acceptable indoor temperature.

High Thermal Mass Wall:
Small Temperature Variation

Low Thermal Mass Wall:
Large Temperature Variation

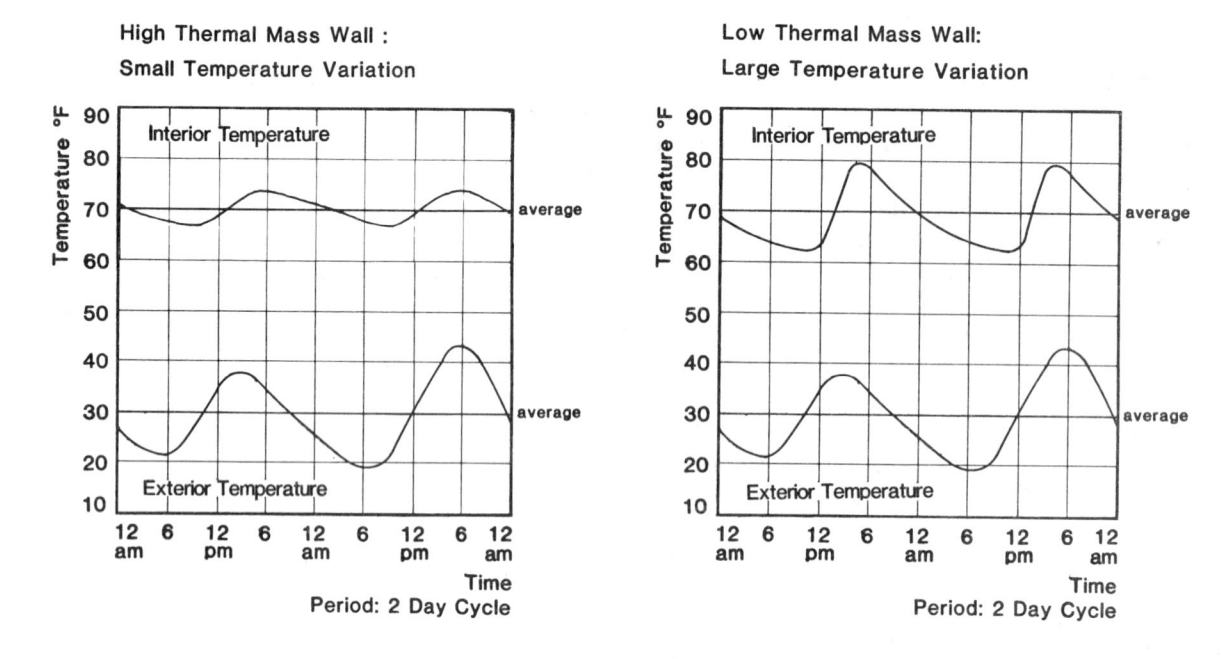

Figure 3.5.2.1 - Average Temperature and Temperature Swing

The volume of heat storage is usually limited as much by building area and construction costs as by solar availability. Storage capacity should generally provide at least enough heat for a one-day cycle.

Commercial buildings with a large internal heat gains can require mechanically controlled heat storage strategies. Heat removed from one zone can be mechanically transferred to another zone or to a remote storage mass. Water source heat pumps can transfer internal heat to the building perimeter and heat recovered from electric lighting can be sent to water storage tanks for future recall.

In residential and light commercial skin-dominated buildings, an uncontrolled heat storage strategy would be based on the thermal flywheel effect. Energy stored in mass of the building (floor, walls or overhead) during solar-charging hours would be released or reradiated from the storage components after sundown. If storage mass is integral with the structure of the building poorly sized mass will provide inadequate heating at night if there is too much mass and overheating in the day if there is too little mass. The major objectives of using thermal mass, whether controlled or uncontrolled storage, is to avoid large temperature fluctuations.

3.5.3 Location of Thermal Mass

Thermal mass in a building can be either an integral component of the structural system (walls, floors and roofs) or isolated in rock beds or water storage areas. In underground construction, the mass is actually the earth surrounding the exterior of the structure.

Envelope

Locating thermal mass within the building envelope can serve as a mediator between the external and internal factors governing the thermal equilibrium. The building envelope will both restrict and delay the energy flow.

Internal Mass

The efficient use of a given quantity of material is achieved by spreading the mass over as large an area as possible. This will minimize the thickness of the mass layer and maximize performance. Charging of the storage mass is most effective when the mass is located in a zone that experiences direct solar gains (see Figure 3.5.3.1). Charging thermal mass can be accomplished with diffuse glazing materials.

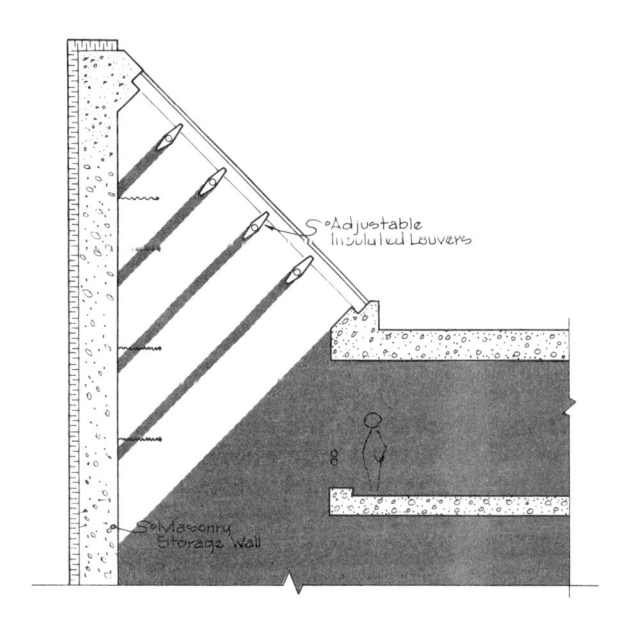

Figure 3.5.3.1 - Interior Thermal Mass

Isolated Mass

If solar charging of a building is not feasible or internal heat gains are significant, energy can be recovered and stored for later use in a remote area within the building. Rock-beds and water tanks are common sensible heat storage systems.

Exterior Mass

Early designs using underground construction as an energy-conserving technique surrounded the structure with earth in order to moderate the extremes of exterior temperature. Designs now use the earth to serve as thermal storage mass as well temperature moderator. Careful detailing and construction attention are required to maintain a dry, insulated earth mass around a building.

Using this technique the underground structure is surrounded by a mass of earth that is covered by an umbrella of insulation and moisture protection. The insulation umbrella and watershed, is covered by a second layer of earth, which isolates the storage mass around the structure. The heat conducted through the building shell to the surrounding earth actually modifies the climate in the soil to produce a new thermal earth environment. This large earth mass, which has a tremendous amount of thermal storage, heats up very slowly and releases heat slowly. Consequently, this heat flow system will maintain an interior temperature which varies only a few degrees all year.

3.5.4 Materials for Energy Storage

Solar heat is stored in two ways: as sensible heat and as latent heat.

Sensible heat energy, which is the commonly understood form of heat, is stored by increasing the temperature of solids, e.g., concrete, masonry, rocks, earth, or liquids such as water.

Latent heat energy storage involve the various heat of fusion chemical compounds, such as paraffin waxes and inorganic salt hydrates. A chemical heat storage medium can absorb and store significant amounts of heat as it undergoes the phase transition from the solid to the liquid state--releasing the heat later as reverts to the solid state. For pure substances, the heat storage takes place at a constant temperature that corresponds to the melting point of the substance. A variety of problems exist for phase-change materials, and they are not yet ready for widespread application.

Structural mass that supports building loads at the wall, floor or roof can provide heat storage, as can architectural (non-load-bearing) elements with significant mass (i.e., coverings of partitions, walls or ceilings).

Common commercial materials used as building mass include concrete, masonry, concrete masonry units, gypsum board, and adobe block. Solid thermal storage materials absorb, conduct and distribute heat throughout the mass. Liquid thermal mass, on the other hand, absorbs heat more effectively because convection loops are established which mix the fluid. This lowers the temperature of the liquid at the container walls and improves its ability to absorb more heat there.

The choice of a thermal storage system (solid vs. liquid, and type of solids and liquids) should be based on the following trade-off criteria:
- high storage capacity per unit mass and volume
- suitable properties in the desired operating temperature range
- uniform temperature of storage mass
- capability to charge and discharge at high heat input/output rates without penalties from temperature gradients
- in remote storage systems, small self-discharging rate, i.e., small heat losses to the surroundings
- long, reliable life
- inexpensive.

Solid Thermal Mass

Solid materials conduct heat from surface to interior at a slow rate. The following rules of thumb can be used to avoid overheating and large

temperature fluctuations:
- Interior walls and floors of masonry should be at least 4 inches in thickness.
- Diffuse sunlight directed over the surface area of the masonry, either by using a translucent glazing material or by reflecting direct sunlight off light-colored interior surfaces first.
- Masonry floors should be of a dark color.
- Masonry walls of any color.
- Use lightweight construction (little thermal mass) for non-storage building components; a light color to reflect sunlight to masonry surfaces.
- Use limited direct sunlight on dark masonry surfaces for long periods of time.
- Use internal insulating devices if needed to control radiation from thermal storage mass.
- Use exterior insulating devices on a glass wall if needed to diminish nighttime heat loss.
- Use exterior sunshading if needed to prevent unwanted heating of thermal storage mass.
- Use exterior vents as needed for the summer cooling mode.

Water Storage

Masonry and water thermal storage walls collect and distribute heat to a space in much the same way. Within the wall, the liquid mass transfers heat by convection rather than by conduction. In a water wall the liquid heats up uniformly, using all the thermal mass. This is in contrast to a masonry wall, heat passes slowly from the surface to the interior. A liquid wall exposed to direct sunlight can be better at both long-term storage and at avoiding immediate release of heat into a space. As in the solid walls, the exterior face of water walls are often painted black or dark colors for maximum solar absorption. Vertical storage tubes and the containers used for roof ponds are often transparent, however.

When using a water wall for heat storage:
- The wall should be located to receive direct sunlight between the hours of 10 a.m. and 2 p.m.
- The surface of the container exposed to direct sunlight should be of a dark color (at least 75-percent solar absorption).
- Roughly one cubic foot (7.48 gallons) of water is needed for each square foot of south glazing. (The designer may want to vary this according to the temperature fluctuation desired in the space.)

Rock-Bed Storage

A rock bed is a remote thermal storage system using uniformly sized rocks that can load and unload heat by means of thermosiphoning. Thermosiphoning relies on the gravity principle of denser cold air falling, and consequently, hot air rising.

As a rule of thumb, if used in conjunction with a solar collector system, about 200 pounds of rock (or 2 net cubic feet) per square foot of collector window should be used.

The cross section of the storage bin should be approximately two-thirds the area of the collector.

Minimum allowable rock size is one-twentieth of rock bin depth.

To avoid reverse thermosiphoning:
- The <u>bottom</u> of the storage bed should be <u>above</u> the top of the collector. In a water thermosiphon, the ideal distance is 2 feet between the top of the collector and the bottom of the storage tank.
- Backdraft dampers should be designed to close and seal air passages when airflow reverses. These dampers can be manually operated.
- Both the inlet and the outlet should be placed at the top of the collector. As a result, a cold air "plug" will develop at night, with both columns of cold air of the same length, tending not to move.
- Clean, round rocks, not broken or flat, and all of the same diameter, should be used. Angular rocks and rocks of varying size pack more tightly in the bin than uniformly sized rocks, causing higher pressure drops.
- Access to rock bin should be provided for cleaning.
- The building should be placed on top of the rock bin so that heat flow can be passive, moving vertically into the usable space.
- The storage bin should be insulated.
- The system should be ventilated during the summer, to avoid heat collection or storage.
- Airflow directions through the rock bin should be vertical. Hot air from the collector should feed <u>downward</u>, with cool air from the bottom returning to the collector. Hot air delivered to building spaces should be taken from the top of the rock bin. Cold air should return at the bottom of the rock bin.

3.5.5 Mass Storage for Heating and Cooling

Heating

Solar charging of a building space is achieved by the sunlight that heats the air or substances within the space. Materials in direct sunlight are slightly more effective than other surfaces. Lightweight, dark-colored materials in the sun can store little heat and thus become quite hot, emitting the absorbed solar heat relatively quickly by

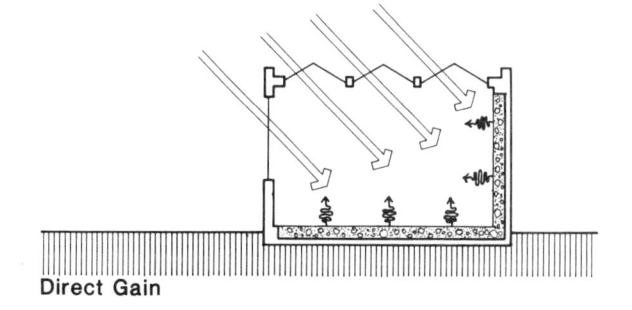

Figure 3.5.5.1 - Thermal Mass for Heating

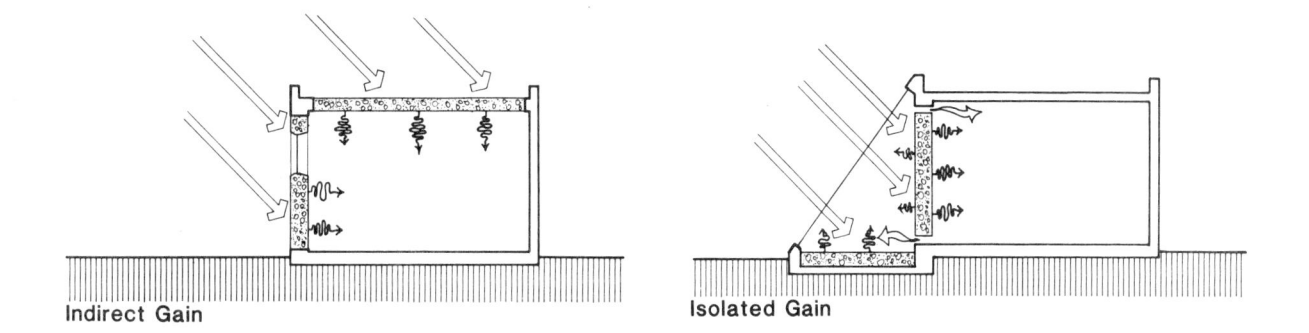

Figure 3.5.5.1 (continued) - Thermal Mass for Heating

convection to the room air or by radiation to other surfaces. If most of the solar energy heats air instead of the storage mass there will be large rapid temperature increases in the space. When the sun is clouded or goes down, there will also be large rapid temperature drops. If the mass is not irradiated by direct or reflected sunlight, both the ability of the mass to moderate temperature swings and to provide heat when the sun is gone are reduced (see Figure 3.5.5.1).

Heat absorbed by the surface of the structural mass wall or floor travels through the solid mass gradually by conduction. As the sun goes down, the heat in the deepest level of the mass gradually returns to the surface conductively. If the mass is too thick, heat will not return to the surface soon enough, possibly 24 hours later when heat is unneeded because the wall or floor is again receiving solar radiation. If the mass is even thicker, the deeper portions do not receive any solar heat.

The thickness or depth of liquid mass storage containers becomes a design or cost issue rather than a thermal concern. There can be temperature stratification in the liquid storage systems, mass temperature is generally uniform because the incoming heat creates convective mixing.

Cooling

If natural ventilation is desired but there is little or no wind, the thermal mass of a building can be designed to induce ventilation by duplicating the natural temperature stratifications that cause wind itself.

In the cooling season thermal storage systems used in the winter for heat collection can be used to complement cooling and night ventilation systems. During the day the building is closed to outside air with the storage mass acting as a heat sink (see Figure 3.5.5.2). Rock beds can be used as thermal storage for night ventilation systems. Cool night air can be stored in the rock bed and, during the day, air from interior spaces can be directed through the rocks to be cooled. Rock beds have the advantage of a large surface area, allowing for rapid heat exchange. At night, the heat absorbed during the day is removed and both the storage

Night Ventilation

Reradiation

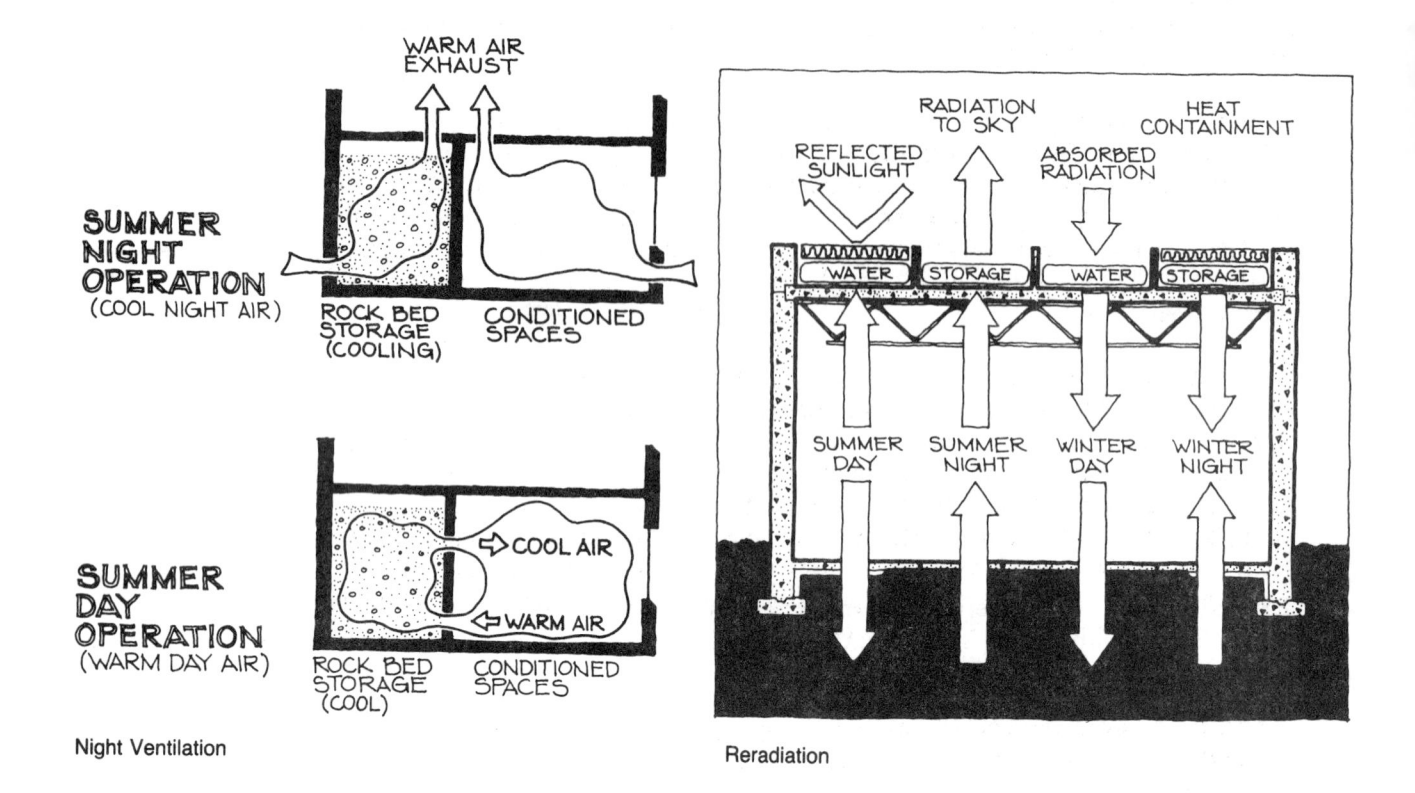

Figure 3.5.5.2 - Thermal Mass for Cooling

and the interior of the building are "flushed out". Cool night air is brought into the building and warm air is discharged. See Section 3.5.7, Passive Cooling Systems, for further detail.

3.5.6 Passive Heating Systems

Solar charging of the building's mass can be achieved by using three basic systems: direct gain, indirect gain and isolated gain.

Direct Gain

Direct-gain systems can be used in climate regions that do not experience daytime overheating or severely cold temperatures, because this solar technology (see Figure 3.5.6.1) requires a great deal of glass exposure in the occupied space.

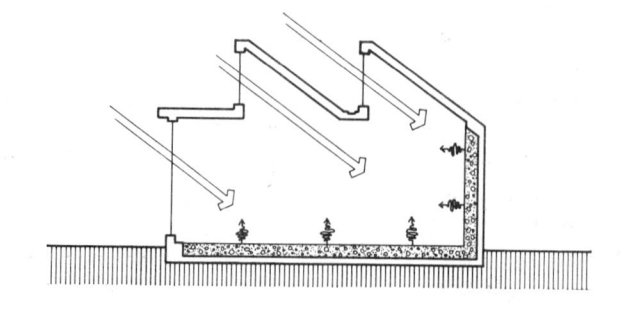

Figure 3.5.6.1 - Direct Gain Storage

The basic characteristics of the direct gain building are: a south-facing collector area, conditioned spaces exposed directly behind, and absorber-storage floors and walls.

Typically, double-glazed windows, clerestories or skylights are used for collection. The floors, walls, ceiling or freestanding masonry elements or water containers absorb heat and store it within their mass. Heat distribution is by reradiation and natural convection, regulated mainly by location of the storage medium within the conditioned spaces. Heat loss to the outside is controlled by insulating the glazing at night and on sunless winter days.

Up to a point, the use of direct gain is fairly straightforward. If the heat from direct gain can be used immediately, there is no need for storage. Direct gain can be used to supply up to 30-40 percent of the building requirements without special concern for thermal storage. As the glazing area is increased, it is necessary to consider how the heat will be stored in the building materials and what temperature swings will result. If very large glazed areas are required, then the designer must use thermal storage carefully to prevent overheating. With large glazing areas, night insulation should be considered.

Advantages:
- flexibility of architectural design
- standard construction materials can be used
- ease of operation
- collection glass area provides light to occupied space and provides views to the outside.

Disadvantages:
- building orientation is dictated by sun position, except for roof monitors
- glare and overheating are possible unless controls are well-designed
- ultraviolet degradation and fading of fabrics occurs without controls
- solar collection temperatures are limited by occupant comfort needs.

Absorber and Storage.
In some direct gain systems, excess heat is ducted from the direct gain space to other spaces and/or to remote rock bed or water storage for later use. More commonly, the heat is stored in structural thermal mass within the direct gain space. If this is the case, the absorber and storage are essentially the same. Absorption and storage

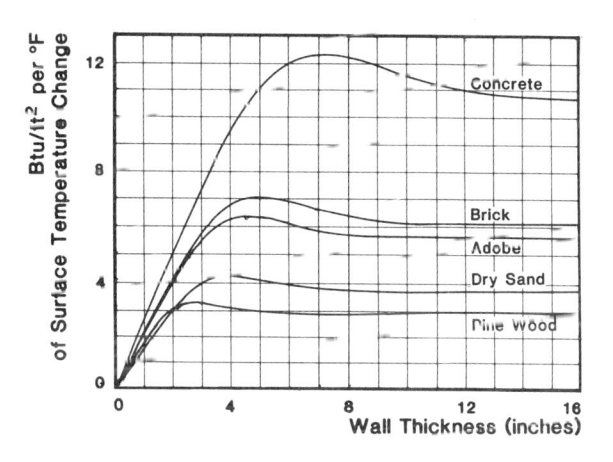

Figure 3.5.6.2 - Heat Capacity

of heat in a space are the primary challenges to the designer of a direct gain system. If a major reliance is to be placed on direct gain for space heating, roughly 65 percent of the solar energy admitted into a space must be stored in the structure (walls and/or floor and/or ceiling) for use during the night.

The graph in Figure 3.5.6.2 shows the diurnal heat capacity of walls and floors made of various thermal mass materials. The diurnal heat capacity of a material surface is the daily amount of heat per unit of surface area that is stored and then given back at night, per degree of temperature difference between day and night. The mass is assumed to be insulated on the side away from the room. Using this curve, it is possible to assess, for example, the value of a 6-inch concrete mass over a 5-inch concrete mass. The extra inch is only 35 percent as effective as the inch at the surface, so the designer might consider placing that extra inch somewhere else where it would be more effective. Note that the effectiveness of concrete mass beyond an 8-inch thickness becomes negative because of time-phasing. Brick and adobe mass walls and floors peak at about 5 inches.

The area of mass surface is the most important variable in direct gain design. A minimum mass area of three times the glazing area is essential and six to nine times is recommended to control temperature swings.

Direct sunlight can be diffused over the surface area of the thermal mass in a space by using a translucent glazing material, by placing a number of small windows so that they admit sunlight in patches, or by reflecting direct sunlight off a light-colored interior surface first, thus diffusing it throughout the space. Figure 3.5.6.3 gives recommended thermal storage mass of water or masonry for each square foot of south glazing, given the percentage of a building's heating load to be satisfied by a direct gain system. This assumes that the mass is in the direct sun all day. In direct gain situations, this is adequate thermal storage, provided:

Expected Solar Savings	Recommended Effective Thermal Storage per sq ft of solar collection area	
	Pounds of Water	Pounds of Masonry
10%	6	30
20%	12	60
30%	18	90
40%	24	120
50%	30	150
60%	36	180
70%	42	210
80%	48	240
90%	54	270

Figure 3.5.6.3 - Sizing Storage

- the mass is within the direct gain space or encloses the direct gain space
- the mass is not insulated from the space
- the mass has an exposed surface area equal to at least three times the glazed area.

Location. The performance of direct gain buildings is relatively insensitive to the distribution of thermal storage mass within a space. The optimal location is in the floor directly behind the glazed area, although buildings with an identical amount of thermal storage mass in the walls will perform within a few percent of the optimal system. If one or more layers of the glazing are diffuse, the significance of mass distribution is further reduced because of the uniform distribution of transmitted solar radiation. Thermal storage mass located on east, west, or north walls is almost as effective as that located on the floor. It is, therefore, generally desirable to distribute mass about the direct gain area as uniformly as possible.

Indirect Gain

Indirect-gain systems can be used in most climate regions. In indirect gain systems, sunlight strikes a thermal mass located between the sun and the space. The sunlight absorbed by the mass is converted to thermal energy and transferred into the conditioned spaces. Because conditioned spaces do not receive solar radiation immediately, indirect gain systems offer greater control over temperature swings and overheating.

Sunspace/Trombe Wall System

Trombe Wall System

Roof Pond System

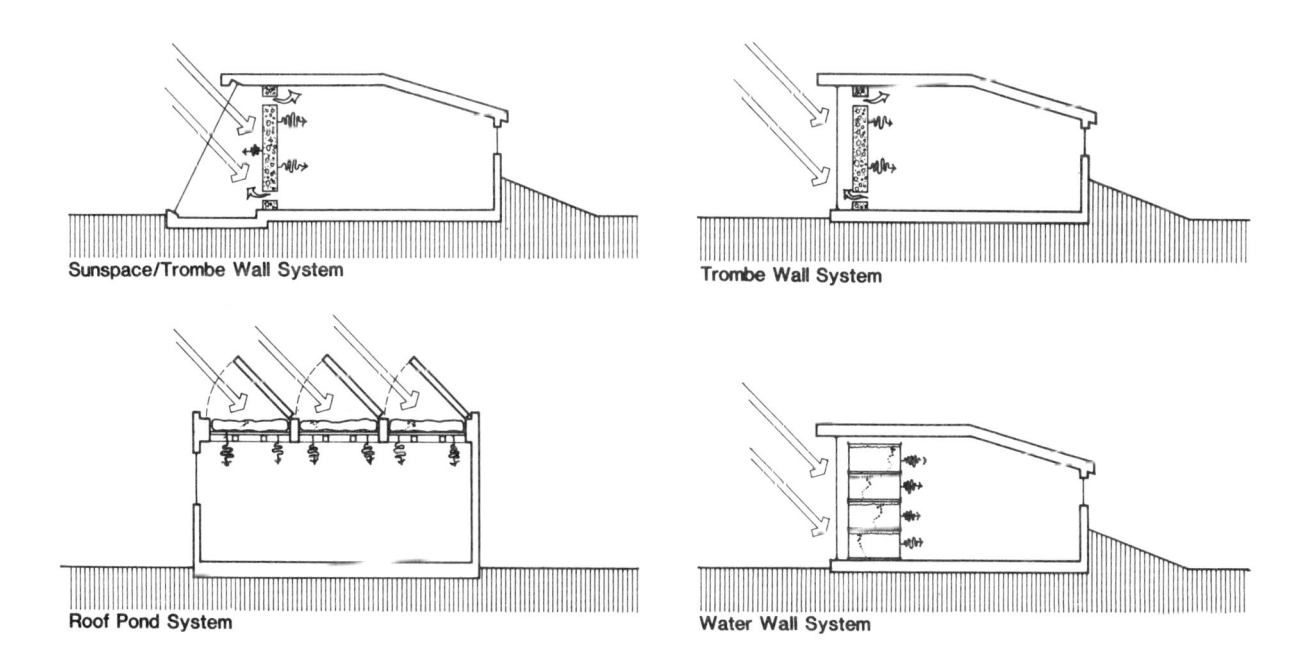

Water Wall System

Figure 3.5.6.4 - Indirect Gain Thermal Storage

The two common types of indirect gain systems are thermal storage walls and roof ponds (see Figure 3.5.6.4). The difference between the two systems is the location of the mass; one is contained in a wall and the other on the roof over the space being heated.

Roof ponds, which use a massive, roof-mounted body of water for heat collection and storage, are most effective in climates that do not experience great snowfalls and have low relative humidities.

<u>Thermal Storage Walls.</u> Thermal storage walls are composed of masonry or water. The south-facing side is covered with glazing to prevent the escape of thermal radiation. The absorbing surface is often painted a dark color for better absorption of sunlight (as discussed in the section on direct gain). The type and thickness of material determines the wall's ability to store and distribute heat to the living spaces during the desired time period. Radiant distribution from the wall can be delayed up to 12 hours by varying the depth and properties of construction.

Masonry wall designs vary. Solid, unvented walls supply only radiant heat to the building. Walls with a number of openings or vents allow light into the living spaces and facilitate distribution of heat by convection from the cavity between the wall and the glazing.

The Trombe wall, a distinct type masonry thermal storage wall, combines radiant distribution with a convection loop that draws cool air from inside the building through low wall vents and delivers warmed air back to the building through upper wall vents. The convective heating is almost immediate, and can provide warmth to the space during the day even though radiant heat is not released by the wall until nighttime.

An air space of approximately 3-1/2 inches must exist between the wall and glazing. Either double glazing with movable nighttime insulation (assumed R-9) or triple glazing--which is comparable to nighttime insulation are recommended. Optimal vent size depends primarily on the percentage of load the designer wants to satisfy with the Trombe wall. Recommended vent areas are shown below in Figure 3.5.6.5. "Vent area" in this table is the area of the lower vents, which is equal to the area of the upper vents, measured as a percentage of the total Trombe wall area.

Percentage of heating load to be provided by thermal storage wall	Recommended Vent Area	Comment
25%	3%	Performance levels off above 3%
50%	1%	Performance levels off above 1%
75%	½%	Performance decreases above 1%

Figure 3.5.6.5 - Recommended Vent Areas

In terms of total heat delivered, Trombe walls tend to perform slightly better than unvented thermal storage walls. For example, a building in Albuquerque that would have satisfied 70 percent of its heating load without vents would satisfy 76 percent with upper and lower vents, (vent area equal to 1/2 percent of the wall area). Use of a Trombe wall or an unvented thermal storage wall depends primarily on when the heat is needed. If heat is needed primarily during the day, then the vents are needed. If not, the vents will lead to daytime overheating.

Many designers prefer to use direct gain windows instead of vents to provide daytime building heating. This can distribute heat gains more evenly and avoid the overheating possible with vented thermal storage walls.

In water thermal storage walls, the water can be placed in a variety of containers, each with different ratios between heat-exchange surfaces and storage mass. Larger containers provide greater and longer-term heat storing capacity, while smaller containers provide larger heat-exchange surfaces and thus faster distribution. Container variations include tin cans, bottles, tubes, bins, barrels, drums, bags and complete water walls.

The primary advantage of using a water wall is the ability to obtain a very high thermal storage value within a relatively small volume. It is impractical to achieve thermal storage values as high as 90 Btu/degrees (F.)/sq ft with a masonry wall because it would need to be 3 feet thick. This would be awkward, uneconomical, and ineffective. However, a water wall having this heat storage capacity could be made only 18 inches thick. It would perform well and only allow small temperature swings.

There are major cost implications to sizing a thermal storage wall. Not only is the wall itself expensive, but the space it takes up within the building is valuable. Performance increases markedly with increasing storage mass up to but only to the point where the mass is sufficient to heat the building during the night. In commercial buildings, occupancy periods and night setback temperature are especially important in determining the optimal amount of thermal mass.

Regardless of type of mass system, the area of a thermal storage wall depends on; absorptivity surface (as discussed under direct gain), heat loss from the conditioned spaces, climate, and amount of incident solar radiation. The rate of heat loss from a space is largely determined by the difference between indoor and outdoor air temperatures. Therefore, in cold climates, a larger thermal storage wall is needed. Local climate and latitude affect the amount of solar energy received during the winter. For example, at 36 degrees North latitude (Tulsa, Oklahoma) each square foot of thermal wall intercepts approximately 1,883 Btu during a clear January day, while at 48 degrees North (Seattle) the same wall receives only 1,537 Btu. As a general rule, a thermal storage wall needs to be larger the farther north or the more severe the winter climate.

Figure 3.5.6.6 provides rules of thumb for sizing double-glazed thermal storage walls to maintain space temperatures at 65-70 degrees (F.) without additional heating. If a wall is too thick, heat will dissipate within it before it can reach the conditioned spaces; if too thin, the heat will reach conditioned spaces during the day, dissipating within the space before the heat is needed during the night and possibly cause overheating. If the surface area of a wall is too great or too small, the spaces will be too cold or too hot, respectively.

Average Winter Outdoor Temperature (°F) (degree-days/coldest month)	Square Feet of Wall Needed for Each One Square Foot of Floor Area to be Heated	
	Masonry Wall	Water Wall
15° (1,500)	0.72->1.0	0.55-1.0
20° (1,350)	0.60-1.0	0.45-0.85
25° (1,200)	0.51-0.93	0.38-0.70
30° (1,050)	0.43-0.78	0.31-0.55
35° (900)	0.35-0.60	0.25-0.43
40° (750)	0.28-0.46	0.20-0.34
45° (600)	0.22-0.35	0.16-0.25

Figure 3.5.6.6 - Mass Sizing

Controls. As in direct gain systems, controls for the operation of thermal storage walls are important, though less so because the space is not directly influenced by solar gain. For optimal efficiency in the winter, external movable insulation or other insulation should be provided to protect the storage mass from wasteful heat loss to the overcast or night sky. In the summer, unwanted heating of the storage mass can be prevented by shading the glazed area with overhangs or closing the external insulation. With a water wall, thermal transfer across the water and radiant distribution from the wall to the interior space are more rapid than the longer time lag of a masonry wall. If heat is not desirable until the cooler evening hours, a water wall requires some storage-distribution control, such as insulation between storage and the space.

Roof Pond. A second indirect gain system is the roof pond, in which the collector-storage mass is placed on the roof the floor or wall of the building. The roof pond system requires a body of water on the roof, exposed to direct solar gain, which it absorbs and stores. The thermal storage in the ceiling will radiate uniform, low-temperature heat to the entire building in both sunny and cloudy conditions. The ceiling must be close to the individuals being warmed, because radiation intensity drops off quickly with distance. This suggests that the storage mass be uniformly spread over all spaces and that ceiling heights not be raised from the normal. Movable insulation is generally required to reduce heat losses on sunless days and winter nights and heat gain in summer. This system is most suitable for heating one-story buildings, or the upper floor of a two- or three-story structure. The system does not dictate building shape or orientation and allows complete freedom with regard to the arrangement of indoor spaces. In addition, the roof pond is invisible from the street level.

The area of roof pond required varies according to whether movable insulation is used and the type of glazing, as well as climate and building load. The recommended ratios of roof pond area to the floor area heated are given below in Figure 3.5.6.7.

Average winter outdoor temperature (°F)	15 to 25 degrees (F.)	25 to 35 degrees (F.)	35 to 45 degrees (F.)
Double-glazed ponds w/night insulation	—	0.85–1.0	0.60–0.90
Single-glazed ponds w/night insulation and reflector	—	—	0.33–0.60
Double-glazed pond w/night insulation and reflector	—	0.50–1.0	0.25–0.45
South-sloping collector cover w/night insulation	0.60–1.0	0.40–0.60	0.20–0.40

Figure 3.5.6.7 - Roof Pond Ratios

Roof pond heating is characterized by stable indoor temperatures and high levels of comfort because of the large area of radiative surface. Daily fluctuations of space temperature are only 5-8 degrees (F.) in a masonry building and 9-14 degrees (F.) in a building constructed of lightweight materials.

Controls. Night insulation provides the means for controlling the heat flow from the pond to the space. The most common movable insulation panels are 2-inch polyurethane foam reinforced with fiberglass strands and sandwiched between aluminum skins. This is a standard item marketed as "metal building insulation." This insulation has been used successfully for up to 40-foot spans before requiring support by metal channels. In the flat roof pond system, the metal frames that support the insulation panels should be designed so that they do not form a straight heat-conducting path from the ponds to the exterior.

Panels should be as large as possible to reduce the amount and cost of hardware (such as tracks, seals). The tracks for the panels must be able to withstand deflection, and should seal tightly. This requires careful detailing. Sometimes the tightness needed can require neoprene curtains and seals that ride along the panels. Studies have shown that 24 percent of the energy striking the ponds on an average winter day was lost through inadequate seals or night insulation. The efficiency of this system can be increased by designing the insulating panels to act as reflectors in the open position, using either a bi-folding or solid panel hinged along its north edge and covering the surface panel with a reflective material.

Isolated Gain

In isolated gain systems, the solar collection and storage elements are in a "sunspace" separate from the spaces they heat. Isolated gain solar technologies can be used in most climate regions.

Solariums, greenhouses, and atriums are used as sunspaces in isolated gain systems. These terms are used somewhat interchangeably in the solar literature. Loosely defined, a solarium is a narrow, one or two-story space on the south side of a building. In contrast, an atrium is a more integral part of the building, adjacent to the majority of spaces in the building. Greenhouses, totally glazed attached rooms, are used predominantly for plant growing and are usually located on the south side of the building.

In all these variations, the sunspace is a direct gain space. Storage materials and location vary and include masonry walls, water-filled drums, concrete or rock floors and pools. Because sunspaces can reach high daytime temperatures, provision is often made for ducting heat to a storage area somewhere in or below the building; a rock bed below the first floor is a common example of this technique. The sizing and location of storage depends on whether the sunspace is used during the evening hours and whether the storage is used to heat the building at night.

An attached sunspace has the following characteristics:
- Thermal control (primarily through shading and natural ventilation) is critical to reduce overheating in the summer.
- The hot air from the top of the sunspace can often be drawn through ducts by a fan to rock-bed storage and back to the sunspace, improving the system efficiency and reducing overheating in the sunspace.
- The occupied space is buffered by the sunspace, temperature swings in the occupied space are small.

The principal method of heat transfer between the sunspace and building is a thermal wall.
- The surface of the wall (sunspace side) should be highly absorptive. In cool and cold climates, thermocirculation vents or operable windows should be located in the wall, and the sunspace thermally isolated during overextended cloudy periods.
- The greenhouse should be elongated along the east-west axis.
- The north wall should be constructed of opaque materials incorporating at least 2 inches of rigid or 3 inches of batt insulation.
- The ceiling and/or upper part of the north wall should be a light color to reflect light back onto the plant canopy.
- In cold climates, 1.4-2.0 square feet of south-facing double glass (sunspace) should be provided for each square foot of (adjacent) building floor area.
- In temperate climates, 0.8-1.4 square feet of glass area should be provided for each square foot of building floor area.

3.5.7 Passive Cooling Systems

As with solar heating, solar cooling techniques are better defined for residential and small-scale buildings than for large-scale commercial buildings. If environmental conditions are right, however, it is possible to take advantage of natural cooling forces in the environment to reduce cooling requirements in most commercial buildings face.

As with heating systems, there are direct, indirect and isolated passive cooling processes. These systems affect air temperature, air movement, humidity and mean radiant temperature.

Direct cooling occurs when the interior surfaces and contents of the space are exposed directly to environmental heat sink(s).

Indirect cooling occurs when the space is cooled by spontaneous radiation of thermal energy to storage (or some exchange surface) that is in turn cooled by exposure to environmental heat sink(s).

Isolated cooling occurs when the space is cooled by mechanically controlled fluid or radiative transfer to storage (or some exchange surface) that is in turn cooled by exposure to environmental heat sink(s). Figure 3.5.7.1 shows an array of passive cooling strategies.

Design Strategies	Air Temperature	Air Movement	Humidity	Mean Radiant Temperature
Shading	●			●
Underground Construction	●			●
Thermal Mass	●			●
Night Sky Radiation	●			
Earth-Air Heat Exchange	●	●	●	
Thermosiphon	●	●		●
Evaporative Cooling	●		●	
Night Ventilation			●	
Day Ventilation	●	●	●	●

Figure 3.5.7.1 - Cooling Strategies

Direct Cooling

Direct cooling is the counterpart of the direct gain heating system. The same elements and principles apply, except that the space is designed to lose heat rather than gain it.

Direct cooling has two major components: keeping heat out and introducing "coolness." Most of the strategies for keeping heat out of a building are the opposite of those for admitting direct solar gain, and include:
- orienting the building away from intense solar exposure
- using indirect daylighting instead of artificial lighting
- shading roofs, walls and windows (overhangs, wing-walls and

vegetation)
- adjusting surface area-to-volume ratios
- using thermal mass.
- Strategies for encouraging direct loss of heat from occupied spaces include:
  - natural and induced ventilation
  - openable windows and walls
  - openable roofs
  - transpiration of plants
  - evaporation of interior pools.

Another method of direct-gain cooling is through the use of desiccant salts to absorb moisture in the air. In regions of high humidity, where moisture in the air prevents the body from cooling itself evaporatively, desiccant cooling is a traditional strategy. Dehumidifiers have replaced the salt barrels that were once ubiquitous in the Southeast, but before energy was plentiful. Desiccant salts were effective coolers, the only drawback being the need to throw them out once they were saturated.

Passive cooling in regions of high humidity remains a problem today and desiccant solutions are a focus of research and current design experimentation. One new hybrid system now in use rotates two desiccant salt plates, one inside the space absorbing moisture from the air; the other, already saturated, outside in the sunlight, losing its moisture through evaporation and being readied for reuse. Another system combines induced ventilation to bring air into the interior from underground over an activated charcoal desiccant. As the air warms and exits high on the south wall, it passes over and warms the saturated desiccant plate, drying it out for reuse.

Indirect Cooling

As with direct cooling systems, indirect cooling systems parallel their heating counterparts. In fact, many of the indirect heating techniques can be adjusted to provide cooling as well. Some examples are:
- underground construction
- Trombe walls
- water walls
- double roofs and walls.

<u>Night Sky Radiation Cooling.</u> Night sky radiation cooling involves cooling a massive body of water or massive building masonry by exposing it to a cool night sky. Although this is most effective when there is a large day-to-night temperature swing, a clear night in any climate will act as a large heat sink and draw away the heat that has accumulated in the building mass during the day. Once cooled by radiation to the night sky, the water or masonry acts as cold storage, drawing heat away from the space throughout the day and providing natural summer cooling.
- The cooling capacity of night ventilation systems is limited to the minimum outdoor air temperature. They are most effective in hot, arid climates, which have a diurnal swing of 20 degrees (F.) or greater.
- The performance of a night cooling system also depends on the capacity

of the thermal storage system. Night air can provide instantaneous cooling, but the extent to which the system can be used to offset warmer daytime temperatures depends on the heat-sink capacity of the structure.
- Rock beds can also be used as thermal storage for night ventilation systems. Cool night air can be stored in the rock bed and, during the day, air from interior spaces can be directed through the rocks to be cooled. Rock beds have the advantage of a large surface area, allowing rapid heat exchange.

Evaporative Cooling. Evaporative cooling technologies can be used in climates with predominantly low humidities. The addition of moisture (with pools, fountains and plants) will lead to its evaporation, which increases the humidity but lowers the dry-bulb temperature of the air.

Evaporative cooling techniques are most effective in regions with high dry bulb temperatures and with wet-bulb temperatures of 65 degrees (F.) or less.

Roof Ponds. Roof ponds can combine both night sky radiation and evaporative cooling. They involve the use of a contained body of water, protected when needed by moving insulation panels (or by moving the water).
- Conventional floor-to-ceiling heights are the most effective for radiant cooling.
- Insulating panels, which are rolled back to expose the water mass or masonry to the clear night sky, allow the stored heat to radiate out, leaving chilled water behind. These panels are closed during the day to allow the chilled storage mass on the roof to absorb heat from the interior spaces.
- The water or masonry roof containers can also be sprayed with water at night to be additionally cooled by evaporation.
- About four times as much heat can be dissipated from the roof pond by evaporation as by radiation. Up to 20-30 Btu per square foot of pond surface per hour can be dissipated by evaporation and radiation under very clear skies with low humidity and cool nighttime temperatures.
- Roof ponds should be 6-12 inches in depth, and are usually constructed of polyethylene, polyvinyl chloride, metal or fiberglass tanks with plastic covers.
- Insulating panels can be 2-inch polyurethane foam between aluminum skins, commonly called "metal building insulation."

Night Ventilation. Like radiative cooling, night ventilation takes advantage of the thermal absorption and lag characteristics of mass; it requires the same 20-degree (F.) diurnal temperature swing to be effective.

The principle is that the transmission of heat through mass--stone, concrete, adobe--is both delayed and attenuated over time. Depending on the material and the thickness of a massive wall, the delay can stretch 2-12 hours, and the greater the lag the greater the attenuation of heat transmitted. Thus less heat reaches the interior spaces, and it doesn't arrive until late evening or night, when ambient temperatures have dropped

and the exterior wall is radiatively cooled. By night's end the wall is again a cold barrier to the daytime transmission of insolation. Exterior sheathing, insulation or shady vegetation can add to that barrier, further flattening the diurnal curve.
- Night ventilation can complement thermal storage systems used in the winter for heat collection. During the day, the building is closed to outside air circulation, while the storage mass acts as a heat sink. At night, the interior of the building is "flushed out," with warm air escaping to the cool night. Cool night air is thus induced into the building.
- The cooling capacity of night ventilation systems is limited to the minimum outdoor air temperature. They are most effective in hot, arid climates, which have a diurnal swing of 20 degrees (F.) or greater.
- The performance of a night cooling system also depends on the capacity of the thermal storage system. Night air can provide instantaneous cooling, but the extent to which the system can be used to offset warmer daytime temperatures depends on the heat-sink capacity of the structure. The amounts of mass recommended for passive heating in Section 3.5.6 generally apply as well to cooling.
- Rock beds can also be used as thermal storage for night ventilation systems. Cool night air can be stored in the rock bed and, during the day, air from interior spaces can be directed through the rocks to be cooled. Rock beds have the advantage of a large surface area, allowing for rapid heat exchange.

Isolated Cooling

Isolated cooling draws in cool air (usually through the ground) from a location remote from the building itself.
- Cool pipes, which are essentially air-to-ground heat exchangers, can be either open systems, which precool ventilation air (natural or induced) or closed systems, which precool return air for a mechanical system. They should be placed at a depth of 6-12 feet.
- Cool air drawn through these pipes in the ground can be stored in rock-bed storage.
- Cool pipes should be pitched down to the building.
- Near the bottom end of the pipe, a condensation drain or humidification pan can be used to adjust the humidity level.
- Cool pipes commonly used are 4-12 inches in diameter and constructed of clay tile or noncorrosive metal.

Longer pipe runs generally result in more effective heat exchange.

3.6 ELECTRIC LIGHTING

3.6.1 Introduction

Electric lighting can account for 35-60 percent of a commercial building's energy use. It is estimated that the use of natural daylighting in conjunction with well-designed electric lighting can reduce this 10-40 percent. Thus as much as 25 percent of a building's energy use can be eliminated by careful lighting design.

There has been considerable debate in recent years on the degree to which lighting levels can be reduced without reducing the quality of lighting. The lighting levels currently recommended by the Illuminating Engineering Society of North America (IES) are based to a limited extent on empirical data and, where data are unavailable, on consensus within the IES based on professional judgment. The current IES-recommended levels (Figure 3.6.1.1) were developed with energy conservation in mind. Unlike earlier IES-recommended levels, which were categorized by building space and based on the most difficult task to be encountered in that space (e.g., 72 footcandles for classrooms), the current levels are recommended according to activity, with weighting factors to account for differences in worker age, task demand, and background reflectance. The new IES system is based on the use of

Task Areas	Footcandles on Tasks
OFFICE	
General	100
Drafting	150-200
Accounting	150
Conference	30
Restroom	30
Elevators, Stairs, Corridors	20
Lobby	50
COMMERCIAL	
Merchandising	100-200
Restaurants (public spaces)	30-50
Kitchens	70
Circulation	30
INDUSTRIAL	
Receiving	20
Fabrication	50-100
Detailed Fabrication	500-1000
Assembly	100
Inspection	50-100
LIBRARY	
Reading Areas	30-70
Card File Areas	100
CHURCH	
Main Area	15-30
Altar Area	100
RESIDENTIAL	
Living	10
Dining	15
Circulation	10
Kitchen	50
Task Lighting	50
EXTERIOR	
Building	15-30
Parking	1-2

Figure 3.6.1.1 - Levels of Illumination

task lighting, which involves providing needed light levels at specific task areas rather than throughout a whole room. Task lighting can save considerable energy by enabling ambient lighting levels to be reduced below the levels needed at task surfaces.

Research to provide much-needed empirical data on lighting quality and quantity is now underway under the aegis of the American Institute of Architects and IES.

Luminance

Luminance (brightness) is critical to lighting quality. The eye does not see illuminance (light). Rather it sees a surface that is illuminated by light and therefore has luminance. This luminance depends on (1) the light falling on the surface and (2) the reflectivity of the surface. A black surface reflects very little light and thus has a low luminance. For the eye to distinguish between different surfaces, those surfaces must have different luminances. White lettering on white paper, for instance, is impossible to see. Contrast between specific tasks and the immediate background increases visibility (the eye's ability to distinguish fine detail) and reduces the need for illumination.

Glare

Although contrast between specific tasks and immediate background increases visibility, luminance contrasts between immediate background and surrounding background can produce eye-adaptability problems, termed glare. Automobile headlights surrounded by darkness, for instance, inhibit a driver from seeing the road. As the background recedes from the center of vision, greater luminance differences are acceptable. Figure 3.6.1.2 gives IES-recommended luminance ratios for projected pictures.

Permissible Luminance Ratios for Projected Pictures: Conventional Screen Luminance[a] vs Screen Luminance Resulting from All Non-Image Luminance[b]

Projection Facility[c] Type					Type of Material	Recommended Ratio[d]
1	2	3	4	5		
x	x	x	x		Motion pictures at optimum.	300:1
		x	x	x	Full scale black and white and color, where pictorial values are important and color differences must be discriminated.	100:1
				x	Color diagrams and continuous tone black and white in high key.	25:1
				x	Simple line material such as text, tables, diagrams, and graphs.	5:1

[a] Measured with no film in the aperture; therefore maximum image high-light luminance will normally be 25 to 60 per cent of the screen luminance.[34]

[b] Measured with the projection lens capped; therefore minimum shadow luminance will approach this screen luminance resulting from all nonprojected illumination.

[c] Type of projection facilities: 1—Review Room; 2—Theatre; 3—Drive-In Theatre; 4—Auditorium; 5—Classroom

[d] Reference 33.

Figure 3.6.1.2 - IES Luminous Ratios

Given adequate lighting <u>levels</u>, glare is the primary factor in lighting quality. Glare can be categorized as direct glare, as reflective glare, and as disability glare (which interferes with vision) and as discomfort

glare (which irritates or distracts). Reflective glare, sometimes
referred to as veiling reflection, is unwanted illuminance reflected off
specular surfaces that makes those surfaces difficult to discern.

A single light source can cause both disability glare and discomfort
glare.

Glare can be caused by incorrectly screened light sources, large or small
luminous surfaces near the work plane, or by light which reflects off a
task into the eye. Two common sources of disability glare are a very
bright light source that prevents discrimination of detail beyond the
light and the reflection of a light source on the specular surface of a
work area which prevents discrimination of detail on the surface itself.

Disability glare, which has been difficult to analyze, can be avoided by--
- raising the luminaire (disability glare is rapidly reduced and at an
  angular displacement of 40 degrees, is almost negligible)
- reducing the size or luminance (brightness) of the glare source or
  shielding it from view with louvers
- increasing the illuminance of the task
- increasing the luminance of the surrounding area.

Discomfort glare is difficult to analyze. Research indicates that the
severity of discomfort glare is related to the brightness and apparent
size of the source, the angular separation between the source and the line
of vision, and the brightness of the background behind the source.

Discomfort glare can be reduced by--
- decreasing the amount of illuminance from the luminaire or shielding it
  from view
- moving the source from the line of vision
- raising background brightness to that of the source level
- increasing the brightness of the source's immediate surroundings.

3.6.2 Light-Distribution Systems

Selection of light distribution systems are significant factors in
lighting quality, energy use and cost. Systems include direct, indirect,
and indirect-direct lighting.

Direct Lighting

Direct lighting usually involves ceiling luminaires which are mounted in
the ceiling cavity, mounted on the ceiling; or suspended below the
ceiling, with all of the light produced directed to the work plane below.
Output from luminaires may be modified by the use of reflectors, lenses,
or baffles. Direct lighting is most commonly used for general lighting
where the level of illumination needed on work planes is relatively
uniform throughout a space. Direct lighting can be used to provide task
lighting in a particular area and general lighting in other areas. This
uses less energy than a uniform direct system but restricts the
flexibility of furniture movement.

Advantages of direct lighting include maximum efficacy (i.e., minimum watts per square foot), simplicity of installation, ease of maintenance and minimum costs. The disadvantages are high potential for both glare and poor lighting quality.

Indirect Lighting

Indirect lighting uses hidden light sources and sources which bounce light off ceilings or other surfaces to the work plane. Indirect lighting virtually eliminates the possibility of glare. Success depends on the proximity and reflectivity of the reflective surfaces. The room in effect becomes part of the luminaire, and the treatment of room surfaces is critical.

Indirect lighting can require excessive energy for task lighting. At the same time, however, with no glare problem, it becomes possible to use efficient high-intensity lamps which are often portable and allow easy relocation.

Indirect-Direct

Indirect-direct lighting, whether provided by dual-purpose luminaires or separate direct and indirect luminaires, offers the possibility of achieving the advantages of both lighting systems, although glare must be avoided.

One method, called task/ambient (T/A), uses task lights at individual work stations supplemented by ambient lighting. Ambient systems can be direct (ceiling mounted luminaires, directed toward the floor) or indirect (floor- or furniture-mounted luminaires) directed toward the ceiling. Such systems can be integrated into furniture. A single light source can provide both task lighting (down to the desk) and ambient lighting (up to the ceiling).

To prevent problems with eye adaptation, ambient lighting levels should be at least 20-30 percent of the task lighting levels. Veiling reflections from task luminaires must be avoided. This is accomplished by proper positioning of lights and by using luminaires with lens controls which shift light output away from the "mirror" angle.

Advantages of T/A systems include adaptability to changes in office plan and the potential for lower wattage per square foot than either direct or indirect lighting alone. Disadvantages include higher electrical distribution costs. The predominant 120-volt system, usually requires more circuits than with the 277-volt system used with ceiling-mounted systems. T/A lighting units usually release their heat into the work area, where it must be removed by the airconditioning system, while ceiling-mounted systems provide opportunities for removing luminaire and ballast before it enters the space.

Light Source	Lamp wattage	Typical Total watts	Mean lumens	Rated lamp life (hours)	Installed, lumens watts (average)
Incandescent	300	300	5 800	1 000	19
	500	500	10 000	1 000	20
	1000	1 000	21 000	1 000	21
Fluorescent	2-40 (430 mA)	97	5 290	20 000	55
	2-75 (430 mA)	181	11 340	12 000	63
	2-60 (800 mA)	140	7 400	12 000	53
	2-110 (800 mA)	268	15 820	12 000	59
	2-110 (1 500 mA)	267	11 000	9 000	41
	2-165 (1 500 mA)	385	15 600	9 000	41
	2-215 (1 500 mA)	480	24 800	9 000	52
Mercury	100	125	3 500	24 000	28
	175	205	7 500	24 000	36
	250	285	11 100	24 000+	39
	400	150	19 800	24 000+	44
	2-400	875	39 600	24 000+	45
	1 000	1 070	47 900	24 000+	45
Metal halide	175	215	10 800	7 500	50
	250	300	17 000	10 000	57
	400	450	25 600	20 000	57
	1 000	1 080	90 200	12 000	83
	1 500	1 625	142 600	3 000	88
Super metal halide	400 (Vertical Operation)	450	32 000	15 000	71
	400 (Horizontal Operation)	450	32 000	20 000	71
	1 000 (Vertical only)	1 080	100 000	12 000	92
High pressure sodium	50	60	2 970	24 000	50
	70	94	5 200	24 000	55
	100	135	8 550	24 000	63
	150	195	14 400	24 000	74
	200	250	19 800	24 000	79
	250	303	24 750	24 000	82
	400	470	45 000	24 000	96
	2-400	950	90 000	24 000	95
	1 000	1 095	126 000	24 000	115
Deluxe high pressure sodium	250	303	22 500	7 500	74
Low pressure sodium	18	40	1 800	10 000	45
	35	64	4 800	18 000	75
	55	80	8 000	18 000	100
	90	125	13 500	18 000	108
	135	163	22 500	18 000	138
	180	205	33 000	18 000	160

Figure 3.6.3.1 - Light Sources

3.6.3 Light-Producing Systems

Lighting systems consist of lamps, luminaires, often ballasts, and controls.

Lamps

Incandescent, fluorescent, and high-intensity discharge (HID) lamps vary in performance, cost, and character of the light produced (see Figure 3.6.3.1).

Incandescent lamps produce light in all parts of the spectrum but tend to have a high level of light in the orange range. They are relatively inefficient (no more than 20 lumens per watt) but are beneficial where--
- use is infrequent or of short duration
- low-cost dimming is required
- minimum initial cost is required
- warm color is desirable, (enhancement of flesh tones)
- short lamp-life is acceptable
- lamp replacement is simple.

Fluorescent lamps are available in a variety of types, with color emphasis in particular areas of the spectrum. Lamps that produce light color approximating that of the sun and sky tend to be less efficient and more costly. They produce 870-16,000 lumens, and their efficacy is 40-85 lumens per watt.

Energy-efficient fluorescent lamps have greater efficacy than standard lamps of similar wattage, but generally output depreciates faster and life is shorter. They should be used where their reduced light output is acceptable.

HID lamps provide 1,100-155,000 lumens and have significantly greater efficacies than fluorescent or incandescent lamps. HID lamps are especially useful in indirect lighting systems, where light output is modified by reflectance from ceiling and wall surfaces.

Mercury HID lamps are long-lived but have efficacies lower than fluorescent lamps'. They produce light in the blue-green spectrum that tends to render color poorly.

Metal-halide HID lamps do not generally last as long as fluorescent lamps but their efficacy is 80-100 lumens per watt. Their light tends to be in the warm range.

Mercury and metal-halide HID lamps require a heating of the electron stream to vaporize the gases. This requires a start-up time of 3-6 minutes to reach full output. If the lamp is extinguished or if there is an energy interruption, another 3-8 minutes is required for the lamps to cool down before restrike is possible. Thus accidentally extinguished lamps can leave an area darkened unless other lighting has been provided.

High-pressure sodium (HPS) HID lamps provide the long life of mercury lamps (16,000-24,000 hours to 7,500-20,000 for fluorescents), with efficacies of up to 140 lumens per watt or, with ballast losses included, 124 lumens per watt. The spectral output of the HPS lamps peaks predominantly in the yellow range, causing objects to appear yellowish in color. Use is usually limited to areas where this yellow color is appropriate and acceptable to users.

Low-pressure sodium (LPS) HID lamps have especially high efficacies--over 150 lumens per watts including ballast losses. They produce a monochromatic yellow light, rendering objects a very dull, grayish-yellow and are usually limited to use in street or other outdoor large-area lighting.

Luminaires

A luminaire consists of a housing unit (with a reflector, lens, louver, one or more lamps, possibly a ballast, and/or lamp brackets), and appropriate wiring for the system.

The efficiency of luminaires depends on materials and finishes used and the design of the reflector and housing. Efficiency can be determined by calculating the coefficient of utilization (CU) for the various generic types of luminaire (see the IES Handbook) or from data supplied by the manufacturer. The CU provides an indication of the effectiveness of a particular type of luminaire in a particular type of space. The CU can be multiplied by the lamp lumen output for the luminaire and footcandle level at the work plane. Low-efficiency luminaires contribute less light and more heat than do more efficient luminaires.

Ballasts

Gaseous discharge and HID lamps require either a ballast or control equipment to provide adequate starting voltage and to limit current after the lamp has started.

Normal ballasts for fluorescent lamps give off up to 12 percent of the energy input as heat. Low-wattage ballasts compatible with 34-watt fluorescent lamps are available that consume 3-5 watts less than the conventional ballast. Very-low-heat (VLH) ballasts operate at lower levels of temperature, thereby increasing ballast life and reducing maintenance. The use of single-lamp ballasts should be minimized, (consumes as much as 17 percent more energy).

Solid-state electronic ballasts now available allow dimming of fluorescent lamps, have higher efficiencies and consume less energy than the conventional core and coil magnetic ballasts. The combination of reduced ballast energy consumption and lower wattage use by the lamps decreases the heat buildup, thus reducing thermal lamp lumen depreciation. Electronic ballasts reduce visible flicker (cycles off and on 44,000 times per second, versus 120 times per second for conventional ballasts.

3.6.4 Lighting Controls

The principal types of lighting system controls are selective switching (on/off), dimming, and variations of the two.

Selective Switching

The simple switching of lamps on and off, either manually or automatically, is referred to as selective switching. It allows the elimination or reduction of lights by level or zone. It effectively in reduces waste by limiting the lighting when it is not needed or when daylight is available.

Switches can be controlled manually, by photosensors responding to the levels of daylight available by preset timers and by occupancy sensors that switch lamps on or off based on the proximity of persons.

Selective switching can be categorized as two-step, three-step, four-step, or five-step. The two-step system is a simple on or off of all lamps on the circuit. The three-step system is used with luminaires with two lamps, or multiples of two. The three steps are: a) all lamps on, b) half of the lamps on, and c) all lamps off. The four-step system is applied to luminaires with three lamps, or multiples of three; the three steps are: a) all lamps on, b) one-third of the lamps on, c) two-thirds of the lamps on, and d) all lamps off. The five-step system is applied to luminaires with four lamps or multiples of four, and the steps are: a) all lamps on, b) one-fourth on, c) one-half on, d) three-quarters on, and e) all lamps off.

Dimming

Most luminaires can now be dimmed. Lamps that require ballasts must be equipped with dimming ballasts. Dimmers allow refined control to provide only the additional footcandles needed to supplement daylighting and maintain the targeted footcandle level.

3.6.5 Illuminance Calculation Methods

An important goal of lighting design is to provide sufficient, but not excessive, illuminance on a visual task. Recommended illuminance values, based upon the best available research, are available from the IES.

Point Illuminance Calculations

In many cases targeted illuminance values are to be provided at specific tasks, rather than for large areas of various tasks. In these cases, a point method of illuminance calculation should be used. The Isofootcandle Method (see Figure 3.6.5.1 and the IES Handbook) of calculating illuminance at a point makes use of predetermined plots of lines of equal illuminance on surfaces.

By locating a point on the Isofootcandle chart with reference to the ratio of distance/mounting height of a luminaire, the direct illuminance at the point can be read directly.

If a number of luminaires are involved, the various contributions can be added together to obtain the direct illuminance at a given point.

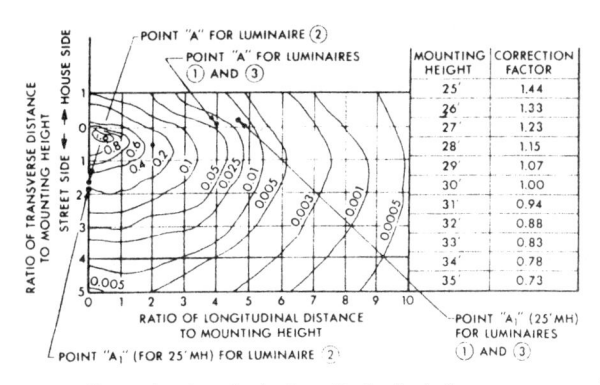

Example of an isofootcandle (isolux) diagram of horizontal footcandles on pavement surface for a luminaire providing a Type III-M light distribution, per 1000 lumens of lamp output times 10.

Figure 3.6.5.1 - Isofootcandle Diagram

Average Illuminance Calculations

Where the target illuminance values are average maintained values, the Zonal Cavity Method can be used to determine the number of luminaires required or the area of floor each luminaire can cover effectively.

It is important that the designer understand the relative influence of various factors on luminaire spacing and design.

Number of Luminaires for a Space

The number of luminaires required for a given space is a product of the illumination (in footcandles) desired and the areas (in square feet), divided by the light (in lumens) provided by each luminaire. In these calculations, this latter quantity is adjusted to account for both the amount of light, generated by the luminaire, that does not reach the work surface (the luminaire's Coefficient of Utilization, or CU) and the degradation of the luminaire's efficiency caused by temperature and voltage variations, dirt accumulation on luminaires and room surfaces, output depreciation, and maintenance conditions (the luminaire's Light Loss Factor, or LLF:

$$\text{Number of luminaires} = \frac{\text{fc} \times \text{sq ft}}{\text{lumens per luminaire} \times \text{CU} \times \text{LLF}}$$

The lumens per luminaire for this calculation is determined by multiplying the number of lamps per luminaire times the lumens produced by each lamp.

The CU is determined from manufacturers' data or from charts in the IES Handbook.

The LLF is determined by multiplying values for room surface dirt, lamp lumen depreciation, lamp burnout rate, and luminaire dirt depreciation,

and an adjustment factor. The values for these five factors are:
- Room Surface Dirt: clean room, frequent maintenance, 0.95; medium conditions and medium frequency of cleaning, 0.9; dirty room, infrequent maintenance, 0.85.
- Lamp Lumen Depreciation: see IES Handbook.
- Burnout Rate: group-replacement, 1.0; individual replacement on burnout, 0.95.
- Luminaire Dirt Replacement: depends on luminaire design and maintenance schedule. The maintenance category can be obtained from the manufacturers' data or from the IES Handbook.
- Adjustment Factor: a factor of 0.9 accounts for voltage variations, ballast differences, luminaire ambient temperature and luminaire deterioration not caused by dirt.

Area Covered by a Luminaire

Determining the area of floor that each luminaire covers effectively can be a more useful procedure for large spaces. The values in the preceding procedure are simply used in a different equation:

$$\text{Area per luminaire} = \frac{\text{lumens per luminaire} \times CU \times LLF}{fc}$$

Zonal Cavity Calculation

The zonal cavity calculation can be used to adjust the luminaire's CU in the foregoing equations to account for the effective (as opposed to nominal) reflectances of walls, ceilings, and floors.

The room is divided into three cavities (see Figure 3.6.5.2): the ceiling cavity is the space between the luminaire and the ceiling; the floor cavity is the space between the work plane and the floor; the room cavity is the space between the work plane and the luminaire centerline. The "H" in Figure 3.6.5.3 below refers to the various heights of the cavities.

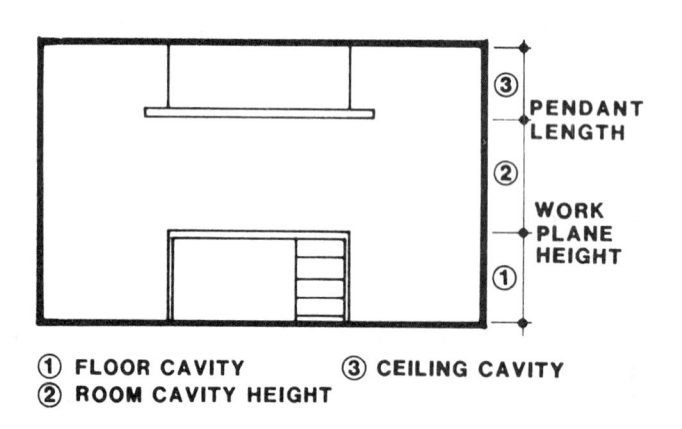

① FLOOR CAVITY   ③ CEILING CAVITY
② ROOM CAVITY HEIGHT

Figure 3.6.5.2 - Three Room Cavities

$$CR = 2.5 \times \frac{\text{area of cavity wall}}{\text{area of work plane}}$$

In a rectangular space the area of the cavity wall is:

$$h \times (2L + 2W) \text{ or } 2h(L + W)$$

from this:

$$CR = \frac{2.5 \times 2h \times (L + W)}{\text{area of work plane}}$$

$$CR = \frac{L + W}{L \times W}$$

$$\text{Ceiling Cavity Ratio, } CCR = 5h \frac{L + W}{L \times W}$$

$$\text{Room Cavity Ratio, } RCR = 5h \frac{L + W}{L \times W}$$

$$\text{Floor Cavity Ratio, } FCR = \frac{L + W}{L \times W}$$

Figure 3.6.5.3 - Cavity Ratio Formulations

The Room cavity ratios can be obtained from the Nomographs above in Figure 3.6.5.4.

Effective ceiling and floor reflectances can be determined on the basis of known or assumed reflectances. If luminaires are surface-mounted or recessed, then CCR = 0 and p = known or assumed ceiling reflectance. If the floor is the working plane, FCR = 0, and P = known or assumed floor reflectance.

Finally, CUs from manufacturers' data or the tables used earlier are used to arrive at an adjusted CU with which to calculate the number of luminaires for an area or the area per luminaire.

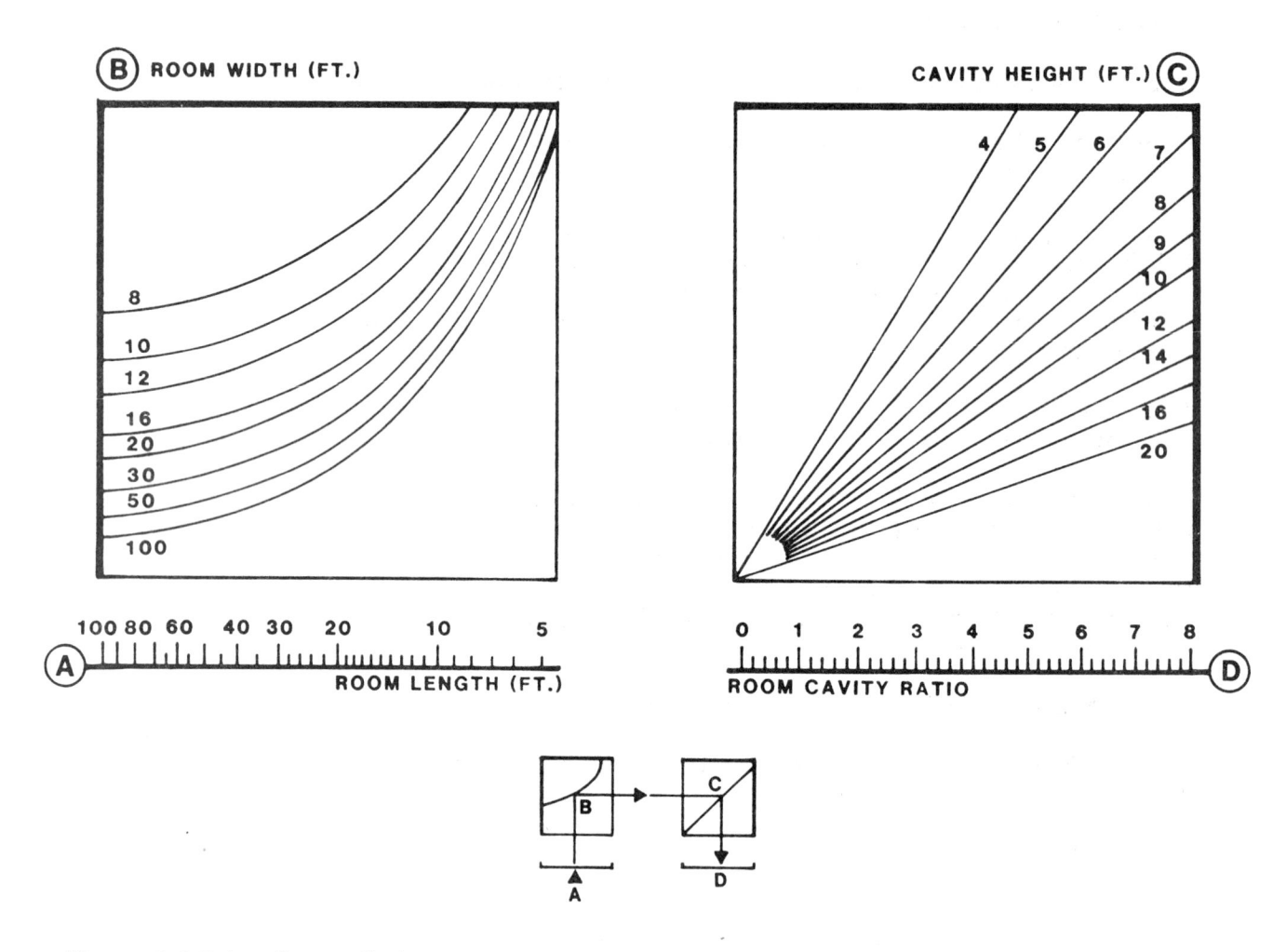

Figure 3.6.5.4 - Room Cavity Ratio Nomograph

3.6.6 Energy Use

Energy-efficient design requires that the designer be concerned with two major aspects of the lighting system: the amount of electrical energy needed to operate the lights and the energy given off as heat, effecting its mechanical system. In commercial buildings, as much as 60 percent of energy use may be for the electric lighting system.

Calculation of the energy needed to operate a lighting system must include the energy consumption of the luminaires in a given space (total watts), multiplied by the hours per day of operation, multiplied by the days per year of operation, multiplied by the utilization factor (percent of total period lights will be on).

Thermal Effects

The following equation can be used to compute the heat gain from lights:

Heat gain (Btu/hr) = footcandles/sq ft x area (sq ft)
x .06 watts/footcandle x 3.41 Btu/hr/watt.

From a use profile for the building, the annual heat gain from the lighting system can be found by the following formula:
Annual lighting heat gain (Btu/yr) = total watts x lighted hours per day x lighted days per year x utilization factor x 3.41 Btu/watt x cooling load factor.

Utilization is the ratio of wattage in use to the total installed wattage (In commercial buildings this ratio is usually one).

The cooling load factor (based on the number of hours per day that the lights are on) can be applied to achieve a more accurate calculation. The cooling load factor equals 1.0 if the cooling system is operated only when the lights are on, or if the lights are on more than 16 hours per day. Cooling load tables are available in the ASHRAE Handbook. For fluorescent lamps, use a cooling load factor of 1.25.

3.6.7 IES Energy Guidelines for Lighting Systems

In 1981, the IES issued the following energy-conservation strategies for optimizing the use of energy for lighting.

Lighting Needs

1. Identify seeing tasks and locations so that recommended illuminance can be provided for tasks, less in surrounding areas.
2. Identify seeing tasks where maintained illuminance is greater than recommended and modify to meet the recommendations.
3. Consider replacing seeing tasks with those of higher contrast, which calls for lower illuminance requirements.
4. Where there are no visual tasks, task illumination is not needed. Review lighting requirements then to satisfy safety and esthetics.
5. Group together tasks having the same illuminance requirements or widely separated work stations, and close off unused space (with minimum heating, cooling, and lighting).
6. When practical, have persons working after-hours work in close proximity to each other to lessen all energy requirements.
7. Coordinate layout of luminaires and tasks for high contrast rendition rather than uniform space geometry. Analyze existing lighting to show where tasks can be relocated to provide better contrast rendition. Use caution when relocating tasks to minimize direct and reflected glare and veiling reflections on tasks.
8. Relocate lighting form over tops of stacked materials.
9. Consider lowering the mounting height of luminaires if it will improve illumination, or reduce connected lighting power required to maintain adequate task lighting.

10. Consider illuminating tasks with luminaires properly located in or on furniture with less light in aisles.
11. Consider wall lighting luminaires, and lighting for plants, paintings, and murals, to maintain proper luminance ratios in place of general overhead lighting.
12. Consider high efficacy light sources for required floodlighting and display lighting.
13. Consider the use of open-plan spaces versus partitioned spaces. Where partitions are tall or stacked equipment can be eliminated, the general illumination may increase, and the lighting system connected power may be reduced.
14. Consider the use of light colors for walls, floors, ceilings, and furniture to increase utilization of light, and reduce connected lighting power required to achieve needed light. Avoid glossy finishes on room and work surfaces.

Lighting Equipment

15. Establish washing cycles for lamps and luminaires.
16. Select a group-lamp-replacement time interval for all light sources.
17. Install lamps with higher efficacy (lumens per watt) compatible with desired light source color and color-rendering capabilities.
18. In installations where low-wattage incandescent lamps are used in luminaires, investigate the possibility of using fewer high wattage (more efficient) lamps to get the needed light. Lamp wattage must not exceed luminaire rating.
19. Evaluate use of R, PAR, or ER lamps to get the needed light with lower watts depending on luminaire types or application.
20. Evaluate use of reduced wattage lamps when the illuminance is above task requirements, and whenever luminaire location must be maintained.
21. Consider reduced wattage fluorescent lamps in existing luminaires along with improved maintenance procedures. CAUTION: Not recommended where ambient space temperature may fall below 60 degrees (F.).
22. Check luminaire effectiveness for task lighting and consider luminaire and component replacement or relocation for greater effectiveness.
23. Consider reduced-current ballasts where a reduction in illuminance can be tolerated.
24. Consider the use of ballasts that can accommodate high pressure sodium or metal halide lamps interchangeably with other lamps.
25. Consider multi-level ballasts where a reduction in illuminance can be tolerated.
26. Consider substituting interchangeable-type metal halide lamps on compatible ballasts in existing mercury lighting systems. Two options: Upgrade substandard lighting in a mercury system with no increase in lighting power, or reduce lighting power by removing luminaires that may increase lighting levels above task lighting requirements.

27. Consider using heat removal luminaires whenever possible to improve lamp performance and reduce heat gain to space.
29. Select luminaires that do not collect dirt rapidly and that can be easily cleaned.

Daylighting

30. If daylighting can be used to replace some of the electric lighting near the windows during substantial periods of the day, lighting in those areas should be dimmed or switched off.
31. Maximize the effectiveness of existing fenestration shading controls (interior and exterior) or replace with proper devices or media.
32. Use daylighting effectively by locating work stations requiring the most illumination nearest the windows.
33. Daylighting, whenever it can be effectively used, should be considered in areas when a net energy conservation gain is possible, considering total energy for lighting, heating, and cooling.

Controls and Distribution System

34. Install switching for selective control of illumination.
35. Evaluate the use of low-voltage (24 volts or lower) switching systems to obtain maximum switching capability.
36. Install switching or dimmer controls to provide flexibility when spaces are used for multiple purposes and require different amounts of illumination.
37. Consider a solid-state dimmer system as a functional means for variable lighting requirements of high intensity discharge lamps.
38. Consider photocells and/or timeclocks for turning exterior lights on and off.
39. Install selective switching on luminaires according to grouping of working tasks at different working hours, and when not needed.
40. Consider coding on light control panels and switches according to a predetermined schedule of when lights should be turned on and off.

Lighting Maintenance

42. Evaluate the present lighting maintenance program and revise it as necessary to provide the most efficient use of the lighting system.
43. Clean luminaires and replace lamps on a regular maintenance schedule.
44. Check to see if all components are in good working condition. Transmitting or diffusing media should be examined, and badly discolored or deteriorated media replaced to improve efficiency (without producing excessive brightness and unwanted visual discomfort).

45. Replace outdated or damaged luminaires with modern luminaires that have good cleaning capabilities, and that use lamps with higher efficacies and good lumen that use lamps with higher efficacies and good lumen maintenance characteristics.
46. Trim trees and shrubs that may be obstructing luminaire distribution and creating unwanted shadows.
47. Analyze use during working and building cleaning periods and institute an education program to have workers turn off lights when they are not needed. Inform and encourage personnel to turn off light sources such as (a) incandescent--promptly when space is not in use; (b) fluorescent--if the space will not be used for five minutes or longer; (c) high intensity discharge lamps (mercury, metal halide, high pressure sodium)--if space will not be used for 30 minutes or longer.
48. Light building for occupied periods only, and when required for security purposes.
49. Restrict parking to specific lots so lighting can be reduced to minimum security requirements in unused parking areas.
50. Schedule routine building cleaning during occupied hours.
51. Reduce illuminance levels during building cleaning periods.
52. Adjust cleaning schedules to minimize the lighting use, such as by concentrating cleaning activities in fewer spaces at the same time, and by turning off lights in unoccupied areas.
53. Post instructions covering lighting operation and maintenance procedures in all management and general work areas.

3.7 THERMAL SYSTEMS

3.7.1 Introduction

Airconditioning can be defined as the process of treating air to control its temperature, humidity, cleanliness and distribution in order to maintain environmental conditions which enhance comfort and productivity of occupants, as well as to accommodate equipment requirements.

Airconditioning systems heat and cool. The heating mode involves the simple addition of heating energy to overcome the net heat loss from the building. The operating principle of the principal cooling mode involves four sequential heat transfer (or removal) processes: 1) air distribution, 2) fluid or water distribution, 3) refrigeration, and 4) heat rejection.

While one or more of the heat transfer processes can be consolidated on smaller unitary systems, all large central systems generally have distinct and separate subsystems to accomplish each of the four processes.

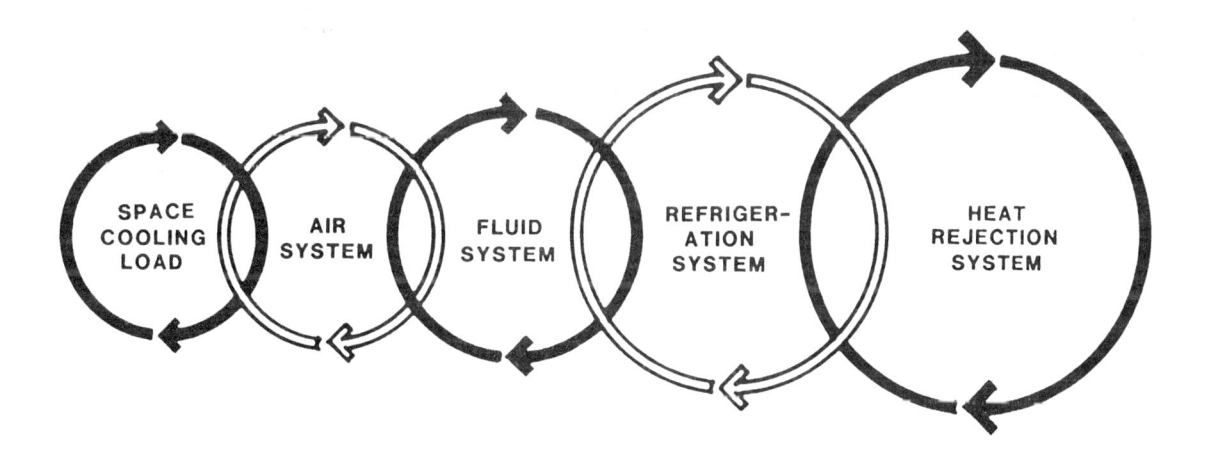

Figure 3.7.1.1 - Cooling Process Sequence

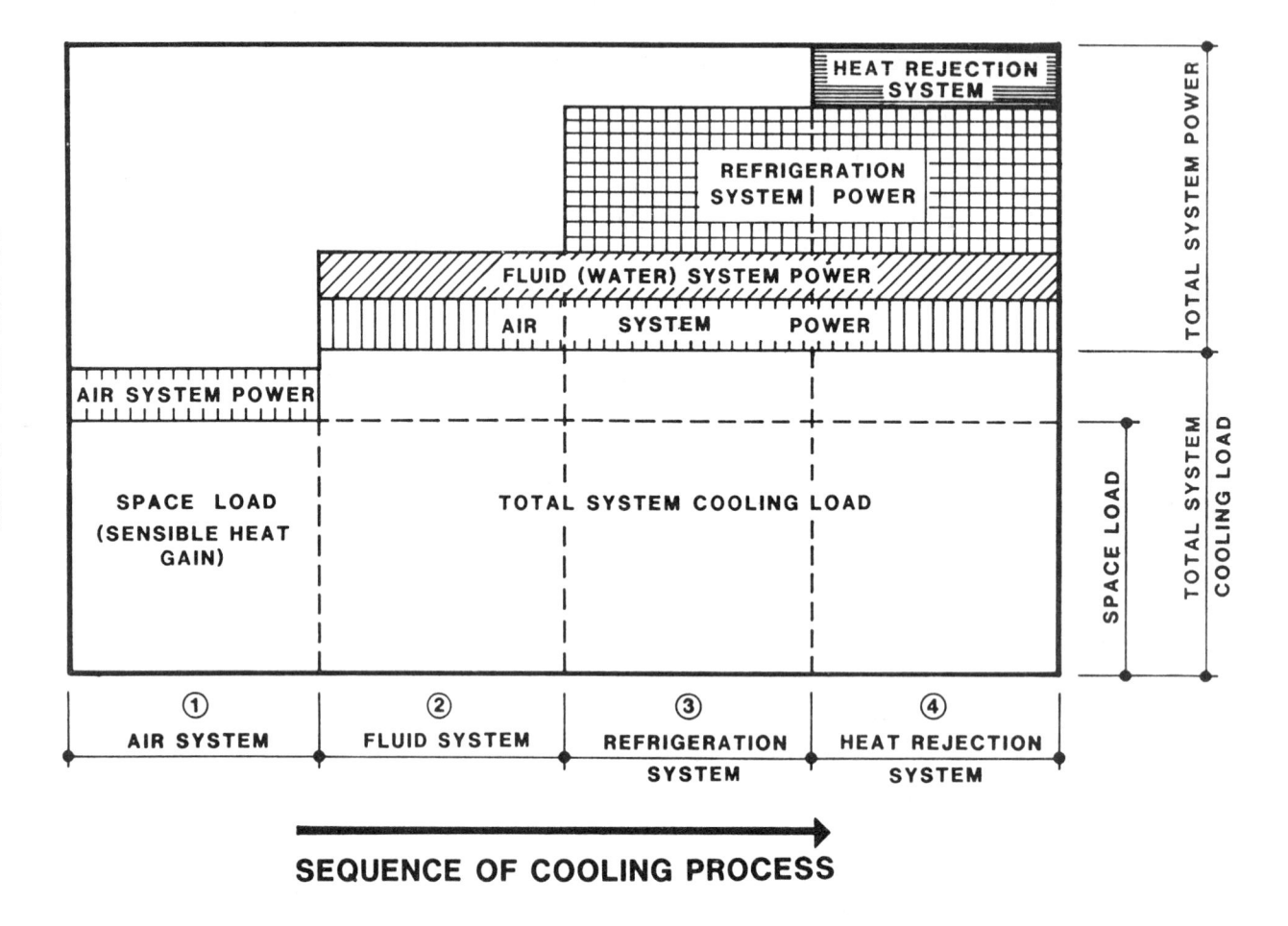

Figure 3.7.1.2 - Cooling Process Sequence

Airconditioning equipment uses power to transfer heat. The power used is generally electric for fans, pumps, and compressors. This equipment is not 100-percent efficient; some of the energy it uses is lost as equipment heat. In the heating mode of operation, equipment heat can be beneficial; in the cooling mode, a liability. The airconditioning system must remove not only heat from the conditioned space, but also this equipment-generated heat.

For example, fan energy absorbed in the air distribution system is added to the load of the fluid system, pump heat is added to the load of the refrigeration system, and compressor heat is added to the load of the heat rejection system which finally transfers the total space and equipment heat to the exterior. The interrelationship between the power (rate of energy) required for each subsystem and the total system cooling load is illustrated in Figure 3.7.1.1.

Coefficient of Performance (COP) is a concept that is traditionally used to quantify efficiency of heat removal:

$$COP = \frac{TOTAL\ HEAT\ REMOVAL}{POWER\ REQUIREMENTS}$$

COP considers the removal of heat attributable both to the building and occupancy requirements and heat attributable to the various components of the airconditioning system itself.

Misleading results can arise if the COP is used to evaluate portions of, rather than overall system performance. For instance, the use of refrigeration equipment with high COP is encouraged; however, the efficiency of this portion of the system is of little value if a major part of the heat removal is done with inefficient fans and pumps.

3.7.2 Distribution Systems

HVAC systems are generally classified according to the fluid delivered to the occupied space: air, air and water, water, or refrigerant.

Systems	Energy Use
Variable-volume interior with perimeter radiant heating VAV and perimeter heating can often oppose each other in perimeter zones with varying solar exposures. It may be necessary to control the perimeter system with an outside air anticipator and solar compensator but these are difficult to coordinate with the VAV system	Lowest
Variable-volume interior with perimeter constant volume VAV with perimeter constant volume theoretically uses a little more energy, but actually uses less by avoiding simultaneous heating and cooling.	Low
Variable-volume, dual-duct	Medium
Variable-volume, with terminal reheat	Medium
All-air induction with perimeter reheat	Medium
Constant-volume, dual-duct and multizone	High
Constant-volume perimeter induction	Very High
Constant-volume single-zone and terminal reheat	Highest

Figure 3.7.2.1 - HVAC System Comparisons

The choice of an HVAC system is based on factors such as the amount of control capability and flexibility required, environmental requirements, cost, energy consumption and system efficiency. Figure 3.7.2.1 gives an indication of various system efficiencies.

All-Air Systems

Advantages
- adaptable to humidification, heat-recovery systems and automatic seasonal changeover
- adaptable to complex zoning schemes, with ability to provide year-round heating and cooling
- adaptable to close control of temperature and humidity, e.g., in computer rooms
- can make greater use of untreated outside air instead of mechanically cooled air more often in summer.

Disadvantages
- special care required with terminal device placement and surrounding structural elements to ensure accessibility to terminal units for maintenance and repair
- in cold climates, radiation heating needed at perimeter during unoccupied hours to avoid having to heat entire building
- higher structural costs and increased HVAC loads, due to large duct spaces that increase building volume.

The available all-air systems are classified as single-duct or dual-duct:
- single duct, constant-air-volume (CAV)
- single duct, variable-air-volume (VAV)
- single duct, reheat CAV or VAV
- dual-duct (including dual-duct VAV)
- multizone.

The single-duct, single-zone system can be quite effective, but has a limited range of application. The single-duct, VAV system is clearly superior to the remaining all-air systems designed to deliver constant-temperature air. This system satisfies the severest zone load and gives smaller volumes of the same constant-temperature air to other zones with lesser loads. This system is especially effective for groups of interior zones where loads vary but not rapidly or frequently. The most serious problems would occur in zones with lesser heat loads but which produce quantities of moisture, dirt or odor that are too large to be eliminated by low volumes of air. Spaces with no cooling loads, but a minimum air supply volume, can also become too cool.

Applications
- where space is truly one zone, with uniformly distributed heat losses and gains

- relatively small buildings
- single rooms within larger buildings.

Advantages
- centralized location of equipment for operation and maintenance
- absence of most equipment in occupied spaces, less infringement on floor space
- outdoor air can be used in place of mechanical refrigeration
- wide choice of zonability, flexibility and humidity control under all operating conditions
- adaptable to heat recovery
- design freedom for distribution systems
- best suited for applications requiring abnormal exhaust makeup
- adaptable to automatic seasonal changeover
- adaptable to winter humidification.

Disadvantages
- additional duct clearance needed
- in cold climates, any system that uses air for perimeter heating requires longer fan-operating hours to take care of heating for unoccupied periods
- in systems with no built-in zone self-balancing devices, air balancing is difficult and may have to be done several times when a common air system services areas that are not vented simultaneously
- air-heating perimeter systems are usually not available for use during building construction as rapidly as perimeter hydronic systems
- accessibility to terminal devices demands close coordination between architectural, mechanical and structural design.

Special Considerations
- prevent simultaneous heating and cooling
- maintain filters to reduce airflow resistance
- maintain insulation.

Dual-duct systems condition all the air in a central apparatus and then distribute it through two parallel ducts to the spaces to be conditioned. One duct carries cold air and the other warm air, providing sources for heating and cooling at all times.

Application
- buildings with multiplicity of zones with highly variable heat loads, e.g., offices and hotels

Advantages
- no electrical equipment, piping, etc., in conditioned spaces
- can be combined with direct radiation systems
- no zoning of central equipment
- system is self-balancing.

Disadvantages
- volume control necessary
- higher velocity and pressure in ducts

- parallel ducts with crossovers require special attention
- less economical than VAV systems.

Special Considerations
- reduce temperature of hot duct and raise temperature of cold duct to that point where loads of the most critical zone can just be met
- if possible, stratify return and outdoor air with splitter so warmest air goes to the warm duct and coolest air to the cold duct, reducing both heating and cooling loads
- reduce system pressure by using lower pressure mixing boxes
- install controls to shut off heating or cooling portions when they are not needed
- provide volume control for supply air fan
- reduce air volume by lowering fan speed when air quantities can be diminished.

CAV multizone systems mix hot and cold air at the central air handler in response to thermostats in each zone. All the intermediate zones are supplied with a mixture of cold and hot air, using energy in a manner similar to the reheat system.

CAV multizone systems can satisfy different loads by varying air temperature only. Unfortunately, the normal control strategy is to cool all of the air to the level required by the severest load and to reheat the air delivered to all zones with lesser loads as necessary. This technique offers finely tuned control but can wastes energy.

Multizone units are now available with individual heating and cooling coils for each zone, using far less energy than units with common coils.

Application
- small and medium-size buildings with two or more individual zones.

Advantages
- same as dual-duct systems.

Disadvantages
- same as a dual-duct systems
- hot ducts are necessary for humidification
- once installed, it is difficult to add an extra zone with different characteristics
- tight dampers and controlled duct temperatures are necessary.

Special Considerations
- zones controlled should be similar to each other
- a thermostat for each room in a zone is more efficient
- hot and cold duct control is recommended
- small and large zones should not be mixed if possible
- cycling rather than modulating is preferable
- treat each zone as a single-zone system, adjust air volumes and temperatures accordingly
- install controls to shut off fans and control valves during unoccupied periods.

<u>Constant-air-temperature (CAT) VAV systems</u> respond to different loads in multiple zones by supplying varying quantities of conditioned air at a constant temperature through a single duct. The air volume is modulated by means of outlet dampers at each zone so that the total supply fan volume can vary in response to demand.

VAV systems can be applied to interior or perimeter zones, with common or separate fan systems, common or separate air temperature controls, and possibly auxiliary heating devices. VAV systems may vary the volume in the total airstream or to the zones of control, or both. Two of the many combinations of the basic concept are VAV terminal-reheat systems and VAV dual-duct systems.

<u>VAV Terminal Reheat System.</u> As a space's need for cooling decreases, the air volume will eventually reach a preset minimum. A reheat coil in perimeter areas is activated. Energy waste is reduced to a minimum before the heating is activated. If the space experiences internal heat gains, terminals without reheat coils can be used in interior spaces.

With VAV dual-duct systems, interior spaces are served with a single cold duct and VAV warm air duct. As a space's need for cooling decreases and the cold-air volume reaches a preset minimum, a damper permits mixing of hot air with the supply air. When there is no requirement for a minimum ventilation rate, energy waste can be reduced because the amounts of hot and cold air to be mixed are kept to a minimum.

Application
- multizoned buildings, for both internal and perimeter zones.

Advantages
- inexpensive temperature controls for multiple zoning
- self-balancing
- "nondumping" systems save fan, pumping, heating and refrigeration energy
- full shut-off for unoccupied areas
- fewer draft problems
- well-suited to laboratories or other applications requiring abnormal exhaust makeup
- provides least infringement on rentable floor space
- does not interfere with window drapes; minimum damage risk to furnishings
- quieter operation
- no zoning for central equipment
- system equipment can usually be smaller because air is not delivered to all spaces simultaneously.

Disadvantages
- perimeter systems not available for use during building construction as rapidly as radiation systems
- absence of built-in automatic zone devices for rapid easy balancing when a single air system serves areas that are not rented simultaneously
- sometimes difficult to prevent unwanted air noise and motion
- often difficult to provide for proper fire safety separations.

Air-Water Systems

Air-water systems combine the cost and energy-efficiency of water systems with the flexibility of air systems, to provide forced-air ventilation, central control humidity and rapid response to load fluctuations in a variety of zones. In these systems, both air and water are delivered to each space, and heating and cooling functions are carried out by changing the temperature of one or both media to control space tempeatures year-round.

Water's high specific heat allows it to deliver a given amount of heating and cooling capacity in a much smaller volume than air requires (see Figure 3.7.2.2). this results in distribution pipes much smaller than comparable air ducts, a feature that makes water attractive in highrise and other buildings where space is at a premium.

Further, the pumping necessary to circulate the water throughout the building is usually about 1/6 the fan power that would be required for an all-air system. The savings on operation cost can be quite substantial when compared with medium- or high-pressure all-air constant-volume systems.

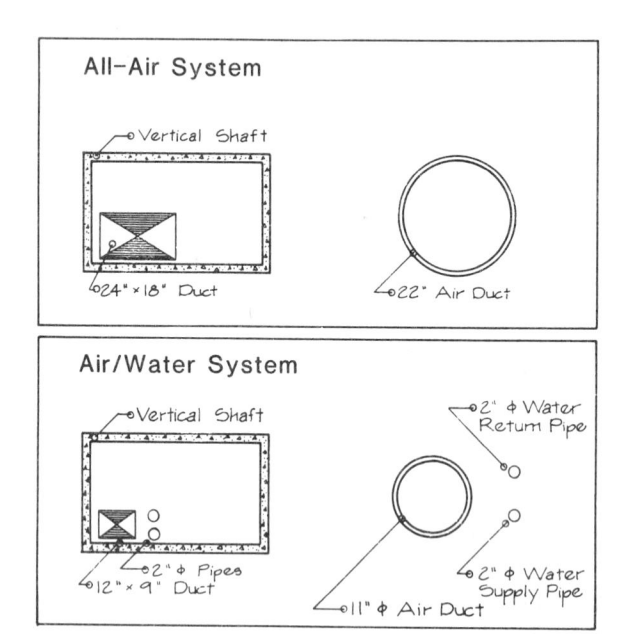

Figure 3.7.2.2 - Comparative Space Needs

When water is the primary conditioning medium, the system can be designed so that the air supply is equal to ventilation or exhaust requirements, eliminating the need for return air ducts and fans.

Air-water systems are primarily applicable to multiple perimeter spaces where a wide range of sensible loads exists and where close control of humidity is not required. Where significant fluctuations in airconditioning requirements can occur at the same time on a given exposure, individual room control is available.

For all systems using outdoor air, there is an outdoor temperature, the changeover temperature, at which mechanical cooling is no longer required. At this point, the system can accomplish cooling through the use of outdoor air; at lower temperatures, heating rather than cooling is needed. With all-air systems capable of operating with up to 100-percent outdoor air, mechanical cooling is often not required at outdoor temperatures below 50-55 degrees (F.). An important characteristic of air-water systems, however, is that the can continue to require refrigeration for secondary water cooling even when the outdoor temperature is considerably less than 50 degrees (F.).

These systems have been commonly applied to office buildings, hospitals, hotels, schools and better apartment houses.

Advantages
- ability to handle a variety of loads through separate sources of heating and cooling in each space
- capacity for centralized humidification, dehumidification, and filtration
- capacity for space heating by water system alone, without fans, at night or during power emergencies if wall units are located under windows.

Disadvantages
- air at low dew point is necessary when primary system accomplishes all dehumidification
- inability to prevent condensation caused by open windows or other sources of humidity
- humidity control requires water chilled to low temperatures or even chemical dehumidification
- can require mechanical cooling even when the outdoor temperature is considerably less than 50 degrees (F.).

The actual equipment used will generally be either induction units or fan coil units.

Air-Water Induction Systems

In an air-water induction unit, centrally conditioned air is supplied to the unit plenum at high pressure. It then flows through induction nozzles and forces air from the room to flow over the water coil and become heated or cooled. The primary and secondary air streams are mixed and discharged to the room.

A wide variety of induction unit configurations are available, including units with low overall heights or with extremely large coil face areas, to suit the particular needs of space or load.

Fan-Coil Conditioner System with Primary Air. Fan-coil conditioner units are versatile room terminals that can be used with both air-water and water-only systems. Despite the shortcomings in the quality of airconditioning achieved with water-only systems, the fan-coil units have been more commonly associated with that type of system than with air-water systems. Many of the standard features of the units are accordingly used for the water-only applications.

The basic elements of fan-coil units are a finned-tube coil and a fan. The fan recirculates air continuously from within the perimeter space through the coil, which is supplied with either hot or chilled water. In addition, the unit can contain an auxiliary heating coil, which usually functions by electric resistance, steam or hot water. The primary air system for areas using fan-coil units need not be integrated with the fan-coil system.

Air-water systems are categorized as two-, three-, or four-pipe systems. Incorporating both cooling and heating capabilities for year-round airconditioning, they all function in the same way, although the details of system design differ significantly.

Advantages
- pipework and ducting lasts up to 20-25 years
- positive ventilation air supply
- recirculation occurs only within each room when all primary air is outdoor air, thus reducing cross-contamination
- high quality air filtration
- reduced cooling capacity, with the building load rather than the sum of room peaks determining capacity requirements.

Disadvantages
- applicable only to the perimeter of most buildings
- usually not possible to shut off primary air supply in individual rooms
- supplementary ventilation air needed for spaces with high exhaust requirements.

All-water systems use fan-coils or unit ventilators with unconditioned ventilation air supplied by an opening through the wall or by infiltration. Cooling and dehumidification are provided by circulating chilled water or brine through a finned coil in the unit. Heating is provided by supplying hot water through the same or a separate coil, using two-, three-, or four-pipe water distribution from central equipment. Electric heating at the terminal can be used to enhance system flexibility.

All-Water Systems

All-water systems can be especially economical and compact, but their effectiveness as space conditioners is limited to buildings with small interior spaces.

Application
- buildings with minimal interior spaces, e.g., motels, apartments and small office buildings.

Advantages
- system is flexible
- pipes need less space than ducts
- low installation costs
- internal zones can be used as a heat source.

Disadvantages
- ventilation and humidity control depend on windows and exhaust system
- energy waste because of different zone loads and during intermediate seasons.

Special Considerations
- reduce flow to the minimum needed to meet space conditions
- for fan-coil systems, install a control to prevent simultaneous heating and cooling
- install a seven-day timer to shut off equipment during unoccupied periods
- close outside air dampers any time infiltration equals ventilation requirements
- if fan-coil units are not located in conditioned areas, insulate casings to reduce heat loss or gain.

Unitary Systems

The foregoing mechanical distribution systems are designed to take advantage of the performance efficiencies of large central plant equipment. Most refrigerant systems, on the other hand, are designed for decentralization. Inefficiencies in performance are offset by the following advantages:
- individual room control, air distribution and ventilation system for each room, usually with simple adjustment by the occupant
- heating and cooling capability always available independently of operation of other building spaces
- only one terminal zone or conditioner affected in the event of equipment malfunction
- usually low initial cost
- reliable, manufacturer-matched components (usually with certified ratings and published performance data), assembled by manufacturer
- ability to shut down equipment in unoccupied rooms for extended periods.

Unitary systems rarely have the variations of coil configurations, evaporator temperatures, air-handling arrangements and refrigerating capacities available in central systems. Thus, unitary equipment often requires a higher level of design ingenuity and performance to develop superior system performance. Unitary equipment seldom experiences serious breakdowns, however, because of factory control in component matching and of quality control in interconnection.

Unitary systems generally locate the fan and evaporator on the roof. The compressor and condensing section can be mounted remotely, but they are more often packaged with the fan and evaporator. The air distribution ductwork penetrates the roof. The complete system consists of the unitary equipment, air distribution and air delivery system(s), interlocking controls, structural supports and vibration-isolation system.

Unitary systems can also be equipped with VAV terminals, either the bypass or squeeze-off type. Unitary systems are designed for CAV control units and do not have the capacity for adjusting fan speeds. For small outside air percentages, bypass terminals avoid increases in duct static pressure and do not allow the cooled air to mix with warm room air before circulating it again.

Unitary units also include window airconditioners or through-the-wall units, also called packaged terminal airconditioners (PTACs). PTACs generally include a heating section; window airconditioners do not.

As indicated earlier, unitary systems are well suited to local zoning, with one unit per zone (see Figure 3.7.2.3). A variation on this is to use a single unitary system to supply preconditioned air to other unitary systems in the building. Under mild weather conditions, such a unit continues in operation even if the zone thermostats turn one or more other units off. This prevents the introduction of hot, humid air into the conditioned spaces under periods of light loading. This strategy can also be adapted to highrise buildings.

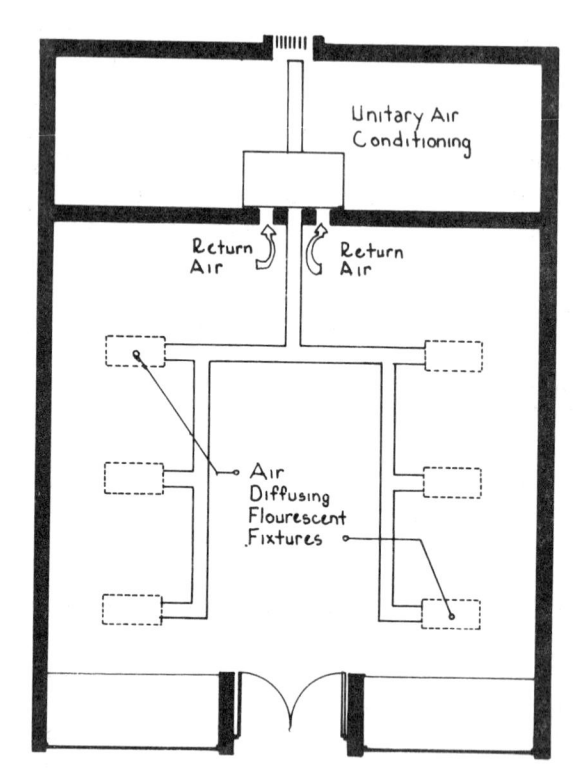

Figure 3.7.2.3 - Single Package Unit

Direct-Expansion, Water-Loop Heat Pumps

Direct-expansion, water-loop heat pumps deserve special attention because heat recovery and redistribution--prime energy-conserving tactics--are among their inherent characteristics.

The direct-expansion, water-loop heat pump is used as terminal equipment to heat and cool a zone when connected to a closed-loop piping circuit with means for adding heat to, or rejecting heat from, the water circuit. With supply loop water temperature maintained at 60-90 degrees (F.) and with a water flow rate of 2-3 gallons per minute per ton, the terminal equipment can either heat or cool to maintain the desired temperature in its zone.

Water circulated within the closed loop becomes either a sink or a source of heat. Units on the heating mode extract heat from the water; units on the cooling mode reject heat to the water. In the heating season, heat rejected from the central core units is carried in the loop water to perimeter units for use. Unlike air-source heat pumps, the heat available for units of this system does not depend on outdoor temperature, since the water loop is the primary source. A secondary source of heat is usually provided.

In the cooling mode, the heat pump operates as a water-cooled airconditioner. In the heating mode, the functions of the evaporator and the condenser are reversed so that the equipment operates as a water chiller. Heat is removed from the water in the water-to-refrigerant heat exchanger, which then acts as the evaporator. That heat, plus the heat from the compressor, is rejected through the refrigerant-to-air heat exchanger (acting as the condenser) and heats the room.

The multiple water-loop heat pump system offers zoning capability, since terminal equipment can be selected with cooling capacity as low as 7,000 Btu/hr. Since equipment can be placed in interior areas, the system can accommodate future relocation of partitions with a minimum of modifications.

This system is twice as efficient in heating than in cooling; waste heat entering spaces from the terminal compressors enhances the system's heating capacity but detracts from its cooling capacity.

Many applications of this system lend themselves well to heat storage. Installations that operate in winter on the cooling cycle most of the day and the heating cycle at night (such as a school) are excellent candidates for heat storage. This can be accomplished by installing a large storage tank in the closed loop circuit ahead of the boiler and adjusting the controls of the heat rejecter to allow the loop temperature to build up to 95 degrees (F.) during the day. The volume of water at 95 degrees (F.) can be used during unoccupied hours to maintain heat in the building, allowing the loop temperature to drop from 95 degrees (F.) to 65 degrees (F.). The storage tank operates as a flywheel to prolong the period of operation between the limits where neither heat makeup nor heat rejection is required.

Terminal units are available in a variety of sizes and types:
- finished console cabinets for window or wall flush mounting
- floor-mounted vertical units for concealed installation
- ceiling-concealed models hung from floors above and connected to ductwork.

Typical Systems

The following are the most common systems used in commercial buildings.

<u>Single-Duct, Constant Air Volume/Variable Air Temperature, Single-Zone.</u>
The single-duct, CAV/VAT single-zone system is perhaps the simplest of all

systems (see Figure 3.7.2.4). An air-handling unit (AHU) located in the mechanical space serves one or more rooms through a single duct, including branches. The AHU can be equipped with coils or a furnace for heating and/or coils for cooling. Coils can be supplied with steam, hot water, electrical power, direct-expansion (DX), or chilled water depending on the services intended. In some designs, a refrigeration compressor is included within the conditioned space; the distribution ductwork may not even be required. A single-room thermostat controls either the heating or cooling mode of operation as well as the space temperature based on the load demand. Since the thermostat can only respond to the conditions in the space where the thermostat is located, the load conditions in the other spaces may or may not be satisfied.

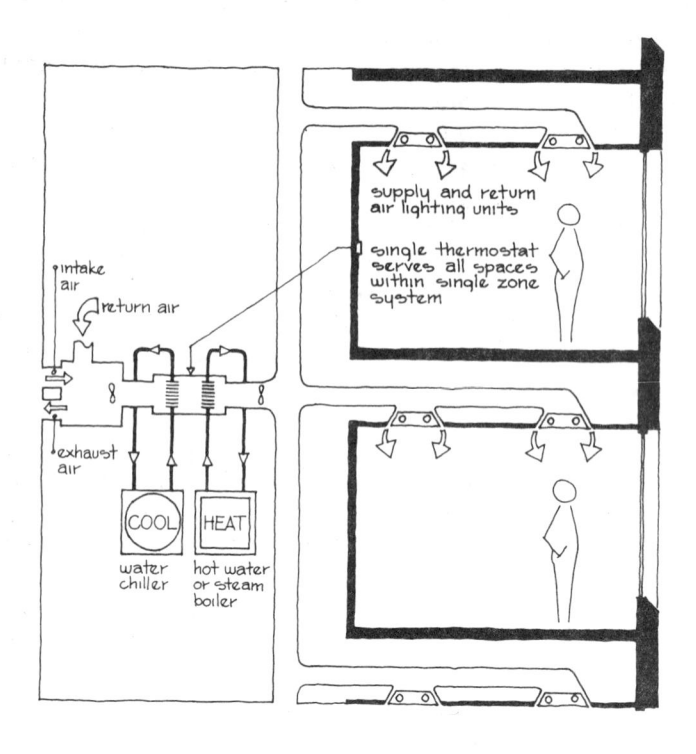

Figure 3.7.2.4 - Single-Duct Single-Zone

<u>Single-Duct, Constant Air Volume/Variable Air Temperature System with Terminal Reheat.</u> The single-duct, CAV/VAT, terminal reheat system is basically an extension of the single-zone system (see Figure 3.7.2.5). However, the size of the system can be expanded to serve

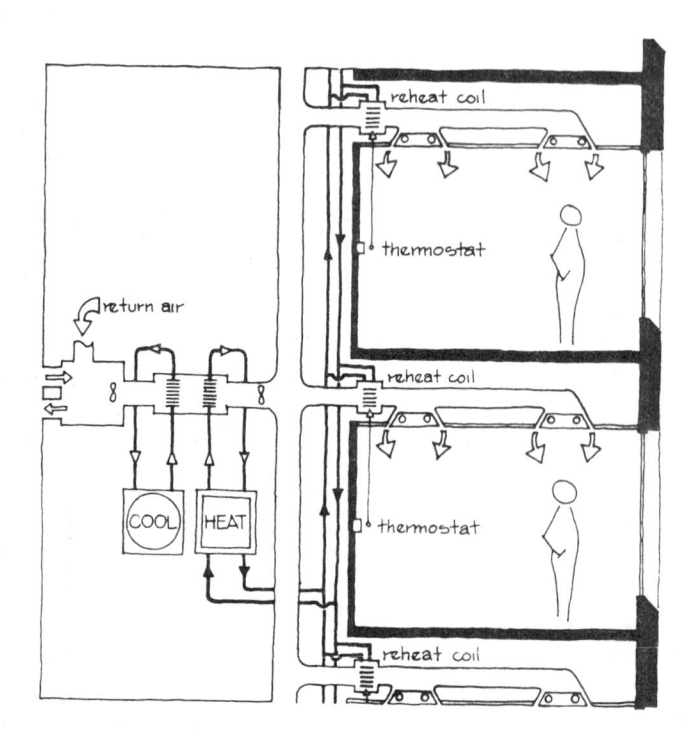

Figure 3.7.2.5 - Terminal Reheat

larger areas since the terminal reheat coils provide the means for temperature control to satisfy individual room requirements. This system is energy intensive as all the supply air must first be pre-cooled to a low temperature--e.g., 55 degrees (F.)--and then reheated again. For energy conservation purposes, terminal reheat systems should not be used unless the source of energy for reheat is solar or recovered from waste energy.

There are, however, applications where a CAV/VAT terminal reheat system is desired, such as hospital surgical suites, research laboratories and computer equipment rooms where humidity control is critical. As an improvement to this system, VAV/CAT reheat boxes can be used where the air volume is first modulated down to 50 percent before the reheat coil is activated. This system has a relatively low first cost.

Single-Duct, Variable Air Volume/Constant Air Temperature System with Perimeter Heaters. With the single-duct, VAV/CAT system with perimeter heaters, VAV/CAT control boxes are used for all interior spaces that require year-round cooling. VAV boxes satisfy the space requirements by varying the amount of air introduced into spaces. However, if the building is in a climate where heating is required in perimeter rooms, a separate heating system will be necessary to offset skin heat loss. In this case, heaters, either hot water, steam or electric, can be installed.

Single-Duct, Variable Air Volume/Constant Air Temperature System with Fan Terminal Units. The single-duct VAV/CAT system with fan terminal units can also serve exterior rooms. A small centrifugal fan inside the fan terminal box draws warm ceiling plenum air, as well as additional heating energy from a tempering coil, to provide heated air into the perimeter space. Cooling is provided from a central system serving VAV dampers in the fan terminal units.

Double-Duct, Constant Air Volume/Constant Air Temperature System with Mixing Boxes. The double-duct, CAV/CAT system with mixing boxes consists of a single-fan air handling unit in a blow-through configuration (see Figure 3.7.2.6. Air is distributed through the two parallel main ducts. One duct carries cold air normally maintained at 75-100 degrees (F.). These ducts provide the capability of cooling

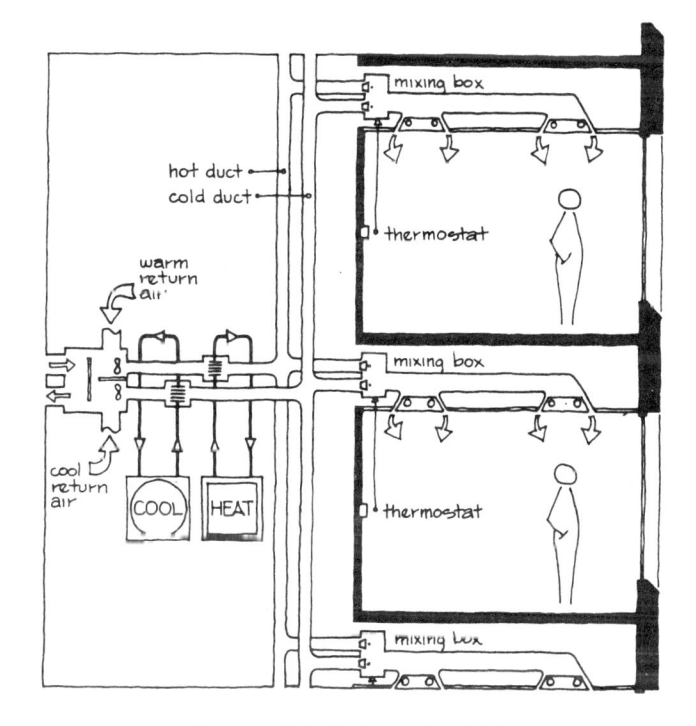

Figure 3.7.2.6 - Dual Duct

and heating at all times. A CAV/VAT mixing box is installed for each space (or zone) to mix the cold or warm air in proper proportion to satisfy the space heat load as indicated by the space thermostat.

Because two main ducts must be installed, double-duct systems generally require more ceiling and shaft space, resulting in higher construction cost. Energy consumption is high due to mixing of warm and cold air.

Multizone System. A multizone system requires a factory-built, multizone air handling unit with separate cold air and hot air compartments that provide mixed air to as many as 12 zone ducts (see Figure 3.7.2.7). Thermostats within each space control the air temperature of the respective zone ducts according to the space demand. This system is normally used in capacities up to 20,000 cubic feet per minute (cfm) even though larger units of up to 50,000 cfm are available. It is ideally suited for small buildings with limited distance for duct runs to the spaces; the cost of construction can vary from very economical for small buildings to considerably more expensive for larger systems.

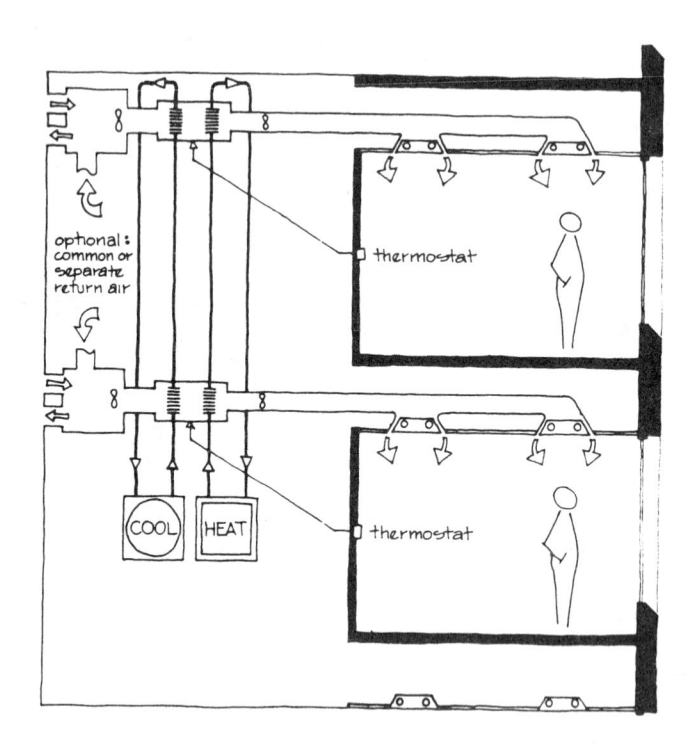

Figure 3.7.2.7 - Multi-Zone

Fan Coil System. Fan coil units, which consist of built-in centrifugal fans and water coils, are essentially small air-handling units (see Figure 3.7.2.8). They are mounted within the space, either below the window, below the ceiling or above the ceiling, and have independent or combined chilled and hot water coils. Because the units are located within the space, the air pressure required for the unit fans is quite low and therefore will be most efficient in terms of its air transport factor (ATF). When the coils are supplied by independent chilled and hot water sources, the system is known as a four-pipe coil system. If the supply system is a changeover between hot and chilled water using the common supply and return pipes, the system is called a two-pipe system. A four-pipe system is expensive but contains a high degree of flexibility because each fan coil unit can be changed over independently of the other.

In general, the ventilating system provides only the minimum quantity of outside air required.

Construction cost of the fan coil system varies from modest to high depending on cabinet design and method of outside air supply.

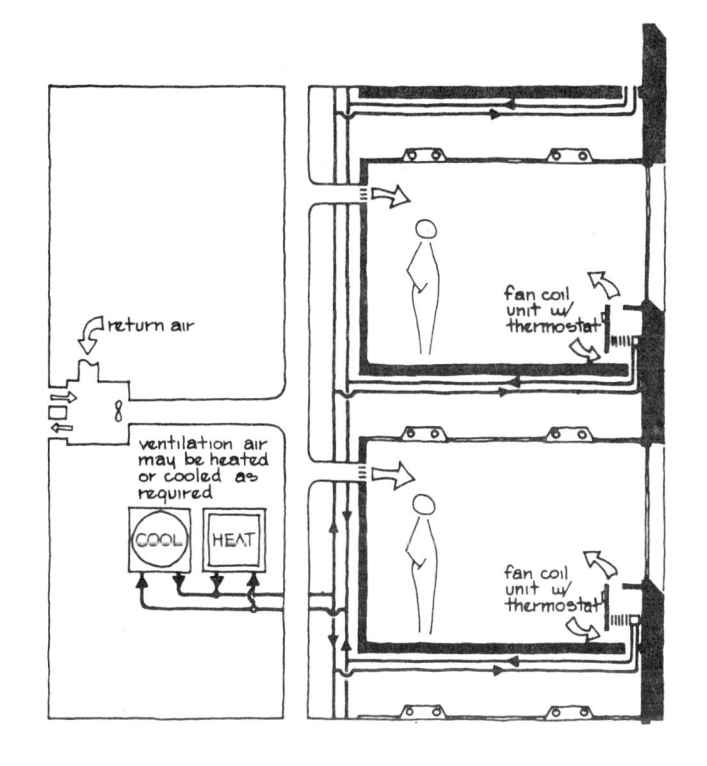

Figure 3.7.2.8 - Fan-Coil

Combination Single-Duct VAV/CAT and Double-Duct VAV/VAT System. The combination single-duct, VAV/CAT and double-duct VAV/VAT system consists of dual air-handling units, with one unit supplying cold air to the cold air duct and another supplying warm air to the warm air duct. It can be considered a combination single- and double-duct system, with the advantage of increased energy efficiency. With this system, VAV/CAT single-duct boxes are normally used for interior spaces, with VAV/VAT double-duct mixing boxes used for exterior spaces. The system has oderate construction cost and low operating costs.

All-Water Heat Pump System. The all-water heat pump system consists of multiple modules of DX cooling units piped with a closed-loop water circuit. The circuit transfers heat removed from a space that requires cooling to a space that requires heating (see Figure 3.7.2.9). Water circulated within the closed loop becomes

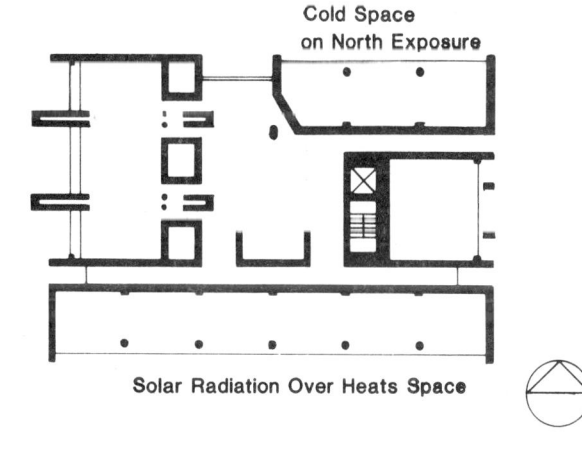

Figure 3.7.2.9 - Water-Loop Heat Pump

either a sink or a source of heat. Units on the heating mode are extracting heat from the water; units on the cooling mode are rejecting heat to the water. During the cooling season, heat rejected to the water loop is cooled through an indirect heat exchanger located outside the building. A boiler should be added to the loop for the heating season.

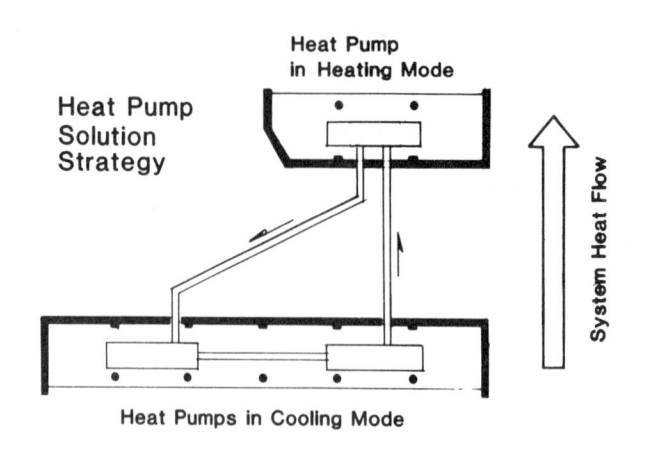

Figure 3.7.2.9 (continued) - Water-Loop Heat Pump

Figure 3.7.2.10 shows an array of typical systems.

CRITERIA	Single-Zone (Self-Contained)	Single Duct Reheat	Single Duct VAV with Heater	Single Duct VAV with Fan Terminal	Double Duct (All Zones)	Multizone (Low Velocity)	Fan Coil (2-Pipe)	Combination Single Duct & Double Duct	All-Water Heat Pump (Above Ceiling)
Operating Principle of Primary Air	CAV/VAT	CAV/CAT	VAV/CAT	VAV/CAT	CAV/VAT	CAV/VAV	CAV/VAT	VAV/VAT	CAV/VAT
Practical Application of Factory Built Unit (cfm)	Up to 40,000	Up to 50,000	Up to 50,000	Up to 50,000	Up to 40,000	Up to 30,000	Up to 800	Up to 40,000	Up to 5,000
Limit of Control Zones	One	Unlimited	Unlimited	Unlimited	Unlimited	Up to 12	Unlimited	Unlimited	Unlimited
Temperature Control Capability	Fair	Excellent	Good	Excellent	Excellent	Excellent	Good	Excellent	Good
Humidity Control Capability	Fair	Excellent	Good	Good	Good	Good	Fair	Good	Fair
Noise	High	Low	Low	Medium	Low	Low	Medium	Low	High
Central Equipment	Low	High	High	High	High	High	High	High	Medium
Air Handling Equipment	Medium	High	High	High	High	High	Low	High	Low
Finished Area	None	None	Low	None	None	None	High	None	None
Ceiling Cavity Height	High	Medium	Low	Medium	High	Medium	Low	High	High
Capital Investment	Low	Medium	Medium	Medium	High	Medium	High	Medium	Low
Energy Consumption	Medium	High	Medium	Low	High	High	Medium	Low	Low
Maintenance	Medium	Medium	Low	Medium	Low	Low	High	Low	High
Ease of Alteration	Poor	Excellent	Excellent	Good	Good	Poor	Good	Good	Poor

Figure 3.7.2.10 - Common HVAC System Types

3.7.3 Components

Cooling Sources

Refrigeration is the heart of the cooling system. Two cycles, or methods, of refrigeration can be used--vapor compression or absorption. In the case of vapor compression, refrigerant gas is compressed and condensed to liquid refrigerant. In the phase-change process of condensing, the refrigerant liberates its latent heat of vaporization to the heat rejection system. When the liquid refrigerant is allowed to expand at lower pressure, it evaporates into refrigerant vapor. In doing so, it absorbs latent heat of vaporization in a second phase-change. Figure 3.7.3.1 shows the coefficients of performance (COP) of various equipment.

Equipment COP	COP
Single stage absorption	0.67
Two stage absorption	1.25
Turbine drive centrifugal	1.0
Turbine drive chiller with piggy back absorption chiller	1.6
Electric driven reciprocating chiller	3.5
Electric driven centrifugal chiller	4.0

Figure 3.7.3.1 - Typical COPs

The absorbing of heat constitutes the refrigerating or cooling effect. Refrigerant can be used directly in the air cooling coil (direct expansion, or DX system), or can be used in a refrigerant-to-water heat exchanger (chilled water system).

Several types of refrigeration compressors are commonly used. Reciprocation compressors range in size from a fraction of a ton to approximately 50 tons in capacity. Rotary helical, or "screw," compressors are also available, in capacities up to approximately 400 tons. Equipment from 200 to 2,000 tons generally uses centrifugal compressors, which are most efficient. Figure 3.7.3.2 shows the compressive refrigeration cycle.

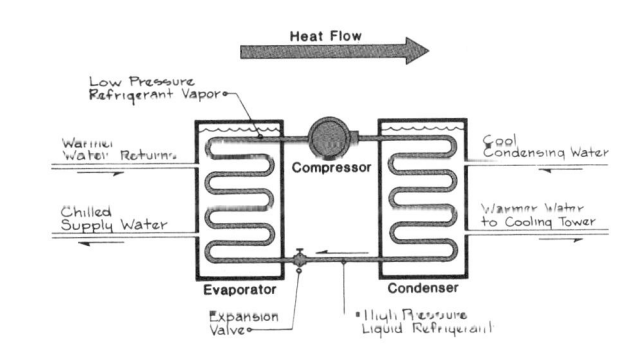

Figure 3.7.3.2 - Compressive Cycle

The COP for refrigerating equipment is calculated by including all the heat being delivered to the refrigeration machine, including heat from fans and water pumps. As stated earlier, this can be misleading in an overall evaluation of an airconditioning system.

Refrigeration involves the moving of heat from one place to another. Generally, heat is removed from the building and rejected to the outdoors. On the other hand, during winter, large buildings can need cooling of interior spaces at the same time heating is needed in perimeter spaces. Heat reclamation refrigeration systems can be used to serve both purposes, thereby saving energy. Domestic water heating can also benefit from heat that might otherwise have been wasted to the outdoors. Large buildings and buildings with intense cooling needs, such as computer centers, are prime candidates for heat reclamation.

The other method of cooling is absorption refrigeration (see Figure 3.7.3.3). The absorption cycle commonly used in commercial and institutional buildings uses water as the refrigerant. Water is evaporated at very low pressure to produce a cooling effect. Water vapor is then absorbed by a strong solution of lithium bromide, a desiccant salt. As the solution becomes weak, heat must be added to drive off excess water, thus reconcentrating the solution. The water vapor is then condensed for subsequent evaporation. Absorption refrigeration uses heat from gas, hot water or steam and a small amount of electric power to operate the assembly's pumps.

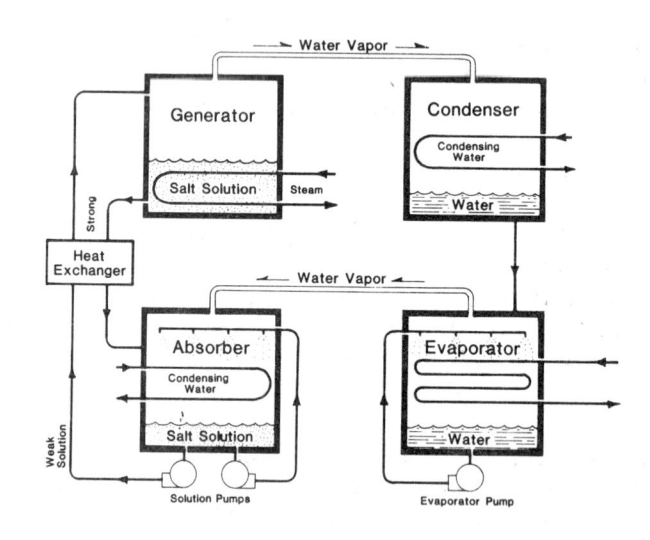

Figure 3.7.3.3 - Absorption Cycle

Absorption refrigeration consumes much more energy than does vapor compression. Absorption will generally be used only when an inexpensive source of heating energy is available, such as solar or turbine generator exhaust.

Heating Sources

Boilers are used in the vast majority of HVAC systems. They should be selected to provide high average efficiency for the predominant load range. Large boilers with modulating burners can operate at constant efficiency down to 25 percent of their maximum rated outputs. The use of two or more boilers in sequential operation can increase boiler operating efficiency when system loads are below 25 percent peak load, with each boiler operating at its highest average efficiency and responsive to an incremental portion of the load.

For small boilers with fixed-firing-rate burners the most efficient boiler arrangement is a modular boiler assembly consisting of multiple boilers.

Each boiler is able to respond to a small increment of load and operate at peak efficiency. Under part-load operation such boiler modules start and stop in sequence to match the load.

For most commercial applications heating is accomplished by circulating air over fin coils supplied with boiler-heated water. The variations primarily involve coil location.

Boilers can be heated by oil, natural gas, coal, or electricity. Oil comes in several varieties. The lighter oils, No.1 and No.2, ignite and burn at lower temperatures and are more satisfactory than heavier oils for intermittent, automatically controlled heating systems. The lighter fuels are also more expensive, and as prices have risen, burners have been developed to make use of the heavier No.5 and no.6 oils. These oils often must be preheated and atomized by being forced under pressure through a nozzle. Gas burning is relatively straightforward. Given the supply uncertainty and price fluctuations for oil as well as natural gas in recent years, multifuel boilers have been developed.

Pumps, Motors, and Fans

Pumps. Properly selected pumps offer high efficiency under part-load conditions. With automatic-throttling-type control valves and multiple pumps that can be started and stopped in sequence, the quantity of fluid in circulation can be reduced to match the load and still maintain high-efficiency operation. This can be especially useful in multiple heat pump systems.

Motors. Alternating current motors vary from low efficiencies at fractional horsepower outputs to higher efficiencies of larger motors. In the last few years, higher-efficiency motors offering significant energy savings have become widely available. Above 3 horsepower, squirrel-cage motors operating at 1/2-3/4 part loads are slightly less efficient than at full-load rating. Below 3 horsepower, for similar load comparisons, losses in motor efficiency are greater.

Fans. Fans should be selected for the highest operating efficiency at predominant operating conditions to minimize energy consumed for air circulation. Centrifugal fans include air-foil, backward-inclined, and forward-curved types. Air-foil and backward-inclined fans have similar efficiencies, with the air foil more efficient in larger sizes. Efficiency of forward-curved fans is lower than the other two centrifugal types.

Vane-axial fans are available with either fixed or adjustable pitch blades. At full-load operation, their efficiencies are comparable to centrifugal fans. At part-load operation, the position of adjustable pitch fan blades can be automatically reset to reduce air quantity and maintain high operating efficiency. Variable inlet vanes used with fixed blade vane-axial fans can vary the quantity of air flow for efficient part load operation.

Heat Rejection

Heat must be removed in order to condense hot refrigerant gas. For heat to flow, the temperature of the heat-removal medium must be lower than the refrigerant-condensing temperature. Generally, the cooler the heat-removal medium, the less power will be required by the refrigerant compressor. Water and ambient air are the most commonly used media. Air-cooled condensers use fans to circulate outside air through a finned coil in which refrigerant gas turns to liquid. For air-cooled condensers, the power used in calculating a unit's heat-removal factor (HRF) will be that of the fan. Values of HRF range from 25 to 60.

Water-cooled condensers most often use pumps to circulate cooling water through refrigerant-to-water heat exchangers. River, lake or well water can be used, but cooling towers are the most prevalent design solution.

A cooling tower is an evaporative cooling device. A portion of the water evaporates in the cooling tower, absorbing heat as the water changes phase from liquid to vapor and cooling the remaining water, which is recirculated to the condenser. Makeup water must be added to compensate for the water lost in evaporation, as well as to dilute dissolved solids, which tend to concentrate as the water evaporates.

Cooling towers may or may not use fans to conduct air past the water. Injection towers rely on spray nozzles to induce air flow and splash. For water-type heat rejection systems, the power used for calculating HRF will be the sum of pump and fan requirements. Typically, HRF will range from 20 to 40.

Heat Exchangers

Thermal Wheels. Thermal wheels, also called heat wheels, are packed with a heat-absorbing material such as aluminum or stainless steel wool. The wheels transfer energy from one airstream to another or, for large boiler plants, from flue gas to combustion air. The thermal wheel can only be installed when the hot and cold airstreams are immediately adjacent and parallel. Two types of thermal wheel are available: one transfers sensible heat only, the other transfers both sensible and latent heat.

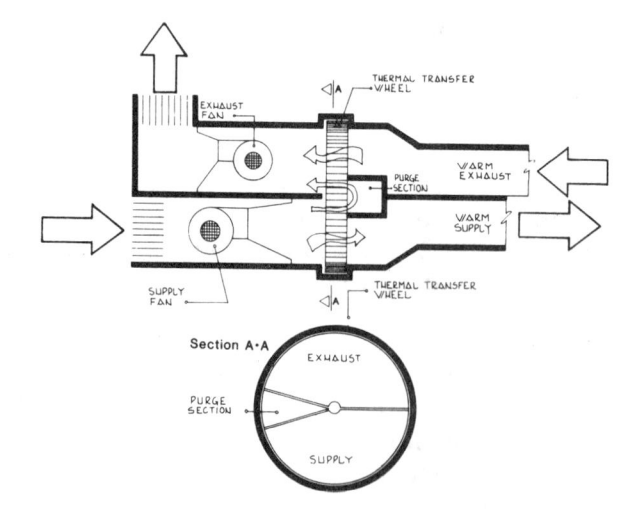

Figure 3.7.3.4 - Thermal Wheels

Thermal wheels are driven by electric motors, which use energy and decrease summer efficiency because of motor-generated heat. Efficiencies are generally 60-80 percent for sensible heat transfer and 20-60 percent for latent heat transfer.

Heat Pipes. Heat pipes running through the adjacent wall of inlet and outlet ducts can be an efficient means of transferring heat from the warmer duct to the cooler one. The heat pipes are short lengths of copper tubing, sealed tightly at the ends with wicks or capillaries and containing a charge of refrigerant. For single-direction heat flow, the refrigerant moves by capillary action to the warmer end of the tube and evaporates, absorbing heat in the process. The warmer end of the pipe is slightly lower than the cooler end, where it condenses, releases its heat to the cooler duct, and remigrates to the lower end. For dual-direction heat flow (summertime cooling recovery) heat pipes must be installed level. All liquid flow is then by capillary action only.

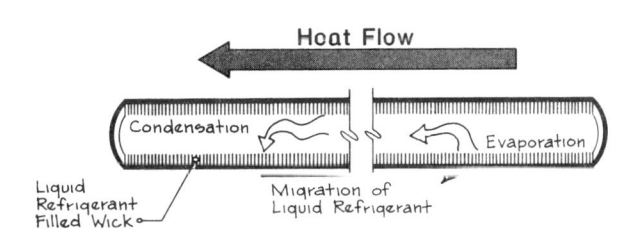

Figure 3.7.3.5 - Heat Pipes

Runaround Coils. A runaround coil system is composed of two or more extended surface fin coils installed in air ducts and interconnected by piping. A heat-exchange fluid of ethylene glycol and water is circulated through the system by a pump; the fluid absorbs heat from the hot air stream and releases it into the cold air stream (or vice versa). A runaround-coil system can be used in winter to preheat cold outdoor air and in summer to cool hot outdoor air. Where there is no possibility of freezing, water can also be used as the heat transfer medium. Runaround coils are most often used when there is difficulty locating the exhaust air duct in close proximity to the make-up air duct. They are substantially less efficient than heat wheels and heat pipe heat exchangers.

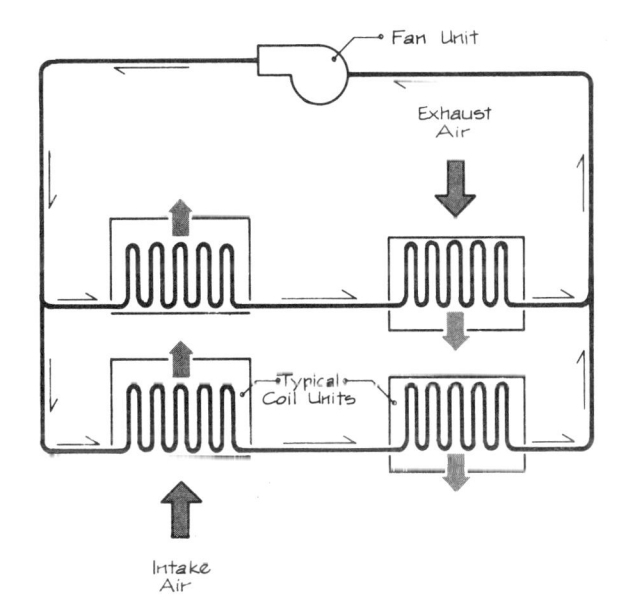

Figure 3.7.3.6 - Run-Around Coils

When double-bundle condensers are used for heat recovery, a cooling coil can be placed in the exhaust air duct to remove the heat before exhausting the air to the outside. This heat is transferred via the chiller to the condenser side. This is one of the most efficient forms of exhaust air heat recovery possible. It should be considered when other system requirements support it.

Air-To-Air Heat Exchanger. An air-to-air heat exchanger transfers heat directly from one air stream to another through either side of a metal transfer surface. This surface can be convoluted plates (for low-temperature use in HVAC systems) or tubes (for boiler flue gas heat transfer). These heat exchangers are available as packaged units or custom-made. Efficiencies tend to be lower than 50 percent, but these exchangers are relatively inexpensive, have low resistance to air flow, require no power input, and are durable.

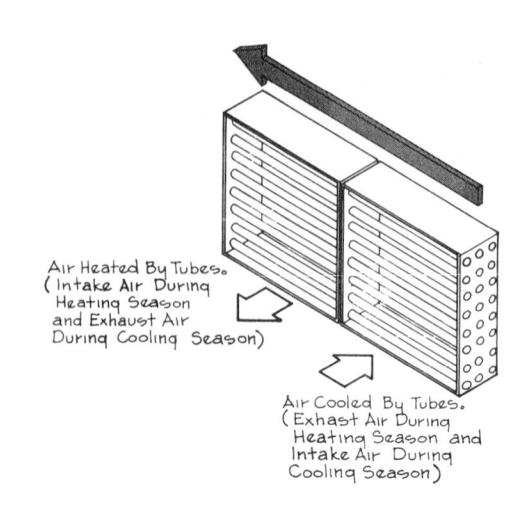

Figure 3.7.3.7 - Air-to-Air Exchangers

Extreme care should be used in the design of flue gas heat recovery systems. Improper design can lead to cooling flue gases below their condensation point. Flue gas condensate, particularly from oil-filtered boilers, is extremely corrosive.

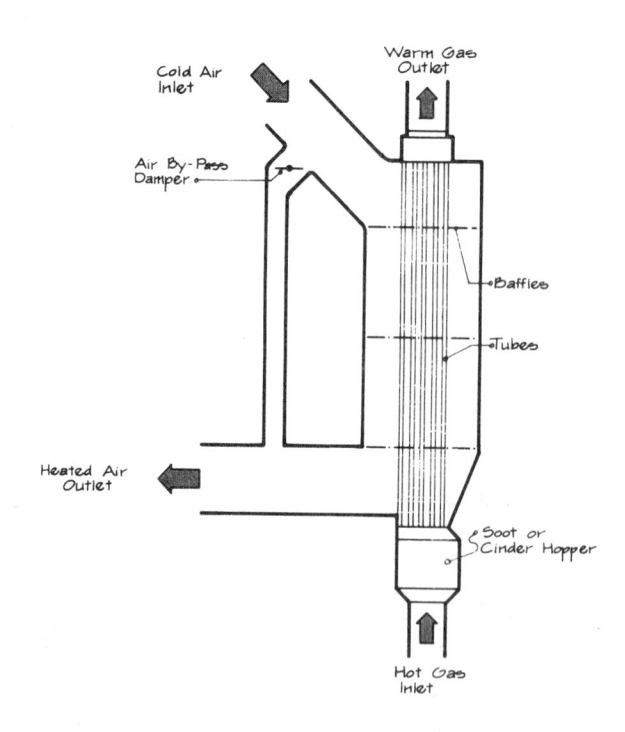

Figure 3.7.3.8 - Flue-Gas Recovery

Heat Pump. Heat pumps are effective heat exchangers in the heating mode. They can be configured in all possible combinations of air and water.

Shell and Tube Heat Exchangers. Shell and tube heat exchangers can be configured to transfer heat to liquid from liquid, steam, or gas. They are especially effective where large temperature differentials exist. Figure 3.7.3.9 lists various applications of heat reclamation devices.

Heat Reclaim Sources	Temper Ventilation Air	Preheat Domestic Hot Water	Space Heating	Terminal Reheat	Temper Makeup Air	Preheat Combustion Air	Heat Heavy Oil	Internal to External Zone Heat Transfer
Exhaust air	1a, 1b, 1c, 2, 3, 4, 5				1a, 1b, 1c, 2, 3, 4, 5	Direct		5, Direct
Flue gas	1b, 3, 4		3, 4		1b, 3, 4	1b, 2, 3, 4		
Hot condensate	3, 6	3, 6	3, 5, 6	3, 6	3, 6	3, 6	6	
Refrigerant hot gas	6	6		6	6			
Hot condenser water	3, 6	3, 6	3, 5, 6	6	3, 5, 6	3, 5, 6	6	5
Hot-water drains		6						
Solid waste	7	7	7	7	7	7	7	
Engine and exhaust cooling systems	6, 8	6	6, 8	6	6, 8	6, 8	6	
Lights Air-cooled condensers	5, 9		5, 9 Direct	5, 9	5, 9			5, 9

Heat Reclaim Devices:
1. Thermal wheel
    a. Latent
    b. Sensible
    c. Combination
2. Runaround coil
3. Heat pipe
4. Air-to-air heat exchanger
5. Heat pump
6. Shell/tube heat exchanger
7. Incinerator
8. Waste heat boiler
9. Heat-of-light

Applications of Heat Reclamation Devices

Fred S. Dubin and Chalmers G. Long, Jr., *Energy Conservation Standards*, © 1978. Reprinted by permission of McGraw-Hill Book Company, New York, New York.

Figure 3.7.3.9 - Heat Reclamation Devices

3.7.4 Controls

Control systems can be divided into two categories: manual and automatic. Manual controls have been in use for many years. Generally speaking, automatic controls, including energy management and control systems (EMCSs), are more popular because they do not depend on people to remember to turn them on or off at appropriate times. At the same time, manual controls operated by building staff can be effective in monitoring for malfunctions. Manual controls are also usually both less complex and more reliable than automatic controls. Manual controls thus can be useful, particularly for very small systems and for large central plant heating and cooling equipment.

Most of today's control devices can be divided into three other categories: localized controls, remote limited and multifunction controls, and centralized, computer-based EMCSs (the latter are discussed in Section 3.9).

Localized Controls

A localized control device provides independent, relatively low-cost control for specified systems and equipment. Each local controller independently controls its operating system or equipment, not acting in conjunction with any other controlling device.

These systems usually are most applicable when:
- the control device is compatible with the system involved and will improve system operation and efficiency
- usage and climatic factors permit
- the HVAC systems involved are relatively simple
- only a single small building with few mechanical equipment rooms is involved, or each building of a complex of buildings has a small, individual HVAC system
- immediate results are desired because, for example, installation time allowable is minimal and/or individual system or component optimization is more important than total system-wide optimization.

Time Controls. Time controls are among the most effective local controls because they are based on the simple principle of turning energy systems on or off -- up or down -- according to a schedule. Some of the common types are:
- astronomical control automatically compensates for seasonal variations in time of sunrise
- delay timer delays on or off switching action for a set interval after automatic or manual actuation
- interval timer is set for a desired elapsed time interval; manually or automatically repeatable
- externally initiated time control starts timing cycle upon initiation by a remote signal
- program time switch is a sophisticated control with programmed signals that can be set as close together as five minutes
- repeat-cycle time control continually repeats a selected cycle of less than 24-hour duration
- seven-day time control allows different cycles each day of the week; each day is divided into morning, afternoon and night with multiple on/off cycles per day; available with skip-a-day feature to omit the cycle(s) on any day
- 24-hour time control continuously repeats a 24-hour cycle with up to seven on/off cycles per day

A variety of these time controls can be applied to various energy systems, as follows:
- building warm-up or cooling-down control on HVAC systems, especially applicable for interior areas which normally follow the warm-up with a

cooling cycle. The cycle should also shut outside air dampers (which normally open with fan start-up) during the warm-up period. Dampers should also be shut during summer cool-down.
- program controls for shut-down prior to the end of the work day to take advantage of the thermal mass storage effect of the building.
- all lighting circuits where potential savings justify cost of the installation. A savings potential exists even in small spaces. Manual occupant override must be developed for individual circumstances. Interval timers can be acceptable for automatic off switching after a preset time period.

Automatic Temperature Setback/Setup Controls. Automatic temperature setback/setup controls essentially combine two thermostats or a thermostat with two set points and a time clock. When two thermostats are used, one thermostat is set for a daytime temperature, the other for a nighttime temperature. The time clock switches control from one thermostat to the other at a preset time.

Economizer Cycle. The use of an all outside-air economizer cycle can be a cost-effective energy-conservation measure, depending on the climatic conditions and the type of mechanical system. Where applicable, the cycle uses outside air to satisfy all or a portion of the building's cooling requirements when the temperature of the outside air is less than that of the return air from the space.

A dry-bulb temperature economizer cycle is regulated by an outdoor air temperature sensor that discontinues compressor operation when outdoor temperature falls below the design supply temperature, normally 50-60 degrees (F.). Cooler outside air is then drawn into the system and used to reduce space temperature. An enthalpy economizer cycle is similar to a dry-bulb temperature economizer cycle, except it takes similar action on the basis of a comparison of the total heat content (enthalpy) of indoor and outdoor air.

Supply Temperature Reset. It is common practice to set boilers to maintain a predetermined water temperature based on the needs of the coldest day. As a result, on most days the water is overheated, wasting energy. An automatic supply temperature reset system compares outdoor and supply-water temperatures and regulates the hot-water system accordingly. Studies indicate potential energy savings of more than 17 percent.

A supply temperature reset should not be used on hydronic systems where service or process hot water is provided by the boiler or where day-night temperature control is used.

Radiator Valves. Radiator valves are used on free-standing radiators, convectors, and baseboard heating units to provide automatic room temperature control of the hot water in two-pipe steam heating systems. The valve body is installed in place of the manual valve; it throttles steam supply to the radiator according to ambient room conditions.

Deadband Control System.
HVAC systems generally are controlled by room air temperature, outside air temperature and fixed equipment settings. Using several factors like this to control equipment settings often wastes energy.

A deadband control system operates solely on the basis of room temperature. As shown in Figure 3.7.4.1, it establishes a relatively wide range (deadband) over which no heating or cooling is provided. As the temperature falls below or rises above deadband settings, heating or cooling is gradually increased to reset the temperature of the air being supplied to the space.

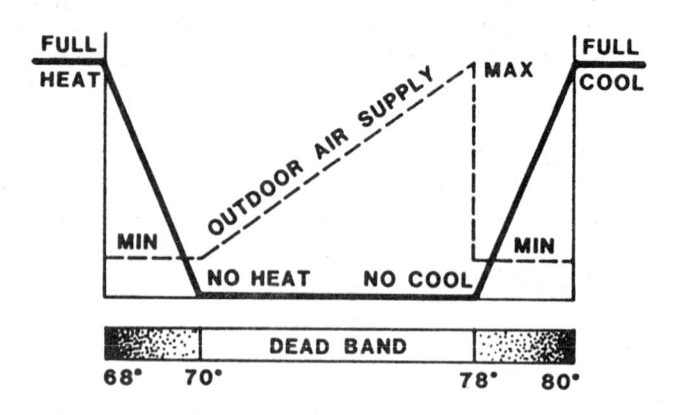

Figure 3.7.4.1 - Dead Band Control

A deadband control is applicable to HVAC systems that provide heating and cooling in sequence; it can be used effectively even when these systems have economizer cycle controls or are interfaced with higher levels of EMCS.

Multizone System Controller. Most existing multizone systems provide heating and cooling simultaneously year round, even though only one or the other is really needed most of the time. In addition, many multizone systems maintain temperatures to meet maximum demand conditions at all times, even when cooling could be supplied with "free" cool air readily available from outdoors.

A multizone system controller can be used to match heating and cooling output to actual demands in the space, relying on outdoor air as much as possible to meet cooling needs. These systems are applicable to almost any building having more than one zone heated by gas, oil, electric, steam, or hot-water radiation and cooled by DX or chilled water.

A multizone system controller typically includes a central processor, hot and cold deck controls, room thermostats, dampers with associated linkages and motors, economizer controller, changeover temperature controller and a morning warm-up thermostat. When the thermostat calls for cooling, the damper for that zone is modulated to admit more air from the cold deck and less from the hot deck. If the zone cooling damper is wide open and the space demand is still not satisfied, the central processor modulates the economizer to bring in more outside air. If a cooling demand still exists after the outdoor air damper is wide open, the central processor turns on mechanical cooling in stages as required.

When a heating demand exists, the space thermostat modulates the damper to admit more air from the hot deck until the demand is satisfied. If the zone damper to the hot deck is fully open but heating requirements are still not satisfied, a stage of heating is activated. The first stage of heating can be condenser heat if the cooling equipment is designed to provide it.

Single-Zone System Controller. A typical single-zone system controller includes a space thermostat, discharge air sensor, economizer motors, enthalpy controller, dampers with associated linkages, and a logic panel consisting of three on/off heat and three on/off cool thermostats, an economizer and an adjustable night setback.

The single-zone system saves energy in a number of ways: use of outdoor air for the first stage of cooling, night and weekend setback, outdoor air damper shutdown, and better system supervision and control. Further savings can be anticipated through increased equipment life due to reduced operation by using the economizer cycle as the first stage of cooling.

Chiller Energy Management Controller. A chiller energy management controller uses programmed logic to load, unload, start, and stop centrifugal chillers. The controller also resets suction temperature automatically by sensing load requirements; remotely monitors and displays inlet vane position in percentages as well as chiller operating hours; and starts the standby chiller automatically, when needed.

Individual Local Controls. Adding individual local controls can frequently be justified when the potential for waste is otherwise uncontrollable, in situations such as:
- changing reheat controls to modified VAV in a zone that has simultaneous heating and cooling--one nullifying the other--instead of sequencing one to a minimum or zero value before starting the other.
- changing to light switches that control relatively few fixtures in large areas such as cafeterias. When only one control is available, all lighting must be either on or off. Local lighting controls permit selectivity.

Remote-Limited and Multifunction Controls

Remote-limited and multifunction controls are typified by a limited function demand controller, which interfaces with numerous energy-consuming devices and systems to limit electrical demand. Many of the newest EMCS devices are programmable through use of microprocessors and provide multifunction capability in the same "black box."

Remote-limited and multifunction EMCS devices usually are most applicable when:
- the functions to be performed are limited
- the number of points to be monitored and controlled are generally fewer than 100.

Scheduled Start/Stop. The scheduled start/stop program is a remote-limited, multifunction control that consists of starting and stopping equipment based on the time of day and day of week and operates in conjunction with optimum start/stop, unoccupied cycle setback, and lighting control programs. Scheduled start/stop is the simplest of all EMCS functions to implement.

This program serves energy-conservation and demand management functions by turning off equipment during unoccupied hours or during periods of maximum electric demand. In addition to sending a start/stop command, it desirable to have a feedback signal indicating the status (on-off or open-closed) of the controlled equipment. The feedback signal verifies the command has been carried out and provides the EMCS operator with an alarm when the equipment fails or is locally started or stopped.

Optimum Start/Stop. The scheduled start/stop program described above can be refined by automatically adjusting the equipment operating schedule in accordance with space temperature and outside air temperature and humidity. In the scheduled start/stop program, HVAC systems are restarted prior to occupancy to cool down or heat up the space on a fixed schedule independent of outside air and space conditions. The optimum start/stop program automatically starts and stops the system on a sliding schedule that takes into account the thermal inertia of the structure, the capacity of the HVAC system to either increase or reduce space temperatures, outside air conditions, and current space temperatures. This program logic determines the minimum time of HVAC system operation needed to satisfy the space environmental requirements at the start of the occupied cycle, and determines the earliest time for stopping equipment at the day's end.

Demand Controller. Most large buildings are billed for electric demand as well as the amount of electrical consumption (see Section 2.3, Cost of Energy). Demand refers to the average rate of use of electrical power for a specified time interval.

A demand controller prevents electrical demand from exceeding a predetermined maximum. Interrruptible or secondary loads are connected to it, and as usage approaches maximum during an interval, secondary loads are shed. When usage subsides, or when the demand interval ends, the secondary loads are restored.

Many demand controllers have been designed to function with specific utility rate structures and metering methods. Local utility companies can provide further information.

Multifunction Programmable Controller. Multifunction controllers perform demand control, time-of-day load scheduling, optimized start/stop, and duty cycling. Duty cycling has become somewhat controversial. It consists of shutting down a system for predetermined short periods of time during normal operating hours. This use is based on the assumption that HVAC systems seldom operate at peak output. Accordingly, if a system is shut down for a short period of time, it still has enough capacity to overcome the slight temperature drift that can occur during the shutdown.

Although the interruption does not reduce space cooling loads, it does reduce net auxiliary loads, such as those contributed by heat from fans and pumps. It also reduces outside air heating and cooling loads since the outside air intake damper is closed while an air-handling unit is off.

Random duty cycling can actually result in an increased electrical peak, with associated utility rate increases (see Section 2.3, Cost of Energy). The computer memory of an EMCS can be used to synchronize the duty cycling of electric loads to minimize the peak electric demand. Normally, each load is assigned a relative priority level, maximum off time, minimum off time, and on-off priority such as "first on/first off" or "first on/last off."

An optional feature of duty cycling is space temperature feedback, in which the on/off interval is fine-tuned according to fluctuating space conditions to prevent the space temperature from rising above a maximum limit. To prevent short cycling of the fan, the space temperature control operates with a deadband temperature range such as off at 72 degrees (F.) and on at 78 degrees (F.).

A major disadvantage of duty cycling is that the continuous cycling of fans can result in increased maintenance costs for belts, sheaves, motors, and electrical starters. Many harmful effects from the continuous duty cycling of fan motors are not immediately visible, but fans, which have very high inertia and torque loads at startup, have high starting currents on motor windings. This results in increased motor temperature and severe electromagnetic stresses on wire, rotor bars, and insulation. While every motor is capable of taking a certain number of starts, trouble can result after only a few years if a motor is cycled on and off, for example, 24 times a day.

Duty cycling can also result in occupant discomfort. Unless building system changes have occurred to allow for a reduced average hourly air flow rate, or unless the HVAC system was originally overdesigned, space discomfort problems can result from duty cycling. Moreover, the air-handling systems in some buildings are not zoned to accommodate duty cycling. For example, if one air flow handler serves both the interior and the perimeter, full air flow rates can be required in the interior zone or one of the perimeter zones at all times; e.g., peak air flow would be required for the east zone in the morning, the west zone in the afternoon, and the south zone in the winter as the sun's rays impinge on it. While the average space temperature can be comfortable with duty cycling, some zones would be uncomfortable.

The following equipment generally should not be duty cycled:
- VAV fans
- fans or pumps larger than 25 hp
- fans for refrigerant cooling coils or heat pumps
- chilled water pumps
- lighting systems.

<u>Programmable Lighting Controller.</u> Programmable lighting controllers can control all lighting inside and outside a building. Typical components of such systems include the central controller, through which a control program is entered via a keyboard, and transceivers that accept signals from the control unit and, in turn, operate the relays with which they are connected. Some systems can accept manual override through direct activation at the keyboard or through use of a pushbutton telephone. Printers can be integrated with the system to provide a hard copy record of activity.

Waste Heat Recovery

Cascading energy systems recover "waste" thermal energy generated by building operations to satisfy part of the building's energy needs. Sources of waste heat include machines, lights and people. Space heating is the most obvious application of a cascading energy system, although many other applications can be easily integrated into conventional building systems.

Air-handling HVAC systems often incorporate energy recovery techniques as standard design. Air, heated by lights, machines and people, is returned to a central location (this may be independent of the central heating and cooling elements). This heated air is then recirculated to other spaces requiring heating. Large buildings, which generate substantial heat in internal zones, may transfer this heat to perimeter zones during the heating season. During the cooling season, hot air from individual zones may be selectively ejected from the building if more favorable outdoor air exists. The appropriate zoning of spaces, their thermal loads and the system can greatly influence the efficiency of systems of this kind.

Heat Recovery From Lighting Systems

There are two major methods for recovering lighting heat: plenum-return systems and water-cooled luminaires. Ducted-air systems can be designed to provide a direct means of controlling and redistributing heat dissipated by lighting fixtures. One approach is to provide the lighting fixture with slots through which return air is drawn into the ceiling plenum. As air passes over the lamps, ballast and sheet metal of the luminaire, it picks up as much as 80 percent of the electrical energy used by the light as dissipated heat, carrying it into the plenum.

Plenum heat can be used in space conditioning systems in a variety of ways. In a double-duct or VAV system, the plenum can be the primary source of heat for air supply, with supplementary heat supplied by duct heaters or water coils piped to the space conditioning water side of a double-bundle condenser.

During the cooling season, heat from air-return lighting fixtures can be drawn off and discharged outdoors. This reduces the cooling load for the building and can result in economies in distribution ductwork and refrigerator equipment. Another advantage is that removing heat from the lighting fixtures may increase their efficiency by 10-20 percent.

3.7.5 Active Solar Systems

Heating

In active solar heating systems for space or domestic hot water heating, either air or a liquid can be used to absorb and distribute solar heat. A solar collector of the liquid- or air-heating type (see Figure 3.7.5.1) usually involves a combination of an insulated storage reservoir and associated pumps (or blowers), piping (or ducting), auxiliary heater and a control system.

For large commercial buildings, liquid systems are often preferred because such buildings' mechanical systems also nearly always use hot water. Air systems can be appropriate for small buildings. Air and liquid systems offer advantages and disadvantages as displayed in Figure 3.7.5.2.

- In sizing a system, it is generally most cost effective to design an active solar system to meet 30-70 percent of annual heating requirements. The backup system should be designed to meet 100 percent of the building's heating or cooling requirements.

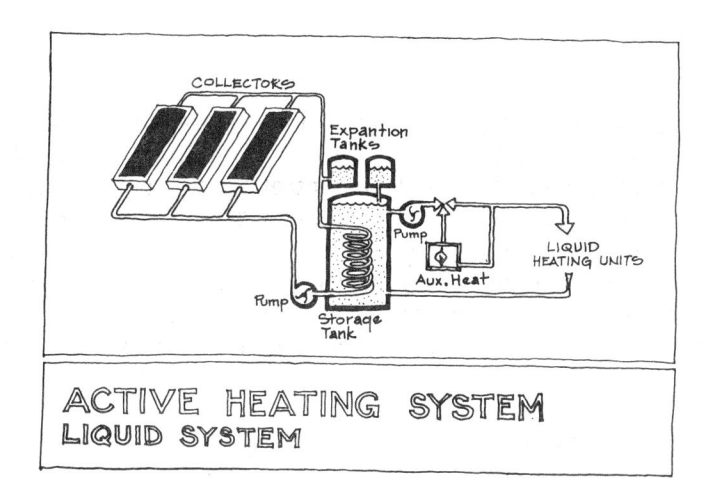

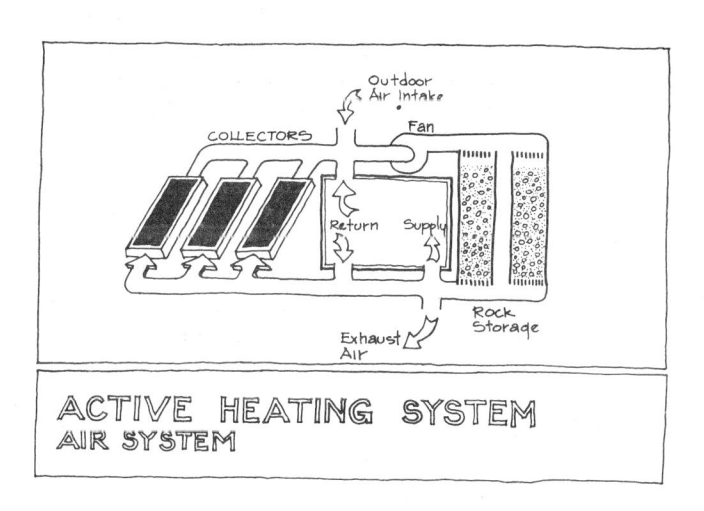

Figure 3.7.5.1 - Active Solar Heating

Liquid	Air
Collectors generally more efficient.	Collectors generally operate at slightly lower temperatures.
Can be combined with domestic hot water and air cooling systems.	Simpler. Space heat can be supplied directly. Can pre-heat domestic hot water. Does not adapt easily to air cooling.
Freeze protection may require antifreeze and heat exchangers. Costlier and reduces efficiency.	No freeze protection required.
Precautions must be taken against corrosion, leakage, and boiling.	Low maintenance requirements. Leaks easily repaired with duct tape.
Insulated pipes take up nominal space. More convenient to install in existing buildings.	Ductwork and rock storage bed bulky.
Higher installation costs for collectors and storage components.	Lower equipment costs.
Has received greater attention from solar industry.	More energy required to drive fans than pumps. Noisier in operation.

Figure 3.7.5.2 - System Comparisons

In general, collector tilt for building heating is approximately the latitude plus 15 degrees. For service-water heating only, the optimum tilt is an angle equal to the latitude.

For the preliminary sizing of an active solar collector array the following information is needed:
- building heat loss for worst month (Btu/Mo).
- insolation for same month on collector surface, at collector tilt and adjusted for average percent sunshine (Btu/Mo/sq ft)
- collector efficiency (from manufacturer). The following formula can be used to derive a collector area for 100- percent solar contribution, which can then be sized down to the desired solar contribution.

$$\text{Collector Area} = \frac{\text{Building heat loss (worst month) (Btu/Mo)}}{\text{Insolation (Btu/Mo/sq ft)} \times \% \text{ Efficiency}}$$

For domestic hot water, a rule of thumb is that 1-1.5 square feet of collector area is required for each gallon of hot water to be delivered.

Cooling

Solar energy can be used to operate cooling equipment by supplying thermal energy for several types of heat-activated cycles, including the gas-absorption, Rankine, and the desiccant absorption cycles.

Solar cooling is applicable to commercial buildings with significant cooling loads during the year. If combined with a solar heating system, it can use collectors that would otherwise not be used during the cooling season. Although conceptually attractive, solar cooling is at an earlier stage of development than solar heating. For example, at this writing, if a solar absorption cooling system alone does not replace 80 percent of the cooling annual energy requirements, it will probably not be cost effective unless it also supplies space heating and DHW and the cooling system is designed with limited electric backup cooling. However, technology for solar cooling is being refined.

Photovoltaics

Solar energy generates direct-current electricity whenever sunlight strikes photovoltaic (PV) solar cells.

PV cells are enclosed in a sealed glass or plastic unit called a module. Any number of these modules can be positioned in a rigid frame to provide a specific power rating. These framed units, called arrays, can be set up in array fields of any size. The wide applicability of PV technology is enhanced by this modularity. A PV system sometimes includes a storage medium (usually batteries) to provide power at night or during cloudy weather. Power-conditioned equipment is also needed if the load requires alternating current, since solar cells produce direct-current electricity. Power conditioning also allows PV systems to be integrated with other electrical generating equipment and the local utility grid.
- The first decision in the design of a PV system is whether the system

will be utility-interactive or a "stand-alone" system. If the system is utility-interactive, it can buy auxiliary power from the utility company during times of need and, in some regions, also sell excess power back to the utility when the PV array produces a surplus. An average "sell-back" rate to utility companies is 50 percent of the rate paid to purchase utility-generated power.
- Another major design decision is whether the PV system will have an electricity storage component. Both utility-interactive and stand-alone systems can use storage systems.
- For rough estimating purposes, a PV array size can be estimated by the following formula:

$$\text{Array Area (sq ft)} = \frac{\text{Load Demand/Day (kwh/Day)}}{\text{System efficiency} \times \text{Insolation (kwh/Day/sq ft)}}$$

An average system efficiency is 10 percent.

3.8 PROCESS LOADS AND DOMESTIC HOT WATER

3.8.1 Process Loads

Process loads--operation loads for equipment--are considered part of the electrical load on the building. For the purpose of this book, process loads are defined as energy needed for uses other than maintaining the internal environment and heating domestic water. (Internal heat gain from process loads is discussed in Section 3.2.2.) Some examples of process loads are:
- energy for vertical transportation
- energy for office equipment
- energy for food service equipment
- energy for computers
- energy for process (non-HVAC) furnaces and boilers.

The annual load for motors and electrical process loads can be calculated on the basis of:
- number and type of each kind of equipment
- operating voltage
- amperage pulled by the motor
- motor horsepower.

The designer can develop an annual use profile for motors and process loads. From the use profile, the annual motor and electric process load can be determined by the following formula:

Annual equipment operating load (kw/hr/yr) =

    total horsepower X operating hours per day X operating days per year X .746 kw/horsepower.

Vertical Transportation

The energy needed for the operation of an elevator and its equipment is a function of the number of stories the car services, the efficiency of the hoisting mechanism, the car's HVAC system, and the passenger capacity.

Escalators are not only expensive to install, they can be costly to operate since they run constantly (even when not transporting people).

Elevators and escalators can add considerably to the cost of running a building. Unnecessary use can be eliminated by encouraging walking, and, during times of low-use, reducing the number of elevators and escalators in operation.

Miscellaneous Equipment

Office equipment--typewriters, cash registers, copying machines, calculators--as well as special equipment such as computers and food service equipment, though relatively small in size, are large in number, and have a significant effect on a building's energy use.

The energy consumption by miscellaneous equipment can be estimated by examining the energy consumption of a few individual pieces and applying the results to the rest of the equipment.

3.8.2 Domestic Hot Water

The amount of energy needed to heat water for domestic use (DHW) varies by building type and level of occupancy. Building types that use large amounts of water--hospitals and apartment buildings--provide the most significant opportunities for energy conservation through efficient domestic hot water systems design.

Active and passive solar systems can be effective in all building types in significantly reducing the energy use for DHW.

To calculate the amount of energy needed to heat domestic water annually, the designer needs to know:
- the building type
- hot water use per occupant
- temperature rise of water (the difference between the water temperature for end use, and the temperature of water entering the heater.)

When the occupant use per day is not known, Figure 3.8.2.1 can be used for estimating purposes.

Building Type	Gallons Per Day Per Occupant Avg. Day	Max Hr.
Office	1.0	0.4
Educational: Elementary	0.6	0.6
Secondary	1.8	1.0
College	0.6	0.6
Restaurant (Full Service)	2.4/ avg. meals a day	1.5/ max. meals/hr
(Fast Food)	0.7/ avg.	0.7/ max. meals/hr
Residential: Hotel Nursing	18.5/bed	4.5/bed
Apartment Houses No. of Apartments 20 or less	42.0/Apt.	12.0/Apt.
50	40.0	10.0
75	38.0	8.5
100	37.0	7.0
200 or more	35.0	5.0
Motel/Hotel No. of Units 20 or less	20.0	6.0
60	14.0	5.0
100 or more	10.0	4.0

Figure 3.8.2.1 - DHW Usage

The yearly average water inlet temperature can usually be obtained from the local water company; if not, use an average of 55 degrees (F.). Hot water demand temperature can be 90-180 degrees (F.), depending on end use.

A use profile similar to the occupancy profile can be developed in terms of gallons/day. This is especially important for buildings with unusual demand loads for workday and nonworkday conditions. From the use profile, the annual energy can be calculated by the following formula:

Annual DHW operating load (kw/yr) =

total gallons per day x operating days per year x temperature rise (_T) x 8.33 lbs/gallon - 3400 Btu/hr/kw.

If electricity is the source for heating water, special consideration must be given to its contribution to peak electrical demand. To calculate the peak electrical demand for DHW, the following information is needed:

- number of electric water heaters
- size of each heater (gallons of storage)
- size of upper and lower heating elements
- type of control on upper and lower element.

A use profile can then be calculated.

The basic goals in DHW conservation are:
- use less water
- limit heat losses
- lower required water temperature

System	Efficiency (%)
Oil-fired heating boilers used year-round but with domestic hot water as the only summer load	45
Oil-fired heating boilers used year-round with absorption cooling in the summer	70
Gas-fired heating boilers used year-round but with domestic hot water as the only summer load	50
Gas-fired heating boilers used year-round with absorption cooling in summer	75
Separate oil-fired hot-water heaters	70
Separate gas-fired hot-water heaters	75
Separate electric water heaters	95

Figure 3.8.2.2 - DHW System Efficiencies

Figure 3.8.2.2 lists efficiencies for different hot water systems.

These goals can be achieved by:
- covering the water storage tanks with a minimum of three inches of insulation
- insulating the entire distribution piping system
- reducing the size of hot water equipment (to minimize losses from operation and stand-by)
- controlling recirculation pumps
- providing for circulation shut-down when the building is vacant
- lowering water temperatures
- selecting end-use products that have minimal water requirements.

Energy-efficient DHW equipment includes:
- flow-restrictors
- orifices in hot water pipes to reduce flow
- spray-type faucets
- self-closing faucets on taps
- pressure-reducing valves in areas that have high water pressure
- flow meters on cold water lines to water heaters, when hot water consumption is greater than 3000 gallons per day.

3.9 ENERGY MANAGEMENT AND CONTROL SYSTEMS

3.9.1 Introduction

Numerous energy management and control systems (EMCSs) on the market offer a wide range of capabilities and features. Various EMCS features save energy, reduce labor, or offer better control. Some are designed to control a group of systems or devices; others are for use primarily to control a single system.

Because there are so many control systems and devices available, it is possible to select a system or group of devices almost ideally suited for a given installation. System selection involves not only the existing or planned building systems, but also the functions being performed in the building and the applicable electric utility rate structure. For example, if a demand rate is not being applied, there is no point investing in demand control equipment. If a demand rate is being applied, however, the demand control equipment must be compatible with the method the utility uses to calculate demand.

In all cases, the designer should confer with utility representatives on EMCSs, applicable rate schedules and the utility's plans for the future.

3.9.2 Centralized Computer-Based EMCSs

A centralized computer-based EMCS consists of a microcomputer or minicomputer to monitor and control various system points. Operator-machine interface usually occurs in a master control room that contains various operator consoles. In some cases the computer and support devices are remote, with data generated in the building being transmitted to the computer via leased telephone lines.

Centralized computer-based systems usually are appropriate when:
- optimization functions are needed
- control decisions are to be based on number of variables and conditions
- operating and maintenance personnel who understand the system either are on-hand or will be hired
- the facility is a highrise building or a complex of buildings with a central plant and several remote mechanical equipment rooms
- there are 200 or more data points.

Functions performed by centralized computer-based systems fall into four categories:
- basic functions, which are generally applicable to a broad range of systems and equipment
- optimizing functions, which improve the operating efficiency of a given piece of equipment or system by monitoring performance and performing adjustments on a real-time basis
- operational functions, which are associated with systems' monitoring, alarm, and development of logs and reports
- other functions not associated with HVAC systems such as lighting, access control, smoke, and fire management.

3.9.3 Basic Functions

Demand control, duty cycling, programmed start/stop and unoccupied hours setback are four of the most important basic functions (discussed in Section 3.7.4, Thermal Systems, Controls).

Optimizing Functions

Hot Deck/Cold Deck Temperature Reset. The hot deck/cold deck temperature reset program is applied to dual systems and multizone HVAC systems in conjunction with the chilled water reset program. These systems use a parallel arrangement of hot and cold decks for providing heating and cooling simultaneously. The hot and cold airstreams are combined in mixing boxes or plenums to satisfy individual space temperature requirements. When the space temperature is acceptable, a greater difference between the temperatures of the hot and cold decks results in inefficient system operation. The hot deck/cold deck temperature reset program, however, can select the areas with the greater heating and cooling requirements and establish the minimum hot and cold deck temperature differentials that will meet the requirements, thus maximizing system efficiency.

Space temperature sensors and mixing box or plenum damper positions are used to determine the minimum and maximum deck temperatures necessary to satisfy the space temperature requirements during the building occupied period. Where humidity control is required, the program will prevent the cooling coil discharge temperature from being set upward when the space humidity setpoint is reached.

Reheat Coil Reset. Terminal reheat systems operate with a constant cold deck discharge temperature in conjunction with the chilled water reset program. Air supplied at temperatures below the individual space temperature requirements is elevated in temperature by reheat coils in response to signals from an individual space thermostat. The reheat coil reset program selects the reheat coil with the lowest discharge temperature or the reheat coil valve most nearly closed (the zone with the least amount of reheat required) and resets the cold deck discharge temperature upward until it equals the discharge temperature of the reheat coil with the lowest demand. Where humidity control is required, the program will prevent the cooling coil discharge temperature from being set upward when the maximum allowable humidity is reached. For airconditioning systems, where reheat coils are not used, the program will reset the cold deck discharge temperature upward until the space with the greatest cooling requirement is just satisfied.

Boiler Optimization. The boiler optimization program is implemented in heating plants with multiple boilers. Optimization of boiler plants is accomplished through the selection of the most efficient boiler to satisfy the heating load. Boiler operating data must be obtained from the manufacturer, or developed by monitoring fuel input as a function of the steam or hot water output. Determination of boiler efficiency also takes into account the heat content of the condensate return in case of steam systems and make-up water. Based on the efficiency curves (fuel input versus steam or hot water output) the boilers with the highest efficiency can be selected to satisfy the heating load. Boilers can be started manually by a boiler operator or automatically by the EMCS depending on site requirements. Burner operating efficiency is monitored by measuring the O_2 or CO in each boiler flue as well as the stack temperature. Note that insurance policies should be checked before applying such a program. Most policies have stringent provisions regarding safety interlocks.

Chiller Optimization. The chiller optimization program is implemented in chilled water plants with multiple chillers. Based on chiller operating data and the energy input requirements obtained from the manufacturer for each chiller, the program will select the chiller or chillers required to meet the load with the minimum energy consumption. When a chiller or chillers are started, chiller capacity must be limited (prevented from going to a full load) for a predetermined period to allow the system to stabilize so that the actual cooling load can be determined. Comparison of equipment characteristics versus the actual operating chiller characteristics can make it possible to determine when heat transfer surfaces need cleaning to maintain the highest efficiency. The program must follow the manufacturer's startup and shutdown sequence requirements. Interlocks between chilled water pumps, condenser water pumps, and chiller must be in accordance with the chiller manufacturer's requirements. Chillers can be started automatically by the EMCS or manually by the chiller operator depending on site requirements.

Hot Water Temperature Reset. Hot water heating systems, whether the hot water is supplied by a boiler or a converter, are designed to supply hot water at a fixed temperature. Depending on the system design, the hot water supply temperature may be reduced as the heating requirements for the facility decrease. A reduction in hot water supply temperature results in reduction of heat loss from equipment and piping. To implement this program, the temperature controller for the hot water supply is reset as a function of outside air temperature.

Chiller Water Temperature Reset. The energy required to produce chilled water in a reciprocating or centrifugal refrigeration machine is a function of the chilled water discharge temperature (leaving chiller). (The refrigerant suction temperature is also a direct function of the leaving water temperature; the higher the suction temperature, the lower the energy input per ton of refrigeration.) Chiller discharge water temperature is selected for peak design times, therefore, chilled water discharge temperatures can be reset upward during nonpeak design operating hours to the maximum that will still satisfy space cooling requirements. The program resets chilled water temperature upward until the required space temperature or humidity setpoints can no longer be maintained. This determination is made by monitoring positions of the chilled water valves on various cooling systems or by monitoring space temperatures.

Condenser Water Temperature Reset. The energy required to operate systems is directly related to the temperature of the condenser water entering the machine. Heat rejection systems are designed to produce a specified condenser water temperature such as 85 degrees (F.) at peak wet bulb temperatures. Automatic controls are provided at some sites to maintain a specified temperature at conditions other than peak wet bulb temperatures. The performance of refrigeration systems is optimized by resetting condenser water temperature downward when outside air wet bulb temperature will produce lower condenser water temperature. The program must incorporate manufacturer requirements governing acceptable condenser water temperature range.

Air Distribution Optimization. The air distribution optimization function involves control of zone dampers to stop the flow of conditioned air to nonessential areas during unoccupied periods. Dampers, which in most cases will have to be installed, are positioned automatically by an optimum start/stop program. Supply fan dampers and associated exhaust fans are positioned by static pressure sensors.

3.9.4 Operational Functions

Chiller Profile Generation. A chiller profile is a printed record of the operating status of chiller equipment and includes such data as demand in kW, return and supply water temperatures, etc. Analysis of these data can identify efficiency and cost factors.

Boiler Profile Generation. Recorded operating data are collected in "profiles," from which curves are plotted to determine operating efficiency. These curves become the basis for developing optimization routines.

Maintenance of Building Systems. A centralized computer-based system can optimize maintenance by scheduling the times maintenance is to be performed either on a calendar basis or according to machine running time. Sensors can warn of impending machine failure or deteriorating unit efficiency.

Safety Alarms. Equipment sensors notify the console operator of abnormal operation by an audible or printed alarm.

Trouble Diagnosis. Mechanical and electrical systems can be monitored for such variables as temperature, pressure, and humidity to help identify causes of abnormal operation.

3.9.5 Other Functions

Centralized Lighting Control. To restrict lighting to only the amount of illumination needed, where and when it is needed.

Access Control Program. To prevent unauthorized use of entrances and exits. Doors can be equipped with electric door locks controlled from the central guard station. An intercom at each door allows the guard to communicate with those desiring entry. For more positive identification, a closed circuit television camera can be located at each door.

<u>Smoke and Fire Management.</u> To optimize life safety and minimize property damage from fire and smoke. The building's heating, ventilating, and airconditioning systems can be controlled to help contain and prevent the spread of smoke through the ducts in the event of a fire.

3.9.6 EMCS Components

Today's computer-based EMCSs are far smaller and perform many more functions, including the critically important function of energy optimization. They are able to take readings from several points and determine the exact second when certain devices should be turned off or on to yield maximum energy efficiency without degrading comfort. Some of the newest systems use distributed processing, which involves individual components that have their own microprocessors, permitting them to operate effectively without having to "ask" the central control unit (CCU) for instructions. This approach frees up CCU capacity, permitting the computer to handle additional functions. A distributed-type effect can sometimes be obtained when pre-existing control units are incorporated into a new central system. This "building bloc" approach to centralization is effective only when the preexisting units are compatible with the new central system.

The modern centralized computer-based EMCS, depending on its size, consists of a central control unit with various combinations of peripheral equipment, data transmission media (DTM), field interface devices (FID), multiplexer (MUX) panels, intelligent multiplexer panels (IMUX), necessary interfacing controls, sensors, and actuators. As shown below in Figure 3.9.6.1, field equipment in medium- and large-sized EMCSs is interfaced with master control room equipment through a communication link termination (CLT) device, which usually consists of communications and signal conditioning equipment in addition to line terminations. Note, however, that some of the equipment does not have to be physically located in the controlled building. For example, in the case of a campus-type facility, the central equipment located in one building would control all buildings. Some school systems have found that all schools can be fitted for master control from one location, and some owners have interconnected buildings located in different cities by means of leased telephone lines.

Through this latter method, building owners can also avail themselves of time-shared systems, in which they receive the services of remote computer-based control equipment for a monthly fee.

The type of signals used by an EMCS is important. An <u>analog</u> signal is a continuously variable signal that bears a known relationship to the value of the measured variable. For example, a thermocouple measures temperature, and emits a signal in the form of a voltage; a resistance temperature device (RTD) measures temperature and emits a signal in the form of an electrical resistance. Such analog signals must be converted to digital form before a computer can use them.

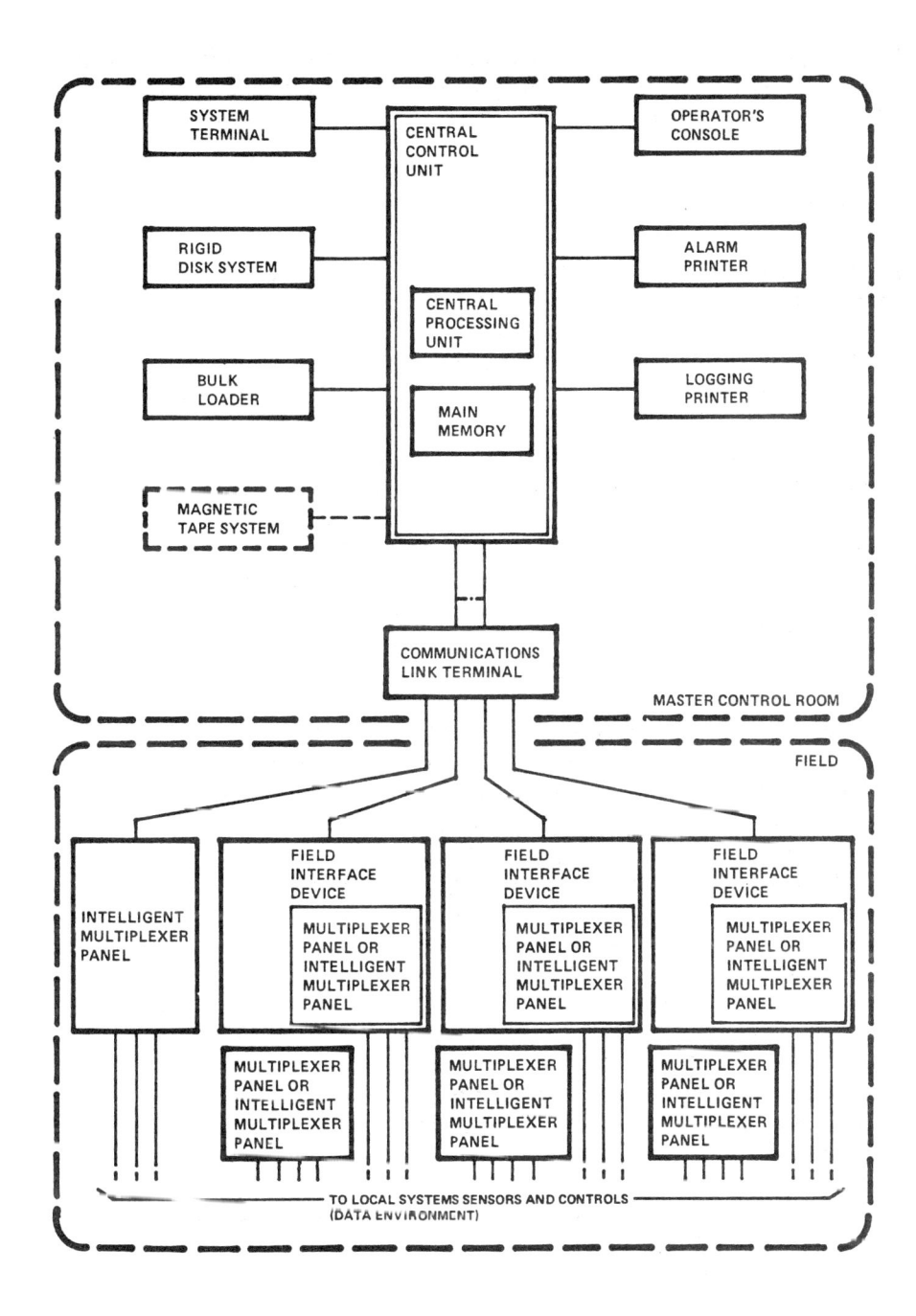

Figure 3.9.6.1 - Energy Management Control System BLOCK Diagram

A <u>binary</u> signal is an input signal equivalent to an electrical contact (switch) that can only be in an open or closed position, as determined by a predetermined condition. Examples include firestats, door contacts, alarm devices, pressure switches, flow switches, and motor-starter auxiliary contacts.

Contemporary EMCSs using distributed processing can also be specified with direct digital control (DDC). DDC provides tighter control than conventional devices because it can perform full proportional, integral, and derivative control. The DDC control action can be customized to meet the specific needs of each loop. Control setpoints are achieved with high accuracy under all conditions, and energy consumption is optimized.

A digital computer is used as the primary controller, which can handle four to eight loops and be reprogrammed for various control functions without hardware changes. No computer-to-controller interface devices are required. A typical DDC loop includes a digital computer, sensor, and actuator, as shown in Figure 3.9.6.2. Actuators can be electronic or pneumatic.

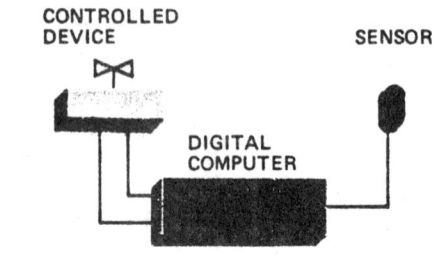

Figure 3.9.6.2 - Typical closed loop, direct control system.

Accessory on/off control and monitoring functions are controlled by the same computer. Each computer can operate independently and perform all essential control functions without being connected to any other computer.

In the case of HVAC equipment, each piece of equipment (air handler, boiler, or chiller) must have its own computer. These units are then tied together into a local network for communications, as shown in Figure 3.9.6.3. Twisted-pair, low-voltage wire normally is used for interconnections. An access computer can be connected to the network at any location. All sensor monitoring and control setpoints and strategies can be controlled from the access computer.

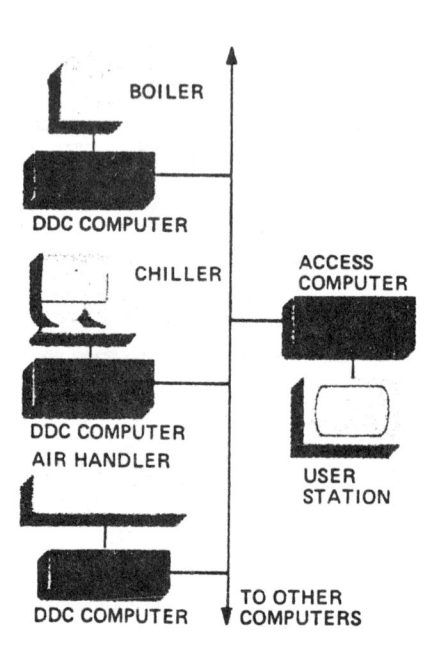

Figure 3.9.6.3 - Digital Control Network

Installed cost of DDC systems is somewhat higher than that of conventional controls for simple applications. However, the price differential narrows considerably with increasing complexity. Little, if any, difference exists for moderately complex applications.

Central Control Unit. The central control unit (CCU) is usually a complete microcomputer or minicomputer system consisting of a central processing unit (CPU) with memory and logical decision functions for performing arithmetic computations and central monitoring and control. Data and programs are stored in and retrieved from CCU memory or mass storage devices. During normal operation, the CCU coordinates operation of all other EMCS components, except safety interlocks.

Peripheral Devices. "Peripherals" are auxiliary input/output devices associated with the computer system, generally at the central station. Typical peripheral devices include operator's console and printers, as well as auxiliary storage equipment such as magnetic and floppy disks. Many individual peripheral devices can function both as combined input and output units and as auxiliary storage devices. Peripherals constitute an important part of the computer system and contribute substantially to the power of the computer and its cost. The success or failure of a computer application often relates directly to the type of peripherals chosen.

Data Transmission Link. Data collected from and commands issued to connected points travel via the system's data transmission link. There are many types available, including coaxial and triaxial cable, telephone pairs, fiber optics, and radio and microwave signals. Qualitative characteristics of the most commonly applied data links are indicated in Figure 3.9.6.4.

	First Cost	Scan Time	Reliability	Maintenance Effort	Expandability	Compatibility with future requirements
Coaxial Cable	High	Very fast	Excellent	Minimum	Unlimited	Unlimited
Triaxial Cable	High	Very fast	Excellent	Minimum	Unlimited	Unlimited
Twisted Pairs	High	Very fast	Very good	Minimum	Unlimited	Limited
VHF FM Radio Signals	Medium	Limited application	Low	High	Very limited	Very limited
Microwave	Very high	Very fast Limited	Excellent	High	Unlimited	Unlimited
Telephone Pairs	Very low	Very slow	Low to high	Zero, if phone co. does it	Limited	Limited
Fiber Optics	Very high	Very fast	Excellent	Minimum	Unlimited	Unlimited

Figure 3.9.6.4 - Transmission Line Characteristics

3.9.7 Field Equipment

The field equipment associated with an EMCS could consist of field interface devices (FIDs), multiplexer panels (MUXs), intelligent multiplexer panels (IMUXs), and sensors and controls.

Field Interface Devices

Field interface devices contain a microcomputer consisting of a microprocessor and its memory, communications interface, digital and analog input and output cards, control panels, and power supplies. Normally, the FID communicates with the CCU. The CCU provides updated data on operational variables, such as start times, calculated by the application programs in the CCU or by operator command. The FID is usually used in applications where stand-alone operation is required, such as in a building complex where one or more FIDs can perform routines using applications software and operating parameters stored in the FID's memory.

Multiplexer Panels

Multiplexer panels serve as the input/output (I/O) device for a FID and its data environment and are considered an extension of the FID. The number of remote MUX panels connected to a single FID is limited only by the maximum number of points addressable by a FID, the number of points allowed on a single data transmission medium, or by the alarm response time. The remote MUX panels continuously transmit their data to the FID via a telephone-"Modem" link or line drivers. The MUX panel normally contains I/O functions to handle digital and analog-data, digital data error detection, and message transmission.

Intelligent Multiplexer Panels

Intelligent Multiplexer Panels are similar to MUX panels, but operate in a "report by exception" mode. IMUX panels perform all functions of a MUX panel and, depending on the manufacturer, are used in place of the MUX panel. The IMUX is allowed to communicate with the CCU in large and medium systems in a monitoring role only, thereby retaining the distributed intelligence inherent in the EMCS architecture. The IMUX is allowed to perform both monitoring and control functions in small systems. The IMUX scans its data environment and compares the data received against the last value and only reports the data that has changed.

Sensors

Sensors are remote input devices connected to the terminal block usually located in the FID. Sensors measure the condition of variables such as temperature, relative humidity, pressure, flow, level, electrical units, and the position of various mechanical devices. They also monitor relay, switch, or other binary devices. The signal from a sensor or other input device is either analog or binary.

Actuators

Actuators are devices that perform control actions at a remote point in response to central system command instructions. Typical actuators connected to FIDs include control motors, valve positioners, damper operators, switches, and relays.

As with input devices, the output signals to the actuators can be classified as either analog or binary.

Software

The EMCS's computer programs are software. Three types of software are used: system software, command software, and applications software.

System Software. System software consists of the basic programs that cause the computer to function. It includes operation procedures for input/output devices and programs that load and unload command and applications software. System software is also used to upgrade the operation of the EMCS by refining existing programs, expanding them, or adding new ones.

Command Software. Command software consists of the programs that permit the operator to communicate with the EMCS and order it to perform required actions, such as monitoring a control point or sending an instruction.

Applications Software. Applications software consists of the programs that specify the details of how various functions, for example, demand control and duty cycling, are to occur.

3.9.8 EMCS Evaluation and Selection

It is difficult to overstate the importance of carefully evaluating and selecting an EMCS for a commercial building.

The first step is to precisely determine the building needs and user requirements. This is time-consuming and must be preceded by a detailed building energy audit and a comprehensive energy management plan. If the requirements are not well defined at the outset, the EMCS selection will not be satisfactory, and the installed system will not attain its maximum potential.

The next step is to evaluate available systems to determine their ability to satisfy the defined requirements. The key is to select the least complicated system that will satisfy building and user needs. In general, larger, more complicated EMCSs become more appropriate as mechanical/electrical systems become more complex, increase in number and become larger and more spread out physically.

Cost Effectiveness

Cost effectiveness is the basic criterion in determining which level of

EMCS is best and, specifically, what type of system will yield maximum return on investment. Cost effectiveness is determined through use of life-cycle cost/benefit analysis (see Section 4.3, Economic Analysis).

Too many building owners have purchased an expensive system with a nominal one-year maintenance service contract, only to find out later that the actual costs of a long-term maintenance contract are much higher.

In some cases, the owner may also be locked into a specific arrangement because other service companies are either not available in the local area or are not qualified to service the proprietary equipment included in the system. To avoid such situations, price quotations for long-term service contracts should be requested and evaluated for competitive systems before final system selection is made.

Adaptability

How well a system can be adapted to an existing facility requires analysis of a variety of questions. Will the system fit into the existing space? If the space is not readily available, can it be made available? Will new construction be necessary? Can the EMCS be interfaced with existing local controls, or will the controls have to be replaced? If much of the existing mechanical equipment is scheduled for replacement, will the new equipment be compatible with the new as well as existing system? If the new equipment will be far more efficient than the existing equipment, is the EMCS needed, or would local controls suffice?

Maintainability

The ability to maintain a system is vital to the system's usefulness. One such concern is the ability to support in-house maintenance through training programs and manuals. Equally important, if not more so, is the availability of professionally trained maintenance persons employed, licensed or authorized by the manufacturer. Without proper maintenance the system will not perform reliably.

Wherever possible, references should be checked to determine whether other users of the proposed system are satisfied with the completeness of preventive maintenance and the responsiveness and capability of outside maintenance (which usually costs 10-22 percent of initial installed cost), and the availability of a service maintenance agreement.

While a high level of sophistication can be desirable, it should be recognized that increased sophistication often results in increased maintenance problems and costs. Trade-offs can be necessary.

Reliability

Reliability involves how well a system performs its stated functions. Built-in system errors often multiply with the complexity of system functions. For example, basic EMCS design features may result in occasional interference with transmission of system signals. A second

reliability problem is whether the system is subject to frequent or
prolonged breakdowns ("downtime"). Information on these question can be
obtained from other users of the system.

Major factors relating to reliability include:
- average length of time the system performs without breakdown
- average extent of downtime
- nature of problems experienced and the degree to which the mission will
  be inhibited.

Expandability

Expandability is the ability of a system to handle additional data points
and equipment added subsequent to initial design. Expansion can require
the purchase of another computer, additional memory and/or more and larger
FIDs. It can cause programming inconvenience, high factory charges, and
disruption of normal operations. These problems can be minimized by
looking ahead during initial design. If a long-range facility plan
exists, both existing and proposed buildings can be identified and points
allocated at the outset. If there is no long-range plan, an allowance for
future growth should be made.

Provisions for future growth affect several elements of the system. The
most critical items are the CPU, memory, and software programs. Equipment
purchased either should have spare capacity for growth or should be
modular, permitting easy addition of more points. Points added later can
cost 50 percent more than those connected at the time of initial
installation.

Field wiring and FIDs can be designed to minimize the impact of future
expansion. If coaxial cable or twisted pair wiring is used between FIDs,
no additional wiring should be needed, assuming all FIDs are purchased
initially. Problems can arise if the FID has not been specified and/or
furnished with adequate spare capacity. It is suggested that FIDs be
selected to handle all known future points, plus an additional percentage
to facilitate more expansion.

Space should be reserved on the CRT format for known future buildings,
air-handling units, and related equipment, with information field-
programmed when the anticipated points are added.

In some cases, suppliers will provide unit prices on items for future
expansion at the time of the original bid. With an agreed-upon cost index
or escalation factor, all future additions can be easily priced using the
unit prices given.

Programmability

Programmability is the degree to which an existing central control unit or
"smart" FID program can be modified. At one time, user programmability
was considered almost essential to ensure that a general program could be
made specific to the unique conditions of a given building. Today, each

supplier has a variety of programs, making it easier to find one that closely matches needs. Furthermore, many of these programs are written in such a way that they can be modified relatively easily, either by the user or by the manufacturer. Generally speaking, it is most effective to have the manufacturer modify programs because of the expense associated with having full-time programmers on staff and the dangers inherent from lack of consistency when, as is common, different part-time programmers are used.

If user programmability is essential, the manufacturer should be asked to furnish the documentation required to modify programs. In most cases, it will be necessary to sign a license agreement that forbids divulgence of the documentation to others. It is also important to determine the degree to which the manufacturer can augment programs, and the number of programs available that will work in the manufacturer's equipment without voiding the guarantee or warranty.

Once the EMCS is operating as designed, it is important to implement an effective preventive maintenance program for the system. Without this, costly problems can occur, causing users to lose confidence in the system.

Various factors should be weighed in selecting the type of maintenance program:
- size and complexity of the control system
- in-house capabilities
- equipment supplier requirements
- annual cost
- diagnostic programs
- wiring diagrams.

Maintenance services are usually available from the EMCS vendor or an independent source. Annual cost is normally 10-12 percent of the EMCS installed cost.

Building Size and Type

Size, type of HVAC system, and systems location within the building affect energy and cost saving. These factors should be examined before determining which buildings are suitable for local or central control purposes.
- Building Size. Building size is usually the most significant factor in the selection of an energy management system. For conditioned spaces, a general rule is the greater the total floor area, the greater the energy consumption. A rule of thumb is that buildings in excess of 20,000 square feet are good candidates for interconnection with central energy management systems. Smaller buildings, especially those with more than one HVAC system type can be more suited to local control.
- Heating and Cooling System. The type of heating and cooling system can influence the potential energy savings and the cost of a central management system. Central management systems can offer the greatest savings potential in larger buildings with central heating and cooling systems. With system components such as air-handling units located in

the same area of the building, thus simplifying control system modifications. Smaller buildings tend to have widely distributed window units and unit heaters, which are difficult and expensive to adapt to a central energy management system. Smaller savings potential can mean that local control is more cost-effective.

- <u>Building Systems Locations.</u> A major factor in central energy management system costs is wiring and communication expense. This interconnection cost is a function of building systems locations. Telephone lines can be used between remote panels and the central console where suitable voice-quality lines exist; otherwise, the installation of additional telephone link capacity must be included in the system cost estimate. Generally, large energy-using facilities require many remote points at considerable distance from other facilities, requiring installation of multiple individual remote panels.

- <u>Integration of Control Systems.</u> Integration of control systems can be improved by providing strategically located vertical wiring conduits or shafts and horizontal distribution points (or closets). To reduce conduit and cable sizes and weight (significant in a tall building), fiber optics can be used between central distribution points and control computers. Twisted (copper) wiring can be used from the distribution point to floor terminals.

3.10 CONSTRUCTION AND COMMISSIONING PROCESS

3.10.1 Introduction

The best designed building will not save energy unless its construction, turnover and operation are performed in accordance with the intent of the design. In effect, the effort spent in achieving a good energy design can largely be wasted unless the building project is "finished right." This can be accomplished by planning and careful oversight. The consequences of slighting or ignoring these steps are all too well known: uncomfortable, unproductive employees; increased energy costs; high maintenance costs; and even safety hazards.

Construction, commissioning and building operation need not be difficult:

- Plan for construction, commissioning, and operation from the early design stages (see Figure 3.10.1.1) onward and continue to check key items throughout the project and into occupancy of the building.
- Include all key players (owner, staff, design team, contractors, subcontractors, and manufacturers), and be sure that each takes responsibility for specific tasks at the proper time.
- Develop Good Project Documentation. In addition to having a good set of drawings and specifications for the building, ensure that several other important elements are made part of the project documents. These include accurate "as-built" drawings for maintenance, and in future years, alteration. Include a complete operation and maintenance (O & M) manual and a listing of HVAC system control strategies.
- Provide for Operational Checks. Be sure that necessary check points, valves, gages and special tools are provided and that equipment, pipes and ducts are properly identified. Make arrangements for long-term maintenance contracts.

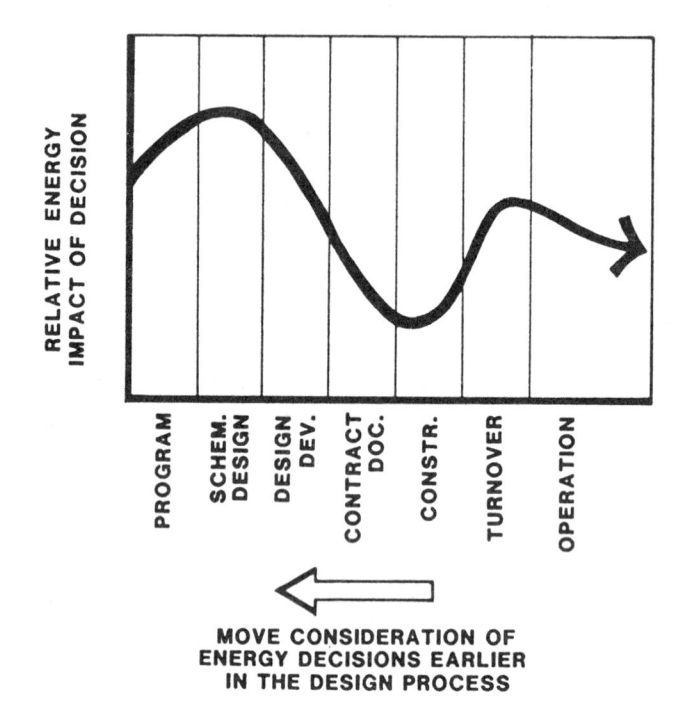

Figure 3.10.1.1 - Timely Effort Curve

	PROGRAMMING	DESIGN	CONSTRUCTION	COMMISSIONING	BUILDING OPERATION
DESIGN TEAM (ARCHITECTS AND ENGINEERS)	Review building proposal Review economic proposal Establish energy economic goals	Document all design assumptions Estimate energy use by subsystem **& For Large Buildings** Document all systems and control strategies Specify contents of O&M Manuals Specify HVAC balancing requirements Specify equipment protection and cleaning Specify on-site instruction Specify access doors, valves, test ports Specify piping system Price quotations on all long-term maintenance contracts	Prepare "as built" drawings Observe construction process for compliance	Conduct "punch list" inspection Visually check for air leakage If possible, participate in on-site training session(s)	
CONTRACTOR AND SUB-CONTRACTORS	**For Small Buildings Only** Review building proposal Review economic program Establish energy/economic goals	**For Small Buildings Only** Document all systems and control strategies Specify contents of O&M Manuals Specify HVAC balancing requirements Specify equipment protection and cleaning Specify on-site instruction Specify access doors, valves, test ports Specify piping system Price quotations on all long-term maintenance contracts	Prepare O&M Manual Final calibration of all controls Hire independent balancing agent or require of subs Protect and clean equipment Provide all access doors, valves, and test ports Place piping system ID tags Prepare "as built" drawings Use HVAC system to "flush" construction odors	Deliver O&M Manual Conduct on-site instruction and training	Warranty and call back as required
EQUIPMENT MANUFACTURERS			Support calibration of controls Provide all special tools required	Support O&M Manual preparation Support on-site instruction and training	
OWNER AND BUILDING STAFF	Develop building program Develop economic program Establish energy economic	Check all key design assumptions	Periodically check compliance on-site	Attend on-site instruction and training sessions	Monitor energy consumption against estimates Periodically test equipment efficiency Periodically sample and test water Inspect and calibrate controls Monitor occupant complaints

Figure 3.10.1.2 - Commissioning Responsibility and Schedule Checklist

- Check Construction and Operation. Periodic checking of the construction work is essential. Once the building is in operation, numerous checks are necessary to ensure efficient, least-cost operation and to predict maintenance needs.
- Conduct a Careful Commissioning of the Building. In commissioning, the building is adjusted, tested, and checked out for proper operation, much as a ship is put into commission. Training in the proper operation of the building is given to the operating staff. Any follow-on warranty work by the contractor is also part of this activity.

A checklist such as shown above in Figure 3.10.1.2 can be valuable in ensuring that construction and commissioning are effective. The checklist is arranged as a matrix to indicate both <u>when</u> a step should occur (programming, design/working drawings, construction, commissioning operations) and <u>who</u> should be responsible (design team, contractor and subcontractors, equipment manufacturer, or building owner and staff).

The matrix clearly illustrates the shift in major responsibilities over time: The owner has primary responsibility during programming, the design team during design, the contractor and subcontractors during construction,

TYPE: OFFICE BLDG.		AREA/FLR: 6,000 S.F.			TOTAL SQ. FT: 48,000
Room Type	Area	No./Flr.	Total Area/Flr.	No./ Building	Area/ Building
Offices (No. 1)	10 X 15	4	600 S.F.	32	2,400 S.F.
Offices (No. 2)	20 X 15	4	1,200 S.F.	32	4,800 S.F.
Conference	30 X 15	1	450 S.F.	8	3,600 S.F.
Computer	15 X 15	1	225 S.F.	8	1,800 S.F.
Copy Room	10 X 15	1	150 S.F.	8	1,200 S.F.
Kitchen/Lounge	15 X 15	1	225 S.F.	8	1,800 S.F.
Restrooms	10 X 20	2	200 S.F.	16	8,200 S.F.
Mechanical	10 X 10	1	100 S.F.	8	800 S.F.
Elevator	20 X 20	1	400 S.F.	1	400 S.F.

Figure 3.10.2.1 - Programming Assumptions

and the building owner or staff again during operation. Note, however, that all players have responsibilities in other phases of the process.

3.10.2 Project Documentation

The building program, developed by the owner, should provide the design team with information essential to the formulation of design assumptions. This would include anticipated building functions, use schedules and occupancy profiles.

It is particularly important that a realistic assessment of these factors be provided to the design team (see Figure 3.10.2.1). Deviation from the schedules and use patterns assumed during this step can significantly hinder the building's ability to perform as efficiently as designed.

Economic Program

The economic program should be developed by the owner. Besides laying out usual economic parameters for the design and construction process, it should offer guidance for establishing energy economic goals.

Energy Economic Goals

Energy economic goals should be established by the owners and designer once the program and overall economic goals have been established (see Figure 3.10.2.2). Based on these the designer should be able to offer energy saving strategies that are appropriate to the owners' needs.

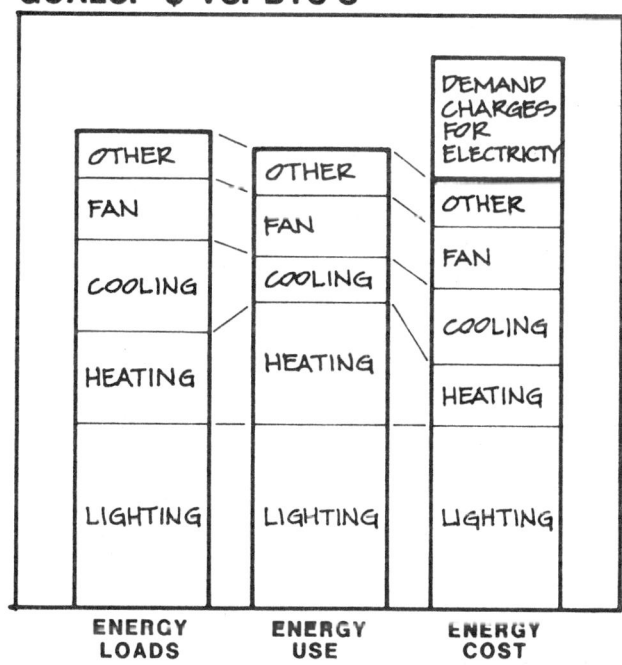

Figure 3.10.2.2 - Economic Goals

Energy Usage by Subsystem

The design team (usually the engineer) should prepare a system-by-system breakdown of estimated <u>annual</u> energy usage (see Figure 3.10.2.3). Depending on the building size, type of systems, and fee for energy analyses, these estimates can range from fairly crude to quite accurate.

258

This breakdown will be used later by the building operating staff in several important ways:
- Operators can review assumptions used in the analyses to determine such items as daytime and night-setback thermostat settings or lighting system switching arrangements for cleaning activities.
- Operators can review energy-use estimates to identify systems causing excessive energy consumption due to a control malfunction (e.g., failure of outside air dampers to close during unoccupied hours or a preheat coil control malfunction that could cause continuous overheating of ventilation air).
- Operators can compare actual monthly energy costs with design estimates to evaluate system performance.

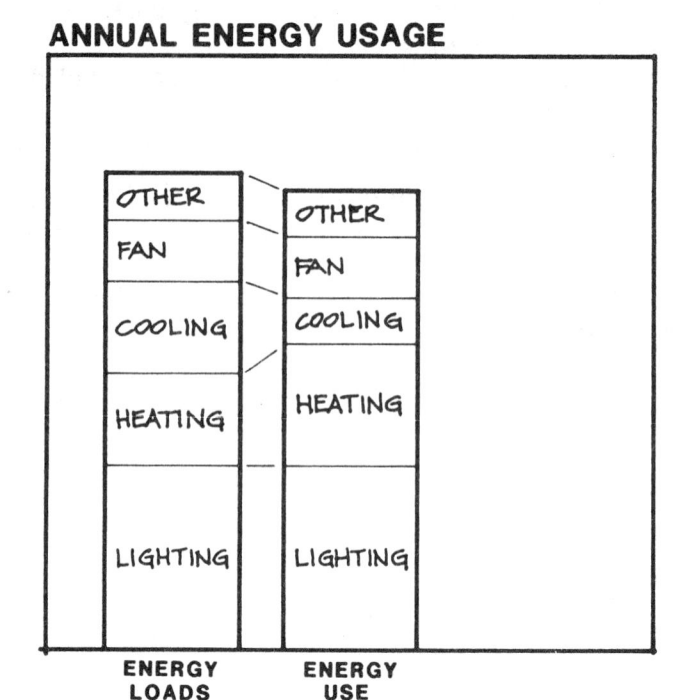

Figure 3.10.2.3 - Energy Usage

Systems and Control Assumptions and Strategies

The owner should be given full documentation of all systems and control assumptions and strategies, including--
- temperature set points for HVAC controls
- minimum and planned ventilation rates
- occupancy schedules and variations for cleaning and maintenance.

The design engineer should prepare schematic diagrams illustrating the major components of each building subsystem, including the proper location of each valve or control device. These diagrams should be accompanied by written descriptions of all control sequences in each mode of operation. Together, these documents will allow the building operating staff to understand how each system is intended to function and to determine if all system components are installed and operating properly.

These diagrams are often placed in glass-enclosed frames and mounted in the mechanical room or maintenance manager's office. They should be made part of the O & M manuals.

Contractor-Supplied Operating and Maintenance Manuals

The design team's specifications writer should provide detailed instructions regarding the content and format of all contractor-supplied O & M manuals. Otherwise, the building operating staff may simply be provided with a set of equipment "catalog cuts" containing little or no useful information. Depending on the type of equipment provided, the O & M manual should contain the following items:
- index
- contractor/subcontractor(s) name, address, and telephone number
- general description of each system and catalog cuts of equipment
- step-by-step equipment start-up, shutdown, and operating settings and procedures under fully and partially occupied conditions
- spare parts lists, including local supplier's name and address
- preventive maintenance and lubrication procedures
- wiring and control diagrams for each piece of equipment, showing "as-installed" conditions
- performance curves for all pumps, fans, refrigeration machines and similar equipment.

O & M manuals can be prepared by the design team. This option should be specified in the original contract for design services, as it is not a standard design service.

3.10.3 Operational Checks

All water and air distribution systems must be properly balanced. Otherwise, thermal comfort conditions designed for individual spaces may never be realized.

For larger buildings, specifications usually require that the contractor who installs a particular subsystem be responsible for hiring an independent agency to complete the balancing in accordance with the procedures specified. A final report should be provided to the owner and signed by a professional engineer. Standard system balancing procedures developed by various trade organization are often referenced in construction specifications.

Independent agency verification that subsystem balancing can cost 5-10 percent of the construction cost. While cost-effective for larger buildings, it is not essential for small buildings. One method of reducing first costs is to place responsibility for balancing with each subsystem contractor, through the general contractor, as described below:
- The contractor who installs a particular subsystem is responsible for balancing that subsystem to achieve the thermal comfort conditions that the system was designed to provide (see Figure 3.10.3.1).
- If, after initial occupancy, the owner is not satisfied with the subsystem performance, an independent balancing agency is hired directly by the owner to document both actual comfort conditions and the adequacy of the original system balancing.
- If the independent agency verifies that the system is balanced and operating as described in the construction documents, the contractor

who installed the
system is relieved of
any responsibility,
and the owner pays for
the independent
balancing report.
However, if it is
found that the system
was not installed or
balanced properly, the
contractor becomes
responsible for the
cost of the indepen-
dent balancing report
and any modifications
required to make the
system perform as
originally designed.

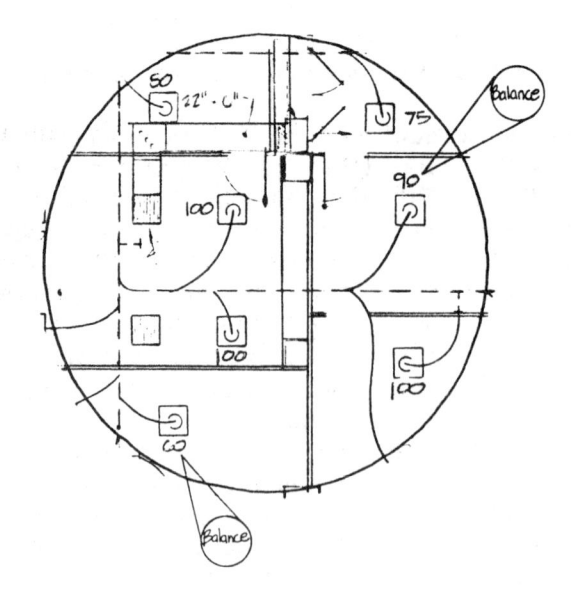

Figure 3.10.3.1 - Balancing Plan

This type of agreement benefits both the owner and the contractor. The owner is protected if the contractor does not perform adequately, and the contractor is protected if the cause of the owner's complaint is a design error or the result of another trade's installation.

Contractor Requirements Prior to Occupancy

Normally, construction specifications require a contractor to protect equipment installed early from damage resulting from subsequent construction operations. The contractor is also responsible for final cleaning and adjustment of all equipment.

These requirements are often slighted as construction draws to a close. The owner's representatives must pay particular attention to ensure these responsibilities have been fulfilled prior to final payment.

Specific areas of concern during construction include the following:
- Protect equipment, piping and ductwork from construction activity, damage and dirt. Vertical sections of piping and ductwork should be capped to avoid dirt accumulation prior to final system hookups.
- Replace air-handling equipment filters. Construction dirt on filters can degrade equipment performance and cause dirt "streaking" of finished ceilings. Periodic filter replacement during the construction phase can be necessary if systems are operated during construction. Care should be taken that no equipment is operated without filters.
- Clean, flush, and sterilize domestic (potable) water piping systems.
- Clean, flush, and protect from corrosion and freezing all piping systems that distribute non-potable liquids.
- Clean, repaint, or refurbish any equipment damaged or soiled during construction.
- Adjust balancing valves, air vents, automatic controls, and similar devices in accordance with specified procedures.

On-Site Instruction and Training

Normally, the contractor who installs a piece of equipment is responsible for providing on-site instruction and training to the building operating staff prior to the owner's final acceptance of the work. In some cases, it is advisable to require that a factory representative conduct these instruction sessions. Contractors may not be qualified to instruct others on operational procedures for complex equipment (such as energy management systems and chillers). This is rarely done on small projects and generally is cost effective only for complex equipment. Training should be coordinated with the preparation and delivery of the O & M manuals.

If at all possible, members of the design team should participate in on-site training sessions. This is a good opportunity for the design team to convey the overall energy efficiency strategy of the building. It is also an excellent time to refocus on key operating assumptions, such as:
- temperature set points for HVAC controls
- minimum and normal ventilation rates
- occupancy schedules and variations for cleaning and maintenance
- operation of special systems and building components (especially passive solar components requiring user interaction).

Training and orientation of the owner's operating staff is a key element in the process of building turnover. These activities are addressed by a new area of professional work known as building "commissioning." This subject is the focus of a Committee of the American Society of Heating, Refrigerating and Air-Conditioning Engineers (ASHRAE), "Systems Commissioning." ASHRAE defines commissioning as follows: "The object of commissioning is to ensure that an installation operates in conformity with the requirements of the design specification." It involves both the "setting to work" and the "regulation" of an installation. It does not include the testing to evaluate the performance of the commissioned installation.

ASHRAE's work in this area is expected to offer product manufacturers, owners, designers and contractors a methodology to determine if the completed installation: 1) operates as designed, 2) fully incorporates the intent of the design, 3) presents a logical format for "setting to work" the system, 4) specifically assigns "certification" responsibilities to the parties involved, 5) outlines suggested performance evaluation procedures and 6) defines reports to be produced.

Access Doors, Maintenance Valves, and Test Ports

Maintenance staff must have easy access to a piece of equipment for it to be maintained properly (see Figure 3.10.3.2). This applies to small items (valves, dampers, etc.), and to large equipment. Maintenance of equipment that is difficult to reach tends to be delayed or forgotten. It is the responsibility of the design team to see that adequate access is specified; the responsibility of the contractor (and subcontractors) to

see that all access
doors are installed; and
the responsibility of
the owner to check on
both.

During construction,
many such items are
omitted in an effort to
reduce first costs.
Even service shutoff
valves are omitted,
preventing the building
maintenance staff from
servicing individual
pieces of equipment
without shutting down
(and possibly draining)
an entire piping system.

Figure 3.10.3.2 - Access Doors

To permit smooth, inexpensive, and long-term operation and maintenance of building systems, adequate service shutoff valves and instrumentation must be specified and installed. Instruments such as thermometers and pressure gauges are necessary to ensure systems and components are performing as designed, to fine-tune systems, and to troubleshoot malfunctioning systems. These devices are very expensive to install after the fact, often requiring lengthy system shutdown.

Provide additional test ports (e.g., capped thermometer pipe wells) at critical points so that troubleshooting devices can be temporarily installed without shutting down entire systems. Location of test ports should be documented as carefully as other system components.

Equipment and Piping System Identification

In large buildings the quality, number, and location of piping system identification tags and flow direction markers are typically spelled out in the construction specifications. Brass or plastic identification tags correspond to the diagrams and written descriptions of each system. These identification markers help construction trades, balancing agencies, building inspectors, and operating staff understand piping systems and components.

3.10.4 Construction

On-site inspection during construction is traditionally part of the design team's responsibility. A number of areas that merit special attention when the design team is attempting to achieve an energy-efficient building:
- Carefully check the integrity of the building envelope. Air leakage (infiltration) is a common reason that buildings do not achieve their

potential for energy efficiency. Areas to be given close inspection are the continuity of insulation and integrity of air/vapor barriers, since both tend to receive less than careful attention from most contractors.
- Check ductwork for air tightness and proper insulation. This is a common area for less than perfect workmanship. Excessive leakage will make balancing difficult and can lead to excessive energy consumption.
- Check all lighting equipment to ensure that the right ballasts and fixtures are supplied. At times, high efficiency ballasts are specified but not delivered. Check to see that fixtures are installed in the proper places. A lighting strategy that mixes high-efficiency and regular fixtures can be confusing to and ignored by installers. Check to see that specified lamps are actually installed. It is essential that the owner or the owner's representative check these items on-site.
- It is especially important to ensure that change orders not have a negative impact on the energy efficiency of the building design.

Record Drawings

If an architect is engaged to provide construction documents, the development of "as-built" drawings is a simple procedure. Subcontractors can simply mark up sepias of original drawings to show changes that occurred during construction. This process requires close supervision by the designer to ensure that all changes are recorded. If the owner works directly with the contractor, the quality and extent of record drawings to be furnished by the contractor should be established as part of the negotiation process.

If inadequate drawings are provided, troubleshooting, system fine-tuning (see Figure 3.10.4.1), and modifications can be extremely difficult or prohibitively expensive. Because of the complexity and interaction of mechanical and electrical systems (even in small, "simple" buildings), it is extremely important to long-term building operation that the "as-built" conditions be thoroughly documented for future reference.

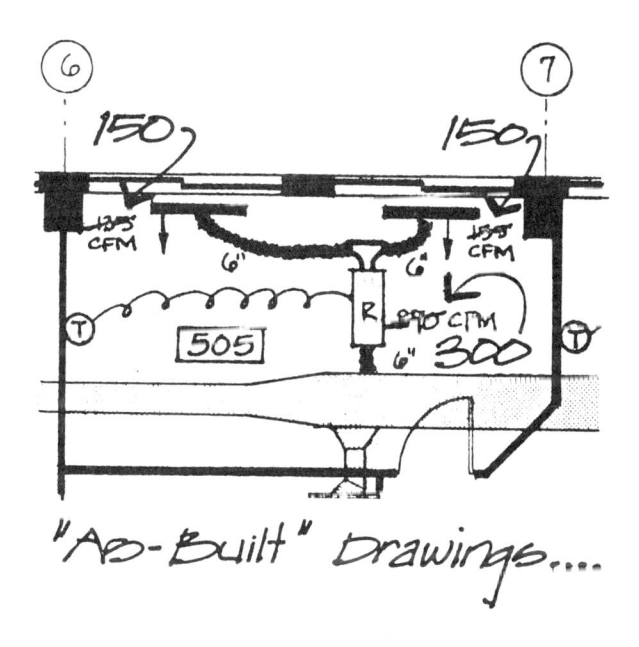

Figure 3.10.4.1 - As-Built Drawings

Special Service and Maintenance Tools

Special tools often are required to service or maintain a particular piece of equipment. Some boilers require a special tool to remove tubes for cleaning and replacement. Any such tools should be included as part of equipment first costs. Responsibility for supplying any spare parts, such as fuses, belts, etc., should be clearly assigned to either the manufacturer or contractor and included in the cost estimate.

Inspection

As part of the normal turnover process, the design team, the contractor, and the owner should jointly inspect the building for items still to be completed before the owner accepts the building and occupies it. This event is an opportunity to double-check items that will have significant effects on energy use. Items to include are:
- visual check for air leakage (around doors and windows)
- operation of the HVAC system within the comfort ranges specified for both heating _and_ cooling in _all_ areas of the building
- delivery of the O & M manuals and holding training sessions
- adequate system identification (tagging)
- clean equipment--including filters--following construction
- delivery of any special tools required by the building maintenance staff.

Warranty Agreements

The owner should work with the maintenance staff to see that energy-related systems are working as expected before contractor and subcontractors are released from obligation.

It can be useful to check actual energy consumption (and costs) during the first year and compare the results to anticipated consumption. It should be expected that the building will use more energy than anticipated until systems are fine-tuned.

Whether fine-tuning should be done by building staff or original contractors depends on the experience of the building staff, complexity of the systems involved, and contractual agreements. Prior to the end of any warranty period, the building owner should be satisfied with the operation of all building subsystems.

3.10.5 Operation

Testing Equipment Efficiency

Maintenance staff should periodically test major fuel-consuming equipment (most notably gas-fired boilers) to determine its actual operating efficiency. Combustion efficiency testing of gas boilers at full and part-load conditions should be conducted at the beginning of each heating season. In many cases, a simple adjustment of controls will return the boiler to its original operating efficiency. The fuel cost savings over a heating season will often more than offset the cost of the efficiency test.

Testing Water Systems

Various types of water treatment may be required to avoid premature deterioration of the distribution system piping. Water treatment chemicals may be required to minimize corrosion and scale build-up. The type and amount of water treatment and the frequency of testing should be specified in the original design. Solar system piping and systems using rooftop air-cooled condensing units with indoor water-cooled compressors should be checked periodically to verify that the proper proportion of ethylene glycol or other freeze-protection additives is being maintained.

These tests and maintenance procedures will normally be done by the building maintenance staff or by a chemical treatment contractor. It is critical to the proper operation of these systems that the specified frequency of testing is adhered to.

Inspecting and Calibrating System Controls

Control components usually are the weakest link in a building's network of environmental control systems. Even the most energy-efficient heating system can perform poorly if a malfunction in the control system causes equipment to receive erroneous control signals.

All controls, even solid-state digital controls, "drift" off setpoints, sometimes within a period of only a few hours. Pneumatic controls are notorious in this regard. Periodic inspection and calibration of controls that tend to drift from their setpoints is necessary. Note should be made of the degree of drift and the date of recalibration so that particularly troublesome items can be identified and inspected more frequently or replaced.

Monitoring Occupant Complaints

After the building is occupied, the operating staff should maintain a log of all occupant complaints regarding the environmental control systems. Pertinent information that might offer clues for future troubleshooting include:
- nature of complaint
- date and time complaint was received
- temperature control zone or room in which the problem occurred
- sky condition (clear versus cloudy), outside air temperature, and relative humidity at the time the complaint was received
- any unusual climatic conditions that may have occurred during the previous night
- corrective action taken and results obtained.

A carefully maintained log of these items over a period of time provides a trail of clues that can be useful in identifying the source of system malfunctions.

4 DESIGN ANALYSIS

4.1 BUILDING TYPES

4.1.1 Introduction

Early design analyses can also be directed toward understanding the inherent energy characteristics of the particular building type being designed. Each building type has peculiar attributes including occupancy, layout, lighting, envelope, glazing, equipment, and zoning characteristics. These attributes and their effect on energy use should be understood. This will give the design a clearer picture of the types of energy problems and constraints he faces. With this understanding he can turn them into opportunities for saving energy.

The building types which architects are accustomed to dealing with are historically based on occupancy patterns considered for the problems of emergency egress from fire. A challenge to the designer is to understand building types in terms of the time frame of occupancy and the energy intensity of the activities and functions which take place. Figure 4.1.1.2 on the opposite page shows a matrix viewing these two categories. Figure 4.1.1.1 shows an enduse breakdown of energy use for the common building types.

The following discussion of basic building types is based on research sponsored by the U.S. Department of Energy and is drawn largely from a series of articles that appeared in "Progressive Architecture" between April 1982 and April 1983.

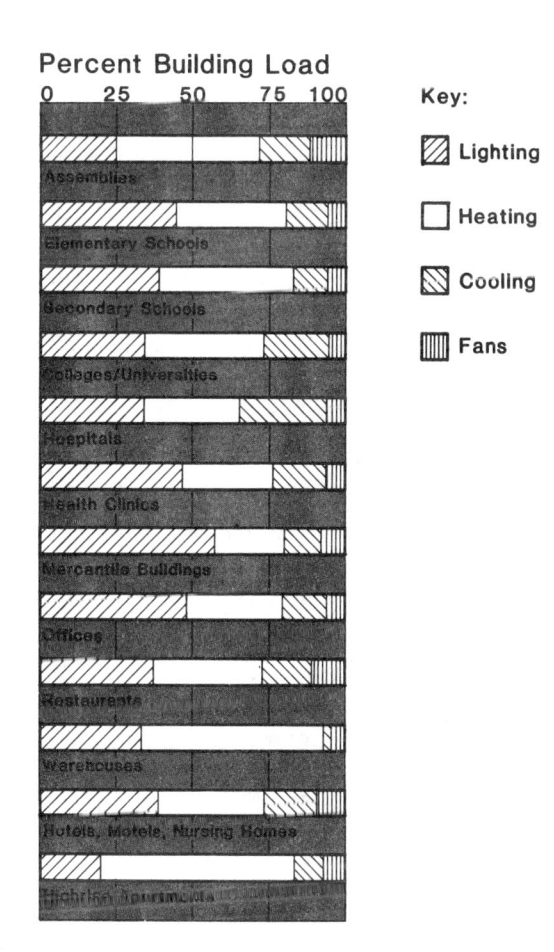

Figure 4.1.1.1 - Energy Enduse by Building Type

FUNCTIONS

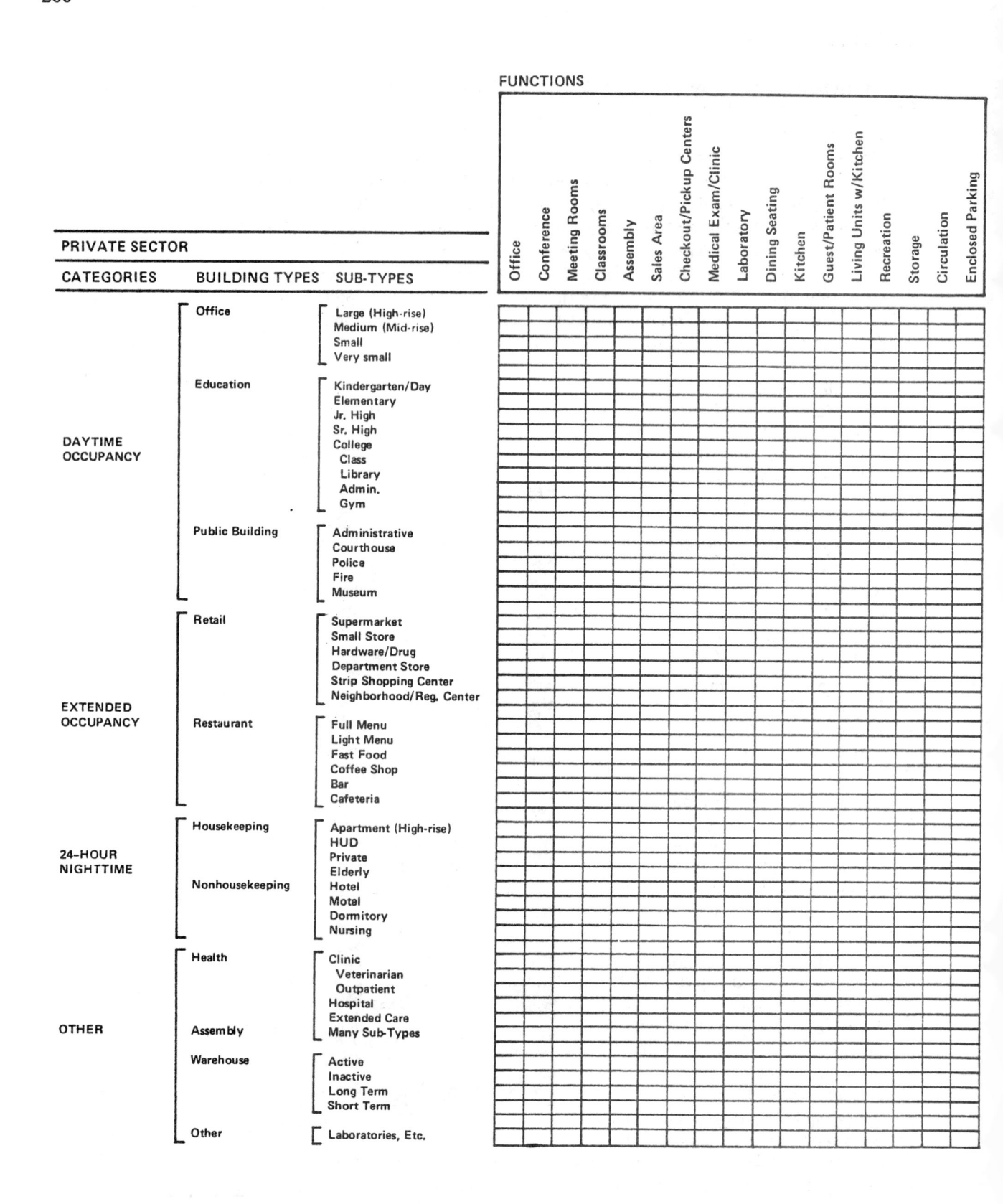

PRIVATE SECTOR			Office	Conference	Meeting Rooms	Classrooms	Assembly	Sales Area	Checkout/Pickup Centers	Medical Exam/Clinic	Laboratory	Dining Seating	Kitchen	Guest/Patient Rooms	Living Units w/Kitchen	Recreation	Storage	Circulation	Enclosed Parking
CATEGORIES	BUILDING TYPES	SUB-TYPES																	
DAYTIME OCCUPANCY	Office	Large (High-rise) / Medium (Mid-rise) / Small / Very small																	
	Education	Kindergarten/Day / Elementary / Jr. High / Sr. High / College / Class / Library / Admin. / Gym																	
	Public Building	Administrative / Courthouse / Police / Fire / Museum																	
EXTENDED OCCUPANCY	Retail	Supermarket / Small Store / Hardware/Drug / Department Store / Strip Shopping Center / Neighborhood/Reg. Center																	
	Restaurant	Full Menu / Light Menu / Fast Food / Coffee Shop / Bar / Cafeteria																	
24-HOUR NIGHTTIME	Housekeeping	Apartment (High-rise) / HUD / Private / Elderly																	
	Nonhousekeeping	Hotel / Motel / Dormitory / Nursing																	
OTHER	Health	Clinic / Veterinarian / Outpatient / Hospital / Extended Care																	
	Assembly	Many Sub-Types																	
	Warehouse	Active / Inactive / Long Term / Short Term																	
	Other	Laboratories, Etc.																	

Figure 4.1.1.2 – Building Types and SubTypes

4.1.2 Offices

For further discussion see "Energy Design of Office Buildings", Progressive Architecture, June 1982.

Office energy requirements for thermal comfort, ventilation, and lighting vary within relatively narrow ranges, except for special functions such as computer centers. Unlike hospitals or restaurants, offices tend to be occupied during regular daytime hours. At night and on weekends, they are often vacant or only sparsely occupied. During office hours, high internal thermal loads can occur from lights, equipment, people, and external solar gain. With a reasonably "tight" envelope, such heat gains can lower the "balance point" (the outside temperature below which a building needs to be mechanically heated) to 40 degrees (F.) or below.

Conversely, the building may need to be cooled while outside temperatures are as low as 40-50 degrees (F.). Control of heat gains during occupied periods can therefore be a predominant energy conservation consideration. At night, during the heating season, peripheral heat gain sources are normally absent and the temperature is lower. Thus, control of conduction and infiltration losses can be a predominant energy factor.

Often superimposed on operational regularity is a fluctuating office building layout, changing with the needs of occupants. A typical design response to the problem of interchangeable space requirements is the use of grid lighting systems that are controlled by banks of circuit breakers. Such systems can cause large areas to be lighted needlessly for cleaning crews and a few off-hour workers.

Lighting is both a major energy end use in office buildings and a major contributor to internal loads. Lighting and space conditioning together account for over 90 percent of total energy use in both small and large office buildings.

Many office buildings, especially larger ones, have varying amounts of non-office-related space. Such multi-use buildings present a more complex analytical and design challenge. Their numerous secondary uses can significantly affect design solutions and annual energy consumption.

Design Strategies

Orientation, form, envelope, and lighting are the basic design strategies used to control thermal loads. In general, treatment of orientation, form, and exposure is interrelated; one cannot be viewed separate from the others.

Overall, energy-conscious design strategies do not need to be exotic. Careful and thoughtful combinations of "conventional" design strategies can be effective for many buildings. Control of heat gains, especially from lighting and solar, is an important design consideration for occupied and unoccupied periods. As a building's design becomes more energy efficient, the major targets of opportunity can shift. Typically, lighting energy strategies become more important after orientation, form, and envelope are optimized.

Orientation. Maximization of solar gain can be achieved by orienting the building's longer elevation along its east-west axis. A small office can orient light scoops and an attached sunspace due south for maximum solar concentration.

Form. Reducing the surface-to-volume ratio can be useful in a climate where cooling loads dominate. Less roof area is exposed to the sun, controlling conductive solar gain. Stairwells and mechanical spaces can be moved to the southern exposure as unconditioned buffer zones for control of solar gain, and glazing can be eliminated from east and west facades. One means of controlling heat loss from glazing, while still admitting natural lighting, is to use a central interior atrium. The building form can be compacted around the atrium, providing a more advantageous surface-to-volume ratio.

Envelope. An important design trend is the nonuniform treatment of glazing and shading for each exposure. In all but the most severe cooling-load climates, glass distribution can be weighted towards the building's southerly exposure and minimized or eliminated on the north, east, and west. The advantages are not so pronounced for large offices, but a combination of glass types and interior shading devices can be selected to provide appropriate window shading coefficients for each exposure regardless of building size.

In buildings where the primary load is heating, glazing (assuming daylighting is not a priority) can be eliminated completely on the north to reduce heat loss and concentrated on the southern exposure. With the glazing shaded in summer (but not in winter, when the sun is lower in the sky) by a series of set-in overhangs or slanted glass, solar gains in the conditioned space can be controlled seasonally. By contrast, in buildings where the predominant load is cooling, glazing can be redistributed to a north-facing clerestory, thus accommodating both daylighting and solar heat control.

Small office designs, predominantly buildings of less than 20,000 sq. ft., can use either direct gain or passive (nonmechanical) thermal storage strategies. Unlike large multizone offices, such buildings require less distinction between interior and perimeter zones, and it is easier to locate the thermal storage mass in physical proximity to both the solar aperture and the conditioned space. Both large and small office buildings, however, can use orientations, form, and fenestration to control and use solar gains on a seasonal basis, even without thermal storage.

Envelope Conduction. Strategies aimed at reducing conduction losses and gains can be important in buildings with climate-dominated loads. The composite "U" factor of the envelope can be improved by manipulating the component "U" values of walls, roof, and glazing. In cooling climates the design trend is to add double glazing. Conduction through glazing should

be a concern in all climates, although this can be outweighed by the
benefits of direct gain strategies, passive thermal storage or
daylighting. Overall thermal integrity in small offices, with their
higher surface-to-volume ratios, is generally more important than in
larger ones.

Lighting. One or more of the following can be used to reduce lighting
(watts per sq. ft.): reduced ambient illumination levels with task
lighting; more efficient fixtures, lamps, and controls; reduced use of
incandescent fixtures; and daylighting. These strategies lower annual
lighting energy consumption and help control heat gain in conditioned
spaces, thus reducing cooling loads on HVAC systems.

On the average, 38-40 percent reductions in annual lighting energy use can
be achieved by improvements in lighting levels, fixtures, lamps and
controls. Daylighting can reduce artificial lighting energy use even
further. Large office lighting system controls are far more complex than
those in small offices. Some automatic controls (e.g., photocell-based)
are used to complement daylighting strategies. Using switches instead of
circuit breakers can also be ineffective in controlling lighting use
during fully or partially unoccupied hours.

HVAC Systems. Experience has demonstrated the value of more energy-
efficient HVAC systems. Larger offices can effectively use variable air
volume (VAV) systems while heat pumps have been successful in small
offices. Less energy-efficient constant-volume systems (either single or
dual duct) should be avoided. The use of a space-temperature deadband
control is almost always advisable.

Small office HVAC systems tend to benefit from unitary or rooftop
equipment; large offices from central systems. In large offices,
moreover, separate heating and cooling plants are less effective that
combined systems using heat recovery. Chiller heat recovery is a useful
option for heating domestic hot water or building areas where heating is
required. Cooling outside air using an economizer cycle is a simple and
reliable strategy.

The control of the total building thermal load through architectural and
lighting strategies can significantly reduce the installed cooling
capacity required, especially in small office buildings.

4.1.3 Educational Facilities

For additional discussion see "Energy: A class by itself", Progressive
Architecture, March 1983.

The intermittent and irregular usage patterns in many school spaces can
significantly influence the selection of energy design strategies. Note
also that these patterns vary considerably between elementary and higher
level facilities.

On a daily basis, areas such as gymnasiums, auditoriums, and to some extent, classrooms are not scheduled for continuous occupancy. Often, however, the energy systems serving these spaces are designed or controlled to operate as if they were.

Internal loads are influenced by the type of activity within the space as well as by occupancy density, lighting, and equipment usage. When cafeterias are used for social activities--dances, for example--higher sensible and latent loads than those experienced during normal lunch periods are placed on HVAC systems. Schools are often used in summer and at night for adult education or civic affairs. Thus HVAC systems and building design strategies must handle both large and small loads efficiently during variable time periods.

All types of schools require large quantities of conditioned ventilation air. In many school spaces, design occupancy densities of 50-75 people per thousand square feet are typical. Ventilation rates are higher than in other building types, often in the range of 10-15 cubic feet of air per minute per person. Infiltration can also be a constant source of outside air due to frequent door openings and normal building cracks. In fact, the inrush of hot outside air when school lets out has been found to be the cause of peak electric cooling demand in some schools.

The high internal heat gains in classrooms and other school spaces often result in only minimal heating loads during occupied periods. On an annual basis, most heating energy is needed to maintain space temperatures when these areas are vacant. Depending on climate, design strategies that control conduction during intermittent and extended unoccupied periods can be effective.

After HVAC, lighting is the largest energy end-use in schools. Because learning spaces can contain various visual tasks, lighting levels are often selected on a "worst case" basis. In many instances, certain school spaces, such as workshops and auditoriums, require multiple lighting systems. Nighttime use of school buildings also contributes to large artificial lighting energy consumption.

Other major energy users in schools include kitchens, cafeterias, and service hot water for showers.

Design Strategies

Design attention to building plan, form, and through the conduction envelope can address the dominant unoccupied status of school spaces and accommodate a variety of complementary natural lighting and solar control schemes for occupied use. Fundamental architectural concepts coordinated with well-controlled mechanical systems can meet both full- and part-load conditions efficiently.

Conduction. Since much of a school's annual heating energy requirements in cold climates are for its considerable unoccupied periods, conduction losses should be minimized where possible. Glass U-values can be improved by double glazing. School administrators generally require that glazing be minimized, usually to 5-10 percent of the wall area--apparently to reduce opportunities for vandalism.

Berming. Earth berming--sometimes enclosing up to 60 percent of a building's mass--has been thought to be effective in all climates at reducing conduction gains and losses. The effectiveness of berming is difficult to assess, however. The thermal behavior of walls below grade has only begun to be well understood, and is influenced by local soil conditions such as composition and average moisture content. This strategy has the advantage, however, of minimizing the temperature difference between the conditioned space and the exterior wall because of the relatively stable earth temperature below the frost line. Berming requires a change in wall construction, depending on the amount of wall below grade, but there is no evident relationship between overall building cost increases and berming. Where vandalism is of concern, the use of extensive berming can have obvious benefits. When not placed on the roof for natural lighting, glazing can be located to the south in cold climates and to the north in warmer climates in bermed buildings.

Where southern exposure is given to windows, massive masonry walls and direct gain passive solar systems can often be used to further offset unoccupied heating loads by taking advantage of time lags in the release of heat from thermal storage. Glazing should be accompanied by solar control measures such as fins, overhangs and interior shading devices that allow entry of sunlight in winter but not in summer, when the sun is higher in the sky.

Other conduction control strategies include the use of non-conditioned spaces such as mechanical rooms as buffer zones on the building's perimeter and the use of compact building forms. Proper use of exterior buffers will differ depending on the basic floor plan chosen to implement various daylighting strategies.

Lighting. In both elementary and secondary schools, artificial lighting accounts for approximately 20 percent of annual energy use. While existing data are not conclusive, it is believed by some that substantial energy can be saved by reducing lighting levels in classrooms without unduly reducing lighting quality.

Daylighting. Clerestories (oriented to either the north or south), monitors, skylights, sunscoops, and windows can be effective in schools. The basic daylighting approach must depend on the internal spatial organization. Side daylighting for perimeter classrooms can be combined with interior circulation to enclose an administration and service core. Clerestories, monitors, and skylights often can be used to locate classrooms on the building's interior with buffer zones on the perimeter.

To accommodate variations in space usage, daylighting strategies should generally include multiple switching schemes and photocell control. The trade-offs between energy savings from reduced artificial lighting and increases in conduction or solar heat gain should be assessed.

HVAC. The most frequently used HVAC control strategy for schools is to set the night heating setpoint at 60 degrees (F.) or less and the cooling setpoint at 78 degrees (F.) or more. Seven-day timeclocks can be installed on hot-water circulating pumps to restrict operation to regular occupied periods. Hot-water temperatures can be reset to match changing space heating loads.

Ventilation air quantities can be reduced where practical. This often allows the use of smaller fan motors. Controls can be installed to keep outside air dampers closed during the morning warm-up cycle. Ventilation fans can be interlocked with heating controls to eliminate operation during unoccupied periods.

Other strategies include reduction of static pressures in the air system and the use of evaporative coolers in hot, dry climates. Heat recovery can be appropriate in all climates. Heat recovery (double-bundle) chillers can be used to preheat ventilation air. Heat can be recovered from locker rooms, general building exhaust and service hot water.

4.1.4 Retail Stores

For additional discussion see "Energy for sales", Progressive Architecture, August 1982.

The merchandising function of retail stores places more design emphasis on the building's interior systems than on its exterior components. The design criteria for lighting systems for promoting merchandising are different from the criteria for increasing worker productivity in office buildings.

Retail buildings, however, share with office buildings the need for "universal" space design. Shops, whether in regional, neighborhood, or strip shopping centers, must accommodate the energy-consuming needs of diverse tenants such as jewelry stores, bakeries, and record shops. Tenant mix and the amount of leased square footage also vary from month to month. These factors strongly influence energy consumption but are difficult to predict or control.

Retail buildings operate longer hours than most other buildings. A six- or seven-day-a-week operation for 10 to 12 hours a day is common. Internal gains from equipment are minimal in most retail operations except for food-related operations such as bakeries and carry-outs. Nevertheless, retail stores are generally considered to be dominated by internal heat loads, primarily due to high uniform lighting loads and high occupant density. As a result, retail energy use is not subject to time-related load swings and is almost "steady state" at given weather conditions.

The form and envelope configuration of retail buildings is frequently dictated by functional space requirements and site constraints. Often there is little flexibility to adjust building orientation for energy concerns. Also, facade treatment may be of secondary importance in malls and department stores.

Lighting systems operate longer and at higher lighting levels than in most other building types. There is a significant need for incandescent display lighting. Lighting accounts for about 35 percent of total annual retail energy usage, and significant energy savings can be achieved here. Unfortunately the designer's influence is often limited; many tenants often furnish their own lighting systems. There are few discernible patterns in the types of lighting fixtures in various retail categories. There is a trend toward replacement of incandescent with fluorescent fixtures.

Conductive losses become more important at night when the daytime problem of internal loads is largely absent. Long hours of operation and the high-ventilation code requirements often dictate time-of-day control of HVAC systems. This can be especially appropriate for fan energy and night heating. Lease arrangements significantly affect HVAC system design criteria; unitary or rooftop systems are a popular means of making tenants responsible for their own energy bills.

Design Strategies

Lighting and HVAC offer the greatest energy saving potential in retail buildings. Major envelope potentials include increased insulation and reflective roofs.

The air system in most retail buildings can effectively use efficient fans, filters, and variable-speed fan drives.

High ventilation rates encourage exhaust air heat recovery. Return and lighting troffers can be used to remove unwanted heat from conditioned space, especially in conjunction with economizer cycle equipment. This exhaust air can be used to condition storage and service areas.

Reducing illumination where appropriate can achieve major energy savings. Time-of-day controls using photocells or timeclocks can be used. Lighting levels can be effectively reduced with manual switching.

HID (high-intensity discharge) fixtures offer potential for significant energy savings. While used infrequently, the higher lumen per watt output of HID fixtures can deliver required lighting levels with less installed capacity.

Daylighting--clerestories and skylights used in conjunction with automatic controls--can be effective in the public circulation areas of regional shopping centers, which constitutes one-third of the total area. Daylighting with manual controls can be used in sales and checkout areas of smaller buildings, such as neighborhood and strip shopping centers.

HVAC. Constant-volume systems are predominant in all types of retail stores, though variable air volume (VAV) systems are sometimes effective. Retail stores are characterized by the near universal use of economizer cycle HVAC systems. Such systems are particularly well suited to retail buildings. The natural resource of cool air is usually available when internal cooling loads are present.

A key strategy for conditioning retail stores is simply to reduce the square footage to be heated, cooled, or ventilated. Storage areas can be left unconditioned or be provided minimal conditioning. Floor-to-ceiling height can also be decreased to reduce the volume of air to be conditioned.

VAV systems with central plants, efficient fans, and VAV boxes are generally used in regional centers. Department stores use central plants but many use constant volume VAV systems. Neighborhood centers commonly use HVAC systems with unitary equipment.

Deadband limits used in temperature control systems can be increased by 6-10 degrees (F.), and the night heating setback temperature difference can be increased by 10 degrees (F.). Improved controls or control strategies that allow equipment to operate on an as-needed basis rather than continuously are beneficial.

Site, Form, and Envelope. The use of insulation in retail stores varies considerably, primarily because building ownership strongly influences the willingness to pay energy-related first costs, such as insulation. Department stores tend to be owner-occupied, while other retail types are generally income properties occupied by tenants. Roof insulation on retail stores has increased potential over other building types. Large roof areas are a significant factor in nearly all retail buildings. Unconditioned or minimally conditioned buffer zones of storage and circulation spaces can be placed on the exterior. These strategies reduce conductive losses through walls, which constitute a relatively small percentage of exposed surface in retail buildings.

Control of solar gain is generally not critical in retail stores where glass area is minimal. Overhangs can be critical in strip shopping centers, which tend to have display glass on exterior circulation areas. Reflective roofs can effectively reduce direct solar gain on significant portions of the retail envelope.

4.1.5 Apartments (Housekeeping)

For additional discussion see "Dwelling with Energy", Progressive Architecture, October 1982.

Apartment buildings have rarely been the subject of published research. This lack of attention is partly due to their hybrid nature. These buildings encompass rental apartments, condominiums, housing for the elderly, and dormitories.
As income properties they can be classified as commercial buildings, yet they share many characteristics with single-family residences, e.g., they can be "skin-load" dominated. The ventilation and infiltration rates are generally high due to frequent opening of windows and doors.

With multifamily buildings, it is important to differentiate energy use in
the public or common spaces from energy use in the living units; their
control can require different strategies. Lighting, heating, cooling, and
ventilating for stairwells, corridors, elevators lobbies (and elevators)
are usually a common obligation, paid for by the building owner,
management group, or condominium association. Typically, these loads are
active 24 hours a day.

Lease arrangements regarding responsibility for energy cost vary widely.
In many instances, domestic hot water is heated by a central facility at
common expense. This is true for heating and airconditioning in some
properties. Although the magnitude of energy usage in common spaces can
vary from one building to another, monitoring responsibility and
management can provide a high degree of control.

Design Strategies

Site and Orientation. Buildings should be oriented for solar access and
control where possible. This can require extensive site planning to
overcome a variety of constraints. Project economics often determine the
number and type of units required for successful marketing, operation, and
return on investment. Site topography, access to views and client
requirements can be overriding.

Conduction. As with other residential buildings, the control of
conduction gains and losses is important. A high level of occupancy
occurs at night when outdoor temperatures are at their lowest and interior
space setpoint temperatures are typically high. In other words,
multifamily buildings experience a higher temperature differential for
longer periods of time than other commercial building types. Night
setback can be used to reduce this temperature difference.

Other strategies include external shading and reflective roofs. External
shading for control of solar gain can be accomplished through the use of
overhangs, louvers, and balconies on apartment units that are stacked.
Reflective roofs are more frequently effective on lowrise apartments,
which have relatively larger roof areas than highrise buildings.

Passive Solar Applications. Passive solar strategies are often limited to
public spaces in lowrise buildings. Substantial passive solar
applications using thermal mass storage at the unit level are quite
feasible. Storage walls, atriums and greenhouses are possible. Passive
features can often be added onto existing buildings as additional public
space.

HVAC Systems. Virtually all major types of heat pump systems can be
effective, the most common being a through-the-wall air-source unit with
electric resistance heat backup. Heat pump applications are often water-
source systems of both the closed and open loop type. Heat pumps are
effective primarily for space conditioning within the dwelling unit. In
common spaces, two- and four-pipe fan coils or other air systems are
generally used.

Multifamily buildings often have central exhaust ventilation from bathrooms and kitchens to roof-top ventilators. Many have both central supply air system and window airconditioners. The exhaust ventilating systems need to be balanced, and supply air must be appropriately controlled to prevent problems created by occupants' frequent opening of windows and doors.

Lighting. A number of lighting strategies can be effective. Nearly all apartments have high percentages of incandescent lighting. The trend is to replace as much incandescent lighting as possible with fluorescent, especially in common areas. Incandescent fixtures in kitchens and baths can be replaced with fluorescent fixtures, and in some instances fluorescents can be used in the living areas as well. Care should be taken, however, to ensure adequate color-rendering in private spaces. HID lighting can be used in public spaces. Daylighting can be used in skylighted central atriums.

Domestic Hot Water. Normally, water heating energy (including water heater standby losses) equals 20-25 percent of annual multifamily energy use. Timeclocks can be used on the water heating equipment, and heat recovery from airconditioning can be used to meet a portion of the hot water load.

Appliances. Recent studies by utility companies and others show that laundry, cooking, and personal appliances can use up to 35 percent of total annual energy in residential buildings. Energy-efficient appliances and residential load-shedding programs sponsored by some utilities can be effective.

4.1.6 Hotels/Motels (Non-Housekeeping)

For additional discussion see "Bed, Board, and Btu's", Progressive Architecture, December 1982.

Residential non-housekeeping buildings (hotels, motels, nursing homes) share certain important functional space type relationships. For example, both a guest room and a patient room need a direct relationship to some type of service area, such as a kitchen, dining, laundry, or assembly area. The resulting mix of functions yields an energy mix of service areas dominated by internal loads and sleeping rooms dominated by external loads.

Energy requirements can vary considerably depending on facility type. Contrast, for example, the functional complexity of the convention hotel and the ubiquitous strip motel. Nursing homes and geriatric centers also share this wide diversity, though not as great.

Usage patterns are perhaps the most significant determinant in energy usage in all buildings. Non-housekeeping facilities are inherently energy intensive because of their 24-hour-a-day nature. Like other residential buildings, nighttime occupancy levels are high. Nursing homes, however, have higher daytime occupancy than hotels and motels because nursing home residents tend to stay at home during the day. Occupant control of HVAC equipment in this building type should normally be available around the clock to meet stringent comfort requirements.

Other characteristics influencing both energy use and conservation opportunities in this building type are high domestic hot water consumption, high ventilation requirements, and large circulation areas, which make up to 20-30 percent of the gross floor area. With all these influences at work, this building type can be among the most energy-intensive of the building categories.

Design Strategies

Strategic location of spaces dominated by external vs. internal loads, outside air reductions, shell tightening, incandescent lamp replacement and heat reclamation can be effective.

Reduction of conduction losses (in colder climates) can be accomplished by increasing insulation levels or reducing exposed wall and glazing areas. Lighting strategies can be less effective in reducing energy use than strategies aimed at mechanical systems.

Form and Space Organization. Two general approaches to space organization and building form are appropriate: opening up the building for solar exposure and tightening the building against the elements. The emphasis on one or the other of these strategies varies according to the individual space mix and function of the building as well as its climate and location.

In sleeping rooms, control of conductive heat loss and gain is of major concern, not only because of the lack of internal gains to offset losses but also because space temperatures are maintained at higher levels of comfort. In heating climates, these spaces can benefit from controlled solar gain by orienting them to the south, while in cooling climates a northern exposure is more beneficial.

Support areas such as laundries and kitchens are typically dominated by internal loads. Generally these spaces can meet much of their own heating requirements even at fairly low outdoor temperatures. In heating climates they are often located to the north. Lighting control, other heat sources and efficient means of cooling such as economizers demand attention. Unwanted or wasted heat from support areas can often be tapped for other uses.

Circulation areas can be strategically placed to serve as barriers to weather-related loads in both heating and cooling climates. Mechanical and storage spaces offer similar potential.

Envelope. Improved control of conduction should be attempted because a large portion of the envelope surrounds sleeping rooms. Insulation can be increased, and the area of the building envelope can be reduced to minimize glazing and surface area exposed to the weather. Living areas and fenestration can be relocated to the south or the north, depending on the geographical location.

Lighting Systems. Nursing homes, hotels, and motels have relatively low levels of installed lighting wattage by comparison to other building types--but have a 24-hour usage profile. Consequently, lighting energy use on a per square foot basis can be comparable to building types with about twice the installed capacity. In hotels and motels, the percentage of floor area illuminated by incandescent lighting is quite high, between 60 and 90 percent. The lighting system design includes all fixtures in guest rooms including table lamps and swag lamps. These types of fixtures are often supplied by tenants in other residential building types. However, not all hotel and motel building owners find fluorescent guest room lighting attractive.
Daylighting has great potential in this building type. Hotels and especially motels are typically low-rise structures and contain a high percentage of floor area for circulation.

HVAC. Code requirements and the need for 24-hour ventilation air can lead to high energy usage. Air-to-air heat exchangers can be used to heat ventilation air with exhaust air.

Other limited heat recovery applications include the reduction of service water heating energy requirements. Waste heat from airconditioning and from laundry wastewater can be used to preheat incoming cold water.

Process Heat. Non-housekeeping residential buildings have numerous heat-generating devices such as dishwashers and clothes washers, and significant amounts of refrigeration. Even the ice machine in the motel hallway can provide enough cost-effective waste heat from its condenser to heat water for a few guest rooms.

4.1.7 Health Facilities

For additional discussion see "Energy to recover", Progressive Architecture, February 1983.

Except for restaurants, hospitals are by far the most energy- intensive of all building types. Even though areas as diverse as surgical suites and patient rooms have different operating hours, internal loads, and use profiles, the predominant 24-hour-a-day operation of hospitals is inherently energy intensive. Strict environmental, life safety, and regulatory requirements affect the design of hospital HVAC systems. Precise control of temperature, humidity levels and high ventilation rates is required.

The widespread perception that hospitals are internal-load-dominated is questioned by past research. In fact, the predominant energy consumption is for heating. Patient areas, corridors, and certain support areas that do not experience high internal loads are often ventilated continuously.

Humidity control of ventilation air in areas that require narrow temperature and humidity ranges is another cause of high heating energy requirements.

Design Strategies

Substantial energy reductions can be achieved in health facilities even though there are more constraints than in other building types. Hospitals are different from other building types in that the major design emphasis can be placed on HVAC systems and heat recovery. Architectural strategies (especially those for patient rooms) can heavily influence the buildings' form and reduce peak heating and cooling loads, but usually do not provide the predominant energy savings.

The three major functional groupings of hospital spaces include: 1) patient areas, 2) ancillary facilities such as operating rooms, intensive care units, emergency rooms and their direct support areas, which have the most strict environmental requirements, and 3) support service areas, including offices, pharmacies, treatment rooms, food service, storage, and other space types.

Patient Rooms. Design strategies in patient rooms should emphasize control of conduction gains and losses. These loads are important because of constant space temperature setpoints and the inappropriateness of night temperature setbacks. Room wall U-values in patient rooms can generally be improved.

Support Areas. Potential energy-conservation strategies include reduction of controlled lighting capacity in patient support areas such as corridors and nurses' stations and the use of improved lighting controls, such as photocells, timeclocks and local two-step switching.

Lighting and environmental criteria can be relaxed in certain areas without detrimental effects on health care. Lighting levels and installed capacity can be reduced in storage areas, mechanical rooms, corridors, and similar spaces. Incandescent lighting can be replaced with fluorescent fixtures using high efficiency ballasts.

In office and administrative areas, VAV systems can be used, as well as task lighting in conjunction with lower levels of ambient lighting.

In hospital kitchens, a prevalent strategy is the use of heat recovery coils in exhaust ducts. Mechanical and storage areas can be located to serve as buffer zones for conditioned interior space.

Building Form and Envelope. Basic decisions on the organization, placement, and treatment of patient rooms usually govern a hospital's form and orientation.

Patient rooms can can account for 75 percent of a hospital's exterior surface areas. Conductive heat loss and gain are of major concern, as is solar control. Exterior exposure of patient rooms can be minimized by locating them around interior courtyards and enclosed atria. Not only can this strategy allow the form to become more compact, but also allows natural light to reach patient rooms.

The overall thermal integrity of the envelope can be improved by a variety of fixed and movable interior and exterior shading devices to control solar gains on a seasonal basis.

HVAC. HVAC zoning can achieve significant reductions in heating and cooling energy requirements. This involves strategic regrouping of the mix of functional spaces assigned to a particular type of HVAC system on the basis of similarities in operational hours, temperature setpoints, and humidification requirements. HVAC systems can be arranged to provide humidity control through reheat at the space level rather than at the central air handler. This also allows more flexible control of ventilation air and minimizes unnecessary system operation and energy required for precision conditioning of supply and ventilation air.

Hospitals offer a near ideal environment for the use of heat recovery and thermal storage strategies. Recoverable waste heat resources are coincident in time with many energy demands, and multiple resources can be tied into the same recovery systems. Resources such as refrigeration and central water chilling equipment and large quantities of exhaust air are plentiful. Combined with thermal storage systems and the central control available at the plant level, heat recovery sources can be matched with energy needs such as heating and preheating of service hot water and ventilation air. In some instances recovered energy can be sent to reheat coils for humidity control or to heating coils in dual duct systems.

Double bundle (heat recovery) chillers can be used in most hospital designs, primarily to help meet hot water loads. Other heat recovery applications included heat wheels, "run-around" loops, variable chilled water pumping, evaporative humidifiers, and the use of separate steam boilers for sterilization processes.

4.2 ANALYTICAL TECHNIQUES

4.2.1 Introduction

Energy analysis methods for building design are becoming available on an increasingly widespread basis. Energy analysis methods can vary from simple manual methods such as a Variable Base Degree Day method with seasonal equipment efficiencies to extremely detailed hour-by-hour computer simulations.

Just a few years ago, the choices were either large, complex (and expensive) methods available only on mainframe computers, or laborious hand-calculation methods. Today, the large, complex programs are improved and less costly to use because of advances in computer technology. Also today microcomputers are in most design offices, and a number of "simpler" energy analysis tools are available to run on them. This includes simplified methods appropriate for both residential and commercial building energy analysis.

4.2.2 Uses of Energy Analysis Methods

Energy analysis methods can be used for decision making in design, code compliance, and cost analysis. Typical energy-related objectives during building design include the reduction of:
- energy loads
- energy use
- peak demand
- energy operating costs
- other operating costs
- first costs.

Energy-conscious design is not simply a matter of reducing the building's loads on its systems. Sometimes major reductions in loads do not produce major reductions in energy use, because of the nature of the building systems. Likewise, major reductions in energy use may not produce major reductions in energy costs, because of the mix of fuels and fuel costs, including utility rate structures.

Code Compliance

In many jurisdictions, energy analysis methods are an optional means of compliance with energy code requirements, especially for innovative building designs. Such compliance is becoming more effective even for smaller buildings as the costs of acquiring and using energy analysis methods decrease with the availability of microcomputer-based analysis methods.

Some firms have developed in-house computer programs that not only perform the necessary calculations but also print out completed forms that can be submitted directly to building officials.

The designer should ascertain whether an analysis tool proposed for use in satisfying code requirement purposes has been certified by the local jurisdiction as acceptable documentation.

Economic Assessments

Economic tools relate construction costs with building operating costs over time for energy, other operating costs and maintenance. Such methods can range from very simple to extremely complex. Complex models can include the time-cost of money, utility rate structures, taxes, and various types of interest. Examples of different methods include:

- simple payback
- discounted payback
- life-cycle cost
- internal rate of return (IRR)
- savings to investment ratio (SIR)
- cost/benefit analysis.

In the short term, the use of energy analysis methods to assist in the reduction of building energy use makes economic sense to a building owner. Often, significant energy cost reductions are possible at little or no increase in first cost. Indeed, it is sometimes possible to reduce both energy operating costs and building construction costs by taking advantage of energy and cost trade-offs among major building systems.

In the long term, reduced building energy use is a powerful hedge against future energy uncertainty. A typical building designed today might last 50 years. Current projections indicate that oil reserves may last 60 years. Irrespective of one's faith in technology to find alternatives, or in the prospective of major new oil finds, it is likely that buildings designed today will operate at some future point within an energy and energy cost scenario quite different from that now prevalent.

Energy Design Tools

Energy design tools can be divided into two groups (see Figure 4.2.3.1): energy strategy tools and energy analysis tools.

4.2.3 Energy Strategy Tools

Energy strategy tools provide guidance to designers about what decisions to make. These tools tell you *what to do*, what major energy opportunity areas are, what strategies to try, what decisions seem best, what directions to try. They often provide a design process for arriving at a solution, as well as means for assessing the effects of the solution. They can be divided into two general groups:
- those that provide a logical structure for determining a solution to specific problems and
- those that have predetermined solutions.

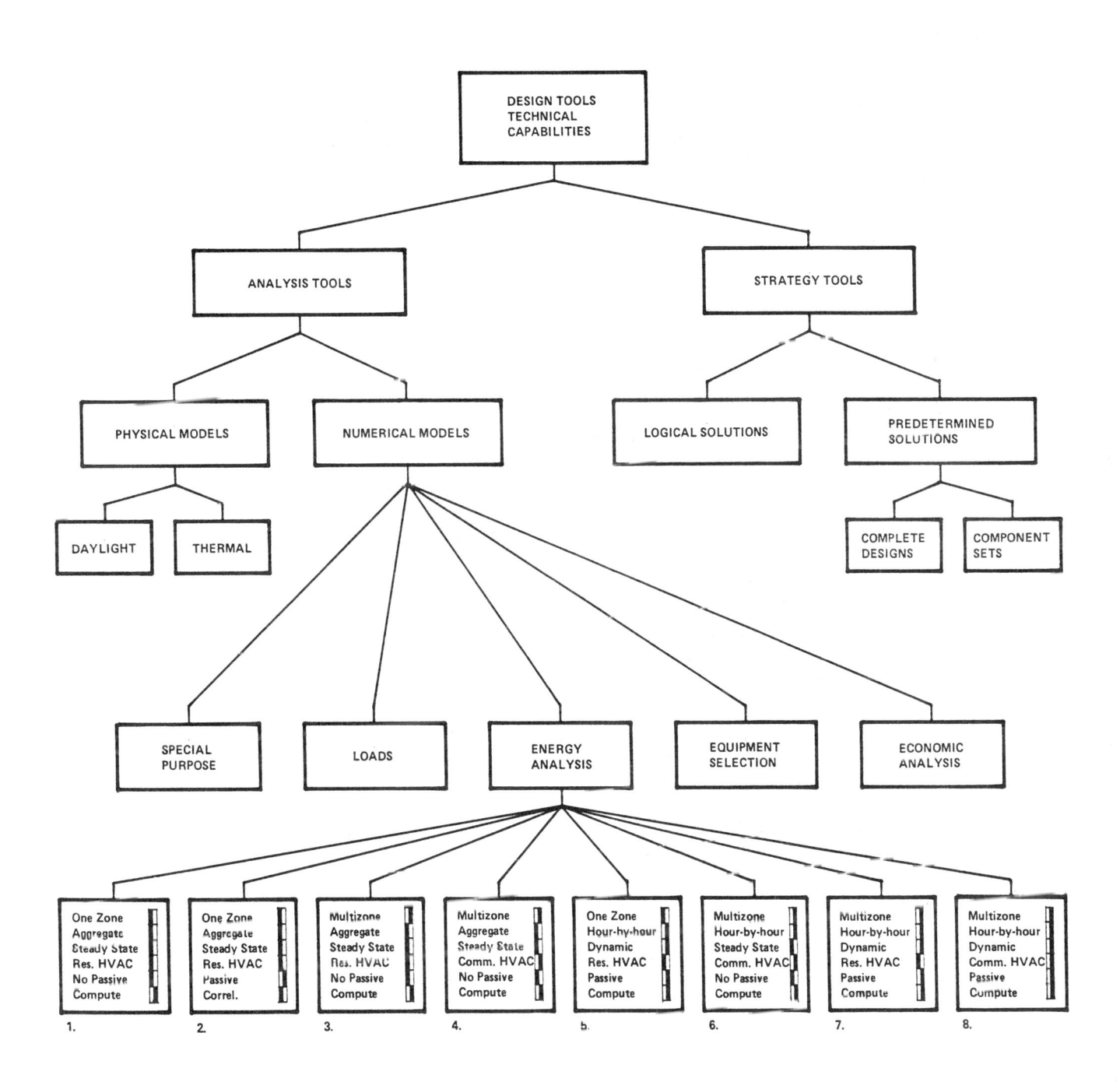

Figure 4.2.3.1 - Design Tool Spectrum

Logical Solution Tools

Unfortunately, very few "logical" solution tools exist, especially those that provide a logical structure for determining solutions to specific problems. Two notable exceptions are:
- Energy Graphics (for U.S. Department of Energy). Booz-Allen & Hamilton, Inc. (Washington, D.C., 1980)
- The Small Office Building Handbook. Burt, Hill, Kosar, Rittelmann Associates (Van Nostrand Reinhold Company: New York, 1985).

Both of these are handbooks that describe a design process for selecting appropriate energy strategies. Both products are appropriate for use in the early design stages.

Such methods depend primarily on logical, or symbolic, analysis rather than on numerical analysis, and incorporate considerable expertise about building energy behavior. While there is considerable interest within the building research community in applying knowledge-based methodologies (including "expert" systems) to building energy design problems, it is unlikely that a general knowledge-based tool useful to designers will be developed for at least several years.

Predetermined Solution Tools

A number of predetermined-solution tools have been developed, primarily for energy code compliance purposes. They are typically based on numerous analyses of various building types that can indicate to designers the likely energy or cost results of certain energy strategies, under the limited conditions included in the analyses. Examples of such predetermined-solution tools include:
- The residential point systems recently developed for several states (California, Pennsylvania, Minnesota, Florida, etc).
- The residential "Slide Rule" developed by the U.S. Department of Energy (DOE), Steven Winter Associates, and the AIA Foundation, and Lawrence Berkeley Laboratory which is currently being packaged as a microcomputer program.
- The Alternative Component Packages portion of the California energy code for office buildings.
- The envelope compliance procedure now proposed for inclusion in ASHRAE Standard 90.

Such predetermined-solution packages have great educational value and are very appropriate for code compliance procedures. However, they have limited application to specific building design problems unless the design alternatives fit within the limits covered by the studies that produced the predetermined solution sets.

4.2.4 Energy Analysis Tools

Energy analysis tools analyze the consequences of decisions. They can predict how well a solution will do, but only after the designer has described the solution (the design characteristics), often in great detail.

A significant limitation on using analysis tools as design tools is that one must develop a design solution <u>before</u> one can use the analysis tool. Many important energy design decisions need to be made <u>before</u> the stage in the design process where solutions are developed sufficiently that detailed building characteristics are available for input to an analysis tool. Thus, it is usually very difficult to use analysis tools early in the design process.

Physical Models

Physical models are generally used for daylight analysis. Such models are excellent for not only assessing the quantity of light in spaces from daylighting solutions but also the quality of the daylighting. Such assessment of lighting quality is not currently possible with numerical models, including computer-based daylighting programs.

Numerical Models

Numerical models are what is generally meant by "energy analysis tools." There are hundreds of tools available to solve many different analysis problems. The categories of analysis tools are:
- special purpose
- loads analysis
- equipment sizing
- economic analysis
- energy analysis.

Special Purpose Tools

Special purpose tools produce answers for building components or for isolated areas. These may be stand-alone methods or may be incorporated into other analyses. Examples include: daylighting methods; infiltration models; subsurface heat transfer methods; and fenestration energy analysis methods.

Load Calculation Tools

Load calculation tools primarily address peak or design-day building thermal loads. Both internal loads (e.g., people, lights, and equipment) and external loads (e.g., temperature, humidity, solar radiation, and wind) for space conditioning are considered at a minimum, but other loads may be considered as well. The calculations' output may also include loads by month, year or other time period. Load calculation models include:
- degree day procedure
- variable base degree day procedure
- bin method (loads portion)
- modified bin method (loads portion)
- graphical/correlation methods
- hourly thermal analysis methods

Load calculation tools can be stand-alone analyses, or incorporated into more comprehensive tools that also model building system energy behavior, use and economics.

Equipment Sizing Tools

Equipment sizing tools include load calculation routines that permit analysis of peak loads to determine the capacities needed to meet such loads. Part-load equipment performance and annual energy estimates are not within this category. Such equipment sizing tools may be included as part of comprehensive energy analysis models.

Energy Analysis Tools

Energy analysis tools produce estimates of building energy use over time, usually annually or monthly, but also daily and hourly. A typical energy analysis method will include:

- <u>Loads analysis</u> to produce estimates of the loads from the spaces in the building on the building's HVAC and lighting systems.

- <u>Systems analysis</u> to determine the energy required by the HVAC distribution systems in meeting the space loads.

- <u>Plant analysis</u> to determine the efficiency of the energy conversion equipment in meeting the requirements of the HVAC distribution equipment.

Applications

<u>Primary Application:</u> Most programs are designed to accomplish a primary objective, whether design, research, or education. The stage of design is also important:
- programming/predesign
- schematics
- design development, architecture and engineering
- construction documents
- construction
- post construction services
- retrofit/rehabilitation.

For existing buildings, the programs diagnose the current energy behavior of the building (and the causes of such behavior) as well as assess alternative ways to improve energy efficiency. Such changes could range from operational improvements, to retrofit of certain building components, to major building rehabilitation.

<u>Applicable Building Type:</u> The limits of end-use calculations, and types of loads and systems that can be assessed will be strongly related to the types of buildings that can be modeled, including:
- single family residential
- multi-family residential

- small commercial
- large commercial.

4.2.5 User Requirements

There are no perfect energy analysis tools. Each is a compromise among often conflicting objectives such as ease of use, simplicity, comprehensive capabilities, speed of calculation, accuracy, precision, and type of equipment required for use.

Types of Users

Different types of users of energy analysis tools can have distinctly different needs. A tool developed with one type of user in mind may be excellent for that type of user, but mediocre or poor in meeting the needs of another type of user. Therefore, it is important to assess user needs and characteristics. Five possible major different user groups for most energy tools are:
- researchers
- architects
- engineers
- educators/students
- building owners and operators.

A researcher may be more interested in rigorously defined, easily modified analysis procedures. The designer may be more interested in user-friendly features, graphic and numerical output, and so on. For students, the ease of use and teaching effectiveness can be paramount.

Availability

Programs vary widely in the availability of information on the origin of the program, the program format, and the specific equipment which it requires:
- origin: public domain, proprietary, or mixed private/public domain
- format: manual, microcomputer, mini/mainframe
- equipment required: RAM, storage (disks), operating system and language, input/output requirements, hardware types (IBM, Apple, VAX, CDC, etc.)

Cost of Use

Purchase price can be significant, but can also be one of the smallest costs of using an energy analysis tool. The time costs for learning to use the tool and the costs of data input preparation can be large. Costs to consider include:
- purchase price
- special hardware or software
- installation and debugging
- learning: operation, capabilities, limitations
- operating: data preparation, input, run cost, run time
- maintenance: day to day (tapes, disks, files), updates.

Documentation

Documentation of energy analysis programs is generally either written in manuals or embedded in software. Full written documentation can include a user's manual, a technical manual, and a programming manual. An important feature of a user's manual is case studies that show the various capabilities of the tool.

Run Time

Even more important from an ease of use point of view is "help" or "run time" information embedded in the program. This is information that is provided to the user at difficult points in the program while the tool is being used. As computer memory and storage gets less costly the extent of such "run time" aids should increase. This information can take various forms:
- context-sensitive "help screens
- defaults: context-sensitive "default" values that show typical or desirable entries for most input requirements. They are among the most useful aids. Defaults can radically reduce the amount of time required for preparing input and reduce the amount of knowledge required to use the tool.
- error-checking: automatic checking for errors and for values outside of expected ranges.
- consistency checking: Many inputs are related and can be checked for mutual consistency. Many tools are very sensitive to the values of relatively few inputs. This can be a valuable feature, but is difficult to develop and is rarely done.

Several other valuable types of information (explanations) can be either written or built into programs. They include:
- input formats and parameters
- output options and formats; many tools include both numerical and graphic output at various levels of detail
- calculation methods
- sources of calculation methods (references to technical volumes, equations, data tables, etc.)
- analysis limitations; this information is often just as important as the tool's capabilities
- computer operations
- weather data; (types used, sources, available files)
- file handling and data storage capabilities
- common operating errors
- document indexing for easier referencing.

User Support

The level and type of support available to the user is very important. Several categories are direct user support, updates, and user groups. Questions regarding user support have to do with the following:
- available from developer, vendor, other
- fee charged

- available through telephone, toll free number, correspondence
- available for document clarification, start-up, technical questions

Input/Output

The important issues regarding input are entry formats and the quantity and complexity of data input that is required. Common formats include:
- interactive
- batch files with (without) editor
- combination of interactive and batch
- input storage and recall.

The major interaction between the user and the tool is via the data input routines; therefore both format and the level of assistance provided are crucial.

Output may be through standard reports or formats that can be specified and tailored by the user.

It is increasingly common for programs to accept inputs from other programs and to provide output files (usually ASCII) that can be read by other programs. This is a powerful feature.

Tool Structure

Developing good program structures is an art, just like designing good buildings. A well-structured program will be easy to operate, even if it is complex, while a poorly structured program will be awkward to use, even if it is a simple one. While it is difficult to define precisely, persons selecting energy analysis tools should investigate the presence or absence of easy-to-use program structure and flow.

4.2.6 Technical Capabilities of Different Tools

From a user's point of view, there are two key questions to be asked about the technical capabilities of any method or tool. The first is, "Is it capable of analyzing the types of energy loads and systems for the buildings I design (or for the particular building in question)?" The second question is, "How accurately, or precisely, does it perform the analysis of importance to me?" These two simple questions are not always simple to answer. Different types of energy tools can be distinguished using the following six pairs of analysis factors. In each of the six features, the right-hand factor indicates a greater level of detail and more precise analysis.

one zone - multizone
aggregate - hour-by-hour
steady state - dynamic
residential HVAC - commercial HVAC
no passive - passive solar
correlation - direct computation

292

1.

One Zone	O		Multizone	EXAMPLES
Aggregate	O		Hour-By-Hour	Degree Day Method
Steady State	O		Dynamic	Degree Hour Method
Resid. HVAC	O		Commercial HVAC	Equivalent Full Load Hours
No Passive	O		Passive	(Cooling only)
Correlation		O	Directly Computed	

2.

One Zone	O		Multizone	EXAMPLES
Aggregate	O		Hour-By-Hour	SLR
Steady State	O		Dynamic	
Resid. HVAC	O		Commercial HVAC	
No Passive		O	Passive	
Correlation	O		Directly Computed	

3.

One Zone		O	Multizone	EXAMPLES
Aggregate	O		Hour-By-Hour	Bin Method
Steady State	O		Dynamic	Variable Degree Day
Resid. HVAC	O		Commercial HVAC	Degree Hour
No Passive	O		Passive	
Correlation		O	Directly Computed	

4.

One Zone		O	Multizone	EXAMPLES
Aggregate	O		Hour-By-Hour	Bin Method/ELE
Steady State	O		Dynamic	Variable Degree Day
Resid. HVAC		O	Commercial HVAC	Degree Hour with commercial
No Passive	O		Passive	HVAC system routines
Correlation		O	Directly Computed	

5.

One Zone	O		Multizone	EXAMPLES
Aggregate		O	Hour-By-Hour	SUNCAT
Steady State		O	Dynamic	
Resid. HVAC	O		Commercial HVAC	
No Passive		O	Passive	
Correlation		O	Directly Computed	

6.

One Zone		O	Multizone	EXAMPLES
Aggregate		O	Hour-By-Hour	AXCESS
Steady State	O		Dynamic	TRACE
Resid. HVAC		O	Commercial HVAC	EMPSS
No Passive	O		Passive	ESP
Correlation		O	Directly Computed	

7.

One Zone		O	Multizone	EXAMPLES
Aggregate		O	Hour-By-Hour	DEROB
Steady State		O	Dynamic	UWENSOL 4.1
Resid. HVAC	O		Commercial HVAC	LPMTZ
No Passive		O	Passive	NBSLD (Depending
Correlation		O	Directly Computed	on interpretation)

8.

One Zone		O	Multizone	EXAMPLES
Aggregate		O	Hour-By-Hour	BLAST 3.0
Steady State		O	Dynamic	BLAST 2.0
Resid. HVAC		O	Commercial HVAC	DOE 2.1A, B, and C
No Passive		O	Passive	
Correlation		O	Directly Computed	

Source: Deringer & Associates, 1984.

Figure 4.2.7.1 - Energy Tool Descriptors

Figure 4.2.7.1 provides examples of tools that fit within eight different groupings of the six key factors. The groupings indicate general differences between tools but are still not detailed enough to assess specific tool capabilities. Examples of more specific capabilities are the following:
- can assess effects of light-dimming controls in perimeter areas or under skylights in daylighting designs
- can assess interzone thermal transfers
- can assess dynamic (over time) effects of building mass (for heating and/or cooling)
- can assess seasonal efficiencies of HVAC systems (residential systems)
- can assess hourly operation of hydronic heat pump system with storage tank
- can assess active solar hot water systems.

Figure 4.2.7.2 provides a much finer breakdown of the capabilities provided by complex energy analysis tools.

4.2.7 Energy Analysis Models

Key issues in energy analysis include steady state vs. dynamic models; the use of single-measure vs. multiple-measure models; effects of building mass; and weather data requirements and availability.

Steady State vs. Dynamic Models

Steady-state models are relatively simple, both analytically and in the effort required to use them. They analyze, or "see" a building's energy systems at single points in time. These times are usually chosen as worst-case weather or loading conditions. This can be useful when sizing equipment or for comparing design alternatives that are not affected by the dynamics of changing weather, internal loads, and so on.

Dynamic models are required to accurately account for changes over time in weather, occupancy profiles, equipment use, and energy use. Dynamic models usually require hourly weather data and profiles of building use for equipment, occupants, and lighting. The solution is usually calculated over a 24-hour cycle. In some cases these models simulate energy use for every hour in a year, while in others a typical day for each month is the basic unit.

Single- vs. Multiple-Measurement Models

The most commonly used single measure method is the traditional degree day procedure for estimating heating requirements. This procedure is based on the assumptions that, in the long term, solar and internal heat gains will on the average offset heat loss when the mean daily outdoor temperature is 65 degrees (F.) and fuel consumption will be proportional to the difference between the mean daily temperature and 65 degrees (F.).

A basic problem with degree day methods is that, except for traditional single-family residences, the 7 degrees (F.) internal heat gain implicit

ENERGY ANALYSIS TOOLS: TECHNICAL CATEGORIZATION FACTORS

1. Building Energy Loads
2. Conventional HVAC Systems
3. Conventional Energy Conversion Plants
4. Component Sizing
5. Control Systems and Operating Modes
6. Mathematical Solution Procedures
7. Economic Models
8. Weather Models
9. Active and Passive Solar Systems
10. Comfort Models

1. BUILDING ENERGY LOADS

Multi-Zone Capabilities:
Interzone Energy Transfer:
Intrazone Energy Transfer:
Internal Radiation:
Material Property Library:
Construction Geometry Library:
Appliance, Equipment, Machinery Loads:
Lighting Loads:
Occupancy Loads:
Fans/Pumps Within HVAC System:
Infiltration Air Loads:
   Sensible Load:
   Latent Load:
Ventilation/Make-Up Air Loads:
   Sensible Load:
   Latent Load:
Moisture Transfer Through Walls (Latent) Load:
Solar Direct Gain Load:
Shading Computation:
View Factors:
Duct Loss and Leakage:
Process/Load Profile:
Other:

2. CONVENTIONAL HVAC SYSTEMS

Single-Zone Fan System (with terminal reheat):
Single-Zone Fan System (with face & bypass dampers):
Dual Duct Fan System:
Variable Volume Fan System:
Multizone Fan System:
Two-Pipe Fan Coil System:
Four-Pipe Fan Coil System:
Two-Pipe Induction Unit Fan System:
All Air Induction System:
Unit Ventilator:
Unit Heater:
Floor Panel Heating System:
Snow Melting System:
Unitary Heat Pump, Water to Air & Air to Air:
Increment Hydronic Heat Pump:
Simultaneous and Changeover Heat Pump:
Double Bundle Heat Pump:
Unitary Cooling Unit with Separate Heating (air or water cooled):
On-Site Generation:
Heating with Waste Water:
Exhaust Air Heat Recovery:
Economizer Cycle, Temperature Control:
Economizer Cycle, Enthalpy/Temperature Control:
Other:

3. CONVENTIONAL ENERGY CONVERSION PLANT

Chillers (Steam Absorption):
Chillers (Reciprocating):
Chillers (Centrifugal):
Turbines (Steam):
Turbines (Gas):
Boilers (Gas-Fired):
Boilers (Oil-Fired):
Boilers (Electric):
Storage, Hot Water:
Storage, Cold Water:
Direct-Fired Hot Air Furnaces:
Piggyback Systems:
Fan and Pumps:
Diesel Generator:
Heat Pumps (Also under HVAC):
Other:

4. COMPONENT SIZING

Design-Day Weather Conditions:
Design Temperatures:
HVAC System Components Sizing:
Energy Conversion Plant Sizing:
Other:

Figure 4.2.7.2 - Analysis Tool Descriptors

5. **CONTROL SYSTEMS/OPERATING MODES:**

    Schedules:
        Outside Air Shutoff:
        Heating System Shutoff:
        Cooling System Shutoff:
        Generator Operating:
        Cooling Equipment Operating:
        Cooling/Heating Equipment Seasonal Operating:
    Shutoff Temperature:
        Heating System:
        Cooling System:
    Fuel Interruption:
        Based on Number of Days:
        Based on Temperature:
    Building Changeover Temperature:
    Economizer Outside Air Cycle:
    Fixed Outside Air:
    Switchover Factor for Generating Sets:
    Supply Air Dry Bulb Reset:
    Supply Air Temperature Reset by Hottest and Coldest Zones:
    Waste Heat Utilization:
    Energy Management/Load Control Systems:
    Solar System Controls:
        Active Solar Systems:
        Passive Solar Systems:
    Other:

6. **MATHEMATIC SOLUTION PROCEDURES**

    Energy Balance (Finite Difference):
    ASHRAE Algorithms:
    Other Solution Method (Describe):
    Time Step (Fixed/Variable and Value):
    Iteration Between Loads, Systems, and Plant:
    Accuracy/Convergence Studies:
    Program Verification Studies:

7. **ECONOMICS MODELS**

    Energy Cost Tables (Input/Default):
    Life Cycle Costs:
    Solar Payback Period:

8. **WEATHER MODELS**

    TMY Model:
    TRY Model:
    Insolation Model:

9. **SOLAR SYSTEMS**

    Active:
        Service Hot Water:
        Space Heating:
        Space Cooling:
        Collector Type:
            Flat Plate, Liquid:
            Flat Plate, Gas:
            Tubular:
            Concentrating:
            User Defined:
    Passive:
        Direct Gain (Mass/Distribution Effects):
        Trombe Wall:
        Greenhouse/Atrium:

10. **COMFORT MODELS**

    Fanger Model:
    Other (Describe):

Figure 4.2.7.2 (continued) - Analysis Tool Descriptors

in the 65 degrees (F.) base temperature (i.e., 65 + 7 = 72 degrees (F.)) is not realistic for other buildings, which can have considerably larger internal heat gains.

Modified degree day procedures developed by ASHRAE and others have greatly improved the accuracy of the degree day method, but multiple-measure calculations are required to model complex nonresidential buildings.

The major multiple measurement method is the Bin method, which can be used to estimate both heating and cooling loads. The Bin Method involves using instantaneous energy calculations at several different outdoor drybulb temperatures and weighting each result by the number of hours of temperature occurrence within each bin, which usually covers a range of 5 degrees (F.) and which are usually separated into three daily eight-hour groups.

Because the Bin method is based on hourly weather data rather than daily averages, it is considerably more accurate than the degree day method. Initial limitations of the Bin method have been significantly alleviated by modifications developed by ASHRAE and Battelle Pacific Northwest Laboratories. The current version is called the Modified Bin Method.

Building Mass

Building mass has been found to have a significant effect on a building's energy use because mass absorbs heat, releasing it gradually over time rather than instantaneously. This greatly complicates analysis of the effects of solar and internal heat gain on the energy requirements of building systems at any point during a day.

ASHRAE has developed a cooling load temperature difference (CLTD) analysis procedure that considers the mass effects of different building elements to yield an effective temperature differential.

Weather Data Requirements and Availability

Multiple-measurement energy analysis models generally require location-specific hourly data on:
- drybulb temperature
- wetbulb temperature (relative humidity)
- global and direct solar radiation or cloud cover
- wind speed.

Weather data are available from the National Oceanic and Atmospheric Administration (NOAA) in five major formats:
- TRY (test reference year) tapes
- SOLMET (solar meteorological) format
- TD-1440 tapes
- TMY (typical meteorological year) format
- WYEC (weather year for energy calculation) format.

These various formats vary primarily by methodology (e.g., TRY gives data on actual years selected for their representativeness, TMY gives data on representative composite years rather than historical years) and by geographic coverage. The TD-1440 tapes, for example, provide the only weather data available for many locations.

Generally, an energy analysis program specifies which of these weather data formats is compatible with its analysis requirements.

4.2.8 Selecting Analysis Tools

A designer's selection of specific energy analysis tools will depend on a wide variety of factors, some based on his or her specific work habits and predilections, some based on well-defined aspects of the available analysis programs (e.g., compatibility with different computer equipment, the specific questions analyzed by the program), and many others factors that are difficult or impossible to define without actually using and analyzing the program. This latter category includes ease of use, reliability of results, usefulness of output formats, the tool's ability to model specific uncommon design elements, and so on.

There is at this writing no comprehensive guide to the available energy analysis tools to give the designer definitive guidance on specific programs.

The *HVAC/Energy Analysis* directory, a part of the *A/E Software Library* produced by the American Consulting Engineers Council, 1015 15th Street, NW, Wash. DC 20005. Produced in cooperation with the AIA and other organizations, the *HVAC/Energy Analysis* lists over a hundred analysis tools.

The Society for Computer Applications in Engineering, Planning, and Architecture, Inc., 15713 Crabbs Branch Way, Rockville MD 20855, makes programs available to its membership.

The AIA Headquarters, 1735 New York Avenue, NW, Wash. DC 20006, has begun a system in which designers are polled on their individual experiences with specific analysis programs.

For the time being, word-of-mouth and personal experience with different analysis tools remain indispensable guides in this area.

4.3 ECONOMIC ANALYSIS

4.3.1 Introduction

Cost/benefit analysis provides an economic assessment of competing design alternatives over the economic life of each alternative. Several characteristics differentiate cost/benefit analysis from other analytical techniques. First, cost/benefit analysis is neither a decision-making process nor a set of economic guidelines. Rather, it is an analytical technique that can be used in the context of a decision-making process to generate economic guidelines.

Second, cost/benefit analysis can be used to assess the consequences of a given decision or to choose among alternatives. That is, it can determine the effects of a decision, or it can play an integral part in the process of making the decision in the first place.

Next, cost/benefit analysis deals only with factors that can be measured in dollars or some other equivalent measure. Because this limitation rules out some important consequences of planning and design decisions, cost/benefit analysis constitutes only part of the larger assessment and decision-making context.

Next, the cost/benefit analysis explicitly measures benefits as well as costs. Thus, while this discussion uses the common acronym LCC (for life-cycle cost), it considers economic benefits--fuel savings, for example--as well as costs.

Finally, cost/benefit analysis examines these consequences over time, permitting consideration of all relevant costs and benefits within a selected period of time, and providing a straightforward methodology for relating them to each other.

Cost/benefit analysis (hereafter termed LCC analysis) uses constant dollars, which are usually in present dollars, and which reflect the general purchasing power of the dollar at the time a decision is made. The basic equations for determining constant dollars appear in the discussion of interest formulas.

Payments that differ in total magnitude but are made at different dates can be adjusted for analytical purposes to be equivalent to one another. Given an interest rate, any payment or series of payments that will repay a present sum of money with interest at that rate is equivalent to that present sum. Therefore, all future payments or series of payments that would repay the present sum with interest at the stated rate are equivalent to each other.

The opportunity rate (i) is the best available rate of return that money could earn if placed in the best (in dollar terms) investment available. The exception to this definition is money that is available only on the condition that it be spent for a specific time such as an earmarked loan. In that case, the particular interest rate paid for that money can be defined as the opportunity rate in developing the life-cycle cost.

The opportunity rate is also called the discount rate. Much of the actual calculation involved in doing LCC analysis involves moving sums of value (dollars) backward or forward in time. If future-invested dollars are brought back to the present they are discounted by the interest rate.

The rate of interest at which a client feels adequately compensated for trading money now for money in the future is the appropriate rate to use for converting present sums to future equivalent sums and future sums to present equivalent sums, i.e., the rate for discounting cash flows for that particular investor.

If a client is unsure of the potential return on an alternative investment, the cost of borrowing can be used as the discount rate. However, the earning rate available on alternative investments should take precedence over the borrowing rate as an indicator of the appropriate discount rate and should be taken into account regardless of whether the money is borrowed or not. In selecting the appropriate discount rate, the client might be asked for the after-tax rate of return on other investments, a factor that can vary considerably. If the evaluation is being made for a governmental client, legislative requirements often exist.

Clients sometimes request that high-risk projects be evaluated with higher discount rates than those with low risk. Risk can also be treated in other ways, such as basing benefit and cost estimates on probabilities of occurrence, incorporating contingency estimates of cash flow into the calculations, or by using sensitivity analysis to assess the effect of different time horizons or of different amounts of energy savings on the profitability of the investment.

Discount rates can be expressed in either "nominal" or "real" terms. Nominal rates reflect the effects of inflation and the real earning power of money invested over time. Real rates reflect only the real earning power of money and therefore are lower that a nominal rate, given the same conditions.

Dollar estimates of benefits and costs and discount values must be made compatible with each other by either including or excluding inflation from all values. A real discount rate is appropriate if inflation is removed from the cash flow prior to discounting. A nominal rate is appropriate if cash flows are inflated.

More than any other variable the discount rate can affect the net benefits of energy conservation investments. The rate selected determines whether a project appears to be economical or uneconomical. For example, a project that has positive net savings when evaluated using a six-percent discount rate might yield negative net savings when evaluated at seven percent.

As the discount rate is increased, the present value of any given future stream of costs or benefits becomes smaller. High discount rates tend to favor projects with quick payoffs over projects with deferred benefits.

LCC analysis rarely examines costs more than 25 to 40 years into the future, and in many instances the time frame is limited to five years. LCC time frames are limited to such periods because of the uncertainties associated with forecasting too far into the future and because this is considered the effective life of many buildings. Furthermore, about 80 percent of equivalent-cost dollars are spent in the first 25 years of most projects.

It is also often useful to examine life-cycle costs for each of a building's components, e.g., HVAC systems. A component's life can usually be determined from manufacturers' data, although this information can be affected by a variety of factors, including maintenance practices and technological obsolescence. Improvements in the state of the art can make it more economical to replace a component before it wears out.

The establishment of the time horizon is a function of the owner's operational and/or economic objectives:
- Functionally, the owner may see the building, or various elements within the building, against a limited time horizon. An assembly plant, for example, may be seen against a 20-year time horizon because the owner does not want to project functional changes in the assembly process beyond that point. The design of an operating suite in a hospital may be seen against a shorter time period due to expected technological changes.
- Economically, owners have a wide variety of goals, and often these goals have reasonably definite time horizons associated with them. An owner may plan to stay in business (and in the facility that houses it) until a specific date, or until it is expected that the community can no longer support it. Similarly, owners may tie their economic goals to the length of leases or to the payback of borrowed money.

These owner objectives tend to limit the horizons for life-cycle cost analyses to five, 10, 15, 20 or 25 years.

Note also that within some schools of thought in the economics profession there is skepticism regarding the value of economic forecasts carried beyond five years. This is based on uncertainty concerning the stability and predictability of overall economic conditions as well as specific cost and income factors.

Through periodic renewal of the elements of a building, it is possible to prolong its physical usefulness for centuries. Individual building elements, however, can have specific useful or economic lives, and very often an LCC analysis is concerned with the replacement or renewal of building elements at the end of such periods. These individual lives do not always conform easily to the overall life cycle being used in the analysis.

Establishing the anticipated lives of building elements is complicated by the wide range of products available and the general lack of documented experience by building owners. In general, the best guide is provided by available owner experience in combination with manufacturers' data.

4.3.2 Constant Dollar Calculations

Equivalence

"Equivalent dollars" provide a means of adjusting present dollars and future dollars to reflect the time value of money, since a dollar received or expended today does not have the same value it would have if it were received or expended in the future. One reason for this discrepancy is that the earning potential of liquid capital is different today, when a dollar received can be put to use to generate additional income, from what it would be at a later date, since a dollar to be received in the future offers no earning potential in the interim. Similarly, an expense that must be paid now draws resources from the client that cannot be used for other productive purposes.

- Equivalent dollars are an integral part of LCC analysis. They are also extremely easy to compute and use: pre-computed factors (taken from Interest Factors Tables) are multiplied by any dollar amount to calculate equivalent dollars. These factors are listed by year (into the future) and by interest rate (or discount rate) and can be chosen to incorporate the adjustment for expected inflation or deflation in the discounting procedure.
- For example, $20,000 received 10 years from now, assuming an interest rate of 10 percent, is worth $7,710 in today's dollars. The Single Present Worth (SPW) factor from the Interest Factors Table for 10-percent interest after 10 years is 0.3855; $20,000* 0.3855 = $7,710. The Single Compound Amount (SCA) factor performs the reverse: $7,710 invested today at a 10-percent interest rate = $2,710 * 2.594 = $20,000 in 10 years.
- Equivalent dollars are determined by one of two methods: the present-worth method and the equivalent-annual-cost method.

Present-Worth Method

The present-worth method converts all present and future receipts and expenditures to today's cost. Initial costs and benefits are already expressed in present worth. Future amounts are multiplied by the appropriate factor, allowing all dollar amounts to be compared, regardless of when they are spent or received.

- The present-worth model has a disadvantage if the alternatives under comparison have different estimated lives. It would be incorrect to compare the total present worth of one alternative, having an estimated life of 15 years, with the total cost of another alternative having an estimated life of 20 years. To reduce these two alternatives to equivalency it would be necessary to study the total cost of each alternative over an equal number of years.
- One method of adjusting alternatives with different lives is to choose a time period for study that is a common multiple of the lives of the alternatives.

- Another method of comparing two alternatives with different lives is to compute the annual cost of each alternative and then to determine the present worth of a given number of years of service.

Equivalent-Annual-Cost Method

The equivalent-annual-cost method converts all amounts, regardless of when they are spent or received, to a uniform annual amount. This allows, for example, a combination of capital expenditures in one year, varying maintenance costs in later years and resale value at the end of a given period to be expressed in terms of a constant amount, in equivalent dollars, each year in the life cycle.

Interest Formulas

Interest formulas are used to move values forward or back in time so that they can be compared on an equivalent basis with other values. Two formulas apply to single payments of money. The single compound amount (SCA) formula is used to determine the future worth F of a present worth P, y years in the future:

$$F = P(1+i)^y$$

This equation sums up the principal P, the interest paid on the principal and any accrued interest each year for a given number of years. If $1,000 (1+i), at the end of the third year it would be worth $1,000 (1+i)(1+i)(1+i). And at the end of y years it would be equal to $1,000 $(1+i)^y$.
- This single compound amount formula is used to find the future worth, F, when there is a single present worth, P, and a given interest rate, i, for the number of years, y, in the future. For any interest rate and for any number of years, the factor $(1+i)^y$ is a constant. Consequently, a table of single compound amount factors can be developed.
- The single present worth (SPW) formula is used to determine the present worth, P, of a future sum of money, F, for a given number of years and a given interest rate:

$$P = F \frac{1}{(1+i)^y}$$

- To determine the present worth of a single future value F, multiply it by the single payment present worth factor (SPW), which is $1/(1+i)^y$. Again, for any one value of i and any one value of y, the SPW factor is a constant.
= The following equations allow one to adjust values (dollars) to present, future and annual increments. Tables derived from these formulas provide a fast, accurate tool for practical application of LCC analysis:

where: P = Present Value
F = Future Value
A = Equivalent Annual Cost
i = Interest Rate (opportunity or discount rate)
y = Study Period (years)

$F = P(1+i)^y$ --Single Compound Amount(SCA) adjusts a single value from present to future (P to F)

$P = F \dfrac{1}{(1+i)^y}$ --Single Present Worth(SPW) adjusts a single sum from the future to the present (F to P)

$F = A \dfrac{(1+i)^y - 1}{i}$ --Uniform Compound Amount(UCA) adjusts a set of equal annual increments to a single future value (A to F)

$A = F \dfrac{i}{(1+i)^y - 1}$ --Uniform Sinking Fund(USF) adjusts a single sum from the future to equal annual increments (F to A)

$A = P \dfrac{i(1+i)^y}{(1+i)^y - 1}$ --Uniform Capital Recovery(UCR) adjusts a single sum to a set of equal annual increments (P to A)

$P = A \dfrac{(1+i)^y - 1}{i(1+i)^y}$ --Uniform Present Worth(UPW) adjusts equal annual increments to a single present value (A to P)

In the manipulation of these formulas, some important aspects of the trade-offs between "present" and "future" dollars emerge.

First, the higher the discount rate, the less important future costs are relative to initial costs, and the less worthwhile it becomes to try to avoid future expenditures by increasing initial costs.

Second, as the life cycle used becomes longer and longer, the annual savings needed to justify an extra initial expenditure flattens out; the savings approaches the discount rate itself. This suggests that:

- analyses with very short life cycles and high discount rates require the greatest accuracy

- analyses with very long life cycles tend to be less valuable than those with shorter life cycles

- the significant trade-offs between "today" and "tomorrow" dollars are best seen when life cycles are in the 10- to 30-year range.

Figure 4.3.2.1 provides a format for completing a life-cycle cost analysis. The format shown in Figure 4.3.2.1 can be used for either the Present-Worth Method or the Equivalent-Annual-Cost Method. Figure 4.3.2.2 on the next page describes different sorts of costs that must be considered in the analysis.

The following steps can be used to fill out the form:

1. Fill out an analysis form for each decision or alternative to be analyzed.
2. Enter the Discount Rate to be used in the analysis.

PW of initial cost:	$ 50,000
PW of the one-time replacement cost:	
P = F × (SPW for 15 years, at 10%)	
P = $20,000 × .2394	4,788
PW of the O & M costs:	
P = A × (UPW for 30 years, at 10%)	
P = $5,000 × 9.427	47,135
PW of the salvage value:	
P = F × (SPW for 30 years, at 10%)	
P = $10,000 × .0573	(573)
PW of the entire system	$ 101,350

Consider the same situation using the equivalent-annual-cost method:

EAC for initial cost	
A = P × (UCR for 30 years, at 10%)	
A = $50,000 × .1061	$ 5,305
EAC of the one-time replacement cost	
PW of this cost is $4,788	
A = P × (UCR for 30 years, at 10%)	
A = $4,788 × .1061	508
EAC of the O & M costs	5,000
EAC of the salvage value	
A = F × (USF for 30 years, at 10%)	
A = $10,000 × .0061	(61)
EAC of the entire system	$ 10,750

Figure 4.3.2.1 - Life Cycle Cost Format

3. Enter the Life Cycle time frame to be used in the analysis.
4. Enter the NonRecurring Costs (See Figure 4.3.2.2) associated with the decision or alternative, and enter the specific analysis year in which each of these costs is to be incurred. (Initial costs in the baseline year should be entered as year "0"; a one-time replacement cost to be incurred after 15 years is year "15," etc.
5. Enter the Recurring Costs (See Figure 4.3.2.2) associated with the decision or alternative, and enter the analysis years in which these will be incurred. (Recurring costs occurring in all 25 years of a 25-year analysis life cycle, for example, should be entered on years "1-25"; costs occurring only in the first ten years as "1-10," etc.)
6. If the objective of the analysis is the assessment of a given decision, enter all relevant nonrecurring and recurring costs; if the objective is choice among alternatives, it is necessary to enter only the differential costs among those alternatives.
7. If the Total Present Worth method is to be used for calculating life-cycle cost, bring all nonrecurring and recurring costs listed to their present worth in the baseline year. Note that there is a place on the form in which to enter the appropriate SPW and UPW factors (for future reference). Total all present worth figures to determine a Total Present Worth for the decision or alternative.

Cost Category	Costs Potentially Included	Use in the Analysis	Sources of Cost Data
INITIAL CAPITAL INVESTMENT COSTS. Costs associated with the initial planning, design, and construction of the facility.	Land costs, including costs of acquisition, options, surveys and appraisals, demolition and relocation, legal and filing fees. Design costs, including cost of consultants and/or in-house staff, as well as required special studies or tests (e.g., test borings). Construction costs, including costs of labor, material, equipment, general conditions (job overhead), contractors' main office overhead, and profit. Other owner costs, including cost of owner project administration, construction insurance, permits, fees and other expenses not included above.	These are usually non-recurring costs, and unless the project development period is a lengthy one, they are usually recorded as occurring in the baseline year. If project development is extended, or if project scheduling alternatives are being considered, it may be desirable to break these costs down year-by-year.	Land and other owner costs usually can be supplied only by the owner. Construction costs can be developed from standard estimating sources and/or from owner, architect, construction consultant, construction manager or cost consultant experience.
FINANCING COSTS. Costs associated with financing capital investment.	Loan fees and one-time finance charges associated with borrowing for the project—both for initial project development as well as major capital improvements. Interest costs for short-term (interim) financing. Note: Interest costs for long-term (permanent) financing usually are considered in establishing the discount rate for the life-cycle cost analysis, and are not included as costs in the analysis proper.	Loan fees and one-time charges are nonrecurring costs and should be recorded in the appropriate year(s). Interest costs which are to be specifically included in the analysis are recurring costs and should be recorded for each of the years in which they are to occur.	From the owner, or the owner's lender or financial adviser.
FACILITY OPERATION AND MAINTENANCE (O&M) Costs. Costs associated with the ongoing operation and maintenance of the facility.	Personnel costs for routine maintenance, cleaning, grounds care, trash removal, space reconfiguration, security, building operation, property management, etc. Costs of fuel, utilities, supplies, equipment and contract services associated with these activities should also be included.	These are usually recurring costs incurred after occupancy of the facility. Some may be incurred during the project development period and should be considered accordingly.	Some O&M costs may be available from the owner, owners associations, and publications. Some manufacturers include O&M data in product literature, but this should be carefully reviewed by owner representatives and other users. Energy efficiency studies can be conducted by designers to predict fuel and utility costs.

Figure 4.3.2.2 - Cost Categories

Cost Category	Costs Potentially Included	Use in Analysis	Sources of Cost Data
FACILITY REPAIR AND REPLACEMENT COSTS. Costs associated with restoring the facility to its original performance.	Costs of major repairs to building elements during the analysis timeframe. Costs of planned replacements of building elements during the analysis timeframe. Includes costs of planning, design, demolition and disposal and other owner costs, as well as costs for labor, materials, equipment, overhead and profit of any outside contractors.	These are usually nonrecurring costs associated with, and recorded in, the specific years in which they occur.	Obsolescence information is often provided by manufacturers, industry associations and sometimes from owner experience.
FACILITY ALTERATION AND IMPROVEMENT COSTS. Costs associated with planned additions, alterations, major reconfigurations and other improvements to the facility.	Costs of all planned capital improvements during the analysis timeframe. Includes costs of land, planning, design, demolition, relocation, disposal and other owner costs, as well as costs of labor, materials, equipment, overhead and profit of any outside contractors.	These are usually nonrecurring costs associated with, and recorded in, the specific years in which they occur.	Information is based on planned functional or economic obsolescence of the facility, and on planned expansion or contraction of the program, as determined by the owner.
FUNCTIONAL-USE COSTS. Costs associated with performing intended functions within the facility.	Salaries and benefits of personnel working in the facility, as well as supplies and services required for the program housed in the facility. Income and real property taxes. Denial-of-use and lost revenue costs associated with delayed or inappropriate scheduling of occupancy, or with using the facility inefficiently; includes continuing rent, unexpired leases, operating in obsolete facilities, etc.	These are usually recurring costs incurred after occupancy. Some (e.g., property insurance and taxes) may also occur during the project development period, and these should be recorded in the appropriate years.	Usually can be supplied by the owner.
SALVAGE COSTS. Costs (or values) of building elements or facilities salvaged during the analysis life cycle.	Costs of salvage operations, including demolition and disposal, if not included above. Salvage values of building elements or facilities recovered as part of replacement, alteration or improvement activities.	Cost of salvage operations are usually nonrecurring and should be recorded in the appropriate year. Value of salvaged facilities or building elements should be entered in the appropriate year as negative numbers (with minus signs).	Information may be available from standard estimating sources, manufacturers, industry associations or owner experience.

Figure 4.3.2.2 (continued) - Cost Categories

8. If the Equivalent Annual Cost method is to be used, convert all costs listed to their uniform annual equivalents. Note that there is a place on the form in which to enter the appropriate UCR and USF factors (for future reference). Total all annual cost figures to determine the Equivalent Uniform Annual Cost for the decision or alternative.

4.3.3 Life-Cycle Cost/Benefit Analysis

LCC analysis expresses the consequences of a choice, as far as practical, in terms of monetary value at stated times in the future. An explicitly defined primary criterion should be applied to such monetary figures. In dealing with certain types of proposals, it can also be desirable to have one or more secondary criteria.

LCC Criteria. The primary criterion to be applied in a choice among proposed alternative options should be selected with the objective of making the best use of limited resources, such as land, labor, capital, materials. But, because the market provides money valuations on most resources, it is usually appropriate to express the overall limitation in terms of money.

In evaluating proposed design options, the important issue is whether the option will be productive enough, that is, will it yield a sufficient rate of return as compared with one or more stated alternatives, all things considered? The minimum acceptable rate of return is often the primary criterion used for investment decisions, although other criteria may be as important.

Even the most careful estimates of the monetary consequences of choosing different alternatives will almost certainly turn out to be incorrect. It is often helpful to a decision-maker to make use of secondary criteria--cash flow differences among alternatives, for example--that argue for or against the necessarily uncertain results of applying the primary criterion.

Often, seemingly minor economic side effects are disregarded when individual decisions are made. If the side effects of a particular decision are sufficiently trivial, a study of them would presumably not change the decision. However, a study of interrelationships among a group of decisions may be needed to provide a basis for judgment on whether the side effects are trivial or important.

LCC and the Design Process. In many cases LCC is applied to single building components, leading to restrictive design solutions. A multi-systems approach to optimization of the building as a whole produces more desirable results.

If LCC analysis is used early in the design process it can help identify major determinants of a project's cost and lead to early design decisions to minimize these costs (see Figure 4.3.3.1). If the costs associated with major design decisions--open plan office space, use of daylighting

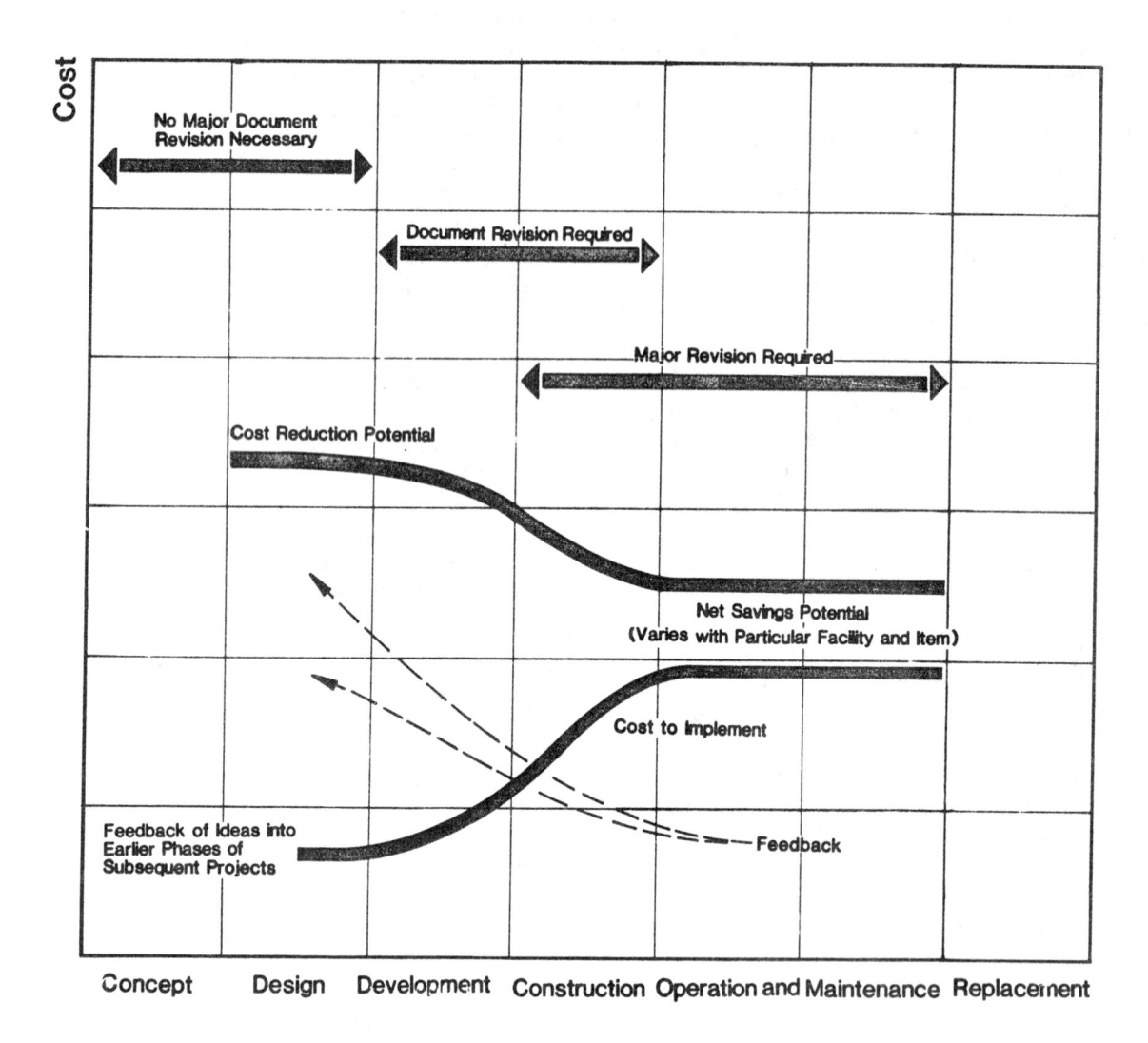

Figure 4.3.3.1 - Time and Life Cycle Cost

and other solar strategies, multi-story versus single-story construction and related costs--are not considered until late in the design process, the design can be so locked in that economic decisions cannot be made practically. In the extreme, LCC analysis early in a project may indicate that the client's funds would be more effectively used renovating an existing facility instead of designing a new one, or used for another type of investment entirely.

LCC Methodology. The following passages present a general overview of the basic steps in the LCC analysis technique.

1. Clarify the objective of the analysis. Is it to assess the consequences of a given decision, or is it to choose among alternatives on the basis of their economic consequences? For the first objective, comprehensive cost information will be required for the analysis; for the second objective, only differential cost information, costs that are different from alternative to alternative, need be considered.
2. Identify the alternative(s) to be analyzed. First, concentrate on those planning and design decisions that might have the greatest economic consequences--both initially and over the facility's use period. For example:
   - The decision must be made either to build or not to build.
   - While the costs of construction are significant, the operational costs of the facility are even more significant. These costs can sometimes be traded off--the costs of a night shift, for example, may turn out to be less than the costs of constructing and operating a new manufacturing facility.
   - A determination should be made of building configuration and orientation, with their resulting cost effects on heating, cooling, maintenance, vertical circulation and other continuing cost items.
   - While some of these cost effects are felt as initial costs (e.g., the cost of elevators for a highrise alternative), many have continuing influence as well (e.g., the cost of operating, maintaining and replacing the same elevators).
   - The choice of mechanical systems is also quite significant, given the importance of fuel, utilities, operating, maintenance and replacement costs for these systems.
   - The design of natural and artificial illumination systems provides another opportunity for useful LCC analysis.
   - Within any of these major decisions are numerous individual options that can also warrant LCC analysis.

   Second, it makes sense to focus on those decisions that rely heavily on what are expected to be expensive continuing cost items. In recent years, fuel and utility costs have risen so sharply that they are in this category. Labor costs--for operating and maintaining a facility and, less directly, for paid occupants of facilities--are always expensive, and it can be useful to look for situations in which the expenditure of extra present construction dollars can save more future operational dollars.

   The selection of alternatives for effective LCC analysis is, in part, a matter of experience. For example, all selected alternatives must meet the performance standards expected of them. Analyzing the economic performance alternatives that must be clearly rejected on other grounds is useless.

3. Establish a time frame for the analysis. Key decisions include the point when the period of analysis starts (its baseline date), how

long it runs (its life cycle) and what useful lives of individual building elements may be involved.

The baseline date is the present, when costs need not be discounted, and, because it is the starting point, the general assumption is that any costs already incurred on the project are met and cannot be recovered.

If the project's development period is a reasonably short one, including time for its planning, design and construction activities requiring capital investment, the period is usually considered as occurring wholly within the baseline year. This allows all initial capital investment costs to be considered either as occurring in the baseline year or in the future.

For larger or more complex projects requiring a longer project development time, initial capital investment costs can be considered either as occurring in the baseline year or in the future.

The latter approach can be useful for a project with a long development time if the designer wishes to experiment with different project scheduling approaches. One scheduling approach includes spending extra dollars to overlap design and construction in order to bring the occupancy date closer; with a long project development period, some of these costs are present costs and some are future costs. LCC analysis can be used to assess the economic implications of these scheduling approaches.

4. Select the cost factors to be considered in the analysis. A long list of cost categories can be considered in LCC analysis. This depends on the objectives of the analysis, the costs the owner considers relevant to decisions and the life cycle selected. Potential costs to be considered include initial capital investment costs, repair and replacement costs, alteration and improvement costs, functional use costs and salvage costs. Figure 4.3.2.2 indicates the nature of these costs, their uses in LCC analysis and where information about them can be obtained.

5. Determine the life-cycle cost "measure" to be used. Decisions can be assessed or alternatives compared in terms of either of two related cost methods: Total Present Worth Cost or Equivalent Uniform Annual Cost.

6. Perform the analysis. Once all of the above is established, the LCC analysis itself is relatively straightforward. The LCC team isolates the significant costs associated with each alternative. These costs are then grouped by year over the number of years equal to the economic life of the facility or, if more appropriate, grouped by time spans equal to the mode of operation. In either case, replacement and alteration costs should be considered. A salvage value, if relevant, is also added for the end of the life-cycle period.

All costs are converted to constant dollars by one of the methods referred to in step 5.

7. Analyze the results. LCC analyses ultimately produce a series of numbers. What do these mean? How do they relate to the initial assumptions used? Is the lowest-cost alternative always the optimal solution for the owner?
   - Normally, final design decisions must take into account non-economic considerations such as politics, esthetics, safety and functional convenience. Therefore, after the economically oriented exercise, non-economic criteria are evaluated, with decisions made on the basis of both sets of factors.

4.3.4 Payback and Break-Even Analysis

Payback

- Payback analysis is used to determine the number of years in which the initial extra expenditures for different alternatives are paid back. The simple payback can be calculated by the following:

$$\text{Simple payback period} = \frac{\text{initial cost}}{\text{annual savings}}$$

- Simple payback analysis is easily misunderstood. The time value of money and future benefits are ignored in this payback formula, which can produce misleading results.
- For clients who seek a rapid turnover of funds, this alternative increases in desirability as the payback period decreases. However a shorter payback period does not necessarily indicate the most economically efficient investment. An alternative with a longer payback period may prove more profitable than an alternative with a shorter payback period if it continues to yield savings for a longer period of time.

Break-Even Analysis

- By altering the value of one of the variables of an alternative and keeping all the other variables between two alternatives constant, a value for the variable that makes the two alternatives equally economical can be found. This value is described as the break-even point.
- Where all costs are known and the discount rate has been established for two alternatives, time can be used as the variable, to solve for the time when one alternative becomes more attractive than another.

4.3.5 Rate of Return on Investment

Many clients look at life-cycle costs in terms of the rate of return on the investment. The rate of return is the interest rate that indicates the return from an investment. A client may determine that the rate of return from investing money in a building is less than the return from using that money for an alternative investment.

- To determine the rate of return on any investment all costs and benefits must be forecast. This technique enables the decision maker to compare the investment with any alternative investments rather than just the alternatives to satisfy a specific need.
- To solve for the expected rate of return a model representing both costs and benefits is developed. The costs are set equal to the benefits, and the unknown in the model is the interest factor that makes the two equal. At some interest rate the conversion factor will make these two equal, and that interest rate is the rate of return on the investment.
- A cash flow chart is most valuable in checking to see if all costs and values have been included. Each value must either be spread out into uniform annual costs over the entire cost study, or they must all be brought back to a Present Worth value to evaluate the rate of return. Either Present Worth models or Annual Cost models can be used in determining rates of return. It is sometimes desirable to calculate the rate of return by both methods to be sure that an error has not been made in the calculation. It is not likely that the same error will be made in an Annual Cost model and a Present Worth model of the same situation, unless it is an error in interpreting input data.

Rate of Return on Extra Investment

- A variation of the rate of return on the investment can be used to compare alternatives, where the decision has been made to use one alternative out of a group, regardless of the rate of return on the investment. Where this decision has been made, the rate of return of the extra investment of one alternative over another can be compared without determining the actual rate of return on either. By determining the rate of return on the extra investment, the decision maker can then decide whether this extra investment is worthwhile.
- If two alternatives will satisfy a given situation, the rate of return on the extra investment can be determined by developing either Present Worth models or Annual Cost models of each alternative and equating like-cost models. The interest rate that makes the two cost models equal is the rate of return on the extra investment.
- Rate of return on extra investment looks only at the additional costs and benefits associated with one alternative or another. This can greatly simplify analysis, because all costs and benefits that are identical in competing alternatives can be ignored.

Figure 4.3.4.1 shows interest tables computed from the previously described formulas.

Year Y	SCA P-F	SPW F-P	UCA A-F	USF F-A	UCR P-A	UPW A-P
1	1.080	.9259	1.000	1.000	1.080	0.926
2	1.166	.8573	2.080	.4808	.5608	1.783
3	1.260	.7938	3.246	.3080	.3880	2.577
4	1.360	.7350	4.506	.2219	.3019	3.312
5	1.469	.6806	5.867	.1705	.2505	3.993
6	1.587	.6302	7.336	.1363	.2163	4.623
7	1.714	.5835	8.923	.1121	.1921	5.206
8	1.851	.5403	10.64	.0940	.1740	5.747
9	1.999	.5002	12.49	.0801	.1601	6.247
10	2.159	.4632	14.49	.0690	.1490	6.710
11	2.332	.4289	16.65	.0601	.1401	7.139
12	2.518	.3971	18.98	.0527	.1327	7.536
13	2.720	.3677	21.50	.0465	.1265	7.904
14	2.937	.3405	24.22	.0413	.1213	8.244
15	3.172	.3152	27.15	.0368	.1168	8.559
16	3.426	.2919	30.32	.0330	.1130	8.851
17	3.700	.2703	33.75	.0296	.1096	9.122
18	3.996	.2502	37.45	.0267	.1067	9.372
19	4.316	.2317	41.45	.0241	.1041	9.604
20	4.661	.2145	45.76	.0219	.1019	9.818
21	5.034	.1987	50.42	.0198	.0998	10.02
22	5.437	.1839	55.46	.0180	.0980	10.20
23	5.871	.1703	60.89	.0164	.0964	10.37
24	6.341	.1577	66.77	.0150	.0950	10.53
25	6.848	.1460	73.11	.0137	.0937	10.68
30	10.06	.0994	113.3	.0088	.0888	11.26
35	14.79	.0676	172.3	.0058	.0858	11.66
40	21.73	.0460	259.1	.0039	.0839	11.93
45	31.92	.0313	386.5	.0025	.0826	12.11
50	46.90	.0213	573.7	.0017	.0817	12.23
60	101.3	.0099	1253	.0008	.0808	12.38
70	218.6	.0040	2720.	.0004	.0804	12.44
80	472.0	.0021	5887.	.0002	.0802	12.47
90	1019.	.0010	12724.	.0001	.0801	12.49
100	2200.	.0005	27485.	.0000	.0800	12.49

8 Percent Interest Factors

Year Y	SCA P-F	SPW F-P	UCA A-F	USF F-A	UCR P-A	UPW A-P
1	1.100	.9091	1.000	1.000	1.100	0.909
2	1.210	.8264	2.100	.4762	.5762	1.736
3	1.331	.7513	3.310	.3021	.4021	2.487
4	1.464	.6830	4.641	.2155	.3155	3.170
5	1.611	.6209	6.105	.1638	.2638	3.791
6	1.772	.5645	7.716	.1296	.2296	4.355
7	1.949	.5132	9.487	.1054	.2054	4.868
8	2.144	.4665	11.44	.0874	.1874	5.335
9	2.358	.4241	13.58	.0736	.1736	5.759
10	2.594	.3855	15.94	.0628	.1628	6.144
11	2.853	.3505	18.53	.0540	.1540	6.500
12	3.138	.3186	21.38	.0468	.1468	6.814
13	3.452	.2897	24.52	.0408	.1408	7.103
14	3.797	.2633	27.98	.0358	.1358	7.367
15	4.177	.2394	31.77	.0315	.1315	7.606
16	4.595	.2176	35.95	.0278	.1278	7.824
17	5.054	.1978	40.54	.0247	.1247	8.022
18	5.560	.1799	45.60	.0219	.1219	8.201
19	6.116	.1635	51.16	.0196	.1196	8.365
20	6.727	.1486	57.28	.0175	.1175	8.514
21	7.400	.1351	64.00	.0156	.1156	8.649
22	8.140	.1228	71.40	.0140	.1140	8.772
23	8.954	.1117	79.54	.0126	.1126	8.883
24	9.850	.1015	88.50	.0113	.1113	8.985
25	10.84	.0923	98.35	.0102	.1102	9.077
30	17.50	.0573	164.5	.0061	.1061	9.427
35	28.10	.0356	271.0	.0037	.1037	9.644
40	45.26	.0221	442.6	.0023	.1023	9.779
45	72.89	.0137	718.9	.0014	.1014	9.863
50	117.4	.0085	1164.	.0009	.1009	9.915
60	304.5	.0033	3035.	.0003	.1003	9.967
70	789.7	.0013	7887.	.0001	.1001	9.987
80	2048.	.0005	20474.	.0001	.1001	9.995
90	5310.	.0002	53120.	.0000	.1000	9.999

10 Percent Interest Factors

Figure 4.3.4.1 - Interest Tables

Year Y	SCA P-F	SPW F-P	UCA A-F	USF F-A	UCR P-A	UPW A-P
1	1.150	.8696	1.000	1.000	1.150	0.870
2	1.322	.7561	2.150	.4651	.6151	1.626
3	1.521	.6575	3.472	.2880	.4380	2.283
4	1.749	.5718	4.993	.2003	.3503	2.855
5	2.011	.4972	6.742	.1483	.2983	3.352
6	2.313	.4323	8.754	.1142	.2642	3.784
7	2.660	.3759	11.07	.0904	.2404	4.160
8	3.059	.3269	13.73	.0729	.2229	4.487
9	3.518	.2843	16.79	.0596	.2096	4.772
10	4.046	.2472	20.30	.0493	.1993	5.019
11	4.652	.2149	24.35	.0411	.1911	5.234
12	5.350	.1869	29.00	.0345	.1845	5.421
13	6.153	.1625	34.35	.0291	.1791	5.583
14	7.076	.1413	40.51	.0247	.1747	5.724
15	8.137	.1229	47.58	.0210	.1710	5.847
16	9.358	.1069	55.72	.0180	.1680	5.954
17	10.76	.0929	65.08	.0154	.1654	6.047
18	12.38	.0808	75.84	.0132	.1632	6.128
19	14.23	.0703	88.21	.0113	.1613	6.198
20	16.37	.0611	102.4	.0098	.1598	6.259
21	18.82	.0531	118.8	.0084	.1584	6.312
22	21.65	.0462	137.6	.0073	.1573	6.359
23	24.89	.0402	159.3	.0063	.1563	6.399
24	28.63	.0349	184.2	.0054	.1554	6.434
25	32.92	.0304	212.8	.0047	.1547	6.464
30	66.21	.0151	434.7	.0023	.1523	6.566
35	133.2	.0075	881.2	.0011	.1511	6.617
40	267.9	.0037	1779.	.0006	.1506	6.642
45	538.8	.0019	3585.	.0003	.1503	6.654
50	1083.	.0009	7218.	.0001	.1501	6.661
60	4384.	.0002	29219.	.0000	.1500	6.665

15 Percent Interest Factors

Year Y	SCA P-F	SPW F-P	UCA A-F	USF F-A	UCR P-A	UPW A-P
1	1.200	.8333	1.000	1.000	1.200	0.833
2	1.400	.6944	2.200	.4546	.6546	1.528
3	1.728	.5787	3.640	.2747	.4747	2.106
4	2.074	.4823	5.368	.1863	.3863	2.589
5	2.488	.4019	7.442	.1344	.3344	2.991
6	2.986	.3349	9.930	.1007	.3007	3.326
7	3.583	.2791	12.92	.0774	.2774	3.605
8	4.300	.2326	16.50	.0606	.2606	3.837
9	5.160	.1938	20.80	.0481	.2481	4.031
10	6.192	.1615	25.96	.0385	.2385	4.192
11	7.430	.1346	32.15	.0311	.2311	4.327
12	9.916	.1122	39.58	.0253	.2253	4.439
13	10.70	.0935	48.50	.0206	.2206	4.533
14	12.84	.0779	59.20	.0169	.2169	4.611
15	15.41	.0650	72.04	.0139	.2139	4.675
16	18.49	.0541	87.44	.0114	.2114	4.730
17	22.19	.0451	105.9	.0094	.2094	4.775
18	26.62	.0376	128.1	.0078	.2078	4.812
19	31.95	.0313	154.7	.0065	.2065	4.843
20	38.39	.0261	186.7	.0054	.2054	4.870
21	46.01	.0217	225.0	.0044	.2044	4.891
22	55.21	.0181	271.0	.0037	.2037	4.909
23	66.25	.0151	326.2	.0031	.2031	4.925
24	79.50	.0126	392.5	.0026	.2026	4.937
25	95.40	.0105	472.0	.0021	.2021	4.948
30	237.4	.0042	1182.	.0009	.2009	4.979
35	590.7	.0017	2948.	.0003	.2003	4.992
40	1470.	.0007	7344.	.0001	.2001	4.997
45	3657.	.0003	18281.	.0001	.2001	4.999
50	9100.	.0001	45497.	.0000	.2000	4.999

20 Percent Interest Factors

Figure 4.3.4.1 (continued) - Interest Tables

Year Y	SCA P-F	SPW F-P	UCA A-F	USF F-A	UCR P-A	UPW A-P
1	1.250	.8000	1.000	1.000	1.250	0.800
2	1.562	.6400	2.250	.4444	.6944	1.440
3	1.953	.5120	3.812	.2623	.5123	1.952
4	2.441	.4096	5.766	.1734	.4234	2.362
5	3.052	.3277	8.207	.1219	.3719	2.689
6	3.815	.2621	11.26	.0888	.3388	2.951
7	4.768	.2097	15.07	.0663	.3163	3.161
8	5.960	.1678	19.84	.0504	.3004	3.329
9	7.451	.1342	25.80	.0388	.2888	3.463
10	9.313	.1074	33.25	.0301	.2801	3.571
11	11.64	.0859	42.57	.0235	.2735	3.656
12	14.55	.0687	54.21	.0185	.2685	3.725
13	18.19	.0550	68.76	.0145	.2645	3.780
14	22.74	.0440	86.95	.0115	.2615	3.824
15	28.42	.0352	109.7	.0091	.2591	3.859
16	35.53	.0281	138.1	.0072	.2572	3.887
17	44.41	.0225	173.6	.0058	.2558	3.910
18	55.51	.0180	218.0	.0046	.2546	3.928
19	69.30	.0144	273.6	.0037	.2537	3.942
20	86.74	.0115	342.9	.0029	.2529	3.954
21	108.4	.0092	429.7	.0023	.2523	3.963
22	135.5	.0074	538.1	.0019	.2519	3.970
23	169.4	.0059	673.6	.0015	.2515	3.976
24	211.8	.0047	843.0	.0012	.2512	3.981
25	264.7	.0038	1055.	.0010	.2510	3.985
30	807.8	.0012	3227.	.0003	.2503	3.995
35	2465.	.0004	9857.	.0001	.2501	3.998
40	7523.	.0001	30089.	.0000	.2500	3.999

25 Percent Interest Factors

Year Y	SCA P-F	SPW F-P	UCA A-F	USF F-A	UCR P-A	UPW A-P
1	1.300	.7692	1.000	1.000	1.300	0.769
2	1.690	.5917	2.300	.4348	.7348	1.361
3	2.197	.4552	3.990	.2506	.5506	1.816
4	2.856	.3501	6.187	.1616	.4616	2.166
5	3.713	.2693	9.043	.1106	.4106	2.436
6	4.827	.2072	12.76	.0784	.3784	2.643
7	6.275	.1594	17.58	.0509	.3569	2.802
8	8.157	.1226	23.86	.0419	.3419	2.925
9	10.60	.0943	32.02	.0312	.3312	3.019
10	13.79	.0725	42.62	.0235	.3235	3.092
11	17.92	.0558	56.41	.0177	.3177	3.147
12	23.30	.0429	74.33	.0135	.3135	3.190
13	30.29	.0330	97.63	.0102	.3102	3.223
14	39.37	.0254	127.0	.0078	.3078	3.249
15	51.19	.0195	167.3	.0060	.3060	3.268
16	66.54	.0150	218.5	.0046	.3046	3.283
17	86.50	.0116	285.0	.0035	.3035	3.295
18	112.5	.0089	371.5	.0027	.3027	3.304
19	146.2	.0068	484.0	.0021	.3021	3.311
20	190.1	.0053	630.2	.0016	.3010	3.316
21	247.1	.0040	820.2	.0012	.3012	3.320
22	321.2	.0031	1067.	.0009	.3009	3.323
23	417.5	.0024	1388.	.0007	.3007	3.325
24	542.8	.0018	1806.	.0006	.3006	3.327
25	705.6	.0014	2349.	.0004	.3004	3.329

30 Percent Interest Factors

Figure 4.3.4.1 (continued) - Interest Tables

GLOSSARY

Absorption: The act of shortwave radiation striking a surface and changing to long-wave radiation. Some of the radiation received at ground level is reflected as well as absorbed by the earth's surface. The total amount of radiation striking the surface equals the amount of energy absorbed by a surface plus the amount reflected.

Active system: A system that uses mechanical means to satisfy loads.

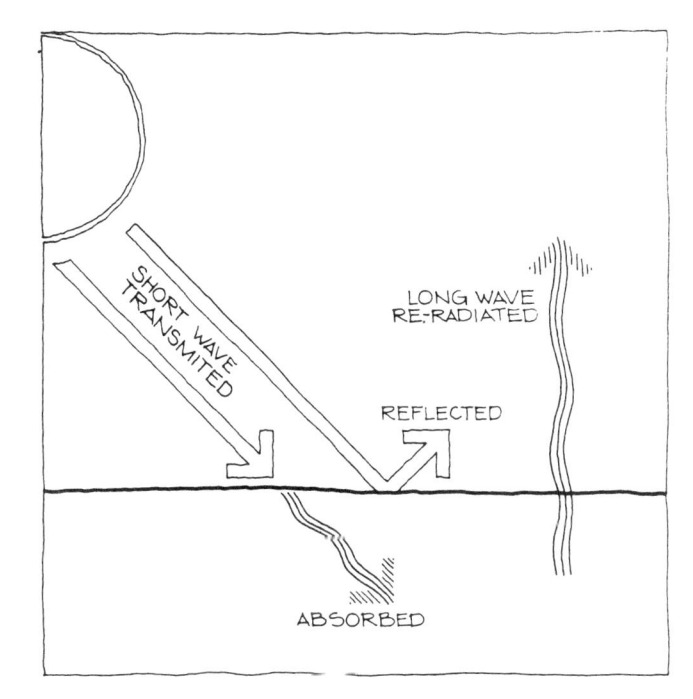

Absorption

Air quality: Relative air composition and, in particular, the level that is healthy for use. Indoor air is made impure by carbon dioxide and water vapor discharged from the lungs, organic materials and bacteria given off by the body, pollutants and radioactive particles emitted by the radon found in some building materials.

Annual value: Benefits or costs occurring in uniform amounts annually, or the uniform annual equivalents of past, present or future benefits.

Brightness ratio: The ratio of the brightness (luminosity) of an object to brightness of adjacent spaces or objects; this ratio describes varying levels of comfort.

British thermal unit (BTU): The amount of heat required to raise the temperature of one pound of water one degree F.

Calorie: The metric unit of the amount of heat needed to raise the temperature of one gram of water one degree C. One calorie equals approximately four BTUs.

Capacity: The ability of a piece of equipment or system to satisfy the maximum anticipated (design) load.

Cascading energy: The process by which recoverable waste heat is used at sequentially lower temperature (quality) levels.

Conditioned and unconditioned spaces: The need for air treatment such as heat addition, heat removal, moisture removal or pollution removal for a space versus the lack of need for such airconditioning in a space.

Conductivity: The measurement of heat energy transfer over time caused by direct molecular interaction. It is a function of the material's thickness, area and thermal conductivity, and the difference in temperature.

Constant dollars: Values expressed in terms of the general purchasing power of the dollar in the base year. Constant dollars do not reflect price inflation.

Consuming system: A system that uses nonrenewable resources to satisfy loads.

Consumption: The using up of nonrenewable or renewable resources so that it is no longer available for work.

Degree-day: The amount of annual heating or cooling demand in a particular geographical area. To determine heating degree-days, sum the temperature difference in degrees F between the interior temperature desired and the average outdoor temperature below the desired temperature for each day of the year. Cooling degree-days are arrived at in a similar manner, except that the average exterior temperatures above desired interior temperatures are used. This will give a quantitative value for how warm or cold a particular area is, relative to other areas.

Degree-hour: Similar to degree-days but, due to smaller increments, gives a more sensitive presentation of temperature fluctuations. To determine the degree-hours, take the temperature difference in degrees F between the desired temperature and the average outdoor temperature for each hour of the day.

Demand: The amount of energy required to satisfy the net utility loads at any given time.

Dew point temperature (DP): The temperature at which moisture from the air begins to condense. Dew point temperature forms the upper curve boundary of the psychrometric chart, the line of 100 percent humidity. It represents the fact that as the temperature falls (from right to left on the

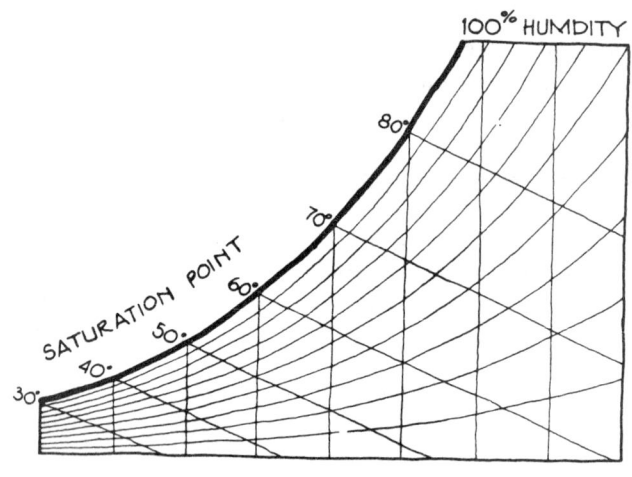

Dew Point

bottom axis), the maximum amount of moisture that the air can hold decreases with it.

Diffuse radiation: Light from the sun passing through the atmosphere which is "scattered" because of suspended dust and air molecules. The distance the sun's beams travel through the atmosphere affects the composition of received radiation, reducing the sun's diffuse energy as this distance increases.

Direct gain: Occurs when sunlight enters a space before being intercepted. Greenhouses, solar floor/wall systems, and skylights are examples. (See Greenhouse effect).

Direct radiation: Light that has travelled a straight path (without interference) from the sun to the earth's surface. Thus, sunlight or insolation strikes a building surface with both direct and diffuse components proportionately. On a cloudy day, more diffuse insolation will be present.

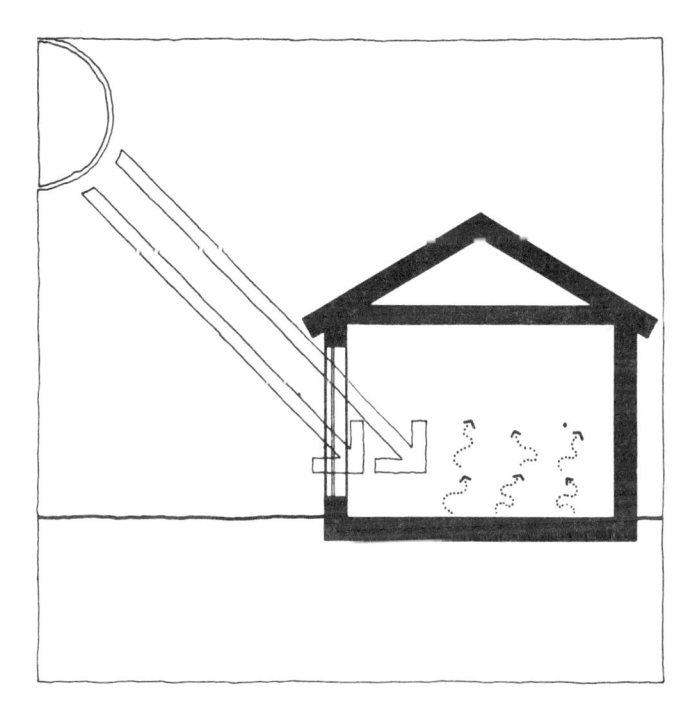

Direct Gain

Diurnal shifts: The difference between day and night temperatures.

Dry-bulb temperature: A measure of sensible heat as read on a standard thermometer and shown on the psychrometric chart as vertical lines read along the horizontal axis.

Earth temperature gradients: The stability of the temperature of dry earth at a certain depth.

Efficiency factor: The ratio of output energy over input energy.

Equivalent temperature differential (ETD): A factor used to determine solar radiation gain through an opaque wall. Based on specific construction types, kit takes into account insolation and ambient air temperatures.

Energy: The capacity to do work. There is heat energy, light energy, sound energy, potential energy, chemical energy, kinetic energy, and electrical energy. All of these energy forms interact and flow into and out of a building.

Energy Equivalents:
1 BTU =
   777.48 foot-pounds
   .29305 watt-hours (W/hr)
   1,055 joules
1 BTU/hr/sq ft/(°F/in)/ = 5.682 x 10^4 Watts/cm^2
1 BTU/sq ft = .271 langleys (cal/cm^2)
1 Calorie = 3.9685 x 10^{-3} BTU
            4.184 joules
1 Horsepower =
   33,000 foot-pounds/min
   42.42 BTU/min
   2.546 BTU/hr
   1.014 metric horsepower (hp)
   7457 kiloWatts (KW)
1 KiloWatt =
   56.98 BTU/min
   1.341 horsepower
1 Lumen = .0014706 watts
1 Watt =
   3.413 BTU/hr
   .00314 horsepower (hp)

Energy management systems: Coordinated manual and/or automatic control and supervision of the operation of active and passive systems within a building.

Enthalpy (h): A mathematical quantity used in thermodynamic calculations and equal to the internal energy of a substance plus ;the pressure times the volume (h = u + pv).

Footcandle: The amount of direct light from one candle ;falling on a square foot of surface one foot away.
Foot lambert: The luminance due to reflection, transmission, or emission of one footcandle from a surface.

Greenhouse effect: Radiation from the sun is primarily shortwave energy. Interior objects absorb shortwave radiation and emit long-wave radiation. Consequently, most of the heat is "trapped" within the space. This collected heat can be stored or used immediately to heat the interior.

Heat capacity: The ability of a material to store heat. Heat capacity is a function of volume, density, specific heat and difference in temperature.

Humidity ratio (W): Also known as absolute humidity, the ratio of the mass of water vapor in each pound of dry air to the mass of air; shown on the horizontal lines of the psychrometric chart and read along the right-hand vertical axis.

Indirect gain: Occurs when the sun's energy is intercepted and stored in proximal storage before it enters the space. Solar masonry walls, water wall collectors, etc., are indirect gain systems.

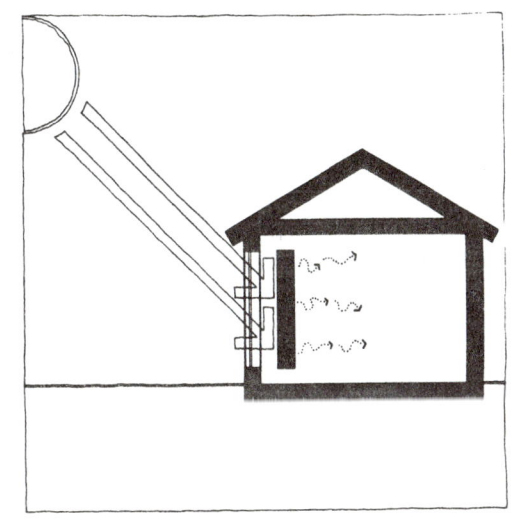

Indirect Gain

Infiltration: Occurs at all cracks in a building and is due to pressure differences between the outside and inside, which are caused primarily by wind and temperature differentials.

Insolation: The amount of solar energy that strikes a surface area at a given orientation. (incident solar radiation).

Insulation: The retardation of heat flow. The ability to do so depends upon thickness and thermal properties of the material.

Isolated gain: Occurs when solar collection and thermal storage are separate from living spaces. This relationship allows the system to function

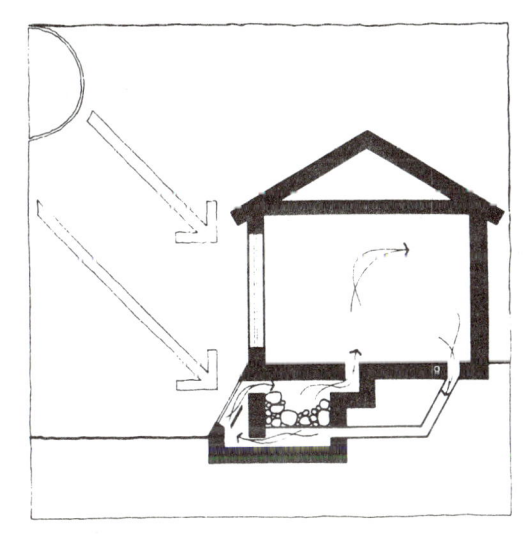

Isolated Gain

independently of the building, with heat drawn from the system only when needed.

Life-cycle cost (LCC) analysis: The total cost of a system over its economically useful life. It includes the appropriate summation of all costs expected to be incurred as a result of choosing and implementing any particular plan or design over the life of the facility.

Load: That demand for energy that is required at any given time to satisfy a need or needs.

Net building load: The demand for energy required to satisfy all space loads.

Night Sky Radiation: A reversal of the daytime insulation principle. Just as the sun radiates energy during the day throughout the void of space, so heat energy can travel unhindered at night, from the earth's surface back into space. On a clear night the earth, like any other warm object can cool itself by radiating long-wave heat energy to the cooler sky. On a cloudy night, the cloud cover acts as an insulator and prevents the heat from traveling to the cooler sky.

Nonconsuming system: A system that uses renewable resources to satisfy loads.

On-and Off-site utility systems: An off-site utility system is a system that satisfies utility loads from an energy supply located at a site separated from the building site. An on-site utility is a system that satisfies utility loads from an energy supply located at the building site.

Opportunity rate: The best rate of return that money could earn if placed in the highest-yield investment available.

Passive system: A system that uses nonmechanical means to satisfy space loads.

Payback period: The time required for the cumulative net benefits derive from an investment to pay back the investment lost, considering the time value of money.

Power factor: The ratio of the working current, including the changing current, supplied to a device.

Present worth: Past and future cash flows expressed in time-equivalent amounts as of the present time, adjusted for inflation and the time value of money.

Process energy: The energy used by a building to provide a specific industrial or commercial service.

Profiles (operation schedules): Descriptions of a building's use during uniform intervals of a day. They may describe occupancy, light usage, mechanical system usage, etc. during each hour of the day.

Proximal storage: Energy storage that is proximal to a space, either located inside the space or integral to the space or envelope.

Psychrometrics: A graphic representation of air temperature, humidity, and other data on a chart.

Rate of return on extra investment: The ratio of savings-to-extra-investment of one energy-conserving design option compared to another.

Recoverable waste heat: That quantity of waste heat that is available for reuse directly or indirectly.

Reflectivity (albedo): The ratio of reflected sunlight to received sunlight. By capturing albedo, more than 100 percent of the direct solar energy on a surface is available.

Relative humidity (RH): The ratio of vapor pressure in an air-water mixture to saturation vapor pressure, shown by the curved lines that climb from left to right on the psychrometric chart.

Remote storage: Energy storage located outside the space and its enclosure. Remote storage is normally used to improve heating or cooling system efficiency.

Resources load: That demand for an energy resource that must be provided in order to satisfy utility loads.

Sensible heat ratio (SHR): The ratio of the sensible heat to total heat in a process. Sensible heat is heat which, when added to a substance, changes only its temperature and not its state.

Sol-air effect: The combined effects of solar radiation and air temperature on a surface. The procedure for analyzing the sol-air effect takes into account the following:
- Solar radiation on all building surfaces
- Outside air temperature relative to time of day and solar position

- Building orientation
- Exterior materials relative to thermal mass, conductivity, color, textures and movable insulation
- Shading on all surfaces
- Window placement.

During cooling periods, the sol-air calculations indicate the net heat gain into a building. During heating periods, sol-air calculations indicate the net heat loss. Solar radiation's effect on a surface is determined by subtracting the sol-air loss from the steady-state loss. Total solar radiation on the building is determined by adding the direct gain through the solar collection surfaces to this sol-air radiation value.

Solar altitude: The vertical angle between the sun's position in the sky and a horizontal plane at a given latitude. The altitude is lowest at winter solstice and highest at summer solstice.

Solar angle of incidence: The angle the rays of the sun make with a line perpendicular to a surface. it determines the percentage of direct sunshine intercepted by that surface, and equals the angle of reflectance.

Solar azimuth: The horizontal angle between the sun's bearing and a north-south line, as projected on a plan horizontal with the earth's surface. The sun comes over the horizon at a different point each day. The daily total arc is smaller in winter, larger in the summer.

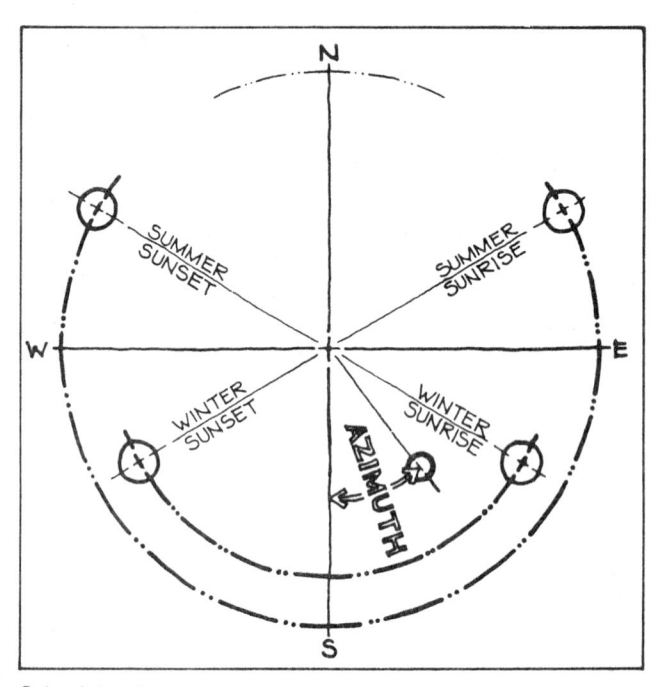

Solar Azimuth

Solar constant: The amount of solar energy received outside the earth's atmosphere. It equals 429 BTU/sq ft. After a portion of this radiation is reflected into space and some is absorbed in the atmosphere, the amount of solar energy available when it reaches the earth's surface averages about 225 BTU/hr/sq ft. Depending on the time of day, latitude, season, and the weather, it varies between 0 and 330 BTU/hr/sq ft.

Solar intensity: The amount of solar radiation striking an area as a function of its perpendicularity to a surface. Imagine a handful of pencils, their points touching a tabletop. They represent the parallel rays of the sun. The marks made by the points represent units of energy. When the pencils are perpendicular to the table-top, the dots are as close together as possible. This shows that energy density per square-inch is at a maximum. When the pencils are inclined toward the plane of the table, the dots cover a larger area. This shows that ;energy density per square-inch decreases.

Solar radiation flow: The flow of electromagnetic waves intercepted by the earth's atmosphere. It is either reflected, diffused (scattered), absorbed, or transmitted as direct sunlight.

Long- and shortwave radiation cycle is the input of shortwave (0.3 to 3.0 microns) radiation from the sun and the outward flux of long-wave radiation (3.0 to 30 microns) from the earth. The invisible, ultraviolet portion is shorter than 0.4 microns in wavelength and makes up 5 percent of the total solar energy that reaches the earth.

The near-infrared portion of the spectrum, 0.7 to 3.0 microns, contains the remaining 48 percent of the total terrestrial sunshine. Once absorbed, it becomes heat, a long-wave radiation, which is between 3.0 and 30 microns.

Space loads: Energy demands resulting from program requirements, external factors, and internal factors. These loads are considered to be placed on the building before energy-conscious design strategies are used.

Specific heat and heat content: The ability of a material to store varying amounts of heat. It is the amount of heat required to produce a unit change in temperature unit mass.

Specific volume (V):
The volume occupied by one pound of a substance and shown on the psychrometric chart as the cubic feet of the mixture per pound of dry air. The reciprocal of specific volume density, pounds per cubic foot.

Stored energy: That quantity of energy that may be accumulated or deleted to satisfy an imbalance between demand and system capacity.

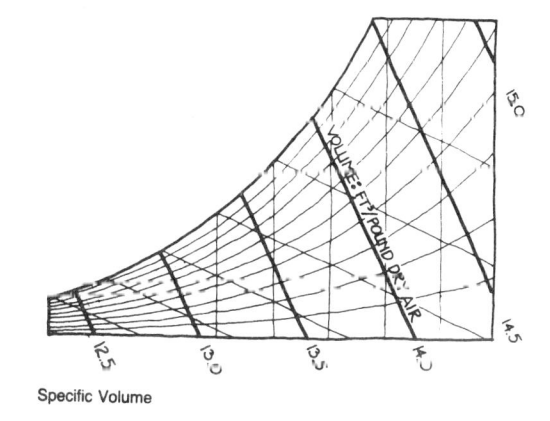

Specific Volume

Stratification: The tendency of warmer fluids, when unevenly heated, to rise and stratify or layer, in a given volume.

System capacity: The sum of the system load, and that quantity of energy used by a consuming system to satisfy the system load.

$$\text{System capacity} = \frac{\text{net system load}}{\text{system efficiency (percent)}}$$

System load: That demand for energy that must be provided by an active system in order to satisfy a space load.

Thermal inertia: The tendency of a massive material to remain at a certain temperature. It is an example of the axiom, "an object at rest tends to stay at rest; an object in motion tends to remain in motion."

Thermal mass: A substance (liquid or solid) in which heat energy is dumped or stored. "Heat storage" and "heat sink" are terms for the same concept. Liquid thermal mass tends to stratify; Warmest liquid rises to the top, cools and falls, creating constant movement. Solid thermal mass's ability to store heat is dependent upon the material's specific heat, conductivity and convective heat transfer.

"U" and "R" values: These values are inversely proportional, $U = 1/R$. The lower the U-value, the better the insulative quality;; the higher the R-value, the better the resistance to heat flow. R-values for individual materials, air spaces, air films, etc., are established; these are used to calculate the coefficient of the transfer for an entire wall. The R-values of the individual materials are added together, then inverted to obtain the overall U-value for the wall.

Utility load: That demand for energy that must be provided by a utility system (on- or off-site) in order to satisfy system loads.

Vapor barriers: Materials in a wall which prevent moisture-laden air from condensing on the inner surface of the outer wall of a building.

Vapor pressure (Pw): The pressure exerted by water vapor in the air.

Ventilation: Airflow through and within an internal space stimulated by two means: 1) the distribution of pressure gradients around a building and 2) thermal forces caused by temperature gradients between indoor and outdoor air. Ventilation of air-flow conditions within a building provides air purity, motion, convective cooling and evaporative cooling which in turn influence the health, comfort and well-being of the occupants.

Waste heat: Heat that is at too low a temperature to do the work for which it was originally intended, but which may or may not be recoverable for some other task.

Wet-bulb temperature: The temperature indicated when a thermometer hose bulb is covered by a wet wick and exposed to a stream of air moving 500--2,000 fpm. Shown on lines that slope down from left to right and read on the curved line on the upper left edge of the psychrometric chart.

INDEX

Absorption, 317
Absorption refrigeration, 220
Acceptable-practice method, 89
Access control program, 243
Active energy systems, 48, 234
Active solar heating
   air/liquid systems comparison, 233
   sizing for, 233, 234
Active solar systems, 233-235
   as design strategy, 78
   standards for, 91
Active system, definition, 28, 317
Actuators, 249
Adobe blocks, for heat storage, 42
Adobe walls, heat capacity of, 173
Adsorbents, 57
Air cavity, heat flow across, 119
Air circulation, code requirements, 83
Air cleaning, 56
Air distribution optimization, 242-243
Air filtration, 56
Air flow. See also Ventilation; Wind
   around building, 103
      effect on air quality, 51
   effects of surfaces on, 103-104
   through windows, 139-140
Air ionizers, 57
Air leakage. See also Infiltration
   code criteria, 89
   during construction, 262
Air movement
   effect on microclimate, 99-100
   for thermal balance, 40
Air pollutants. See Pollutants
Air quality. See Indoor air quality
Air spaces, U-values of, 137
Air transport factor (ATF), 216
Air velocity, and comfort, 46
Airconditioning, 75, 201

   standards for, 91
   U.S. rate of use, 1
Airconditioning systems, smoke and fire management of, 244
Air-cooled condensers, 222
Air-exhaust system, for transporting lighting waste heat, 25
Airflow, use for energy design, 99
Air-flow windows, 139-140
Air-handling unit (AHU), 214
Airlocks, 136
Air-to-air heat exchangers, 224, 280
Air-washing, 57
Allergens, 50
All-water heat pump system, 217-218
Ambient temperature, and human comfort, 45
American Society for Testing and Materials. See ASTM
American Society of Heating, Refrigerating and Air-Conditioning Engineers. See ASHRAE
Ammonia fumigation, in pollution control, 54
Annual value, 317
Apartment buildings
   design analysis and strategies for, 276-278
   DHW usage in, 237
   highrise
      exterior walls in, 119-120
      heat gain per occupant, 107
      occupant space requirements, 106
   thermal distribution systems for, 210
   thermal systems for, 209
Apertures
   for daylighting, 152-156
   placement of, for ventilation, 134
Appliances
   energy use, 74
   in predesign energy budget, 74
   usage in apartment buildings,

278
Architectural Graphics Standards, 72
Architectural programming factors, 78-79
Area, in mass heat storage, 174
Arenas, heat gain per occupant, 107
Artificial lighting. *See* Lighting; Lighting systems
Asbestos, 50
ASHRAE, 89
ASHRAE Standard 90, 83, 85, 89, 121
　criteria for curtain walls, 129
Asphalt, for heat gain, 102
Assembly-use buildings
　heat gain per occupant, 107
　occupant space requirements, 106
ASTM, 85
　Standards in Building Codes, 91
Atriums
　for daylighting, 151
　in heat gain systems, 180
　and solar heat gain, 35
Attic spaces, insulation of, 124, 125
Auditoriums, lighting needs of, 108
Azimuth. *See* Solar azimuth

Balance point, 31-32
Ballasts for lamps, 191
Banks, lighting needs of, 108
"Base case" building energy analysis, 76-77
Basic Building Code, 85
BEPS. *See* Building Energy Performance Standards
Berming
　in construction, 97
　in educational facilities, 272-273
　of foundation and basement walls, 129
Boiler optimization programs, 241-242

Boiler profile generation, 243
Boilers, 220-221
　efficiency in DHW systems, 238
　special maintenance needs, 264
Break-even analysis, 311
Brick
　heat capacity of, 173
　for heat storage, 42
　R-value of, 121
Brightness ratio, 317
British thermal unit. *See* BTU
BTU, definition, 29, 317
Buffered spaces, for controlling heat gain, 35, 38
Building code compliance, 83
Building components, lifespan of, 300
Building configuration
　in conservation design strategy, 77
　for daylighting, 34, 77, 94
　designs for daylighting, 151
　in economic analysis, 309
　for energy conservation, 93-95
　for hospitals, 281
　for hotels/motels, nursing homes/geriatric centers, 279
　and infiltration, 136
　length-to-width ratio, 35
　for office buildings, 270
　related to external factors, 93-95
　related to solar heat gain, 35-36
　for retail stores, 274, 276
　in roof pond systems, 178
　surface area-to-volume ratio, 35, 117
Building design. *See also* Design strategies
　analytic techniques, 283-297
　and indoor air quality, 51, 52-57
　and outdoor temperature, 66
Building design process, 73-84
　goals, 73
　predesign energy analysis, 73-

79
Building Energy Performance Standards (BEPS), 9, 65
Building energy performance targets (BEPTs), 79
Building envelope, 36
  code requirements, acceptable-practice method, 89
  in conservation design strategy, 77
  construction monitoring of, 262-263
  design for thermal comfort, 48
  in design strategy, 117-130
  for educational facilities, 273
  in energy budget, 74
  energy use, 74
  heat gain/loss, 36-39
  of hospitals, 281
  for hotels/motels, nursing homes/geriatric centers, 279
  increasing thermal mass in, 41
  for office buildings, 270-271
  for retail stores, 274, 276
  for thermal mass storage, 167
  total performance, 130
  U-value code compliance, 87
  and U-values, 117-119
Building form. *See* Building configuration
Building lifespan, 300
Building loads, energy analysis descriptors of, 294
Building mass, in energy analysis, 296
Building materials, as pollutants, 51
Building occupants. *See* Occupants
Building orientation
  for apartment buildings, 277
  for daylighting, 151-152
  in economic analysis, 309
  effect of, on solar heat gain, 35
  for office buildings, 270
  and passive heating, 173
  related to external factors, 93-95
  in roof pond systems, 178
  and shading devices, 146
  and space planning, 115-116
  and ventilation, 40, 133
Building owner in construction and commissioning process, 254-265
Building shape. *See* Building configuration
Building site
  effect on air quality, 51
  for retail stores, 274, 276
Building size, and EMCSs, 252
Building type
  and design analysis, 267-282
  and EMCSs, 252-253
  energy analysis for, 285-289
  heat gain per occupant by, 107
Buildings systems integration, 19

Calibration of system controls, 265
Calorie, 317
Capacity, 317
Capital investment costs, 305
Cascading energy, definition, 28, 317
Cathedral ceilings, insulation of, 124
Caulking, 129
Cavity ratio formulations, 195
Ceiling panels, 155
Ceilings
  colors for energy conservation, 198
  height
    and daylighting, 153
    for radiative cooling, 183
    in roof pond systems, 178
    in isolated heat gain, 180
  Model Energy Code Criteria, 88
  OTTV, 88
  reflectance of, 109
  as source of indoor pollutants, 51

Cellulose, R-value, 118
Central control units (CCUs) in EMCSs, 247
Centralized lighting control, 243
C-factor, for building envelope, 117-119
Charcoal filters, 57
Chemical heat storage media, 168
Chiller energy management controller, 229
Chiller optimization program, 242
Chiller profile generation, 243
Chiller water temperature reset, 242
Chimney effect, 40
Churches, recommended lighting levels, 185
Clay, construction on, 96-97
Clerestories, 153
   for educational facilities, 273
   for passive heating, 173
   for retail stores, 275
Climate, 64-67
   data sources, 71-72
   and design strategies, 70-71
   designs for severe, 95
   regional data, 64, 65
     limitations of use, 66, 70
Clinics, heat gain per occupant, 107
Closed circuit television, 243
Coaxial cable
   in EMCSs, 251
   transmission characteristics, 247
Code compliance, by energy analysis methods, 283-284
Code requirements, of floors, 128
Codes, for energy conservation, 85
Coefficient of performance (COP), 203
Coefficient of Utilization (CU)
   for illuminance calculations, 193
Coefficients of performance (COP), 89
Cogeneration, 63
Colors
   for absorption of sunlight, 176
   for daylighting, 152
     with shading devices, 147
   effect on heat penetration, 123
   effect on reflecting surfaces, 101-102
   for energy conservation, 198
   for heat storage, 170-171
   in isolated heat gain, 180
   in light sources, 190
   in light wells, 151
   in passive heating systems, 174
   for roofs, 124
   use for reflectivity, 108
Combustion appliances, and indoor air quality, 54, 55
Comfort zone, 48, 49
Commercial buildings
   absorption refrigeration systems in, 220
   active heating systems for, 233
   energy use by, 2-5
   heat storage strategies for, 166
   median size, 2
   recommended lighting levels, 185
   thermal distribution systems in, 213
   use of glass in, 123
   use of thermal storage walls in, 177
Commercial energy end use, 1
Commissioning process, 254-265
   responsibility checklist, 255
Component life, in economic analysis, 300
Component performance, in design strategy, 87
Compressors, 213
Computer rooms, placement of, 111
Computers, for EMCSs, 240, 244, 249

INDEX

Concrete
  in construction, 119
  heat capacity of, 173
  in heat gain systems, 180
  for heat storage, 42, 168
  R-values of types of, 121
Concrete-masonry units, for heat storage, 42
Condensation, 38
  in air-water thermal systems, 209
  on glazing, 132
  prevention, 120
Condenser water temperature reset, 242-243
Condensers, 213, 222
  for heat recovery, 224
Conditioned spaces, 318
Conduction, 23, 119, 171
  in apartment buildings, 277
  in educational facilities, 273
  of heat through building, 36
Conductivity, 318
Conference rooms, lighting needs of, 108
Configuration. *See* Building configuration
Constant dollar calculations, 301-307
Constant dollars, 318
Constant-air-temperature (CAT), variable-air-volume (VAV) thermal distribution, 207
Constant-air-volume (CAV) multizone thermal distribution, 206
Construction
  energy use in, 2
  on-site inspection during, 262, 264
  operational checks during, 259-264
  record drawings, 263
Construction costs, in economic analysis, 309
Construction documentation, 83
Construction process, 254-265
  programming assumptions, 256
  scheduling checklist, 255
Consuming system, 318

Consuming system, definition, 28
Consumption, 318. *See also* Usage
  definition, 29
Contaminant control devices, 55
Contractors, preoccupancy responsibilities, 260
Control systems
  energy analysis descriptors of, 295
  individual local, 229
Controls, for thermal systems, 225-229
Convection, 23, 119, 171
  for heat distribution, 173
  for heat gain or loss, 42, 107, 176
  in heating, 176
Cooling, 49
  active solar, 234
  design strategies for, 49
  in passive systems
    direct, 181-182
    indirect, 181, 182-184
    isolated, 181, 184
  use of microclimate for, 99
Cooling absorption cycle, 220
Cooling load, by fuel type, 5
Cooling load factor, 110-111
  of lighting systems, 197
Cooling process sequence, 201-202
Cooling towers, 222
Cost categories for economic analysis, 305-306
Cost/benefit analysis, 298-311. *See also* Life-cycle cost analysis
Courtyards
  for daylighting, 77, 151
  and solar heat gain, 35
Crawl spaces, 127
Cross ventilation, 133

Data transmission links in EMCSs, 247
Data transmission media (DTM), 244
Daylight apertures, 152-156

INDEX

Daylighting, 102-103, 149-164
  and aperture height, 153, 155
  and building orientation, 93-94
  for educational facilities, 273
  for energy conservation, 199
  Lumen method analysis, 159-164
  measurement of illumination, 159-164
  model geometry, 157-158
  model testing, 158
  in passive cooling systems, 181
  physical models for, 156-169
  physical models for analysis of, 287
  published data, 72
  qualities, 109
  with shading devices, 147
  site criteria, 151
  target height for, 153, 155
  use for energy conservation, 34, 199
Daylighting configurations, 150
Deadband control system, 228
Decrement factor, 41
Degree days/hours, 67, 318
Dehumidification, 49, 68, 210
  in pollution control, 54
Dehumidifiers, 182
Demand, 318
Desiccant salts
  in absorption refrigeration, 220
  for cooling, 182
Desiccants, for humidity control, 182
Design analysis, 267-312
Design concept analysis, 43
Design of Energy-Responsive Commercial Buildings, 83
Design strategies
  for apartment buildings, 277-278
  architectural program factors, 78
  and economic analysis, 307-308
  for educational facilities, 272-274
  for energy conservation, 77-79, 82-84
  for hospitals, 280-282
  for hotels/motels, 279-280
  for humidity control, 68
  for indoor air pollution abatement, 52-57
  for lighting systems, 197-200
  for nursing homes/geriatric centers, 279-280
  for office buildings, 269-271
  for passive cooling, 181
  for retail stores, 275-276
  for thermal comfort, 49
  for thermal mass, 168-169
Design With Climate, 94
Dew-point temperature, 48, 318-319
DHW. *See* Domestic hot water
Diffuse radiation, 319
Direct digital control (DDC) in EMCSs, 246-247
Direct gain. *See also* Solar heat gain
  definition, 319
Direct heat, U.S. rate of use, 1
Direct solar gain. *See* Solar heat gain
Discount rates, 299-300
Distributed processing in EMCSs, 244, 246
District heating/cooling, 63
Diurnal shifts, 319
Domestic hot water (DHW)
  in apartment buildings, 278
  calculating peak electrical demand for, 238
  energy conservation for, 238
  energy efficient equipment for, 239
  energy needs of, 237
  solar systems for, 237
  system efficiencies, 238
  usage, by building type, 237
Domestic water heating, 220
Doors, controlled access of, 243
Double envelope structures, 130
Double-duct, constant air volume

INDEX

(CAV)/constant air temperature (CAT) system with mixing boxes, 215-216
Drafting areas, lighting needs of, 108
Draperies. *See* Shading devices
Dry-bulb temperature, 48, 65, 319
Dry sand walls, heat capacity of, 173
Dual-duct thermal distribution, 205-206, 216
Duty cycling, 231-232

Earth, for thermal mass storage, 166, 167-168
Earth temperature gradients, 319
Earth temperatures, use of, for heating and cooling, 38
Earth-air heat exchange, in passive cooling systems, 181
Earth-integrated construction, 38
Economic anaylsis, 298-312
Economic forecast timeframe, 300
Educational buildings
 DHW usage in, 237
 heat gain per occupant, 107
 occupant space requirements, 106
Educational facilities
 design analysis and strategies for, 271-274
 lighting needs of, 108
Efficiency factor, 319
Eh, measurement, 159
Electric lighting. *See* Lighting
Electric power, code criteria, 89
Electrical services, U.S. rate of use, 1
Electrical unit sensors, 248
Electricity
 cost computation, 58-62
 ratchet clause, 60
 demand charges, 60, 61
 demand-control equipment, 60, 230
 pulse initiated meters, 60
 use of, in office buildings, 4
Electrostatic precipitators, 56
Elevators
 energy use, 74
 lighting needs of, 108
 operating costs, 236
 in predesign energy budget, 74
EMCS. *See* Energy management and control systems
Energy, definition, 29
Energy analysis
 cost of, 289
 program documentation, 290
 tool descriptors, 293, 294-295
Energy analysis methods, 283-284
 design tools for, 284-286
Energy analysis models, 293, 296
Energy analysis tools
 input/output, 291
 selection of, 297
 structure of, 291
 technical capabilities of, 291, 293
 user support, 290-291
Energy auditing, 89
Energy budget, 79
 in predesign, 74
Energy codes and standards (chart), 86
Energy conservation, for DHW systems, 238
Energy conservation guidelines, 91
Energy Conservation in New Building Design. *See* ASHRAE, Standard 90
Energy conservation investments, in economic analysis, 299
Energy conservation targets, by state and building type, 80-82
Energy conversion plants, energy analysis descriptors of, 294
Energy cost estimates, in design

process, 8-9
Energy costs, 58-63
　delivered fuel, 62-63
　electricity, 58-62
　natural gas, 62
Energy demand estimates in design process, 8-9
Energy design, timely effort curve, 254
Energy design procedure flow chart, 7-20
Energy design process, 6-20, 43
Energy diffusion, 41
Energy efficiency, 2, 25
Energy efficiency ratios (EER), 89
Energy end use
　commercial, 1
　in commercial buildings, 4
　by fuel type, 5
　industrial, 1
　in office buildings, 4
　residential, 1
　space heating, 4
　in United States, 1-2
Energy equivalents, 320
Energy estimates in design process, 8-9
Energy flow, 25-29, 27
　of a building, 27
Energy management and control system (EMCS) block diagram, 245
Energy management and control systems (EMCSs), 225, 228, 229, 231, 240-253
　adaptability factors, 250
　components of, 244-247
　cost effectiveness evaluation, 249-250
　evaluation and selection of, 248-253
　expandability, 251
　field equipment, 248-249
　maintainance, 250, 252
　maintenance contracts for, 250
　optimizing functions, 241
　programmability, 251-252
　reliability, 250-251
　remote control in, 249
　time-sharing systems, 244
　type of signals used, 244-245
Energy management systems, 320
Energy needs in underground construction, 97
Energy profiles, 75-77
Energy requirements for building, 74-77
Energy storage. *See* Heat storage; Thermal mass storage; Thermal storage
Energy storage systems
　for storing waste heat, 27
　use, 27
Energy transformation processes, 1-2
Energy usage
　in apartment buildings, 276-277, 278
　in educational facilities, 273
　in hospitals, 280-282
　in hotels/ motels, nursing homes/geriatric centers, 278-280
　planning documentation, 258
　of retail stores, 274-275
Energy use. *See also* Energy end use
　in absorption refrigeration, 220
　factors affecting, 75
　for lighting systems, 196-197
　in United States, 1-5
Energy use groups, and zoning, 116, 167
Energy-flow diagram, 26-29
Energy-flow system, 26
Enthalpy (h), 320
Envelope. *See* Building envelope
Equipment
　access to, for maintenance, 261-262
　computed heat gain, 111
Equipment identification, 262
Equipment loads, controlling, 14
Equipment maintenance, special service and tools for, 264
Equipment operation, during

INDEX

construction, 264-265
Equipment sizing tools, 288
Equivalent dollars, in economic analysis, 301
Equivalent temperature differential (ETD), 319
Equivalent-annual-cost method of economic analysis, 302, 304, 307, 312
Error checking in energy analysis programs, 290
Escalators, 236
Ethylene glycol, in heat exchangers, 223
Eutectic salts, for heat storage, 42
Ev, measurement of, 159
Evaporative cooling, 49, 183
  as design strategy, 78, 102
  in passive systems, 181
Evaporators, 213
Exhibition halls, lighting needs of, 108
Exterior spaces, recommended lighting levels, 185
External factors in design elements, 93-105
External loads, controlling, 14-15

Facility alteration and improvement costs, 306
Facility operation and maintenance costs, 305
Facility repair and replacement costs, 306
Fan coil thermal distribution system, 216-217
Fan coil units, 209, 210, 211
Fan-coil conditioner systems, 209-210
Fans, 221
  energy use, 74
  in predesign energy budget, 74
Fenestration, 131-164. *See also* Apertures; Windows
Fiber optics
  with EMCSs, 253
  transmission characteristics, 247
Fiber tube containers, for heat storage, 42
Fiberglass, R-value, 118
Field interface devices (FIDs), 244, 245, 248, 251
Financing costs, 305
Finned-tube coil, 210
Fire management, 244
Floor materials, 128
Floors
  colors of, for energy conservation, 198
  insulation of, 127-129
  model energy code criteria, 88
  for passive heating, 173
  reflectance of, 109
  as source of indoor pollutants, 51
  for thermal storage, 166
  vapor retarders for, 128
Florida, South, weather anomalies, 70
Fluorescent lights, 25, 189-190, 198
  characteristics of, 109, 189-190
  cooling load factor, 111
Food facility areas, lighting needs of, 108
Foot lambert, 320
Footcandle, 320
Forced-air ventilation, 208
Formaldehyde, 50, 52, 54, 57
  source control of, 54
  urea, R-value, 118
Fossil fuels, 1, 2
Fountains, cooling with, 183
Fuel adjustment charges, 62
Fuel costs, in economic analysis, 309
Fuels
  for boilers, 221
  delivered, 63
Functional-use costs, 306
Furniture, reflectance of, 109

Garages, effect on indoor air quality, 50

Gasketing, 129
Glare
  description of, 186-187
  luminance ratios for, 186
  with passive heating systems, 173
  reduction of, 187
Glare control, 155, 156
Glass
  in commercial buildings, 123
  conduction heat loss through, 137
  transfer of solar radiation through, 36
Glass blocks, 142
Glass coating materials, 142
Glass coatings, 138, 140
Glazing
  anti-reflective coatings, 143
  characteristics, 113
  condensation on, 132
  double, 155
    for passive heating, 173
    in thermal storage walls, 176, 177
  in heat storage systems, 176
  insulated, for passive heating, 173
  low-emissivity coatings, 141, 144
  multiple, 137-140
  properties of, 145
  solar heat gain through, 132
  transmission of heat through, 113
  transmittance, 145
  triple, 155
  types of, performance of, 138
  U-values, 132, 145
Glazing materials, 140-145, 167
  in passive heating, 174
Goals, in design strategies, 78-79
Grass, use for design strategy, 99
Greenhouse effect, 320
Greenhouses, in heat gain systems, 180

Heat capacity
  definition, 320
  of walls, 173
Heat exchange
  earth-air, in passive cooling systems, 181
  for heat transfer, 25
Heat exchangers, 54, 56, 63, 222-225
  for hotels/motels, nursing homes/geriatric centers, 280
  for passive cooling, 184
Heat flow, 22
  across air cavity, 119
Heat gain. *See also* Solar heat gain
  components of, 29-32
  decreasing, 37
  direct, 170
    in passive heating systems, 172-173
    windows for, 177
  effect of asphalt on, 102
  from equipment, computed, 111
  indirect, 171, 175-180
  internal
    factors causing, 106
    occupant effect on, 106-107
  isolated, 171, 179-180
    definition, 321-322
  from lighting, computed, 110
  from lights, 197
  through building envelope, 36-39
  through walls, 118
Heat gain/loss
  and building configuration, 95
  and thermal mass, 165
  total, computed, 117-118
Heat loss. *See also* Heat gain
  decreasing, 37
  movable insulation for reducing, 42
  strategies for, 182
  through glazing, 137-139
Heat of fusion, for heat storage, 42
Heat penetration, types of, 123
Heat pipes, 223
Heat pumps, 56, 166, 212-213,

INDEX

217-218, 224
  for apartment buildings, 277
  standards for, 91
Heat reclamation, 220
Heat reclamation devices, 225
Heat reclamation refrigeration systems, 220
Heat recovery, 224
  in all-air systems, 204, 205
  in all-water thermal systems, 212
  flue-gas systems, 224
  for hospitals, 282
  from lighting systems, 111, 232
Heat rejection, 222
Heat removal coefficient of performance, 203
Heat removal luminaires, 199
Heat storage, 36, 41-43, 165-180
Heat storage capacity, 41
Heat transfer, 22
  C-factor, 117
  for cooling, 201
  in isolated heat gain, 180
  mechanical, 25
  in underground construction, 96
Heat transmission, through glass, 113
Heat wheels, 222-223
Heat-absorbing glass, 142
Heated air, to induce air movement, 40
Heating, 49
  in active solar systems, 233-234
  design strategies, 49
  use of microclimate for, 99
Heating and cooling, simultaneous, 241
Heating and cooling systems, and EMCSs, 252
Heating load, by fuel type, 5
Heating sources in thermal systems, 220-221
Heating systems, smoke and fire management of, 244
High pressure sodium lamps. *See* Sodium lamps

High-intensity discharge lamps, 188, 189, 190-191
High-risk projects in cost analysis, 299
Hospitals
  design analysis and strategies for, 280-282
  heat gain per occupant, 107
  occupant space requirements, 106
  as source for district heating, 63
  thermal systems for, 209
Hot deck/cold deck temperature reset programs, 241
Hot water heaters, efficiency in DHW systems, 238
Hot water heating systems, 242
Hot water systems, standards, 91
Hot water temperature reset programs, 242
Hotels
  design analysis and strategies for, 278-280
  DHW usage in, 237
  heat gain per occupant, 107
  lighting needs of, 108
  thermal systems for, 209
Human comfort
  with duty cycling, 231
  factors affecting, 44-45
Humidification, 49
  in thermal systems, 204, 205
Humidity
  and comfort, 46, 68
  control
    and EMCSs, 241
    for thermal comfort, 48
  desiccant salts for, 182
  design strategies, 68
  effect on indoor air quality, 52
  low
    cooling with, 183
    effect on indoor air quality, 52
    effects of, 68
    and indirect gain systems, 176
  source of high indoor, 52

in underground construction, 97
Humidity ratio (W), 321
HVAC systems. *See also* Thermal distribution systems; Thermal systems
  for apartment buildings, 277
  classification and description, 203-218
  comparison charts, 203, 218
  for educational facilities, 273-274
  and EMCSs, 252
  energy analysis descriptors of, 294
  for hospitals, 281-282
  in hotels/motels, nursing homes/geriatric centers, 280
  for office buildings, 271
  for retail stores, 274, 275-276
  zone considerations when planning, 115-116

Illuminance
  calculation methods for, 192-195
  values by type of activity, 110
Illuminating Engineering Society of North America, 85, 91
Illumination, recommended levels of, 185
Illumination measurement
  of daylighting, 159
  on ground, 160
  from ground on window, 160
  from ground on work plane, 164
  from sky on work plane, 164
  total, on work plane, 164
  on window, 160
Incandescent light, 189-190, 198
Incident solar radiation. *See* Solar radiation
Indirect gain, 321
Indirect heat, U.S. rate of use, 1

Indoor air quality, 50-57
  assessment of, 52
  definition, 317
  effect of building design on, 51
  effect of humidity on, 52
  effect of occupancy patterns on, 52
  effect of outside sources of pollutants on, 51
Indoor pollutants. *See* Pollutants
Indoor thermal air quality, factors affecting, 48
Induced ventilation cooling system, 134
Induction units, 209
Industrial buildings, recommended lighting levels, 185
Industrial energy end use, 1
Infiltration, 129-130, 321. *See also* Air leakage
  decreasing, 37
  in educational facilities, 273
  through apertures, 135-136
  in underground construction, 96
Infrared energy, 24
Infrared radiation, 140, 141, 142, 143, 144, 145
Insolation. *See also* Solar heat gain
  definition, 321
Inspection
  during construction, 264
  of system controls, 265
Insulation, 36
  characteristics and selection of, 120-121
  definition, 321
  effect on U-value, 119
  of floors, 126-129
  for heat storage, 41
  movable, 42, 155
  movable panels, 176, 178, 179
  of perimeters, 128
  of retail stores, 276
  of roofs, ceilings, and attic spaces, 124-125

INDEX

and R-value, 118
in thermal storage walls, 178
types of, 120
  R-values of, 121
in underground construction, 96, 97
uses for, 38
for water storage tanks, 238
Insurance policies and EMCSs, 242
Intelligent multiplexer panels (IMUX), 244, 245, 248
Interest formulas, 302-307
Interest tables, 315
Internal load, controlling, 13
Internal loads, in educational facilities, 273
Isofootcandle method, 192-193
Isolated heat gain
  definition, 321-322

Joists, and U-values, 128

Kilowatt hour, definition, 29
kw-hr. *See* Kilowatt-hour

Labor costs, in economic analysis, 309
Laboratories, thermal systems for, 207
Latent heat energy storage, 168
Libraries
  lighting needs of, 108, 185
  recommended lighting levels, 185
Life-cycle cost, in design process, 307-308
Life-cycle cost analysis, 298-311, 323
Life-cycle cost criteria, 307
Life-cycle cost format, 304
Life-cycle cost methodology, 309-311
Life-cycle cost/benefit analysis, 307-311
Light
  availability for daylighting, 150-151

electric
  specifications, 189
natural. *See* Daylighting
reflection effects, 101-102
Light
  electric
    types of, 189-191
Light shelves, 149
Light wells, for daylighting, 151
Lighting
  comparison of types of, 109
  computed heat gain from, 110
  direct, 187-188
  electric, 185-200
    amounts needed, 107-111
    code criteria, 88
    as heat source, 34
  indirect, 188
  natural. *See* Daylighting
  needs, by type of activity, 110
  as source of waste heat, 25
  standards, 91
  U.S. rate of use, 1
Lighting load, by fuel type, 5
Lighting systems
  in apartment buildings, 277-278
  calculating needs for, 192-196
  centralized control, 243
  computed operating load, 110
  controls and switches for, 192, 199
  in educational facilities, 273
  energy use, 74, 196-197
  energy-conservation strategies for, 197-200
  heat recovery from, 232
  for hospitals, 281
  in hotels/motels, nursing homes/geriatric centers, 279-280
  maintenance, 199-200
  for office buildings, 271
  in predesign energy budget, 74
  programmable controls for, 232

for retail stores, 274, 275
task/ambient method, 188
thermal effects, 197
utilization factor, 110
Lights. *See types of light*
Liquids, for heat storage, 168
Lithium bromide, in absorption refrigeration, 220
Load calculation, tools for energy analysis, 287
Load estimates in design process, 8
Load reduction concept, 25
Loads
  balancing, 15-16
  definition, 27, 322
Local Climatological Data, 71
Los Angeles, CA, distinct weather pattern of, 70
Louvers, 149, 152
Low-e coatings. *See* Low-emissivity coatings
Low-emissivity coatings, 141, 144
Lumen method analysis, 159-164
Lumen method factors, 159
Lumen method tables, 161-164
Luminaires, 187, 188, 191-192
  calculation of area covered by, 194
  calculation of numbers needed per space, 193-194
  in heat recovery systems, 111
  heat removal, 199
  water-cooled, 232
Luminance, 186
Luminance measurements, 157

Macroclimatic regions, 65
Maintainance costs in economic analysis, 302
Maintenance
  of building systems, 243
  of equipment, access for, 261-262
Maintenance costs, with duty cycling, 231
Manufacturers product standards, 91
Masonry
  for heat storage, 168
  for passive heating, 173
  recommended thermal storage mass, 174
  sizing for thermal storage walls, 178
Masonry walls
  in heat gain systems, 180
  for thermal storage, 176-177
Mass heat storage, area factor, 174
Mass storage
  for cooling, 171-172
  for heating, 170-171
Mass systems, types, for heat storage, 42
Mathematic solution procedures, energy analysis descriptors of, 295
Mean radiant temperature, 45
Mechanical spaces, placement of, 111
Mechanical ventilation, 40, 54, 56
Mercantile buildings
  heat gain per occupant, 107
  occupant space requirements, 106
Merchandising, recommended lighting levels, 108, 185
Mercury vapor lamps, 109, 189-190
Metal building insulation, 179
Metal halide lamps, 109, 189-190, 198
Metal vapor lights, 25
Microclimate
  and building design, 97-101
  use for cooling/heating strategies, 99
Microprocessors in control systems, 229
Microwave transmission characteristics, 247
Model Energy Code, 87-89
  criteria, 88
  publication, 89
  U-values, 90
Modems in EMCSs, 248
Motels
  design analysis and strategies

INDEX

for, 278-280
  DHW usage in, 237
  lighting needs of, 108
  thermal distribution systems
    for, 210
Motors, 221
  energy use, 74
  in predesign energy budget,
    74
MRT. *See* Mean radiant
  temperature
Multifunction controls, 229-232
Multiple glazing. *See* Glazing
Multiplexer (MUX) panels, 244,
  245, 248
Multizone system controller, 228-
  229
Multizone thermal distribution
  system, 216
Municipal buildings, lighting
  needs of, 108
Museums, lighting needs of, 108

National Oceanic and Atmospheric
  Administration (NOAA), 71
National Woodwork Manufacturers
  Association (NWMA), 91
Natural gas, 63
Natural light. *See* Daylighting
Negative-ion generators, 57
Net building load, definition,
  27, 322
Night sky radiation, 322
Night ventilation, in passive
  cooling systems, 181
Noise pollution, 51
Nonconsuming system, 322
Nonrenewable energy sources, 1
Numerical models for energy
  analysis, 287
Nursing homes
  design analysis and strategies
    for, 278-280
  DHW usage in, 237
  energy usage in, 278
  heat gain per occupant, 107

Occupant complaints, 265
Occupants
  effects of, on heat gain, 106-
    107
  energy use, 74
  in predesign energy budget,
    74
Office buildings
  design analysis and strategies
    for, 269-271
  DHW usage in, 237
  heat gain per occupant, 107
  occupant space requirements,
    106
  small, thermal distribution
    systems for, 210
  thermal systems for, 209
Office design, and indoor
  pollution, 51
Office equipment, energy use,
  236
Offices, recommended lighting
  levels, 185
On-site energy, 2
Operating and maintenance (O &
  M) documentation, 259
Operating modes, energy analysis
  descriptors of, 295
Operation loads for equipment,
  calculation of, 236
Operational checks during
  construction, 259-264
Operational costs, in economic
  analysis, 309
Opportunity rate, 298-299, 322
Orientation. *See* Building
  orientation
OTTV
  of roof, 126-127
  for roof/ceiling, 88
  terms from Model Energy Code,
    123
  for walls, calculated, 123
Overall Thermal Transfer Values.
  See OTTV
Overall U-value. *See* U-values
Overhangs, 152
Ozone production, 57

Paraffin waxes, for heat
  storage, 168
Parking, lighting and energy

conservation, 200
Parking areas, recommended lighting levels, 185
Partitions, and ventilation, 134-135
Passive cooling systems, 180-184
Passive design, for thermal comfort, 48, 179
Passive heat storage, 42
Passive heating systems, 172-180
Passive solar design, for apartment buildings, 277
Passive solar heating, 49
Passive system, definition, 28, 322
Payback analysis, 311
Payback period, 322
Perimeter insulation, 128
Peripheral devices in EMCSs, 247
Perlite, R-value, 118
Phase changes, 24
Phase-change materials, for heat storage, 42, 168
Photoelectric controls, 111
Photovoltaics, 234-235
Pine wood walls, heat capacity of, 173
Piping identification, 262
Plantings, use in design strategy, 99-100
Plants. *See* Trees; Vegetation
Plastic bags, for heat storage, 42
Plastic sheets
  for apertures, 145
  in pollution control, 54
Plenum-return systems, 232
Plenums, 241
Pollutants
  control of. *See* Pollution-abatement strategies
  factors affecting concentration of, 51
  generation of, 51, 55
  sulphur, 63
  types of, 50, 55
Pollution-abatement strategies
  absorption, 57

adsorption, 57
air cleaning, 56
air filtration, 56
air ionizers, 57
concentration reduction, 55
contaminant control devices, 55
electrostatic precipitators, 56-57
source control, 52-55
source removal, 54
source substitution, 54
ventilation, 55-56
Polyisocyanurate, R-value, 118
Polystyrene, R-value, 118
Pools
  for cooling, 182, 183
  in heat gain systems, 180
Power, definition, 29
Power factor, 322
Present worth, 322
Present worth method of economic analysis, 301-302, 303, 304, 312
Pressure sensors, 248
Process energy, 322
Process heat, in hotels/motels, nursing homes/geriatric centers, 280
Process loads, 236-239
Profiles (operation schedules), 323
Project development period, in economic analysis, 310
Project documentation, 257-279
Proximal storage, definition, 28, 323
Psychrometric charts, 47-48, 65
Psychrometrics, 323
Pumps, 221

Radiant energy, as source of heat gain, 38
Radiant heat distribution, 176
Radiant slabs, for heat storage, 43
Radiant temperature, 45, 48
Radiation, 23-24, 119, 171
  for heat distribution, 173
  in passive cooling systems,

INDEX

181
Radiation cooling, night sky, 182-183
Radiator valves, 227
Radon, 50, 56, 57
  entry paths, 53
  filtration of breakdown products of, 56
  source control of, 54
Rain water, effect on building, 120
Rate of return
  on extra investment, 312, 323
  on investment, 311-312
Record drawings, 263
Recoverable waste heat, definition, 29, 323
Reflectance, of various surfaces, 102
Reflectance measurements, 157
Reflectance values
  of indoor elements, 109
  of types of light, 109
Reflective glass, 142-143
Reflectivity (albedo)
  definition, 323
  effect on lighting needs, 108
Refrigerant systems, 211
Refrigeration, 220
  U.S. rate of use, 1
Regional architecture, 64-65
Regional weather, 70
Reheat coil reset programs, 241
Relative humidity, 46, 48, 66, 67, 323
Relative humidity sensors, 248
Remote input devices in EMCSs, 248
Remote storage, definition, 28, 323
Remote-limited controls, 229-232
Renewable energy
  on-site use, 25
  sources of, 1
Renovation, and indoor pollution, 51
Residential buildings
  DHW usage in, 237
  energy use, 2
  heat gain per occupant, 107
  recommended lighting levels, 185
Residential energy end use, 1
Resource load, definition, 28, 323
Restaurants
  DHW usage in, 237
  heat gain per occupant, 107
  occupant space requirements, 106
  recommended lighting levels, 185
Retail stores, design analysis and strategies for, 274-276
R-factor. *See* R-value
RH. *See* Relative humidity
Risk factor in economic analysis, 299
Rock beds
  in heat gain systems, 180
  for thermal storage, 43, 166, 167, 169-170, 171, 173
  thermal storage for night ventilation, 183
Rock floors, in heat gain systems, 180
Rocks, for heat storage, 168
Roof
  for heat storage, 42
  insulation, in underground construction, 97
  OTTV, 88
  sawtooth, 154
Roof ponds, 175-176, 178-179
  in passive cooling systems, 183, 184
Roof sections, 124
Roofs
  calculated U_o-values, 125
  for energy storage systems, 42
  insulation of, 124
  model energy code criteria, 88
  openable, 182
  OTTV, 126
  TD_EQ, 127
  for thermal storage, 166
  types of, R- and U-values of, 125-126
Room cavity ratio nomograph,

196
Run time information in energy analysis programs, 290
Runaround coils, 223
R-values
   for building envelope, 117-119
   of building materials, 118
   definition, 326
   of materials, 122

Safety alarms, 243
Salt hydrates, for heat storage, 168
Salvage costs, 306
Sawtooth roof, 154
Scale models, for daylighting, 156
School EMCSs, 244
Schools, thermal systems for, 209
Screens, 147
Scrubbing, 57
Sealants, 129
   with low-e window coatings, 144
Sealants, in pollution control, 54
Sensible cooling, 49
Sensible heat energy, 168
Sensible heat ratio, 323
Sensible heating, 49
Sensors in EMCSs, 248
Shading
   for heat reduction, 38
   in passive cooling systems, 181
   to reduce solar heat transfer, 36
   and solar heat gain, 35
   use for energy design, 99
Shading coefficient, 113
   of glazing, 138
Shading coefficients, of various glazing, 145
Shading devices, 36
   for apertures, 146-149
      effect on U-values, 148-149
   interior, 147-148
   in passive cooling systems, 181
   for skylights, 155
   trees as, 101
Shading patterns, 101
Sheet Metal and Air Conditioning Contractor's National Association, Inc. (SMACNA), standards and guides publications, 91
Shell and tube heat exchangers, 224-225
Shutters, 147
Single compound amount (SCA) formula, 302
Single-duct, constant air volume (CAV)/variable air temperature (VAT)
   single zone system, 213-214, 218
   with terminal repeat, 214-215, 218
Single-duct, constant air volume (CAV)/variable air temperature (VAT) system
   single zone, 213, 218
Single-duct, single-zone thermal distribution system, 204-205, 218
Single-duct, variable air volume (VAV)/constant air temperature (CAT) system
   with fan terminal units, 215, 218
   with perimeter heaters, 215, 218
Single-duct VAV/CAT, double-duct VAV/VAT combination system, 217, 218
Single-zone system controller, 229
Site factors in building design, 98
Siting
   in building design, 93-105
   criteria for daylighting, 151
Sky, light intensity of, 150
Skylights, 154-155
   for educational facilities, 273
   for passive heating, 173
   for retail stores, 275

INDEX

shading devices for, 155
Skyvaults, 102-103
Slabs
    insulation of, 128-129
    Model Energy Code criteria, 88
Sliding patio doors, wood, standards for, 91
SMACNA. *See* Sheet Metal and Air Conditioning Contractor's National Association, Inc.
Smoke and fire management, 244
Snow, indirect gain system with, 176
Sodium lamps, 109, 189-191
Software
    for code compliance and energy analysis, 283
    in EMCSs, 249, 251
Sol-air effect, 323-324
Solar altitude, 324
Solar angle of incidence, 324
Solar azimuth, 98, 324
Solar cone, 101
Solar constant, 324
Solar energy, 25
    and building orientation, 93, 94
Solar Energy Code, Uniform, 91
Solar energy systems, use of skylights for, 155
Solar heat gain, 34, 71, 71, 111-112. *See also* Heat gain
    effect of underground construction on, 38
    effects of variables on, 35-36
    in roof ponds, 179
    through glazing, 113, 131-132
Solar heat storage. *See* Heat storage; Thermal mass storage; Thermal storage
Solar heating, standards, 91
Solar illumination, measurement of, 159-164
Solar intensity, 325
Solar path diagrams, 98-99
Solar radiation, 35. *See also* Heat gain; Solar heat gain
    by orientation and month, 112
    transfer of, 36
    through glass, 36
Solar radiation flow, 325
Solar systems, tool descriptors for, 295
Solar transmission, through glass, 139
Solar transmittance, through glazing, 144
Solariums, in heat gain systems, 180
Source energy, 2
Southern Building Code, 85
Space conditioning requirements, 115-116
Space heating, U.S. rate of use, 1
Space load, definition, 27, 325
Space organization, for hotels, motels, nursing homes/geriatric centers, 279
Space planning, 106-116
    by zone, 114-116
Space requirements, by building type, 106
Specific heat and heat content, 325
Specific volume (V), 325
Stack effect, 135
Stairways, lighting needs of, 108
Standards, for lighting, 91
Standards-developing organizations, 89-91
Steel
    in construction, 119
    for heat storage, 42
Stone, for heat storage, 42
Stone panels, R-value of, 121
Storage heat gain, 41-43
Storage-wall heating systems, 42
Stored energy, definition, 28, 325
Stratification, 325
Sun
    effect on building, 68-69
    factors affecting design strategy, 101-102
    position of, in design strategy, 98
Sunlight. *See also* Daylighting

components of, 140
Sunscoops, for educational facilities, 273
Sunspaces, 42, 179-180
Sunspace/Trombe wall system, 175-177
Supply temperature reset system, 227
System capacity, 326
System controls, inspection and calibration of, 265
System load, definition, 28, 326
Systems analysis for energy code compliance, 87

Task areas
  lighting for, 186
  recommended lighting levels for, 185
TD_EQ
  for cooling model codes, 89
  for roofs, 127
Telephone pairs transmission characteristics, 247
Temperature
  average, and swing, 166
  and comfort, 44-45, 66
  effects on air movement, 135
  microclimate variations, 99-100
  outdoor, effect on building design, 66
  patterns, 66
  soil/surface relationship, 96
  and thermal mass storage, 165
Temperature contol devices, 227
Temperature difference. See TD_EQ
Temperature differential, decreasing, 37
Temperature economizer cycle, 227
Temperature sensors, 248
Temperature zones, 114
Temperatures
  underground, 95
  of various cover materials, 102
Terrain, effect on microclimate, 99-100
Theaters, heat gain per occupant, 107
Thermal balance, 31-32, 165
Thermal chimney, 134
Thermal comfort, 44-45, 119
Thermal distribution systems
  air-water, 208-209
  air-water induction, 207-210
  all-air, 204-207
  all-water, 210-211
  in commercial buildings, 213-214
  direct-expansion, water-loop heat pumps, 212-213
  unitary, 211-212
Thermal effects, of lighting systems, 197
Thermal flywheel, 165, 166, 213
Thermal inertia, 326
Thermal lag, 41
Thermal mass
  definition, 326
  description, 41
  in design strategies, 49, 168-169
  location of, 166-168
  in passive cooling systems, 181
Thermal mass storage, 42, 165. See also Heat storage
Thermal resistance, 41
Thermal storage, 42
  for hospitals, 282
  indirect gain, 175-180
  materials for, 168-170
Thermal storage mass
  location, 175
  recommended
    for masonry, 174
    for water, 174
Thermal storage walls, 175-178
Thermal system components, 219-225
Thermal systems, 201-235
Thermal transmittance, U-value, 117
Thermal wheels, 222-223
Thermodynamics, first and second laws, 21-22
Thermosiphoning, 40, 169-170

in passive cooling systems, 181
Thermostat control, 212, 214
Thermostat controls, 216
Time, as factor in energy use, 25
Time and life cycle cost, 308
Time control devices, 226-227
Time horizon
  in economic analysis, 300
  and economic goals, 300
Tobacco smoke, 50, 52, 56
Topography, use for energy design, 99-101
Transmittance spectrum, 140
Trees
  and daylighting, 151
  use in design strategy, 99-100
  as windbreaks, 105
Triaxial cable transmission characteristics, 247
Trombe walls, 42, 175, 176-177
  for cooling, 182
Trouble diagnosis in EMCSs, 243
Tube containers, for heat storage, 42
Twisted pair wiring
  in EMCSs, 251
  transmission characteristics, 247

U.S. Department of Housing and Urban Development, 91
Ultraviolet light
  degradation from, with passive heating systems, 173
  transmittance of, by glazing type, 144
Ultraviolet radiation, 140, 141, 142, 143, 144
Unconditioned spaces, 318
Underground construction, 38-39
  in passive cooling systems, 181, 182
  thermal mass in, 166, 167
Underground degree day lag, 96
Underground design, 95-97
  infiltration in, 96
Underground temperature, annual, in Minneapolis, MN, 96
Underground temperatures, 95
Uniform Building Code, 85
United States
  macroclimatic regions, 65
  state-by-state energy conservation targets, 80-82
Usage, definition, 29
Utility loads, definition, 28, 326
Utility systems, on- and off-site, definition, 28, 322
U-values
  and building configuration, 34
  for building envelope, 117-119
  definition, 326
  of glazing, 132, 138, 145
  for walls, 90

Vapor barriers. *See* also Vapor retarders
  definition, 326
  use, 38, 120
Vapor migration, 38
Vapor pressure (Pw), 326
Vapor retarders, in crawl spaces, 127
Variable base degree day method, 283
Variable-air-volume (VAV) terminal reheat systems, 207
Vegetation
  for cooling, 182, 183
  and daylighting, 151
  effect on microclimate, 99-100
  in passive cooling systems, 182
  use
    in design strategy, 99, 100-101, 102
    for windbreaks, 104, 105
    for wind speed reduction, 104
Venetian blinds, 133, 152
Vent area, in Trombe wall system, 176
Vent stacks, 40

Ventilation
   and air quality, 50, 51, 54, 55, 56
   in apartment buildings, 277
   and comfort, 46
   definition, 326
   in design strategies, 49
   in educational facilities, 273
   energy use, 74
   induced, 171
      cooling system, 134
   natural, through apertures, 132-135
   night, for passive cooling, 183-184
   in passive cooling systems, 181
   in predesign energy budget, 74
   for retail stores, 275
Ventilation heat gain/loss, 39-40
Ventilation systems, smoke and fire management of, 244
Vermiculite, R-value, 118
Vertical transportation in buildings, 236
VHF FM radio signal transmission characteristics, 247
Visible light, 140, 141, 142, 143, 144, 145
Vision strip, 155

Walls
   characteristics of types of, 118
   colors for, for energy conservation, 198
   computed U_o value, 118
   heat capacity of, 173
   for heat storage, 42
   masonry
      in heat gain systems, 180
      for thermal storage, 176-177
   model energy code criteria, 88
   for passive heating, 173
   reflectance of, 109
   sections, types of, 119
   as source of indoor pollutants, 51
   subgrade, heat loss through, 96
   for thermal storage, 166
   U-values of, 90
   wood frame, 124
Walls, exterior, 119-124
   ratio to floor area, 35
Warehouses, heat gain per occupant, 107
Warranty agreements, 264
Washrooms, lighting needs of, 108, 185
Waste heat. See also Heat recovery
   cascading use, 28
   definition, 28, 326
   from lighting, 25
   and storage systems, 27
   use, 27
Water. See also Domestic hot water (DHW)
   in heat exchangers, 223
   for heat storage, 42, 43, 168, 169, 173
   for passive heating, 173
   recommended thermal storage mass, 174
   for thermal storage, 177-179
Water bodies
   effect on microclimate, 99-100
   use for energy design, 99
Water heating. See Domestic water heating (DHW)
   energy use, 74
   U.S. rate of use, 1
Water heating, in predesign energy budget, 74
Water pipes, insulation of, 125
Water storage tanks, insulation of, 238
Water systems, testing during construction, 265
Water tanks, for thermal storage, 167
Water thermal storage walls, 176-177
   containers for, 177

sizing for, 178
Water treatment, 265
Water wall system, 175
Water-cooled condensers, 222
Water-cooled luminaires, 232
Watt hour, definition, 29
Weather data
   for energy analysis, 296-297
   on magnetic tape, 72
Weatherstripping, 129, 136, 137
Wet-bulb temperature, 48, 65, 326
w-hr. *See* Watt-hour
Wind
   analysis of, 69
   control of, in design strategy, 103-104
   U.S. pattern, 69
   use for energy design, 99
Wind flow tests, 105
Wind rose, 69-70
Wind speed
   in design calculations, 123
   reduction by vegetation, 104
Wind ventilation, 40, 69
Windbreaks
   in design strategy, 103-104
   effects of, 105
   use for energy design, 99
Window airconditioners, 212
Window frames, 136-137
Window louvers, 146-147
Window seals, 136-137
Windows. *See also* Apertures; Fenestration; Glazing
   in direct heat gain, 177
   for educational facilities, 272, 273
   and EMCSs, 253
   infiltration rates, 129
   infiltration through, 135-136
   in isolated heat gain, 180
   types of, 131
      air-flow, 139-140
      and ventilation, 133
   wood, standards for, 91
Winter solar cone, 101
Wood frame walls, in construction, 124
Wood windows and sliding patio doors, standards for, 91

Work stations, locations for, 199

Zonal cavity method, 193, 194-196
Zone planning, 114-116
Zoning. *See* Zone planning
Zoning schemes, and thermal systems, 204, 205, 206, 207, 212